ma.org.uk

D1494793

BMA LIBRARY
BRITISH MEDICAL ASSOCIATION

THE GOOD GP

TRAINING GUIDE

BRITISH MEDICAL ASSOCIATION

0781005

WITHDRAWN FROM LIBRARY

THE GOOD GP

TRAINING GUIDE

EDITED BY MATT BURKES & ALEC LOGAN

BMA LIBRARY

BRITISH MEDICAL

RC
GP
Royal College of
General Practitioners

The Royal College of General Practitioners was founded in 1952 with this object:

'To encourage, foster and maintain the highest possible standards in general practice and for that purpose to take or join with others in taking steps consistent with the charitable nature of that object which may assist towards the same.'

Among its responsibilities under its Royal Charter the College is entitled to:

'Diffuse information on all matters affecting general practice and issue such publications as may assist the object of the College.'

British Library Cataloguing-in-Publication Data
A catalogue record for this book is available from the British Library

© Royal College of General Practitioners, 2014
Images in this book © Helen Wilson, 2014

Published by the Royal College of General Practitioners, 2014
30 Euston Square, London NW1 2FB

All rights reserved. No part of this publication may be reproduced, stored in a retrieval system or transmitted, in any form or by any means, electronic, mechanical, photocopying, recording or otherwise, without the prior permission of the Royal College of General Practitioners.

Disclaimer
This publication is intended for the use of medical practitioners in the UK and not for patients. The authors, editors and publisher have taken care to ensure that the information contained in this book is correct to the best of their knowledge, at the time of publication. Whilst efforts have been made to ensure the accuracy of the information presented, particularly that related to the prescription of drugs, the authors, editors and publisher cannot accept liability for information that is subsequently shown to be wrong. Readers are advised to check that the information, especially that related to drug usage, complies with information contained in the *British National Formulary*, or equivalent, or manufacturers' datasheets, and that it complies with the latest legislation and standards of practice.

Designed and typeset by Sheer Design and Typesetting
Printed by Martins the Printers
Indexed by Susan Leech
ISBN 978-0-85084-348-4

This book is dedicated to anyone involved in general practice training, most particularly the trainees themselves.

CONTENTS

Foreword   x
Preface   xii
Contributors   xv
Acknowledgements   xxvi

Introduction: on being a patient   1
Introduction: doctoring   3

I TIPS FOR TRAINEES WORKING IN THE HOSPITAL SETTING   7

1   The basics   8
2   Acute medicine   11
3   Breast surgery   16
4   Cardiology   20
5   Colorectal surgery   27
6   Ear, nose and throat   32
7   Emergency medicine   37
8   Endocrine medicine   43
9   Family planning   48
10 Gastroenterology   56
11 General medicine   62
12 General surgery   68
13 Genitourinary medicine   72

14 Geriatric medicine   77
15 Haematology   84
16 Obstetrics and gynaecology   90
17 Old-age psychiatry   97
18 Oncology   102
19 Ophthalmology   107
20 Oral and maxillofacial surgery   112
21 Paediatrics   116
22 Palliative care   122
23 Psychiatry   128
24 Public health   133
25 Respiratory medicine   138
26 Rheumatology   143
27 Stroke medicine   147
28 Trauma and orthopaedics   151
29 Urology   157
30 Vascular surgery   163

II TIPS FOR TRAINEES WORKING IN THE GP SETTING   168

31 Your first GP rotation   169
32 Introduction to the registrar year   175
33 Less than full time: a personal view with practical advice   178
34 How much does it cost to be a GP trainee?   181
35 The ePortfolio   185
36 Workplace-Based Assessments in the registrar year   188
37 The Applied Knowledge Test   195
38 How to pass and fail the Clinical Skills Assessment   199
39 Audit for improvement   206
40 Learning from error   213
41 The home visit   220
42 Out-of-hours care   224
43 How to get the most out of the radiology department   227
44 How to get the most out of the biochemistry department   230
45 How to get the most out of the microbiology department   233
46 On being a 'good' GP trainee: an ethico-legal lexicon   237
47 Rash decisions: dermatology in general practice   244
48 Everything you ever wanted to know about neurology but were afraid to ask   249
49 Child and Adolescent Mental Health (CAMHS) in a ten-minute consultation   253
50 Remote and rural medicine   260

51 The new therapeutics: ten commandments   265
52 Ten commandments for testing   266
53 *A la carte blanche*: leaving GP training   270
54 Minor surgery   273

III BEYOND TRAINING   278

55 Academic general practice: off all summer   279
56 Academic general practice: a coda   282
57 Commissioning   284
58 On diagnosis   290
59 Interacting with the Department for Work and Pensions   295
60 How to write a paper   297
61 Events medicine   301
62 First5   305
63 Tips for teaching   309
64 Getting a job   315
65 Appraisal and revalidation   320
66 General practice and money   326
67 Health is global   331
68 How to become a GP trainer   337
69 How to stay out of trouble   343
70 Sessional locum work   350
71 Kindness as a basic clinical skill   355
72 Social media: a startup guide   360
73 Shared decision making made easier: using a three-step framework 363
74 Staying up to date: a personal view   372
75 Working outside the UK: a postcard from Australia   377
76 Social violence   380

IV PERSONAL DOCTORING   385

77 Personal medicine   386

Glossary   395
Index   402

FOREWORD

These days very few things make me wish that I was younger and I am rather shocked to discover this book to be one of them. The editors have taken their inspiration from travel guides and they have succeeded to a remarkable degree. A good guidebook places your destination within its geographical and historical context. It tells you how to get there and how to get around and it points out places that might interest you. It makes suggestions about how you should behave when this is appropriate and how to avoid getting into trouble. Such a guidebook allows you to travel with confidence, to feel safer and to learn, in the richest and broadest sense of that word, while you are enjoying yourself. This book has just the same aspirations but this time the journey is not to an exotic location but the one that takes you successfully through general practice training.

Just like a good travel book, every one of the possible stopovers on the journey through training is introduced and made to feel safe, doable, potentially rewarding and even fun. I found myself wanting to start GP training all over again and to sample all of the possible stopovers – even orthopaedics! Yet this is not a book to indulge in the simplistic or the merely comforting. It is quite clear that, like any other traveller, what the trainee gets out of any attachment is likely to be directly proportional to the amount he or she puts in – a lesson that once learnt will stand the reader in good stead for a career in which nothing is routine and within which one must be prepared to learn from patients, colleagues and the research literature every working day if one is going to be both safe and effective as a general practitioner and to find joy in that extraordinary and privileged work.

In his autobiography *Errata: an examined life*, the writer and thinker George Steiner writes:

There could be, I knew, no finality to the raindrops, to the number and variousness of the stars, to the books to be read, to the languages to be learned. The mosaic of the possible could, at any instant, be splintered and reassembled into new images and motions of meaning.

General practice seems to me to be a discipline that offers precisely this limitlessness of observation, learning and meaning. This makes it terrifying but also a constant source of excitement and delight – just like travel but this time professional and intellectual rather than geographical.

Travelling requires a map and for doctors the professional map is that of biomedical science and you have a profound responsibility to have studied it well. This book will help you to do this. However, there is always a gap between the map of medical science and the territory of human suffering in which your patients will find themselves floundering. You will need to try to bridge this gap by paying very particular attention to the details of the patient's story and by seeking to understand the various ways in which they are struggling, and the effect that these struggles are having on those around them and on their life's aspirations and hopes. Only then will you be able to see the disease through the lens of the patient rather than the other way round and only then will you be able to resist the contemporary malaise of medicalisation, over-diagnosis and over-treatment. Only then will you be in a position to care for those who are dying and for those who see no further point in living. This book will help you to do all these things too. I wish you courage and joy on your journey.

Iona Heath CBE FRCGP
Past President, RCGP

PREFACE

Being a GP trainee isn't easy.

I know. I was one very recently.

During your hospital rotations it feels as if the moment you approach any degree of mastery (cynics might say competency) in your current job, you swap rotations and are thrown headlong into a new voyage of exploration.

'Hey, tonight you're the paediatric doctor on-call. Tomorrow you will be a gynaecologist.'

Your patients, not unreasonably, will expect you to be 'a specialist'. This mismatch between expectation and experience can lead to anxiety. On all sides.

Your consultants may have little idea of what you don't know or, for that matter, what you need to know to get through the job.

Some will have little idea of what their junior doctors actually do.

This book aims to help with this.

Then there's the GP placements and registrar year. The pressure is now really on as this is what you are SUPPOSED to be good at! But sometimes you won't be. And sometimes you won't like it. And there's so much to learn! And then there's all the assessments! And don't even mention the EXAMS, the very thought of which can induce chest pain in the coolest trainee.

This book aims to help with this.

Then, almost before you know it, you have finished training and you are at last a grown-up GP, who has seen it all. Except you haven't. You will face a whole world of job insecurity, accountants, ethical dilemmas and, even though you have only just finished training, avoiding burnout and staying up to date.

This book aims to help with this.

This book is not about ivory-tower medicine, it's about real-world medicine.

Its style is unapologetically direct and in places irreverent. If you are after a formal textbook, buy a different book instead. If, on the other hand, you have had enough of textbooks and are after something to help with the more tricky bits of your training, then this might be what you've been waiting for.

It's your training. Make the most of it. Enjoy it.

This book aims to help with this.

Let me know how it goes.

Matt Burkes

Morning, branch surgery, then a house call. *Patient number 14.* I'd put that one in our house call book. A sixty-something retired business lady, attitude of a thirty-something. In April she'd perforated her bowel at 40,000 feet *en route* to Miami and a dream cruise. Imminent cruising alters pain perception, and after a torrid night in a Miami hotel room she felt a little better and joined the ship. First night at sea, high fever, collapse at dinner and so to sickbay. Airlifted to somewhere in Mexico and 38,000 dollars' worth of emergency surgery for perforated colon secondary to large malignant tumour. Back home for general evisceration then heroic chemo. A hospice discharge letter earlier in the week suggested she might be at home, so I scribbled a note offering to say hello. My visit the result. I was expecting a harrowing encounter. I rang the doorbell. Through the frosted glass I spotted my patient jinking sideways to hip-charge a black Labrador into the kitchen. I didn't know she had a dog, such a good prognostic indicator. Door open, into front room, do have a seat doctor, so nice of you to visit. Hospice? Marvellous! Sorted the pain relief. And the incontinence. Partner appears, Labrador owner. Labrador appears and sits down to be patted, sniffing my trousers. I have Pointers. Can I help you with anything? How are things going? You are halfway through chemo, how is that? All fine. She radiates vivacity. Thank you so much for coming. I'll come again. I clasp hands. The bravest and most scintillating woman I've ever met.

Back at the Health Centre, soon to be razed, meeting with architects next week. We have a new one a'comin'. An inverted ziggurat, all glass and flying bridges, five storeys' high.

Review results. One stands out. New patient registered a fortnight previously. *Patient 16.* Hypertension and microalbuminuria to an extent that would make a spoon stand upright. Quick phone call, come and see me, works in a nuclear power station. Receptionists, please chase blood results fast. Quick talk with younger partner who knows more about renal biochemistry than I do.

On-call doctor early afternoon, two late calls, second, *Patient 17*. Elderly lady with breakthrough cancer pain. Her daughter-in-law used to play tennis with me when I was ten. Another Labrador! Adjust the dose of long-acting opioid. More clasping of hands, always an ordeal for Scots. Thankfully no kissing. Yet.

Afternoon surgery. Start with Proteinuria Man, *Patient 16 redux*. He's doing a lot of training and body-building. On a high-protein diet. The Byelorussian version with stacks of anabolic steroids. And he's jaundiced. Nope, I haven't sorted him yet.

I finish almost on time. *Patient 35.* He is the perfect last patient this particular day. Thirty-ish, with a tiny skin tag left upper eyelid and mild folliculitis.

Hip hop! Soon to go home.

'So, am I your last patient of the week?'

'Yes', I say, still marvelling at the simplicity of his lovely skin tag, the absence of psychomorbidity.

We chat about football.

'You'll be glad to finish the week', he says. 'You guys must be sick and tired of dealing with the same things all of the time.'

Er … no!

Alec Logan

CONTRIBUTORS

EDITORS

Matt Burkes, a former psychologist and bass player, went to medical school when he realised he would never be on *Top of the Pops*. He graduated from St George's Graduate Entry Programme in 2006 and moved to Chichester, West Sussex. His foundation and training jobs at St Richard's Hospital inspired him to create the 'Tips for Trainees' series for the *British Journal of General Practice*. After a wonderful registrar year at Flansham Park Health Centre, he worked at Maywood Healthcare Centre in Bognor before landing up at Langley House Surgery in Chichester, where he works as a salaried GP. He is married with three children and is involved in a number of educational projects, both medical and non-medical. He enjoys the delicate art of hedgerow wine production and hopes to learn to sail.

Alec Logan is a Glasgow graduate and a full-time GP in Wishaw, Lanarkshire, Scotland. He spent just enough time as a young doctor with the Royal Navy to open his mind. Then his deputy trainer showed him how to top and tail an onion. Such vision! At heart a frustrated journalist, Alec created *Rocket* as a West of Scotland Faculty newsletter, then *hoolet* for RCGP Scotland, then the Back Pages of the *British Journal of General Practice*, which he edited for almost 15 years. He sails when he can. Hebrides; enough said. Look to windward!

CONTRIBUTING AUTHORS

Robert Adam graduated from St George's Hospital Medical School in 2006 and became a member of the Royal College of Physicians in 2010. He currently works as a Specialty Doctor in Cardiology at William Harvey Hospital, Kent.

Ade Adeniyi graduated from St George's Hospital Medical School in 2005, and worked in the hospital's sexual health clinic as part of her postgraduate training. She is currently working as a GP in Croydon with interests in sexual health and contraceptive services.

Ben Atkinson is an emergency medicine trainee (ST5), Southampton University Hospital, Wessex Deanery.

Michael Banna is a GP at Grove House practice in Bognor Regis. He has an interest in medical education and music journalism. He is currently running 43 minutes' late.

Pete Basford is an Endoscopy Research Fellow at Queen Alexandra Hospital, Portsmouth. He is a gastroenterology trainee in the Wessex region with a special interest in advanced endoscopic imaging and therapeutics.

David Beattie qualified from Guy's Hospital in 1990 and was Lecturer in Surgery at Imperial College prior to completing specialist vascular training on the North West Thames Programme at Charing Cross, St Mary's and the Hammersmith Hospitals. He was appointed Consultant Surgeon at the Royal West Sussex NHS Trust (now Western Sussex) in 2002, where he is Chief of Service, Core Division, and Director of Medical Education.

Victoria Beattie trained at University College London Medical School and qualified in 1995. She is a GP partner in Bognor Regis and is a GP and family planning trainer. Her special interests include family planning/women's health and fertility.

David Blane is a GP in Glasgow and Clinical Academic Fellow at the University of Glasgow. His research interests are in multimorbidity and health inequalities.

Veronica Boon is a GP registrar who is currently doing an Academic Clinical Fellow post in education alongside her training. She is currently undertaking the Certificate in Teaching and Learning for Health Professionals (TLHP) and teaching communication skills to undergraduate medical students.

Paul Bowie is Associate Adviser in Postgraduate GP Education with NHS Education for Scotland and is based in Glasgow. He has educational and research interests in improving the quality and safety of primary care.

Deborah Bowman is Professor of Bioethics, Clinical Ethics and Medical Law at St George's. She is a programme consultant and regular panellist on Radio 4's *Inside the Ethics Committee*. When she's not teaching in Tooting or pontificating in a subterranean recording studio, Deborah writes plays and stories to put in drawers and practises playing her cello, sometimes even in tune.

Mhairi-Clare Bradshaw is a GP partner working in Lanark, Scotland. She is just newly qualified, having completed her registrar year in 2012.

Kate Bunyan trained at Guy's and St Thomas's Hospitals, London, qualifying in 2002. She has had a portfolio career, including basic surgical training, emergency medicine and pre-hospital medicine, before setting sail as a doctor onboard cruise ships. She is now Medical Director for Carnival UK, responsible for all aspects of medical and public health in the P&O Cruises and Cunard fleets.

Niall Cameron has been a GP in Govan, Glasgow, since 1986, working in a practice that has a significant involvement in undergraduate and postgraduate teaching. He has been involved with appraisal since 2003 as an appraiser, lead appraiser and latterly as National Appraisal Adviser for Medical Appraisal in Scotland, employed by NHS Education Scotland (NES). The NES has responsibility for appraiser training and developing systems to support appraisal and the roll-out of revalidation.

Antony Chuter lives in Sussex and has lived in physical pain for over 20 years. He volunteered for the RCGP for six years. He says his driving force is to help make things better for patients and to help GPs in their role as carers and healers. His motto is 'It's no good standing on the side and moaning. The only way to change things is to get involved.'

Neil Cripps is a District Hospital General Surgeon with a major coloproctological interest. Within this, his main areas of interest are colorectal cancer and screening for it, anorectal conditions and the surgical treatment of inflammatory bowel disease.

Anne M. Cruickshank is a Consultant Medical Biochemist and Clinical Director, Laboratory Medicine for NHS Greater Glasgow and Clyde and an Honorary Clinical Senior Lecturer at the University of Glasgow Medical School.

Gordon Cruickshank is senior partner at Thomas Barrie & Co., a firm of chartered accountants based in Glasgow who have acted for the medical profession for many years. When not at work your best chance to find him is at Dullatur Golf Club.

Ross Cruickshank graduated from Aberdeen Medical School in 2007 and completed core surgical training before moving to begin training in anaesthetics. He is currently working in Devon and has a special interest in critical care.

Peter Davies is a GP in Halifax and a member of Calderdale Clinical Commissioning Group. He thinks the challenges of commissioning are immense, but the processes will ultimately be very valuable for patients and the NHS. If as a profession we don't take the opportunities of commissioning then we risk being consigned to obsolescence.

Edward Dawe is a specialty registrar Year 6 trainee in orthopaedic and trauma surgery.

MeiLing Denney is a portfolio GP in Edinburgh. She has been a trainer for many years and is currently Training Programme Director in Southeast Scotland. She has also had extensive involvement with MRCGP assessments at the Royal College of General Practitioners (RCGP).

Polly Duncan is an Academic Clinical Fellow in General Practice in Bristol. She has a particular interest in international health and spent a year of Out of Programme Experience (OOPE) working in rural South Africa. She has recently completed the Certificate in Teaching and Learning for Health Professionals (TLHP) in Bristol and is returning to South Africa this year to run a workshop to improve nurse-led management of hypertension in community clinics.

Glyn Elwyn is a clinician-researcher with an interest in shared decision making, user-centred design of decision support tools and their integration into routine health care. His affiliations are Cardiff University, UK; Dartmouth College, USA; Radboud University, Nijmegen, Netherlands.

Greg Fell is a Consultant in Public Health in Bradford. Greg's current role is to advise the Clinical Commissioning Groups on clinical and cost-effectiveness, healthcare economics, epidemiology and prioritisation. Greg is also a member of a National Institute for Health and Care Excellence (NICE) Technology Appraisal Committee and works with the Strategic Clinical Networks, Senates and with the West and South Yorkshire Commissioning Support Unit. In his spare time, Greg looks after his kids and occasionally runs.

John J. Frey III is an Emeritus Professor of Family Medicine at the School of Medicine and Public Health at the University of Wisconsin. He is a US-trained family doctor who served as an assistant in general practice in the NHS in 1979–80 in Glyncorrwg, Wales, with Julian Tudor Hart. His interests are in the ethics of medical journalism and publishing, community-engaged research, and the social and intellectual history of US family medicine in the twentieth century.

Tony Foley works in a family practice in Kinsale on the south coast of Ireland. He is a GP trainer and Member of the Irish College of General Practitioners (MICGP) examiner, and has an interest in dermatology. He is a Lecturer in General Practice at University College Cork.

Julia Gallagher trained at Guy's, King's and St Thomas's Medical School and qualified in 2006. She is currently completing her GP training in Chichester. Her special interests include family planning and women's health.

Simon Glew is a GP registrar on the Brighton training scheme. He is an Academic Clinical Fellow with a special interest in medical education and likes to cycle wherever and whenever he can.

Cliff Godley trained in general and respiratory medicine. He has practised traditional patient-centred family medicine in wettest Lanarkshire for almost 30 years.

Alexander Goodman undertook rotations in paediatrics and obstetrics and gynaecology while a Foundation Year 2 doctor at Western Sussex Hospitals NHS Trust. He is now an obstetrics and gynaecology specialist trainee at the Wessex Deanery.

Trish Greenhalgh is a GP in North London and Professor of Primary Health Care at Queen Mary, University of London.

Marjory Greig completed her microbiology training in Glasgow and Bristol. She was briefly a consultant in Glasgow before migrating south to Chichester in 1990 where she spent 15 years as a single-handed consultant in microbiology and infection control. Since then she has had the pleasure of life with colleagues and now works across Chichester and Worthing.

Anna Gruener is a fifth-year ophthalmic specialty registrar on the London/Kent, Surrey and Sussex rotation. Her sub-specialty interests are glaucoma and vitreoretinal surgery.

Laurine Hanna received a Physics BSc from Durham University, followed by a two-year stint in the oil industry, before qualifying at St George's, London Medical School in 2006. She is now a specialty registrar in general adult psychiatry with South London and Maudsley NHS Foundation Trust.

Rob Hendry has been a GP in Dundee for 11 years and is currently Deputy Medical Director of the Medical Protection Society.

Honor Hinxman is currently an ST3 trainee in anaesthetics at Wessex Deanery, having completed the ACCS training programme as an acute medical trainee. In her spare time, Honor enjoys singing opera and loves the great outdoors on foot, horseback or paddling in a canoe.

David Hogg is a GP on the Isle of Arran. Qualifying in 2009, he is a director of BASICS Scotland, sits on the RCGP Scottish Council and is a member of the Remote Practitioners Association of Scotland. He is editor of RuralGP.com and believes that rural practice offers a feast of interest to new GPs.

Gillian Horne is currently a Wellcome Trust Research Training Fellow with a specialist interest in haematology and the signalling pathways that influence disease progression in myeloid disease. Her other interests include medical education, pottery and sea kayaking.

Richard Imonikhe is an ophthalmology registrar in North Thames with an interest in novel medical devices and business models.

Max Inwood has been a nine sessions per week GP in Edinburgh for the past 20 years. He likes to keep busy and he spends his notional half-day sitting in tribunals deciding on ESA and DLA appeals. In his spare time, he fits in one session per week in out-of-hours care. He qualified from the University of Glasgow in 1982 and spent time in the Royal Navy as a doctor before settling in Edinburgh.

Neil Iosson is a partner at Worthing Medical Group. He carrys out eight sessions per week and still enjoys working as a locum on his day off. Prior to partnership he worked full time as a locum for four years after completing his vocational training scheme (VTS) in West Sussex.

Bhautesh Jani is an academic GP based at the University of Glasgow. He is currently undertaking a clinical fellowship funded by the Chief Scientist Office of Scotland.

Rob Jones is a former oncology trainee who is now training in general practice. He has a special interest in medical education and Tottenham Hotspur.

Matt Knapman originally qualified in 2004 from Guy's and St Thomas' Medical School, London. He trained and then practised as a GP in West Sussex prior to emigrating to New South Wales, Australia, with his family. He is currently dividing his time between learning to surf and working in general practice.

Yolande Knight is a GP registrar on the Mid-Sussex scheme, undertaking dual training as an academic fellow in public health. She completed her Masters of Public Health and early public health training years in London. Her special interests include travel medicine, headache and pain.

Ken Laji is a consultant endocrinologist and lead clinician in his specialty at West Sussex NHS Trust, St Richard's Hospital.

Mayur Lakhani is a former Chairman of the RCGP. He is a practising GP and a member of the CCG governing body. He is working on projects to improve the quality and safety of primary care. He chairs the National Council for Palliative Care.

Richard Lehman is presently working on 'Sharing Medicine' with Harlan Krumholz at Yale, based around 75 or so 'disruptive assertions' or precepts: 'Harlan is coming at it from the viewpoint of a visionary leader in US medicine and the best outcomes researcher there has ever been, whereas I'm a semi-retired GP in Banbury.' Still doing out-of-hours work. Richard's weekly literature reviews for the BMJ are at http://blogs.bmj.com/bmj/category/richard-lehmans-weekly-review-of-medical-journals/.

Murray Lough, an untrained GP, has worked in an even darker part of Lanarkshire than Alec Logan. To shine some light he developed an interest in pharology (look it up) and to rise above the day-to-day traumas became a fully paid-up member of the cloud appreciation society. The message is that to fully appreciate the wonderful world of general practice think big and think differently. Training isn't enough.

Rhianydd McGlone is a part-time GPST3 in Chichester. She spent eight months working in a sexual health clinic as part of her GP training and hopes to combine her interest in sexual health and family planning with a career in general practice.

Alex Mackay is a GP trainee on the Kings VTS. He lives and works in South London.

John McKay is a GP in Glasgow and Associate Adviser (Quality Improvement) with the NES. He has been interested in audit, significant event analysis (SEA) and patient safety for 20 years, and has published widely on these topics. He has coordinated a peer review system for educational feedback on audit and SEA quality for GPs and GPSTs in the West of Scotland Deanery.

Alexander C. Maclennan graduated in 1985 from the University of Aberdeen, then completing the three-year GP Training Scheme in Dumfries. He switched to radiology, training in Glasgow and Vancouver, and is currently a consultant radiologist at the Royal Alexandra Hospital in Paisley. This gives him plenty of free time for golf, hillwalking, diving and sailing.

Elaine McNaughton is a GP and Programme Director of Postgraduate GP Education in the East Deanery, based in Dundee.

Tim Martindale is an anaesthetic and intensive care registrar in Chichester.

David Matthews is a GP partner at Forest End Surgery. His interests include child health, palliative care and joint injections.

Michael Norbury has previously worked as an NES GP Health Inequality Fellow as well as a GP Academic Fellow. He now works as a GP in a deprived practice in Edinburgh and is an Associate Clinical Director with LUCS, the GP out-of-hours service provider for NHS Lothian. He was co-author of an appraisal toolkit 'Appraisal Evidence for Out of Hours GPs in Scotland' in 2011.

Tom O'Dowd was appointed to the Chair of General Practice at Trinity College Dublin in 1993, having previously held posts at two UK universities. In addition to his academic and research roles, he is a principal partner in a large urban practice in Dublin.

Matthew Oliver is a GP in a small town in New South Wales, Australia. His special interests include his family, church and getting out on his bike as much as possible.

Caroline Page is a GPST3 in the Kent, Surrey and Sussex Deanery and is a medical officer in the Royal Army Medical Corps. Her professional interests include occupational medicine, mental health and ophthalmology in primary care.

Luisa Pettigrew is a sessional GP in London. She has had a passion for global health since medical school and has undertaken a Diploma in International Health and an MSc in Health Policy, as well as having worked in Mozambique and various Latin American countries. She is currently the RCGP representative for the World Organization of Family Doctors (WONCA).

Jim Pink is a GP in Cardiff with an interest in medical education and chronic lung disease.

Katie Pink is a respiratory specialty registrar in South Wales with an interest in lung cancer, pleural disease and palliative care.

Alexandra Pitt Ford is a specialist trainee in geriatric medicine in the Kent, Surrey and Sussex Deanery.

Kingsley Poole trained at the University of Oxford (matriculated 1987) and gained Doctor of Medicine (DM Oxon) in 2003 for epidemiological work in the care of people with epilepsy in the UK. He qualified as a GP in 2003 and spent two years as a clinical assistant in the neurology clinic at St Richard's Hospital, 2003–5. He currently works as a GP in West Sussex.

Michael Power is currently Evidence-Based Practice Lead at the Newcastle upon Tyne Hospitals NHS Trust. For the ten years before that he wrote evidence-based guidance for CKS (which trainees and even GPs might find useful). And before that he was head of the paediatric rheumatology service at the University of Cape Town teaching hospitals.

William Reeve studied at St George's Medical School in London, including a degree in anatomy at King's College London. He is currently working as a trauma and orthopaedic registrar in the southeast having completed core surgical training.

Thomas Renninson trained in Birmingham, leaving in 2010, and after completing a foundation programme in Truro has moved to Bristol to start training as an anaesthetist.

Fiona Robbie is a locum GP who trained as a GP in Chichester, qualifying in 2011. She enjoys the variety that working as a locum has given her. Her interests include health promotion and disease prevention, areas in which she hopes to expand her knowledge over the coming years.

Jane H. Roberts is an academic GP in the northeast of England. She has an MSc in medical anthropology and a doctorate exploring how GPs respond to adolescents presenting with emotional distress. Jane is the Chair of the RCGP Adolescent Health Group. This group promotes youth-friendly primary care and supports GPs in offering care to adolescents.

Paul Ryan is a GP trainee on the Cork GP training scheme and is also a qualified pharmacist who has a special interest in therapeutics.

Helen Salisbury is a GP in Oxford and leads the communication skills teaching for the medical school there. She is also medical adviser to the Health Experiences Research Group at the Department of Primary Care Health Sciences.

Tom Saunders is a consultant geriatrician with an interest in community geriatrics. He has worked in a variety of hospitals both teaching and district general, developing a broad experience of general and geriatric medicine. When not working, he can usually be found out running on the South Downs.

Ha-Neul Seo is a sessional GP in the UK and an Administrative Fellow in Health Care Management in Boston, Massachusetts. She is pursuing interests in population health and US payer/provider issues following an MPH at the Harvard School of Public Health. She joined McKinsey and Company as an Associate in 2013.

Sam Sewell dabbled in mental health and motherhood before retraining as a GP in 2009, less than full time of course.

Laura Smith went to medical school at George's, before completing F1 and 2. She then promptly escaped to New Zealand to travel and live her life. However, the UK and NHS managed to lure her back to a more 'conventional' career path, where she works as a general surgical registrar with an interest in colorectal.

Ottilia Speirs is a consultant stroke physician at Frimley Park Hospital. She initially trained as a geriatrician before specialising in stroke medicine and was one of the first trainees to gain CCST in stroke medicine in 2006. Her interests include atrial fibrillation in stroke and TIA mimics.

Mary-Jo Sommerville is a graduate of the University of Glasgow. She is a GP trainer and has been providing medical services to the music industry for over 20 years. She has really excellent wellies.

Clare J. Taylor is an academic GP in inner-city Birmingham. She was Chair of the RCGP Associates-in-Training Committee 2008–9 and the inaugural RCGP First5 Clinical Lead 2009–13.

Anne T. Thompson has been a GP partner and trainer in South Lanarkshire, Scotland, for 25 years. Her main interests are in general practice, women's health, rheumatology and palliative care.

Richard Townsley is a specialty registrar in ENT at the West of Scotland Deanery and dedicated rugby fan. He spends his free time repairing the damage his sons do to his house. He is generally very pleased with his lot.

Neal Tucker was always destined for general practice. He trained as a GP on the Oxford VTS, completing the MRCGP in 2010. He now divides his time between being a GP partner in Oxford and working with NB Medical Education as E-learning Lead and lecturer on the ever-popular Hot Topics course.

Kieran Tunnicliffe is a GP in the Witterings. He has an interest in palliative care.

Daniel R. van Gijn is currently a core surgical trainee working in London. He graduated with honours in both medicine and dentistry and is a member of the Royal College of Surgeons of England and the Faculty of Dental Surgeons of Ireland. He aims to pursue a career in oral and maxillofacial surgery.

Simon van Lieshout is a First5 GP who trained in an urban practice in Edinburgh but wanted to explore rural general practice. An NES Rural Fellowship in Lochaber gave him more than just a taste of rural practice, working single handed in a dispensing practice in his second week. Simon particularly enjoys knowing a small community, longer appointments and the more hands-on approach that rural practice offers.

John Vrahimides trained at Guy's, King's and St Thomas's Medical School and qualified in 2003. He is a GP in Bognor Regis. His special interests include general medicine and postgraduate medical education.

Victoria Welsh completed academic GP training in North Staffordshire. She currently works as a GP locum and Doctoral Research Fellow at the Arthritis Research UK Primary Care Centre, Keele University.

James Willis was a GP, trainer and course organiser. After writing his book *The Paradox of Progress* from his experience in practice he became a regular contributor to the BJGP and other medical journals, wrote a second book, and delivered numerous talks and lectures, including the opening keynote of the annual congress of the Dutch College of GPs in The Hague. He served as Provost of the Wessex Faculty and was on the organising committees of two national college conferences. His website is www.friendsinlowplaces.co.uk.

James Woollard is an ST6 specialty registrar in child and adolescent mental health in London, UK, who was a GP trainee for a year before embarking on a continuing career in psychiatry. His research interests are in the use of digital technology in health care, social media and young people's mental health, and trainee leadership in healthcare policy.

Matthew Yates is an Army GPST2 working at Frimley Park Hospital on the Defence Deanery VTS. Sandhurst trained, he spent time working as a Regimental Medical Officer to an infantry battalion before embarking on GP training. Prior to that, he spent ten years working in various financial positions in the City of London.

John S. Yudkin is Emeritus Professor of Medicine at University College London. His clinical and research interests have focused on diabetes and obesity, recently concentrating on the false assumptions of 'glucocentricity'. He has a longstanding interest in global health, and founded UCL's International Health and Medical Education Centre, which launched the UK's first Intercalated BSc in International Health.

ACKNOWLEDGEMENTS

Matt Burkes would like to thank Ruth, Leif, River and Flint. Also my Nan (who has always believed in me, even when I didn't). Thanks to David Haslam, who encouraged me to keep writing, and to Bill Rogers – a truly great trainer.

Alec Logan would like to thank Janice and the boys. And three generations of general practice Logans, especially his father Jim who first enthused him. And salty chums. And Chris.

Red Roses is an exhibition of texts and linocuts inspired by the vignettes that appear in this book. The vignettes were written by Matt Burkes, David Haslam, Dougal Jefferies, Helen Lester, Alec Logan, Faye McCleery, Hans Pieper and Deborah Swinglehurst. We are grateful to the artist Helen Wilson for allowing the reproductions of her original linocuts to appear in this book.

INTRODUCTION

ON BEING A PATIENT

Antony Chuter

When I was asked to write this I wondered what I should focus on. Should I write about the importance of listening and hearing? Well, I thought that would be covered already. Should I write about care and compassion? But all the GPs I know in the RCGP are the epitome of care and compassion. In fact, it was their wish to be caring and compassionate that led them into general practice in the first place. If you are training to be a GP, and reading this book, I am sure you will recognise these feelings.

I thought about my mother and what she would want a training GP to know. She would say: 'Start from the beginning when looking for answers.' This is because she lived with an undiagnosed overactive thyroid for a number of years. She lived with it until a locum one day decided to 'Start from the beginning' with her.

I wondered what has made the biggest difference to me as a patient. What is it that helps me connect with a GP? I decided that, for me, it is humanity and humility. This is because for years I felt a failure. Doctors said to me, 'This test is normal' or 'This test is negative'. No doctor would say to me, 'I don't know what is wrong with you.' I felt that they did not believe me. AND – I was still in pain.

The revolution in the doctor/patient relationship happened to me when I met a GP who was not afraid to say, 'I don't know, but together we will find out.' He also respected me as a self-manager. He would ask me how I was and what I was doing to help myself. He would then support and encourage me. He always congratulated me when I was doing something well. This helped build my trust in him and my confidence in my ability to manage my health. This positive circle continues.

Two other things you should never forget when you are with a patient are fear and frustration! When someone goes to their GP, the emotions they are most likely to be experiencing will be fear, frustration or a mixture of the two. Typical thoughts are:

'What is wrong?' 'Will it go away?' 'Can you fix it?' 'Can I fix it?' and 'What if it can't be fixed?' Reassurance is key. But you knew that, didn't you?

It is a new world in many ways for GPs. A world where other skills are needed in addition to taking a history and giving a diagnosis. We are told that the future is one of growing long-term conditions where the need for 'shared decision making' is key. But, in reality, it is a world where the core attributes I have been talking about will be the key for patients to trust and work with you.

So caring, compassion, searching and not giving up, humanity, humility, not being afraid to say 'I don't know'. These things all make you human. Supporting, encouraging and congratulating are all essential components of a GP. Add to this the RCGP motto of 'Cum Scientia Caritas' (i.e. Caring with Science) and I think you have the core of what you, as a young GP, need to aspire to.

INTRODUCTION

DOCTORING

John Frey III

In a career that began 45 years ago with entry into medical school, I often have difficulty remembering, with any specificity, how I learned doctoring. The diseases were quite different then. The tools and the places where we worked were as well. Problems were skewed heavily towards infectious disease, surgical problems and trauma. Access to laboratories was limited by what we could do right then and there and the availability of someone to do it. None of the current office-based tools was around – no dip-sticks, no glucometers – only gram stains, spun urines and blood agar for strep cultures. Some things, such as MRI, were not even invented and most of the just-in-time assays of everything from RSV in children to drug screens were not even dreamed of. Lipid measurement took days to weeks to return. The other day, when following up on a patient with hypothyroid disease, I thought to myself that obtaining a TSH wasn't possible when I started because, at that point in time, the existence of TSH – much less all the other hormone assays that we routinely follow – could only be inferred and not measured.

But the changes that have happened from then to now in the technology and the diseases and the pharmaceuticals and the management are all ones, with application of reading and listening and consulting with others in medicine, that can be kept up with. I have attended endless conferences, meetings and continuing education courses filled with content that I would learn, then change when the next development came along. Anyone beginning their training or starting practice now can be reassured, as we would reassure ourselves in the early 70s, that everything will change all the time and be comfortable with the thought. The tools that allow access to both new information via the internet and, more importantly, distillation of that new information by thoughtful intermediaries through hand-held digital communication will only become easier. Facts at one's fingertips are a reality, even facts that have been refereed by colleagues or experts. It should not be unsettling that whatever information you learn now will be less relevant over time. You will get new information about new things or about old problems.

On the other hand, what I learned from patients over these intervening years has been universal. Julian Tudor Hart said that the correction of social ignorance is one of the chief purposes of general practice education. Although I have become less socially ignorant over time, the process never ends. Kafka famously said, in his short story 'A Country Doctor', that 'to write prescriptions is easy, to come to an understanding with people is hard'. Coming to an understanding with people will always remain the work of general practice and it comes, in great part, from living with and listening to our patients. In 1970, Philip Tumulty wrote that 'managing a sick patient is entirely different from diagnosing an illness and prescribing something for it. … the ways of management of a sick person can only come out of an understanding spirit, and a sensitive as well as perceptive and educated mind'. Tumulty goes on to say that 'a first rate clinician trains himself to do two things exceedingly well: to talk to his patients and listen to them'.

Having taught medical students and physicians in training for all these years, I can attest that listening does not always come naturally. We come with a life experience that is quite different from most of the people we care for in communities. We have an education, engage in satisfying work, have a good income and have prestige that we may or may not have earned. We often believe that our life experience, within a narrow range, is that of most of the people we care for. It isn't, of course. That reality rarely enters into our formal education but it does intrude into the realities of daily work. It is not just social class differences that demand admitting our social ignorance but the continuous daily weighing of what we think we would do if we were in the place of our patients, often with a comparison that favours us rather than our patients. We assume that we would assiduously follow our GP's instructions, we would eat right, we would exercise, we would avoid risky behaviour, we would love, honour and obey our spouses, we would follow directions and avoid excessive use. But, of course, we don't. No one does all the time.

When we see how our patients struggle with the burden of illness that affects their lives in every way, when they try to do what they are supposed to do only to have chronic illness and time and age wear them down anyway, when anger and helplessness, loneliness and isolation, fear and pain all gang up on people who have the best intentions and drag them down, again – when we see all this, we realise that there are forces working against our patients and our desire to help them that we simply don't understand. It is then that we realise that working and hoping for small victories rather than dramatic triumphs is the real task of daily practice. But patients let us into their lives as friends and treat us with respect and value what we do for them, even when we feel, in our hearts, that we have done very little. They not only correct our social ignorance but also they enrich our humanity, they temper our arrogance, they teach us to be humble and help us when we feel we have failed. 'It is all right doc, you did the best you could.' And they believe it and we, despite second thoughts and self-recrimination, begin to believe it ourselves. We accept that our role as healers is rarely heroic but more often simply being present, listening and promising to stay with our patients, no matter what. If they are willing to try, then we are willing to help them do it. That is what we learn if we listen to our patients.

All that can happen in the office and it is quite a lot indeed. When we live among our patients, or try to spend time in their world, be that home visits, nursing homes, schools or, in widening circles, their workplaces, neighbourhoods and social gatherings, then everything we observe is data and the experience informs our understanding of their lives. We are closer to learning what Kafka described as the hard work. We come to an understanding with people. The parent at a sporting outing with their children, lovers walking along the street, the way pictures are arranged on walls in old people's houses, how a waitress treats her customers, how a workman stands with his shovel and looks at the product of his labour – how our patients appear in their world gives us some idea of how that world bears down on them or bears them up. I drove by a housing project in the city on one of the first real spring days this year and caught sight of a father, a patient of mine, sitting on the front stoop of the house in the late afternoon sunlight with his little son snuggled up under his arm, just looking at the world together. Now I understand something more of who this man is and what gives him joy, and it is not contained in his medical record.

All this is doctoring. It includes all the things I know about medicine from those guidelines, websites, databases and protocols as applied to this complex, remarkable, flawed and hopeful human being who sits with me in my clinic office and where I negotiate what needs to happen, possibilities for their future, or sit in silence when it all seems too much. It is a gift for us, a place of stories, a life of service and a source of heartache. It is much more than we thought and much harder, too. But, once into it, you will never regret that it is the path you took because, even when it seems hard or frustrating, someone will look up from the seat opposite you or the sick bed and say, 'Thank you, doctor.' It is the best reward.

RED ROSES

It was the end of my first house job and life was wonderful. I was working on a mixed medical ward with many dermatology patients (it was the day when your boss could be a generalist with an interest) and I'd just had an amazing weekend away in the middle of the Yorkshire Dales with my other half (fellow houseman – met as medical students) when I thought he might propose. I got back on the ward on the Monday morning to find the biggest bunch of red roses I'd ever seen waiting for me on the nursing station. I thought I'd find a ring in the middle of one of the stems but no – it was from one the elderly ladies who'd been discharged home the previous week. She'd been admitted with uncontrolled psoriasis and the treatment included quite aggressive fluid restriction. The note read, 'To Dr Burgess – thank you for arguing with the consultant that I needed an extra 100 ml for a cup of tea to get me going every morning. It made such a difference to me.' It's always the little things, the personal things, that people appreciate most.

Postscript: I've spent most of my adult life 'arguing' with authority one way or another, usually about ways to improve patient care – and Huw proposed the following week in the much more romantic setting of the hospital canteen.

Helen Lester

PART I

TIPS FOR TRAINEES WORKING IN THE HOSPITAL SETTING

1

THE BASICS

Matt Burkes

Congratulations! You have secured a place on a general practice training scheme. If you play your cards right you will become a fully fledged GP in no time at all! The years of hospital training rotations may look daunting as they stretch out in front of you, but they will pass more quickly than you can imagine. Consider the positives! You are in secure employment and learning skills that will (mostly) be useful to your future career. This section of the book will take you through common training posts and give you some idea of the basics. The more basic knowledge you turn up with, the more you can potentially get out of the attachment.

Before we get started, though, there are a few basic points that apply to any hospital post for GP trainees.

› Don't be late.

› Get on with your colleagues.

› Remember that the people you meet and work with in the hospital may well be your colleagues (and patients) for many years to come, so making a good impression now will make your life in general practice easier in the future.

› Watch experienced colleagues at work. They will all do it differently. Take the aspects of their work that you like and integrate them into your own style.

› Listen to the nurses and do not needlessly get involved in confrontations/power struggles.

› Be respectful when making/taking referrals.

› Work hard.

› Get your hands dirty.

› Know where to find the resuscitation trolley on every ward, what's on it and how to use it.

› Know your local antimicrobial policy, or where to access it.

› Keep a jobs list and ensure that specific jobs are allocated to specific individuals. Make sure everyone is clear on their responsibilities.

› Develop a list of useful phone numbers within the hospital and add this to your list.

› Talk to your patients. Listen to your patients. Be their advocate when required.

› Look out for the vulnerable adult. If you have any concerns, speak to your consultant.

› Ensure that you view the patient in the context of his or her social milieu, rather than just his or her bed number.

› When you first start a specialty rotation you will find some patients know more about their condition than you do.

› Hospital admissions tend to be complex with numerous problems and medication changes. Try to provide GPs with as much information as possible on discharge. It will be you on the receiving end soon.

› Be aware of, and receptive to, learning opportunities in your jobs. Be proactive – find the experiences you need if they are not handed to you on a plate. This is especially true since the introduction of the European Working Time Directive – there is much less 'firm working' and exposure to learning opportunities.

› Take every opportunity to teach junior team members/medical students/peers/ allied health professionals while in your post. Teaching it to others is one of the best ways of learning about a subject!

› Plan your learning with a personal development plan (PDP).

› Talk to your clinical supervisor in the first week of the job. Go to this meeting with your PDP. Give him or her a copy and work out together how best your clinical supervisor can help you achieve the learning you need.

› Some GP trainees feel that anything that doesn't involve sitting in primary care and seeing patients is not relevant to their future career. This obviously isn't true. If you don't learn core skills in your hospital jobs, when you can ask your boss for help, then prepare for a scary ride in primary care when you are alone in a room with the patient.

> Being positive and having a 'can-do' approach to the job will be appreciated by your seniors. This in turn will generally lead to a better experience.

> Don't be pressurised to perform procedures that you are not comfortable doing but do be prepared to learn how to do them safely, according to local protocols.

> If you are having problems in a job then DO SOMETHING ABOUT IT. Let someone know while there is still time to change things. This could be your consultant, your educational supervisor or your course director.

> All jobs will have an aspect of service provision, and you need to accept this. However, if service requirements are preventing you from meeting your learning needs, you should seek help. Your argument will be more credible if you have a detailed and realistic PDP.

> Keep in touch with your primary care educational supervisor.

> Do your assessments – plan to do them early, and try not to leave them to the last week of a job.

> Keep an eye on the future – What do you need to achieve at the end of your training? How will you do this? An excellent CV can be built from scratch in two years. What will you put on yours? What sort of GP do you want to be? What skills/experiences will help to fulfil this goal?

> Have fun. The hospital is a vibrant social environment. Once you've left it, you've left it. Enjoy it while you can.

2

ACUTE MEDICINE

Honor Hinxman, Tim Martindale and Matt Burkes

Working on the Medical Admissions Unit (MAU) is a perfect opportunity to hone your skills in history taking, examination, investigations and management of both common medical presentations and some more rare conditions. It also provides an environment where you can develop communication and management skills while running the take, delegating to your on-call team, and prioritising unwell patients. Depending on your local policy, you may be expected to 'hold the phone' and accept referrals from the community as well as from the Accident and Emergency (A&E) Department. These interactions will be very helpful in improving your telephone consulting skills and referral technique. Increasingly, however, this role is now filled by nursing or more senior medical staff.

This chapter provides a guide to help you through a typical job on the MAU that will allow you to feel more prepared for the days ahead and the expectations on you as the GPST doctor, as well as covering your educational needs.

THE BASICS

1. Your F1/medical student days are over. When clerking you have to 'hang your hat' and diagnose! Base your diagnosis on a clinical assessment; don't just hang on for chest X-rays (CXR) and bloods. Try to come up with differentials and write them down, because this will help you to plan your investigations and make you think!

2. Familiarise yourself with the common and serious presentations to the MAU and the immediate management of these patients. These include chest pain, shortness

of breath, sepsis, cough, weakness, 'off legs', diabetic ketoacidosis, hyperosmolar hyperglycaemic nonketotic coma and renal failure, to name but a few.

3. Undress the patient to examine him or her.

4. Remember that the notes you make could be read out in court, so ensure good documentation at all times.

5. You're going to be busy. Learn to deal with it. Book holidays early.

THE PATIENTS

6. The time you spend with a patient and his or her relatives in the MAU will influence the patient's entire admission. Inevitably, the diagnosis you make will shape the patient's management on the post-take ward round and the course of action for the next few days. The way you treat the family will shape their expectations for the next few years.

7. Remember, hospitals are really scary places. We see them day in, day out so we forget the impact of the loss of autonomy and privacy that often go with acute admissions. Strive to maintain and protect your patient's dignity at all times.

8. When discharging a patient, make sure you understand the diagnosis and follow-up arrangements. Take the time to explain to the patient and/or relatives what the diagnosis/suspected diagnosis is, what the investigations have found (if appropriate), what treatment has been started and why. Patients are much more likely to take medication if they understand what it is for. Give them the opportunity to clarify details and ask questions.

9. Explain what, if any, follow-up is planned, even if that is just to see the patient's own GP if symptoms recur. Patients really appreciate this. Also, try to convey this information to the patient's GP on the discharge letter; if your patient hasn't understood what has happened then the GP will be his or her first port of call.

REFERRALS AND TEAMWORK

10. If you are taking referrals, listen before asking questions. You need to know: Why does the patient need to come in? What is the possible diagnosis? Most importantly, how sick is he or she? And, therefore, how soon do you need to see the patient?

11. If the referral is from A&E, ask what appropriate investigations have been done before referral (and, if needed, politely request these are done before transfer, for example bloods, electrocardiogram, CXR). If the referring doctor has a specific

diagnosis in mind, check if he or she has started appropriate treatment, as there may be a time delay before you are able to see the patient.

12. Don't be rude to referring doctors on the telephone – it just makes everyone's day unpleasant. Interrupting referrals to make people justify themselves causes the referring doctor to become flustered and annoyed, rapport breaks down, and the information delivery stalls.

13. 'Bouncing' referrals is rare. Another doctor has seen the patient and believes he or she needs to come in for further management. Remember, it is extremely unlikely that, over the phone, you can accurately and safely make a judgement to the contrary. If referrals are noted to be inappropriate, as some are, you have senior colleagues/consultants who can address this. You can always get the A&E team to call/bleep the on-call registrar and remove yourself from the equation.

14. Bear in mind that not everyone is 'good' at making referrals, especially early in the process, so try to make their job as easy as possible.

15. Do not venture negative opinions of other doctors to patients; it is unnecessary and unprofessional.

16. You may have several other doctors (and nurses) who you work alongside in acute medicine. One skill to develop early is the ability to delegate effectively, for example asking a nurse to take bloods on a patient you have clerked so that you can review a sick patient in A&E.

17. You will learn a great deal from the nursing staff, many of whom have worked in their area for many years, such as those who work in coronary care. Their knowledge is invaluable. But remember the patient and his or her treatment is still your responsibility.

18. Always listen to concerned nursing staff. If they are worried about a patient, you should be too. While it is common practice to see patients in time order, that is not always clinically appropriate, and if a patient looks unwell or has abnormal observations then someone (not necessarily you) needs to see him or her sooner rather than later.

SKILLS AND DEVELOPMENT

19. Acute medicine is a great opportunity to become competent and confident in a variety of practical procedures, such as lumbar puncture and chest drain insertion. Some people will actively avoid such things. However, at night when there are fewer people around and something needs to be done quickly, you will be glad of having experience of carrying out such procedures under supervision and with guidance.

20. Take every opportunity to gain the knowledge and procedural skills in a safe environment; observe and assist others before undertaking procedures independently. Never perform a procedure you do not feel comfortable doing.

21. As part of the acute medical team, and during on-call, you will usually form part of the 'crash team'. For confidence, the Advanced Life Support (ALS) course is very useful. This will help you to develop skills in running arrests when necessary – there is nothing worse than an arrest with no team leader! For practice, ask your registrar if you can lead any arrest calls during a shift. That way, they are there to guide you if needed. Confidence, deep breaths and ABC are all you need. And use your team – you are all working towards the same goal.

22. Attend medical meetings, for example grand rounds, departmental meetings and junior teaching. Offer to present if you see something rare or interesting. The more you do, the easier it gets and it looks good on your CV. Also look out for relevant courses you may wish to attend. You have a study budget for the purpose of learning.

23. This job really lends itself to audit projects and completing the audit cycle during your rotation. Express an interest early and let your seniors guide you as to what would be useful, interesting and easy to audit.

24. There is a huge capacity to learn during your daily job and your knowledge base will expand dramatically. You will rapidly feel comfortable with common presentations and their management, but do take every opportunity to learn from peers, seniors and your consultants at the bedside or on ward rounds if anything is less familiar. What you learn now will be taken with you to your future career as a GP, so keep yourself open to new knowledge and skills.

25. Pass on what you have learned – there are lots of opportunities for bedside teaching in acute medicine. And learning comes through teaching others!

26. Most of all, enjoy it!

POTENTIAL PDP POINTERS

› Learn to prioritise patients clinically as they are admitted to the MAU.

› Further develop existing time management skills to manage the busy acute workload.

› Learn to delegate and use medical and ancillary personnel appropriately.

› Develop skills in the prompt and accurate assessment of acutely unwell patients, including attending and leading cardiac arrest situations.

› Build on existing skills in X-ray, blood gas and ECG interpretation.

› Improve knowledge of the management of common acute cardiac presentations including myocardial infarction and heart failure.

› Improve knowledge of the management of common acute gastroenterology presentations including upper GI bleed, inflammatory bowel disease and liver disease.

› Improve knowledge of the management of common acute metabolic presentations including diabetic ketoacidosis.

› Improve knowledge of the management of common acute neurological presentations including headache, transient ischaemic attack (TIA) and cerebro-vascular accident (CVA).

› Improve knowledge of the management of common acute respiratory presentations including asthma, exacerbation of chronic obstructive pulmonary disease (COPD) and pleural effusion.

3

BREAST SURGERY

Laura Smith

Breast surgery is very different from any other surgical specialty and has become very sub-specialised with the evolution of oncoplastic breast surgery.

Time is divided mainly between clinic and theatres, with very few inpatients. Most of the patients are fit and well, so hospital stays are short, and post-op complications are rare.

Breast surgery is very much a consultant-led specialty with seniors expecting to be consulted by trainees about the majority of patients. This is wholly reassuring for any junior, GP trainee or otherwise.

THE BASICS

1. Despite the sub-specialist nature of breast surgery, the evaluation of patients is approached in a systematic fashion with the triple assessment. This consists of clinical examination, imaging (mammogram/ultrasound scan [USS]) and tissue sampling (cytology ± biopsy).

2. When taking a history of the lump, ask about: time scale, nipple discharge and changes in the lump during the menstrual cycle.

3. Family history is so often forgotten beyond medical school, but is of particular relevance here, as is smoking and alcohol history.

4. Risk factors for malignant breast disease are mostly related to hormone exposure. This helps when trying to remember the list:

a) Early menarche <11 years
b) Late menopause >54
c) First pregnancy >40
d) Hormone replacement therapy use
e) Not breast feeding
f) Nulliparity
g) Family history of breast/ovarian/bowel cancer.

5. The specifics of breast assessment are abbreviated to palpation (P), radiology (R), cytology (C) and histology (H). These are then graded 1–5 ranging from normal to malignant. This seems like a foreign language initially, but learning it is essential to understand multidisciplinary team meetings, and simple clinical discussions.

6. If the patient has felt a lump, ask the patient to point it out, as this can save some embarrassment when you can't find it on examination.

7. Compare and contrast the two sides.

8. When examining a lump, the most important thing to determine is discrete lumps vs. nodularity. Discrete lumps stand out from the surrounding tissue with definable borders, and hence can be measured. Nodularity is ill defined, and may fluctuate with the menstrual cycle.

9. Think skin changes.

10. Never forget the axilla, even if the problem seems entirely benign.

THE PATIENTS

11. Patients attending breast clinic tend to be in a fragile emotional state, whether they have found a lump or are attending after screening. These patients are in need of emotional care, as well as medical. Bear this is mind, and always have some tissues to hand.

12. Breast examinations are intimate, and unnerving for the patient. Ensure there is a chaperone, and only expose the patient when you need to.

13. Cancer will be on everyone's mind; don't avoid saying the word.

14. Seeing young patients with the potential of any breast pathology can be traumatic, for them and you. This is especially true as breast cancer can affect this younger age group.

15. Men can get breast pathology. As embarrassing and emotional breast problems are for a woman, it will be magnified in a man.

BREAST CANCER

16. Patients with a new diagnosis will fall into new lumps vs. screening identified. Both of these groups will be fearing the worst.

17. Think about the treatment in terms of:
    a) The patient
    b) The breast
    c) The axilla
    d) Adjuvant treatment, e.g. hormonal modification, chemo- or radiotherapy.

18. Breast-conserving surgery is very much in vogue at the moment, but don't let your team's enthusiasm for fancy operations mask the patient's best interests. A 30-year-old woman has very different needs from an 80-year-old.

19. Cancer will be *in situ* or invasive, ductal or lobular.

20. Axillary surgery varies from sentinel node biopsy, axillary node sampling to clearances (of which there are three levels).

21. Never remove an axillary drain without confirming it with someone more experienced.

BREAST SEPSIS

22. Unlike any other abscess, in the breast we aim not to 'incise and drain', and this is in fact the last resort. Initial treatment is antibiotics ± aspiration (usually ultrasound guided).

23. Most breast sepsis occurs in lactating women, and they should be advised to continue feeding/expressing from the affected breast.

24. Non-lactating breast abscesses are associated with smoking in 90% of cases. Continuing to smoke leads to a high recurrence rate. Make sure your patient is aware of this.

MASTALGIA

25. Always think cyclical vs. non-cyclical.

26. Cyclical is never caused by cancer, while non-cyclical is very, very rarely caused by cancer, so you can reassure the patients.

27. Pain is treated exactly as you would a sprained ankle: support (i.e. a well-fitting bra) and non-steroidal anti-inflammatory drugs (NSAIDs) (topical or oral). After these simple interventions, things get a little more complicated and senior input should be sought.

POTENTIAL PDP POINTERS

› Become comfortable and confident with breast examinations. Patients will be nervous, and your confidence will put them at ease.

› Breast cancer follow-up is routine and protocol driven so become familiar with this – some NHS trusts are pushing for it to be more primary care driven.

› Gaining knowledge of the after care for mastectomy, wide local excision and axillary sampling/clearance will help your patients know what to expect. In addition, learn the management of common post-operative complications.

› One-stop breast clinics exist in most trusts to speed the diagnosis and treatment of breast pathology. Insight into how these run, and briefing your patients accordingly at the time of referral, means they won't be shocked when going for a mammogram/ultrasound ± biopsy on the same day.

4

CARDIOLOGY

Robert Adam

At some point during your GP training you may find yourself slotted into a cardiology firm. It may seem daunting when you first arrive on the Coronary Care Unit (CCU), but remember many have gone through this before and most have survived to tell the tale.

During this training period you should try to gain exposure to a wide range of cardiac presentations, investigations and treatment strategies. This will hopefully build your confidence and ability when tackling these issues in the community.

Keeping things simple is the key to making the most of this attachment. If you approach your cardiology tenure with a positive, inquisitive attitude, you are likely to find it a great learning experience.

Below are a few tips, which will hopefully help you through your placement.

THE BASICS

1. Remember that patient safety is your ultimate priority at all times. If you have doubts or are unsure seek senior help a.s.a.p.

2. Revise your Advanced Life Support (ALS) manual. If you haven't done ALS, seriously consider it.[1] The course will greatly improve your confidence when dealing with unstable patients.

3. Find the resuscitation trolleys. It is highly likely that you will need one at some point. Get to grips with the style of defibrillator on the ward.

4. Locate the cardiac nurse specialists. They will know how the hospital works and often help you in 'sticky' situations.

5. Learn how to use the CCU telemetry system. Being able to review the recorded data without disturbing the nurses will make your ward rounds easier and keep everyone happy.

6. Pin a copy of the latest Driver and Vehicle Licensing Agency (DVLA) cardio-vascular disorder guidelines[2] to the wall of the doctor's office. Patients ask about driving and it is good to have the facts.

7. Know where exercise tolerance tests are undertaken and remember the quickest routes there. At some point you will be fast bleeped to review a patient.

8. Ask questions. Most cardiologists will be more than happy to take you through what they know.

9. Stay calm. CCU can be a stressful place when things aren't going to plan. One cool head can go a long way in these situations.

THE PATIENTS

10. Remember that a patient's main concern might not be how many leads their pacemaker has or which coronary artery has been stented. Uncertainty about the potential impact to their employability, exercise tolerance, driving status, diet or sex life can often cause greater confusion and anxiety. These issues can sometimes be overlooked on busy ward rounds, so make yourself available to discuss the patient's ideas, concerns and expectations, as these are the problems you are more likely to encounter in general practice. And remember that many of your patients think that they will die soon, another MI just waiting around the corner.

INVESTIGATIONS

11. Don't be afraid of ECGs. Remember the basics: RATE, RHYTHM and AXIS.

12. Remember the mnemonic 'WiLLiaM MaRRoW' when assessing prolonged QRS complexes:

    › W pattern in leads V1–V2 and M pattern in leads V5–V6 is Left bundle branch block

    › M pattern in leads V1–V2 and W in leads V3–V6 is Right bundle branch block.

13. Remind yourself of what an ST elevation myocardial infarction looks like. At some point an orthopaedic junior will wander up to you and hold up an ECG covered in ST elevation. Make sure you can recognise it!

14. Always look at the QT interval on an ECG, especially in patients who have presented with collapse. A prolonged QT interval increases the risk of ventricular tachyarrhythmia such as torsades de pointes.

15. Sit in on a few echocardiography sessions and try to learn the basics. This will improve your understanding of the reports you receive.

16. The National Institute for Health and Care Excellence (NICE) published new guidelines regarding the investigation of patients with *Chest Pain of Recent Onset* in 2010.[3] This is not the most exciting thing you will ever read, but a quick review will bring you up to date with the current recommendations. Find out which services are available at your hospital.

CLINICAL SKILLS

17. Polish your stethoscope skills. Cardiology wards are awash with different heart sounds. Many of your patients will have an echocardiogram, so test your ability to detect and identify murmurs.

18. Perfect the art of assessing fluid status. Being able to do this accurately will help you in the community.

CHEST PAIN

19. Not every chest pain is an acute coronary syndrome (ACS). I know that it has been drilled into you since your first day of clinical medicine, but a good history and examination are the key to assessing any patient. Approach every patient with an open mind.

20. Ask patients about cardiac risk factors.

21. Ensure an erect chest X-ray has been done before any ACS medication is given. Patients with thoracic aneurysms and perforated peptic ulcers don't tend to do well if given loading doses of aspirin, clopidogrel and enoxaparin!

22. Troponin tests can be very useful, but only when interpreted correctly in the clinical context of the patient. A negative troponin doesn't rule out ischaemic heart disease.

23. Thrombolysis In Myocardial Infarction (TIMI)[4] or Global Registry of Acute Coronary Events (GRACE)[5] scoring systems can be used to assess the risk of death and ischaemic events in patients with an ACS. A basic understanding of these will be useful when considering further investigations or treatment plans.

24. Locate the cardiac catheterisation lab. If there isn't one in your hospital find out where the nearest one is and whom you need to talk when patients need to be transferred.

25. Post-myocardial infarction (MI) clinics will mostly be allocated to the junior doctors as a 'good learning experience'. Prevention guidelines are a useful resource.[6]

ARRHYTHMIAS

26. If a patient with an arrhythmia has any of the following symptoms, IMMEDIATE treatment is needed:
    › hypotension (systolic <90 mmHg)
    › syncope
    › heart failure
    › myocardial ischaemia
    › extremes of heart rate (<40 b.p.m. or >150 b.p.m.).

27. Beware of broad complex tachycardia. Contact a registrar or consultant a.s.a.p. if you encounter one. Get the defibrillator pads on the patient and follow ALS guidelines if you have to wait for the cavalry to arrive.

28. If you are unsure about how to externally place using a defibrillator ask one of the registrars to show you. This can be a lifesaver.

29. Check the potassium, magnesium, calcium and thyroid function of patients with arrhythmias, fast or slow.

30. Atrial fibrillation (AF) and atrial flutter are the most common arrhythmias you will encounter both in the hospital and in general practice. Familiarise yourself with the NICE 'quick read' guidelines on atrial fibrillation.[7] Try to get comfortable with the main drugs used to rate control.

31. Don't give beta-blockers and rate-limiting calcium channel blockers (diltiazem or verapamil) together. This will only cause trouble!

32. If the onset of AF/atrial flutter is within 48 hours DC cardioversion may be an option.[7] Make the patient nil by mouth and ask a senior to review the case.

33. Go to the elective DC cardioversion lists. This will increase your confidence when using the defibrillators. Always check that the defibrillator is synchronised before cardioverting a patient.

34. The CHA_2DS_2-VASc score is a useful tool when assessing the stroke risk of AF patients. Knowing this system will help you make decisions regarding anti-coagulation therapy.

35. Any patient being considered for anticoagulation should have his or her risk of major bleeding assessed prior to starting therapy. The HAS-BLED score can be used to help assess this risk.[8]

HEART FAILURE

36. Continuous Positive Airway Pressure (CPAP) is a useful tool when dealing with acute heart failure. Find out where you can access this and review the local guidelines.

37. Don't use beta-blockers in the setting of acute heart failure. They are useful further down the line, just not at the front door.[9]

38. Treating heart failure can be a fine balancing act. Introduce new medications at low doses and titrate slowly.

39. When large doses of diuretic are being used, check renal function and electrolytes on a regular basis.

40. Ensure patients have daily weights. This is a crude but very useful way of assessing fluid status. Ensure the patient's final weight is included in the discharge summary.

41. Find out if there are community heart failure nurses attached to your hospital. If there are, get them involved early as this will often lead to a safer discharge.

AND FINALLY

42. Enjoy your attachment. Don't be overawed by the experience. Like everything in life you will get out of it what you put in.

POTENTIAL PDP POINTERS

Prior to starting your cardiology placement set yourself some learning goals. Discuss these with your clinical supervisor and try to focus on areas where you feel your knowledge could be improved.

Statement 3.12 (*Cardiovascular Problems*) of the RCGP curriculum sets out what you should be aiming to accomplish during your training. Below are the most important points.

› Become familiar with and feel comfortable managing ACS, arrhythmias and acute heart failure.

› Become familiar and up to date with the latest treatment protocols for chronic cardiac conditions, including angina, hypertension and chronic heart failure.

> Attend cardiology outpatient clinics to gain valuable experience in the assessment and management of common cardiac conditions.

> Show evidence of understanding of the importance of primary and secondary prevention of cardiovascular problems. Get to grips with the most recent guidelines during your attachment. Use mini-clinical evaluation exercise (mini-CEX) and case-based discussion (CbD) assessments to show that you understand the principles involved.

> Use your attachment to gain experience and understanding of the services available to you in the community, including:

- rapid-assessment chest pain clinic
- cardiac specialist nurses
- community heart failure nurses
- physiotherapist-led cardiac rehabilitation
- dieticians
- smoking cessation team.

REFERENCES

1. Resuscitation Council UK. *Advanced Life Support*. London: RC, 2010, www.resus.org.uk/pages/als.pdf [accessed March 2014].

2. Drivers Medical Group. *At a Glance Guide to the Current Medical Standards of Fitness to Drive*. Swansea: DVLA, 2013, www.dft.gov.uk/dvla/medical/ataglance.aspx [accessed March 2014].

3. National Institute for Health and Clinical Excellence. *Chest Pain of Recent Onset: assessment and diagnosis of recent onset chest pain or discomfort of suspected cardiac origin*. London: NICE, 2010, www.nice.org.uk/nicemedia/live/12947/47918/47918.pdf [accessed March 2014].

4. www.timi.org/ [accessed March 2014].

5. www.outcomes-umassmed.org/GRACE/acs_risk/acs_risk_content.html [accessed March 2014].

6. National Institute for Health and Care Excellence. *MI – secondary prevention. Secondary prevention in primary and secondary care for patients following a myocardial infarction*. London: NICE, 2013, http://guidance.nice.org.uk/CG172 [accessed March 2014].

7. National Institute for Health and Clinical Excellence. *Atrial Fibrillation: the management of atrial fibrillation*. London: NICE, 2006, www.nice.org.uk/nicemedia/pdf/CG036niceguideline.pdf [accessed March 2014]

8. Pisters R, Lane DA, Nieuwlaat R, *et al*. A novel user-friendly score (HAS-BLED) to assess 1-year risk of major bleeding in patients with atrial fibrillation: the Euro Heart Survey. *Chest* 2010; **138(5)**: 1093–100. Epub 18 March 2010.

9. National Institute for Health and Clinical Excellence. *Chronic Heart Failure: management of chronic heart failure in adults in primary and secondary care*. London: NICE, www.nice.org.uk/nicemedia/live/13099/50526/50526.pdf [accessed March 2014].

SEQUELAE MI

My patient is an 82-year-old lady who had an MI six weeks ago – full on whizz-bangery, three stents, no messing!

'Are you getting lots of help from the family?' I enquired.

'Ah, ma son. He won't let me do anything. Follows me around like a wee collie dug!'

Red Roses *collection curated by Alec Logan and illustrated by Helen Wilson.*

5

COLORECTAL SURGERY

Laura Smith and Neil Cripps

As a GP trainee covering a colorectal team, you will encounter a variety of pathologies and patients. This can range from a younger population with inflammatory bowel disease (IBD), older patients with bowel cancers and those of any age with anorectal complaints.

Colorectal cancer is common; it's the third most common cancer in men, and the second most common in women. It is, however, very treatable; survival rates are increasing all the time with the introduction of screening programmes using faecal occult blood. The throughput of patients needing to be seen, investigated and treated by colorectal surgeons is also increasing. Patients will understandably have questions, which, with the help of a colorectal placement, you will be able to answer.

Your attachment will give you a huge insight into the investigation, operations and complications that your patients in primary care could have. This understanding will help enormously when counselling patients and following them up in primary care.

THE BASICS

1. Colorectal surgery requires a rounded approach to patient care, as well as close relationships with other professionals including gastroenterologists, radiologists, stoma nurses and dieticians.

2. Attending outpatients will give you a clear picture of what represents a high-risk pattern of symptoms in bowel cancer. This will stand you in great stead for the remainder of your clinical career.

3. Be aware of the different type of stomas and what they produce (see Box 5.1).

4. Colonic resections are determined by the blood supply to that part of the bowel (see Box 5.2).

5. A chaperone should be used in clinic for invasive examinations from a PR to rigid sigmoidoscopy. It is reassuring for the patients to have someone else there, and covers your back.

6. IBD patients will sometimes know more about their disease and its treatment/ complications than any junior doctor. They are the experts, so try to learn from them.

BOX 5.1: STOMAS

- Ileostomies are (generally) right sided, spouted and produce a more liquid effluent.

- Colostomies are (generally) left sided, flat to abdominal wall and produce more solid stool.

- Ileostomies are formed because:
  - they divert bowel contents to allow a more distal anastomosis to heal without complication
  - the distal bowel has been resected, i.e. an end ileostomy.

- Colostomies are formed:
  - because they protect a distal anastomosis (rarely)
  - because at operation it is deemed that a primary anastomosis is likely to fail. This is usually the case in an emergency operation with peritoneal contamination, i.e. a Hartmann's procedure
  - because the distal bowel has been resected, i.e. after an abdominoperineal resection for low rectal cancer
  - to defunction a diseased segment, e.g. an obstructing tumour.

BOX 5.2: RESECTIONS

- Right hemicolectomy: caecum → first third of the transverse colon. Primary ileocolonic anastomosis, usually avoid a stoma.

- Left hemicolectomy: last third of the transverse colon → rectum. Primary anastomosis, usually avoiding a stoma.

- Sigmoid colectomy: the diseased area of the sigmoid is removed. Primary anastomosis ± covering ileostomy.

- Hartmann's procedure: is a sigmoid colectomy without primary anastomosis and is usually an emergency operation. The proximal bowel becomes an end colostomy. The distal bowel, i.e. the rectal stump, is either oversewn or brought to the surface as a mucous fistula.

- Anterior resection: sigmoid colon → upper third of rectum. Covering ileostomy is required.

- Abdominoperineal excision of the rectum (APER): sigmoid → anus. Usually for tumours less than 5 cm from the anal verge. The proximal colon becomes a permanent end colostomy.

An increasing number of laparoscopic colorectal resections are being performed throughout the country. Some of the above operations require bowel preparation, but it is very consultant specific, so find your local protocol.

THE PATIENT

7. Bowel problems are embarrassing. Never forget this. We may be used to dealing with it on a day-to-day basis, but most patients find it very odd talking to a stranger about their poo.

8. Every two-week rule referral will be concerned about cancer. Remember that this is not the only diagnosis that can cause a change in bowel habit but it is important to exclude it, or diagnose it early and treat accordingly. The outcomes from bowel cancer are good, but better the earlier it is diagnosed, especially if it prevents emergency presentation to hospital.

9. Each patient should be treated as an individual. What is best for one is not necessarily what is best for the next. Think about the whole patient and not just his or her disease. This can be easier said than done.

CANCER

10. Most colorectal cancers have a natural history starting from benign adenomas or polyps. If detected, these can be treated early at colonoscopy so they will never develop into cancer. This is the basis of screening.

11. Colonoscopy is invasive, with risks of bleeding and perforation. Bowel preparation can cause significant dehydration and acute kidney injury, especially in the elderly. Consent is taken with this in mind.

12. Right-sided bowel cancers often present late with symptoms of obstruction, or earlier with iron deficiency anaemia.

13. Left-sided tumours present earlier with change in bowel habit (to looser stools) ± blood PR.

14. Even with metastasis colorectal cancer is treatable, and patients with liver metastasis are often now undergoing liver resections.

RECTAL BLEEDING

15. We all know that blood loss is deceptive and difficult to measure. This knowledge doesn't make it any less frightening for the patient having a PR bleed, especially when you say there is nothing you can do to stop it.

16. PR bleeds are generally managed conservatively, and investigated once they have stopped, usually with a flexible sigmoidoscopy or colonoscopy. The exception would be continued bleeding resulting in an unstable patient, and here angiography can provide a diagnosis and potential intervention. If this fails, a laparotomy with colonoscopy and colectomy is the last resort.

INFLAMMATORY BOWEL DISEASE

17. Beware of masked abdominal and systemic clinical signs in those patients on steroid therapy.

18. Remember that post-operative complications such as sepsis and fistula are much more common in patients with Crohn's disease than those with ulcerative colitis (UC). In general, surgery in Crohn's disease is avoided if at all possible but delaying surgery unnecessarily may lead to greater morbidity.

19. Surgery is undertaken in UC because the disease is limited to the colonic mucosa, and is therefore curative of its complications, e.g. malignant transformation, bleeding or loose stools. Segmental resection is rarely undertaken – total colectomy (± proctectomy) with ileostomy is the usual surgery. Ileo-anal pouch surgery is the modern gold-standard treatment in the non-urgent setting.

20. Successful management of IBD and its complications requires close surgical and medical collaboration.

ANAL AND PERI-ANAL COMPLAINTS

21. Haemorrhoids are frequently found at 3, 7 and 11 o'clock positions, and are classified according to degree of prolapse: first degree never prolapsing; fourth degree irreducible.

22. Anal fissures are longitudinal tears in the lower half of the anal canal. They usually lie in the midline. Non-healing fissures not in the midline should be suspected to be due to other pathology, e.g. malignant disease or infection such as syphilis.

23. Anorectal abscesses are dealt with acutely by incision and drainage, but if they are related to a sinus or fistula formal treatment has to wait till the acute infection has settled. Antibiotics seldom, if ever, have a role in the acute management of anorectal sepsis.

24. Pilonidal sinus is unusual in the over-40s.

POTENTIAL PDP POINTERS

› If possible gain experience in rigid sigmoidoscopy and proctoscopy – these can aid or provide a diagnosis without a more formal investigation.

› Learn about the complications of bowel surgery including 'medical' problems such as LRTI, DVT and thrombotic events, to procedure-specific complications like anastomotic leaks, wound infections or fistulae.

› Become familiar with managing stomas and be aware of the common problems.

› Be able to confidently discuss stomas with patients and answer the common questions and address the common anxieties.

› Become comfortable with the diagnosis and management of colorectal cancer.

6

EAR, NOSE AND THROAT

Richard Townsley and Matt Burkes

A rotation in ear, nose and throat (ENT) is becoming increasingly common in general practice specialty training and not before time, given the amount of GP consultations that relate to this specialty. This is an ideal opportunity to pick up knowledge and skills that will serve you well in day-to-day practice in your registrar year and beyond. You may even consider using this experience as a springboard to build a career as a GP with a Special Interest (GPwSI) in ENT.

It is important, then, to get the most out of your time in the specialty. Few trainees will have much experience in this area and therefore may initially find it daunting.

THE BASICS

1. ENT doctors know you won't have had much exposure to their specialty, so they don't expect you to know it all on your first day, or your last day.

2. ENT doctors are generally a happy bunch, so don't be afraid to ask for help.

3. Head and neck patients can get very sick very quickly, so keep an eye on them and remember A for airway comes first in ABC. You will be dealing with a lot of patients with airway problems.

4. ENT is a specialty in which the multidisciplinary team is important. Discuss cases with allied health professionals and involve them in the development of management plans for complex patients.

THE PATIENTS

5. ENT is a specialty that treats all ages. It can involve the planning and management of anticipated complex airway problems identified in antenatal scanning, neonatal airway emergencies, a wide variety of paediatric conditions and the management of elderly patients.

6. You will encounter patients suffering from chronic conditions that affect their day-to-day lives, with hearing loss or chronic infective conditions of the upper aero-digestive tract and ears. You will also see patients with acute life-threatening conditions such as penetrating neck injuries, airway emergencies and haemorrhage.

7. In addition to managing the patient you will need to manage the worried parents of your paediatric patients, the families of your older patients and the carers and families of your elderly patients.

EARS

8. The ear canal is sensitive, so be careful with the micro-suction.

9. Otitis externa generally requires topical antibiotics and/or steroids. However, for the medication to work the canal must be cleared of debris and mucopus. Aural toilet, whether by micro-suction or syringing, is as important in these patients as the antibiotics.

10. Aminoglycoside antibiotics are ototoxic. Do not use them in non-infected ears. When they are used in cases of infection they should be used in short courses, i.e. one week.

11. 'Dizzy' patients can be fun and interesting, honest! Know the important things to ask and do a full neurological and vestibular exam. This skill will be invaluable in general practice.[1]

12. Dizzy does not equate to vertigo. A good history is key to diagnosing the 'dizzy' patient.

13. In older diabetic patients (although not exclusively) with otitis externa, consider malignant otitis externa.

14. Before you start the job, look at a colour atlas of tympanic membranes to help you recognise common pathology.

15. Know what cholesteatoma looks like and its presenting symptoms.

NOSE

16. Try to treat epistaxis by cautery first before resorting to packing. However, be aware that a patient with epistaxis can lose a lot of blood. So, if need be, pack the nose, but consider obtaining intravenous access first.

17. In patients with epistaxis, a thorough history and examination, full blood count and coagulation screen should be performed to identify the underlying cause of the bleeding and to look for hypovolaemic shock.

18. Nasal packing for epistaxis should not be viewed as the definitive treatment; it is a holding measure. Be aware that nasal packing causes trauma to the nasal mucosa and can cause further epistaxis.

19. Inserting nasal tampons is uncomfortable for the patient. Merocel packs can be coated in Aquagel or Naseptin and rhino packs should be soaked in sterile saline to make insertion easier. When inserting packs aim along the floor of the nose. Properly inserted packs will be flush with the alar margin and not look like walrus tusks.

20. Peri-orbital cellulitis is potentially life and sight threatening. It is often secondary to acute sinus infection. Nasal decongestants, intravenous antibiotics and an ophthalmology referral for visual assessment are necessary. The patient may require CT imaging and surgical drainage, so keep the patient nil by mouth until you have discussed the case with the senior on-call.

21. Chronic sinusitis can also rarely cause meningitis and intracranial pathology. Always look for signs of these.

22. Patients referred with nasal trauma should all be assessed for a head injury and other facial skeletal injuries.

23. You'll be amazed at what children will put up their nose. And how much of it they can get up there.

24. When removing foreign bodies from young children's ears or noses you will only get one attempt. If the 'parent's kiss'[2] doesn't work then tell the parents what you want them to do before you start, wrap the child firmly in a blanket and hide the big scary wax hook from sight. Beware of batteries or magnets as a foreign body; these must be removed as a matter of urgency.

25. Unilateral nasal polyps should be treated with suspicion; biopsy may be required to exclude a neoplasm.

THROAT AND NECK

26. If a sick patient has a sore throat and tender neck with a normal-looking oropharynx, have a good look at his or her epiglottis and larynx with a fibreoptic scope (unless the patient is a child). Warning signs of epiglottitis include drooling, an unwell patient and stridor.

27. When managing a patient with stridor, stay calm, implement appropriate first aid and initial treatment (sit the patient up, oxygen, nebulised adrenaline, consider steroids and antibiotics) and seek senior help, both ENT and anaesthetics.

28. Know where the emergency tracheostomy kit is and how to get access to it out of hours.

29. Always consider that neck lumps may have a sinister cause.

30. Hoarseness should not be ignored and the patient should be scoped with a fibreoptic nasendoscope. Formal microlaryngoscopy may be required depending on the findings.

31. Don't give ampicillin or amoxicillin to patients with tonsillitis. It could be glandular fever and they could develop a rash.

32. Anyone with tonsillitis severe enough to warrant admission should be tested for glandular fever.

33. Speech and language therapists have a wealth of expertise to support you. Treat them with respect and they will make your life easier.

34. Patients who have had a laryngectomy breathe through their neck. Putting an oxygen mask on their face achieves nothing.

35. Always assess nutritional status in head and neck cancer patients. They frequently have problems maintaining adequate oral intake and alternative methods of nutrition may be required.

36. If a patient has had a prolonged period of poor nutritional intake, be aware of refeeding syndrome and obtain a dietetics opinion a.s.a.p.

37. Patients who have undergone a total laryngectomy or who have a tracheostomy may have difficulty in communicating. Recognise this and be patient.

38. Food bolus obstruction is common, especially in the elderly. Any food bolus obstruction that contains bone should be removed as an emergency to reduce the risk of perforation and subsequent infection. Soft bolus obstruction can have a trial of medical treatment first.

POTENTIAL PDP POINTERS

During this rotation it is important that you pick up the required specialist knowledge and skills to enhance your subsequent performance as a GP. Discuss your educational needs with your clinical supervisor and try to construct a PDP that will allow you to fulfil this goal. Here are a few ideas to get you started. Ensure you review your PDP regularly to ensure that you are gaining the knowledge and experience you need to be a good GP.

> Use your ward, clinic and on-call time to gain experience and knowledge of common ENT presentations and management, including epistaxis, nasal polyps, foreign bodies (in nose, ears, pharynx and oesophagus), acute otitis media, otitis media with effusion, cholesteatoma, facial nerve palsy, neck and thyroid lumps, tracheotomies, sinusitis, hoarseness, and head and neck malignancy.

> Learn about 'red flag' symptoms for ENT conditions.

> Learn to use the micro-suction and gain a Direct Observation of Procedural Skills (DOPS) in its safe use.

> Gain experience and insight into end-of-life care and the role of the multidisciplinary team in providing individualised, patient-centred palliation.

> Learn about the expected post-operative course of common ENT operations. This will allow you to understand what is an expected consequence of surgery and what is a potential complication requiring specialist review.

REFERENCES

1. Voelker CCJ, Goebel JA. Evaluation of the dizzy patient. *Journal of ENT Masterclass* 2009; **2(1)**: 128–36.

2. Fisher J. Nasal foreign bodies. http://emedicine.medscape.com/article/763767-overview#a1 [accessed April 2013].

7

EMERGENCY MEDICINE

Matt Burkes, Ben Atkinson and Kate Bunyan

Spending time in the Emergency Department is something that every doctor should experience, but most particularly the GP trainee. Emergency medicine represents the front line of secondary care and experience accrued here is very relevant to the GP. There is no substitute for experience. You will see a lot. You will do a lot. You will experience medicine, surgery, trauma, psychiatry, paediatrics, gynaecology, orthopaedics and often social work all in the same shift.

You will be expected to work hard. The hours are long and the rota can be punishing. The pace can be unrelenting. However, you will learn more about pathology, injury and 'real world' presentations than you ever have before. Many GP trainees love the Emergency Department setting as it has all the variety of general practice but with ready access to investigations. Teamwork is important, communication is key and work can be rewarding, stimulating, challenging and fun!

THE BASICS

1. Take your allotted breaks. You'll need them. Remember to keep hydrated.

2. Be on time.

3. Try not to 'shop around' for opinions.

4. Write a differential list and plan before you discuss with a senior.

5. The nurses and Healthcare Assistants (HCAs) are your friends. Be nice and courteous from the start of your job and they'll save your bacon when you need them later on. Be rude and impolite and your life can be made very difficult!

6. The *Oxford Handbook of Emergency Medicine*[1] and Raby's *Accident and Emergency Radiology*[2] are both worth owning.

7. Always check patient details before requesting investigations/tests on the computer or sending bloods.

8. Try to avoid handing patients over if possible. If it isn't possible, hand over a clear management plan that covers the likely outcomes. Your colleague doesn't want to have to re-clerk the patient.

9. Many Emergency Departments have a folder or intranet links outlining local and national protocols and policies for treating various conditions. Seek this information out early and become familiar with it.

10. Your department may have a 'handbook' for managing common acute conditions. If not, consider writing one with the help of senior staff.

THE PATIENTS

11. Be patient with your patients and most particularly beware the patient you don't like. Make sure that he or she is investigated properly.

12. Remember – the general public doesn't have the same knowledge as you but try not to be patronising or condescending when communicating.

13. Always explain to patients and relatives what you are doing; it may seem obvious to you but they may be scared and/or unfamiliar with hospital procedure.

14. Avoid arguing with patients who are drunk and remember that the 'drunk' patient may be more complicated than on first impression. He or she may be hypoglycaemic or have an intracranial bleed.

COMMUNICATION AND DOCUMENTATION

15. Always document discussions with relatives and collateral history as the specialty you refer to may not have the luxury of this information when they get to the patient.

16. Always document medication lists accurately, not just 'see list with patient', as pieces of paper go missing and the referring team will be unaware of the details. Don't forget that beta-blockers mask a tachycardia; check the drug list for clues to potential causative agents for admission – just over 1% of hospital admissions are due to adverse drug effects.[3]

17. Don't forget to comment on the effect of treatment and clearly state the time after it was administered (i.e. wheeze/recession in children post-bronchodilators, chest pain after glyceryl trinitrate [GTN]).

18. Be professional when making a referral, even if the person you're referring to isn't.

19. Encourage patients who don't have a GP to register with one. This is better for them and can save you work in the future.

SKILLS AND MANAGEMENT

20. Learn how to put in nasal packs.

21. Learn to suture before you start the job.

22. Learn the resuscitation guidelines for common presentations including asthma, anaphylaxis, arrhthymias and so on. Most smartphones have useful apps; do a search for the latest.

23. Don't avoid the resuscitation room. Skills learnt there will be vital in whichever career path you choose.

24. Learn your local acute coronary syndrome (ACS) management pathway inside out – you'll be seeing a lot of it.

25. Always examine the abdomen in patients with back pain or chest pain. If you don't look for an abdominal aortic aneurysm (AAA) you are unlikely to find one. Anticoagulating a leaking AAA misdiagnosed as ACS would be a bad mistake for the sake of a thorough physical examination and appropriate investigation.

26. Beware diagnosing first-episode renal colic in the elderly. It's a leaking AAA until proven otherwise.

27. Be suspicious of constipation that requires morphine for analgesia. Make sure a more significant cause of pain has been excluded.

28. When examining an undressed patient keep an eye out for malignant melanomas (MMs), regardless of their presentation. MM kills young people and is on the increase.

29. Missing testicular torsion can be catastrophic – be very sure of your diagnosis before discharging epididymitis without a urology opinion.

30. Epistaxis management is ALWAYS airway, breathing, circulation (an elderly patient could have significant blood loss prior to attending the Emergency Department).

31. A venous blood gas is a good investigation for diabetic ketoacidosis (DKA) and other presentations requiring serial gases. Only do an arterial blood gas if clinically indicated. The monitored saturations are <92% on air or if the patient desaturates off oxygen.

32. Don't overlook other parameters on the blood gas, e.g. carboxyhaemoglobin (COHb), particularly in someone non-specifically unwell or presenting with lethargy or a headache.

33. All women of childbearing age are pregnant until a urinary β-HCG test says they are not.

34. You will see a lot of children. Most love stickers. If possible spend a minute talking to the parents to put them and their child at ease. Use this time to observe the child before examining. Obviously this isn't practical in an acute emergency.

35. Don't discharge a febrile child on antibiotics without finding a source of infection.

36. Don't ever forget the glucose test.

37. The Emergency Department is a great environment to develop your ophthalmology skills so make the most of this opportunity. Learn to use the slit lamp (preferably before you use it on a patient) but don't become too dependent on it as few GP practices have one. Always document visual acuity and eye movements in any eye/facial injury.

38. Don't forget to check paracetamol levels (and salicylate if showing signs/ symptoms of toxicity) in all overdoses and serious deliberate self-harm (DSH) no matter what the patient reports to have taken (or not taken) – they are the things that CAN be treated.

39. Always check renal function before any procedure requiring radiological contrast, e.g. CT scan or intravenous urogram (IVU).

40. Beware non-steroidal anti-inflammatory drugs (NSAIDs) in the over-60s.

TRAUMA AND INJURIES

41. Know the Ottawa Ankle and Knee Rules inside out – this will save time and worry later.

42. Always examine the joint above and below the site of injury. Document these findings.

43. Always check hand dominance and profession, and accurately document neurovascular status and tendon function in hand injuries.

44. In suspected scaphoid injuries you must document the presence or absence of tenderness in three or more areas, e.g. anatomical snuff box, volar pole and telescoping (not just anatomical snuff box).

45. Don't miss the second fracture after noticing the obvious one that jumped out at you from the screen first.

46. Fractured neck of femur in the under-65s is an orthopaedic emergency. It's bread and butter for the orthopods in the over-65s but a fracture in a young patient of working age has a different set of guidelines and targets.

47. In trauma, bear in mind the concept of distracting injury. Don't let the obvious gross injury make you miss the subtle, more serious one.

48. Familiarise yourself with the National Institute for Health and Care Excellence (NICE) guidelines for managing head injury.[4] Check how these fit with local guidelines.

49. The phrase 'collapse query cause' is still used; however, 'transient loss of consciousness' is more appropriate. The NICE guideline for transient loss of consciousness in adults and young people [5] will help you to avoid missing any potentially serious diagnoses and help you to initiate appropriate follow-up.

POTENTIAL PDP POINTERS

The usual caveat applies that a personal development plan (PDP) works best when it is just that: personal. However, here are some things to think about to help you get the most from your rotation.

› Gain experience working as part of the multidisciplinary Emergency Department team. Work alongside, and in partnership with, nursing staff, emergency nurse practitioners (ENPs), occupational therapists, specialty doctors, A&E doctors, ambulance crews, police and other healthcare providers. Learn what each one does.

› Spend time in all aspects of the Emergency Department, minors, majors and resus, to experience the full range of pathology the department sees and to develop accompanying skills. This includes dealing with the very sick as they will present like this to your GP surgery one day!

› Gain skills and knowledge with regards presentation and management of common ophthalmological and ear, nose and throat (ENT) complaints if your rotation does not include these specialties.

› Improve knowledge of musculoskeletal medicine, including diagnosis and management of fractures and sprains, by seeing these common Emergency Department presentations.

› Gain skills and knowledge with regards minor wound management, dressing and closure.

REFERENCES

1. Wyatt J, Illingworth R, Graham C, *et al. Oxford Handbook of Emergency Medicine.* Oxford: Oxford University Press, 2012.

2. Raby N, Berman L, De Lacey G. *Accident and Emergency Radiology: a survival guide.* London: Elsevier Saunders, 2005.

3. Wu T, Jen M, Bottle A, *et al.* Ten-year trends in hospital admissions for adverse drug reactions in England 1999–2009. *Journal of the Royal Society of Medicine* 2010; **103(6)**: 239–50.

4. National Institute for Health and Care Excellence. *Head Injury: triage, assessment, investigation and early management of head injury in children, young people and adults* (Clinical Guideline 176). London: NICE, 2014, http://guidance.nice.org.uk/cg176 [accessed March 2014].

5. National Institute for Health and Clinical Excellence. *Transient Loss of Consciousness in Adults and Young People.* London: NICE, 2010, http://guidance.nice.org.uk/CG109 [accessed March 2014].

8

ENDOCRINE MEDICINE

Ken Laji

To many trainees, endocrinology is an unfathomable and elitist intellectual blur. This perception is perpetuated by the lack of structured teaching on the subject in many medical schools, the need for a high level of specialism, unpredictable clinical presentations of even the most common endocrine pathologies and confusing test results. It needn't be this way!

Endocrinology has a very broad reach and therefore exposure to the specialty can help you become a better clinician. Furthermore, you will acquire some real confidence tackling the MRCGP exams, where endocrine topics often crop up. Endocrinology is mainly an outpatient specialty, although teams are often called to unpick metabolic puzzles in inpatients. The specialty is an embodiment of multidisciplinary working and you will find the constant reference to basic sciences very stimulating.

THE BASICS

1. It is useful to consider endocrinology in the context of prevalence. The temptation is to jump in and learn esoteric pathology early on – don't succumb to this. You need to build confidence in dealing with common presentations. From this point of view, concentrate on learning about diabetes, thyroid and parathyroid disease, electrolyte imbalance and calcium metabolism first.

2. Get hold of a simple, broad-based book right at the start of your posting in the specialty.[1]

3. Befriend a diabetes specialist nurse and acquire some working knowledge of insulin types and devices. Demystifying insulins is as simple as understanding their time-action profiles, which helps define dose and regimes.

THE PATIENTS

4. Every patient you see will have an interesting twist to his or her pathology – so start collecting short summaries into a 'clinical diary'. This can be useful for your portfolio, great for your assessments and can be used as a refresher while cramming for exams.

5. Your patients will generally have been diagnosed with a chronic condition that may have a major impact on their lives. Try to understand this and in you interactions with them.

6. Endocrinology is complex! If you find it confusing, how will your patients feel?

7. Learn some motivational interviewing techniques when approaching poorly controlled diabetic patients, but remember to view the patient as more than an HbA1c – be aware of his or her social milieu.

OUTPATIENTS

8. This is where you will have a chance to learn the trade – do not treat this as just a service commitment. Ask to sit in as an observer for a couple of sessions, then get stuck in.

9. Discuss interesting cases at the end of the list and any you are not sure of prospectively.

10. Always go back and catch up with tests you arrange and follow them through.

11. Do not follow up patients unnecessarily. Chronic disease clinics are very full, and there is no need to follow up stable patients (like those on thyroxine in established hypothyroidism).

12. Ask to get involved in dynamic function testing. Establish a rapport with the clinical biochemists – they are central to diagnosing endocrine pathologies accurately. Spend a bit of time understanding the principles of biochemical testing. This will help in interpreting results in primary care.

13. Always have a go at interpreting test results – but do discuss your findings with a senior member of the team.

DIABETES

14. Secondary care involvement in the management of diabetes is increasingly in categorising diabetes in atypical presentations, dealing with complex therapeutic decisions, managing complications and treating patients in specific situations like pregnancy and young age.

15. Though national guidelines are applicable to the majority of patients, individualising treatment is necessary in certain situations so spend a bit of time deciding what form of diabetes you are dealing with.

16. Consider maturity onset diabetes of the young (MODY), or monogenic diabetes, in apparent 'Type 2' diabetes in a relatively young, thin patient with no family history of diabetes.[2] This is important because the patient will benefit from introduction of insulin early in an attempt to preserve beta cells.

17. Tests like insulin, C-peptide, glutamic acid decarboxylase and islet cell antibody, as well as genetic tests, are often available to help categorise diabetes. Discuss with your team.

DIABETIC KETOACIDOSIS (DKA) AND HYPEROSMOLAR NONKETOTIC STATE (HONK)

18. Make sure you know the hospital guidelines for these important acute complications of diabetes.

19. Once the patients are better and able to tolerate oral intake, switch to regular insulin early to facilitate discharge.

20. *Make sure the basal insulin dose is met before switching off the insulin infusion.* This may mean having to 'fill in' with an intermediate-acting insulin if the patient is not due for the basal insulin for several hours. For example, if the patient's basal dose is due at 10 p.m., do not just prescribe short-acting insulin like NovoRapid and take the insulin infusion down in the morning. Looking at intravenous insulin requirements will help you to arrive at the required dose.

21. Always alert the diabetes specialist nurse of an admission with DKA.

THYROID DISEASE

22. Remember that 'hyperthyroidism' is not a final diagnosis. Try to establish the underlying pathology – like Graves', thyroiditis, multinodular goitre (MNG), etc.

23. Examine the neck for a goitre and assess and document thyroid bruit and any eye disease (Graves'). Check thyroid antibodies (thyroid peroxidase (TPO) and thyroid-stimulating hormone (TSH) receptor antibodies), consider ultrasound imaging (MNG vs. other pathologies) and a technetium scan (single adenoma).

24. Always seek guidance on appropriate starting doses of antithyroid medication. Remember to discuss side effects with the patient.

25. Eye disease with conjunctival injection and oedema needs urgent MRI scan and steroid treatment. Alert a senior member of staff promptly – eye changes can be permanent.

ELECTROLYTE IMBALANCE

26. This is a common reason for inpatient and outpatient referral, and time spent reading a well written article or textbook will be very useful.[3]

27. In hyponatraemia, carefully document the patient's volume status. Send off paired serum and plasma osmolality as well as urinary sodium before asking for senior help.

28. In all cases of hyponatraemia and hyperkalaemia, it is important to make sure that cortisol axis is assessed to check for glucocorticoid insufficiency. Random cortisol is of limited use unless interpreted in the context of time of day and physical stress, and a Synacthen test of adrenal function is usually needed.

29. In all cases of unexplained hypokalaemia, record blood pressure and consider checking aldosterone/renin ratio.

HYPERCALCAEMIA

30. Acute treatment often forms part of the 'endocrine emergencies' section of hospital guidelines, so look these up.

31. Always attempt to diagnose the underlying cause. The key test is serum PTH, which can be expedited in most places with a call to the biochemistry lab.

POTENTIAL PDP POINTERS

› Learn how to spot, diagnose and treat the common endocrine emergencies, such as DKA, HONK and hypercalcaemia. Learn, and become familiar with, the common treatment regimes for diabetes.

›   Become familiar with the different forms of diabetes and how to manage them.

›   Develop an understanding of the various endocrinology lab tests and know how
    to interpret them.

REFERENCES

1.   Sam AH, Meeran K. *Lecture Notes: endocrinology and diabetes.* Chichester: Wiley-Blackwell, 2009.

2.   Thanabalasingham G. Diagnosis and management of maturity onset diabetes of the young
     (MODY). *British Medical Journal* 2011; **343**: d6044.

3.   Hoorn EJ, van der Lubbe N, Zietse R. SIADH and hyponatraemia: why does it matter? *NDT Plus*
     2009; **2(Suppl 3)**: iii5–iii11.

9

FAMILY PLANNING

Julia Gallagher, Victoria Beattie and John Vrahimides

A family planning post offers a unique and valuable opportunity to build confidence, knowledge and skills that are essential during a career in general practice. Doctors may be expected to answer complicated queries about contraceptives and this can be challenging if experience of family planning is limited.

Unfortunately gaining practical experience can be difficult. Contacting local faculty-registered trainers and the regional family planning consultant is a sensible starting point when organising training.

THE BASICS

1. Always take a full medical history and blood pressure, and calculate body mass index. Offer Chlamydia screening to any individual under 25. Don't forget to give advice about attending the local sexual health clinic and offer condoms if appropriate. Ensure cervical screening is up to date.

2. The UK Medical Eligibility for Contraceptive Use (UKMEC)[1] offers guidance on prescribing different methods of contraception in a variety of clinical situations.

   The four categories that relate to safe prescribing of contraception are:

   – UKMEC 1 'unrestricted use'
   – UKMEC 2 'benefits outweigh risks'
   – UKMEC 3 'risks outweigh benefits'
   – UKMEC 4 'unacceptable health risk'.

Experience in family planning helps guide decisions when multiple risk factors are combined. For example if an individual has several UKMEC 2s, a doctor may consider that the *risks outweigh the benefits* when prescribing the combined contraceptive pill (i.e. manage the patient as per UKMEC 3 and above). In such cases it may be safer to prescribe a progestogen-only form of contraception.

3. Ensure patients are not pregnant before commencing contraception.

4. Doctors who hold moral reservations about any contraceptive method are still encouraged to undertake family planning training. Termination of pregnancy is separate from the regular provision of contraception and doctors can refer to colleagues if they are unable to provide care relating to a termination.

5. When prescribing contraception use a prompt to ensure all the necessary information is appropriately given and documented. The Family Planning Association (FPA) leaflets provide information on common problems (e.g. diarrhoea, vomiting, missed pills, etc.) and the mode of action of contraceptives.

THE PATIENTS

6. Be sensitive. There may be emotional elements in any consultation involving contraception, relationships and obstetric and gynaecological history. A non-judgemental approach will help to ensure the best outcome for the patient.

7. Patients can have very interesting ideas when it comes to contraception, menstruation and fertility. It is essential to explore these ideas and concerns to achieve an effective consultation.

8. Women are often concerned about the association between some types of contraception and weight gain. Developing a patient-centred approach to consultation may enhance compliance more than just quoting evidence from the latest research.

9. Young and vulnerable patients (both under and over 16) may present for contraception and this can be an opportunity to explore any issues they may have. Become familiar with local referral pathways for child protection and document Fraser competency carefully.

10. There has been a rise in the number of women having terminations in their forties over the last decade.[2] Women in this age group are often surprised when they become pregnant and it is essential to explore their health beliefs and discuss contraceptive choices.

METHOD-SPECIFIC GUIDANCE – SOME HANDY HINTS!

COMBINED CONTRACEPTIVE PILL

11. The combined pill contains synthetic oestrogen and progesterone (except Qlaira), which inhibit release of FSH and LH from the pituitary and prevent ovulation.

12. There are many contraceptive pills on the market. The *British National Formulary* (BNF)[3] can be consulted for a comprehensive list. Below is a simple guide that covers the basics.

TABLE 9.1: CONTRACEPTIVE PILLS

	Oestrogen content	Progestogen content	Example brand
First line	Ethinylestradiol 30 micrograms	Levonorgestrel 150 micrograms	Microgynon 30 Rigevidon
Second line	If problematic oestrogenic side effects occur, such as nausea, dizziness or breast tenderness, try a lower dose of oestrogen but warn about the increased risk of breakthrough bleeding:		
	Ethinylestradiol 20 micrograms	Desogestrel 150 micrograms	Mercilon Gedarel 20/150
	If problematic progestogenic side effects occur, such as vaginal dryness, increased weight, depression, lethargy or acne, try an oestrogen-dominant pill:		
	Ethinylestradiol 30 micrograms	Desogestrel 150 micrograms	Marvelon Gedarel 30/150
Third line	Ethinylestradiol 30 micrograms	Drospirenone 3 mg	Yasmin
	It is good practice to counsel women regarding the increased risk of venous thromboembolism with third- and fourth-generation progestogens, i.e. desogestrel, gestodene and drospirenone.[1]		
New	Estradiol valerate	Dienogest	Qlaira

13. *Missed-pill advice.*[1] Become familiar with missed-pill guidelines. It is essential to ascertain exactly when the omission occurred in order to give the correct advice. For example, extending the pill-free interval (and missing a pill in week one) has been associated with increased risk of ovulation, and emergency contraception is often advised.

14. *Antibiotics.* Additional precautions are not required when using non-enzyme-inducing antibiotics,[1] although extra precautions are recommended if the antibiotics cause diarrhoea or vomiting.

15. Combined contraception is also available as a transdermal patch and vaginal ring. Both methods are more expensive than the combined pill. However, they avoid first-pass metabolism and can be useful in women with conditions such as inflammatory bowel disease.

PROGESTOGEN-ONLY PILL (POP)

16. Cerazette (which contains desogestrel 75 micrograms) has revolutionised the market in progestogen-only contraception. It is the POP most likely to prevent ovulation (in about 97% of cycles) and unlike other POPs (which need to be taken within three hours of the same time every day) it has a 12-hour window period.

17. The POP has few contraindications and can be used much more widely than the combined contraceptive pill.

18. It is important to obtain a full medical history because enzyme-inducing drugs can reduce the efficacy of the POP. Therefore it should be used with caution in patients with HIV, epilepsy, TB, etc.

19. The most common side effect of the POP is irregular bleeding. This can be distressing and cause non-compliance.

20. *Missed-pill advice.* If a traditional POP is taken more than three hours' late or Cerazette is taken more than 12 hours' late the current advice is:

    a) Take the missed/late pill now and continue pill taking as normal
    b) Use extra precautions for the next 48 hours.[1]

LONG-ACTING REVERSIBLE CONTRACEPTION (LARC)

PROGESTOGEN-ONLY INJECTABLES

21. Depo-Provera (150 mg in 1 ml) is the most widely used injectable. It is given every 12 weeks and inhibits ovulation.

22. Depo-Provera has all the advantages of the POP but major disadvantages include a delay in return to fertility and patients needing to return every 12 weeks (maximum 14 weeks) for repeat injection.

23. It is good practice to review this contraceptive choice regularly as use of Depo-Provera is associated with a loss of bone mineral density. This is an important concern in young women (who have not reached their peak bone mass) and women approaching the menopause (when bone loss will occur).

24. *Late injections* (>14 weeks and one day). Emergency contraception, alternative contraception and pregnancy testing (at least 21 days following unprotected sexual intercourse) may be required but must be assessed on an individual basis. See Faculty of Sexual and Reproductive Healthcare guidance for further information.[1]

IMPLANTS

25. Nexplanon has replaced Implanon as the only subdermal implant available in the UK. It gives effective, reversible, progestogen-only contraception for three years. Unlike Implanon it is radio-opaque and therefore easier to locate in the event of loss.

26. The most common reason for patients not tolerating an implant is erratic bleeding. A trial of Cerazette prior to implant insertion is good practice and may help avoid early removal. (Nexplanon contains the active metabolite of the same progestogen found in Cerazette.)

27. NICE guidance recommends that Nexplanon needs to be used for contraception for a year to be cost-effective.[4]

28. Insertion is much easier with the new device and should help decrease problems with deep insertions and difficult removals. Training and a letter of competency are required before it is possible to fit the device unsupervised.

INTRAUTERINE DEVICE (IUD)/INTRAUTERINE SYSTEM (IUS)

29. This is a popular, effective, safe, reliable and reversible method of long-term contraception for five years. The copper IUD works primarily by prevention of fertilisation. The Mirena IUS works by thinning the endometrium and thickening cervical mucus.

30. It is good practice to offer swabs to all women (regardless of risk of sexually transmitted infection [STI]) and ensure microbiology results are available before fitting. This should minimise the risk of pelvic infection.

31. Remember to explain the three risks of the procedure when gaining consent, i.e. expulsion, perforation and pelvic infection. Above all ensure the patient is not pregnant and explain the importance of the six-week follow-up, which should be used to exclude infection, perforation and expulsion.

32. Prepare the patient for the problematic side effects and explain that irregular bleeding will settle with the Mirena as the endometrium thins.

33. If you are fortunate enough to have practical training and gain your letter of competency it is a good idea to develop a pro forma to ensure valid consent is obtained.

EMERGENCY CONTRACEPTION

34. Three options are available:

    a) Levonelle 1500 – licensed for use up to 72 hours following unprotected sexual intercourse (UPSI)
    b) Ulipristal acetate (EllaOne) – licensed for use up to 120 hours following UPSI, but not for use more than once in a cycle
    c) Copper intrauterine device – this can be inserted up to five days after the earliest expected date of ovulation (day 19 of a regular cycle).

35. Don't forget to address the issue of effective regular contraception to avoid the need for emergency contraception in the future. Give advice about LARC. If quick-starting a new form of contraception (in addition to giving emergency contraception), ensure the patient returns for a pregnancy test at least three weeks following the episode of UPSI.

FINALLY

36. Ensure you enjoy your family planning post and make the most of the advice and information obtained from your consultants; this will be invaluable in your future career as a GP.

POTENTIAL PDP POINTERS

At the start of your family planning placement consider your specific learning objectives. These can be documented in your personal development plan and discussed with your clinical supervisor to tailor your experience to your learning needs. Some relevant examples are given below.

› Learn the advantages/mode of action/side effects and failure rate of each type of contraception available.

› Become competent and confident in counselling for individual contraceptive choices considering both patient preference and relevant medical history.

› Complete modules on sexual and reproductive health on the e-Learning for Healthcare website.[5]

› Learn the appropriate local referral pathways for child protection issues and appropriate documentation of Fraser competency.

› Gain awareness of the management and treatment of victims of sexual abuse.

› Develop the necessary communication skills to discuss personal information and explore sensitive issues appropriately.

› Improve knowledge of STI counselling and testing, and ensure Chlamydia screening is offered. If possible organise a complementary placement in the local genitourinary medicine (GUM) clinic.

› Gain Direct Observation of Procedural Skills (DOPS) in female genital examination and cervical cytology.

› Complement training with a diploma from the Faculty of Sexual and Reproductive Healthcare (DFSRH). This promotes an excellent foundation for further practical training and professional development.

› Become confident in counselling, and in fitting and removing LARC including Nexplanon, the copper IUD and the IUS.

› Gain the letter of competency from the Faculty of Sexual and Reproductive Healthcare to allow you to practise fitting LARC independently.

REFERENCES

1. Faculty of Sexual and Reproductive Healthcare of the Royal College of Obstetricians and Gynaecologists. *Clinical Guidance*. London: UK, 2012, www.fsrh.org/pages/clinical_guidance. asp [accessed March 2014].

2. Department of Health. *Abortion Statistics, England and Wales: 2010*. London: DH, http:// data.gov.uk/data/resource_cache/74/74a7525c-9814-4946-b5be-21c3de7d6ae8/DH_126769 [accessed March 2014].

3. *British National Formulary*. Combined hormonal contraception 2012. http://bnf.org/bnf/index. htm [accessed March 2014].

4. National Institute for Clinical Excellence. *Long-Acting Reversible Contraception: the effective and appropriate use of long-acting reversible contraception* (Clinical Guideline 30). London: NICE, 2005.

5. Department of Health. *E-Learning for General Practice*. London: DH, www.e-lfh.org.uk/ programmes/general-practitioners/ [accessed March 2014].

REACHING AGREEMENT ON THE REASON FOR THE PATIENT'S VISIT

One of a range of useful things to establish early on in the consultation, but not always as easy as it might seem.

Patient: Can I have some contraceptive pills for my bruvver-in-law?

Doctor: Sorry?

Patient: Can I have some contraceptive pills? Bruvver-in-law.

Doctor: I'm sorry, but you've completely lost me.

Patient: BREVINOR

Doctor (embarrassed laughing): Oh I'm really sorry. I thought you said BROTHER-IN-LAW!

Patient: I did. That's how I remember it.

BRUVVER-IN-LAW.

BREVINOR.

God, I wouldn't want a brother-in-law, though.

(Phew. That's settled then.)

Red Roses *collection curated by Alec Logan and illustrated by Helen Wilson.*

10

GASTROENTEROLOGY

Pete Basford

A gastroenterology placement can be a valuable experience for a GP trainee. You will gain plenty of experience of general medicine but also be exposed to patients with many conditions commonly seen in general practice such as inflammatory bowel disease (IBD), peptic ulcer disease, upper gastrointestinal (GI) cancer and complications of cirrhosis. As in primary care a significant, and rising, proportion of the work is related to diseases caused by excess alcohol consumption.

Gastroenterology jobs tend to be busy but you will learn lots and develop many skills along the way. Here are a few tips to help you get started.

THE BASICS

1. Ensure the surgical team is aware of all patients admitted with severe colitis. If medical treatment fails they may require a colectomy, so it's best the surgeons are aware of them in advance.

2. Be familiar with your local alcohol detox regimen and know the details of your local alcohol support services.

3. Be nice to the blood bank staff – you may need them in a hurry.

4. Ensure all ward patients due for an endoscopy have working intravenous (IV) access.

THE PATIENTS

5. Gastroenterology inpatients are often sick and have complex medical needs. Many patients will have a very poor prognosis or terminal disease, so you will frequently care for dying patients and work with palliative care services.

6. Young patients with IBD often need further explanations, information and a chance to express anxieties following a busy consultant ward round. Your role in this regard can be invaluable.

7. Patients with alcohol dependence can be a challenge to your patience in terms of their behaviour on the ward and repeated admissions after failed detox. Be familiar with assessment of capacity and remember that, despite your best efforts, patients may continue to drink.

INFLAMMATORY BOWEL DISEASE

8. Ensure any patients with Crohn's disease have had a proper peri-anal examination – if you don't look, you won't find the fistulae.

9. Active IBD is a thrombogenic disease. The risk of venous thromboembolism (VTE) is high. Prescribe deep-vein thrombosis (DVT) prophylaxis, even in those patients with bloody diarrhoea.[1,2]

10. *Clostridium difficile* infection is common in patients with colitis. Always test for it in any patient admitted with a flare of colitis.

11. Remember all patients admitted with a flare of colitis need a plain abdominal X-ray (AXR) to check for toxic megacolon (transverse colon diameter >6 cm).

12. Prescribe calcium/vitamin D supplements when starting a course of steroids for IBD. If someone thinks of it two months later the patient may already have significant loss of bone density. Patients over the age of 65 should in addition be prescribed bisphosphonates.[1]

13. All IBD patients in whom anti-TNF therapy (infliximab, adalimumab) is being considered should have a careful history of tuberculosis (TB) exposure, chest X-ray and tuberculin skin test/interferon-gamma release assay to exclude latent TB. [1]

14. IBD patients on large doses of steroids often develop hypokalaemia due to the mineralo-corticoid effects.

15. Avoid opioids in patients with severe colitis – they may increase the risk of toxic megacolon.

LIVER

16. Learn to spell caeruloplasmin (and what it is). Ditto asterixis.

17. Read up on acute alcoholic hepatitis – you will see it frequently. Treatments for severe cases include steroids, pentoxifylline and importantly nutrition.

18. Read up on the correct technique for paracentesis and the relevant anatomy (what bits to avoid) *before* you have to do it.

19. One of the commonest infections in patients admitted to hospital with cirrhosis and ascites is spontaneous bacterial peritonitis (SBP) – an ascitic tap for microscopy, culture and white cell count is a mandatory investigation. Normal ascitic white cell count (WCC) is <500 cells/μL, or neutrophils <250/μL.

20. Know your 'liver screen' for investigating patients with unexplained jaundice or abnormal liver function tests (LFTs) (see Box 10.1). Get the alcohol and drug history – prescribed and over-the-counter (OTC) are crucial. Ask about herbal teas and remedies. And protein supplements and steroids.

BOX 10.1: LIVER SCREEN

- Ultrasound liver + dopplers.

- Hepatitis A/B/C, cytomegalovirus (CMV) and Epstein-Barr virus (EBV) serology.

- Ferritin.

- Copper and caeruloplasmin in those <40 years.

- Anti-nuclear antibody (ANA), autoimmune profile and serum immunoglobulins.

- TTG (coeliac disease can present with abnormal LFTs).

- Fasting glucose and cholesterol (non-alcoholic fatty liver disease [NAFLD]?).

(This list is not exhaustive.)

21. Prothrombin time is the most sensitive laboratory measure of liver failure. Always request a PT/INR on bloods for any liver patient.

22. If you have a smartphone, download an app to calculate the various gastro prognostic scores (e.g. Maddrey's discriminant function, Child–Pugh score, Rockall score).

23. Patients with a severe paracetamol overdose should be discussed with a liver centre at an early stage.

24. The serum-ascites albumin gradient (SAAG) = (albumin concentration of serum) - (albumin concentration of ascitic fluid). SAAG >11 g/L suggests ascites due to portal hypertension rather than non-portal hypertensive causes. It is accurate in 97% of cases.

25. Make sure you know your local protocol for ascitic drains – how much albumin to give and how soon the drains need to be removed.

26. Hepatic encephalopathy has four grades:

   a) No effect on consciousness. Impaired higher mental functions
   b) Personality change and disorientation. Asterixis usually present
   c) Increasing drowsiness. Very disorientated. Asterixis usually present
   d) Coma.

27. Patients with ascites should be on a low salt diet.

NUTRITION

28. Beware refeeding syndrome. Start feed slowly in malnourished patients; monitor and replace potassium, magnesium and phosphate.

29. Malnutrition and weight loss are common in inpatients – remember to prescribe nutritional supplements (e.g. Fortisips, Fresubin) and involve your ward dietician.

30. Malnourished patients are at risk of Wernicke's encephalopathy, particularly when given nutrition or even intravenous dextrose – ensure they are prescribed intravenous thiamine (Pabrinex) first.

ENDOSCOPY AND GI BLEEDING

31. Try to observe at least a couple of endoscopy lists (oesophago-gastro-duoden-oscopy (OGD) and colonoscopy). Having first-hand experience will equip you better to communicate to your patients what these investigations involve.

32. Management of acute upper GI bleeds is about doing the basics well:

   a) Two big IV lines and fluid resuscitation

   b) Bloods including group and save/cross-match

   c) Think about the cause – non-steroidal anti-inflammatory drugs (NSAIDs)/liver disease

   d) Risk stratification (Rockall/Blatchford score)

   e) Early communication with the endoscopist; however, remember patients need to be adequately resuscitated before endoscopy is performed.

33. Learn how to write up an omeprazole infusion (8 mg/h, 40 mg omeprazole in 100 ml saline over 5 h).

34. An isolated rise in urea (without a change in creatinine) is a good marker of significant upper GI bleeding.

35. Gastric ulcers may be malignant – they require a repeat endoscopy 6–8 weeks after diagnosis to confirm healing or to repeat biopsies if not healed. Duodenal ulcers are virtually always benign and do not usually require a repeat endoscopy.

36. Antibiotic prophylaxis is no longer recommended for prevention of endocarditis in patients with prosthetic heart valves or valvular heart disease who undergo routine upper or lower GI endoscopy.[3]

37. All patients with suspected or proven variceal haemorrhage should be prescribed IV antibiotics – approximately 60% of these patients have a bacteraemia and infection often precipitates the bleed by increasing portal blood flow (check local guidelines for choice of antibiotic).

38. Learn the system for booking endoscopies in your hospital and make friends with the people who organise the lists.

39. Patients with obstructive jaundice can develop a coagulopathy due to lack of vitamin K absorption. Ensuring they are given IV vitamin K (three doses of 10 mg is sufficient) will avoid postponing an endoscopic retrograde cholangiopancreatography (ERCP).

40. Learn to love the smell of melaena in the morning.

POTENTIAL PDP POINTERS

There are several conditions that rarely require admission and are dealt with on an outpatient basis (IBS, coeliac disease, mild-to-moderate IBD, non-ulcer dyspepsia). For this reason attendance of at least 3–4 outpatient clinics is strongly encouraged, even if this does not form part of your regular duties/timetable. It is worthwhile discussing this with your supervisor at the start of the attachment and getting some suitable dates in the diary.

› Achieve competency in the recognition, assessment and management of upper GI bleeding.

› Attend an upper GI cancer multidisciplinary team meeting to improve knowledge and understanding of how these patients are managed.

› Improve understanding of common endoscopic procedures by attending endoscopy lists.

› Improve knowledge of diagnosis, investigation and management of severe IBD.

› Spend time with the local alcohol support team.

› Improve knowledge and management of conditions resulting from excess alcohol use (acute alcohol withdrawal, alcoholic hepatitis, cirrhosis).

› Attend outpatient clinics to gain experience in managing chronic GI conditions (IBD, coeliac disease, IBS, cirrhosis).

REFERENCES

1. Mowat C, Cole A, Windsor A, *et al.* BSG Guidelines for the management of inflammatory bowel disease in adults. *Gut* 2011; **60(5)**: 571–607. doi: 10.1136.

2. Irving PM, Pasi KJ, Rampton DS. Thrombosis and inflammatory bowel disease. *Clincial Gastroenterology and Hepatology* 2005; **3(7)**: 617–28.

3. Allison M, Sandoe J, Tighe R, *et al.* BSG guidelines on antibiotic prophylaxis in gastrointestinal endoscopy. *Gut* 2009; **58**: 869–80.

11

GENERAL MEDICINE

Tom Saunders and Pete Basford

During your GP training you will spend time working in general medicine, a period that may daunt you. Ward rounds can be long and patients may be complex, have multiple problems, and often be seriously unwell. Remember you are part of a team and people are there to help you. The majority of the skills that you need will have already been developed during your foundation years, and the idea is to expose you to common conditions that you will encounter during your career as a GP.

You will also learn leadership and management skills. As the firm's senior house officer (SHO), it's your job to ensure the ward round goes smoothly and that things get done. Lead and look after your house officers – they will probably come to you first with any problems. Try to remember what it was like when you first arrived from medical school.

An area in which you can make a real difference to your patients' care is communication – this rotation is, alas, an opportunity to practise your skills in breaking bad news. It is also good training in explaining procedures, diagnosis and management, all of which are common fodder of the Clinical Skills Assessment.

No one expects you to make a diagnosis of Rocky Mountain spotted fever, but simply to develop your skills as a clinician, and become confident in differentiating the sick from the well. Make the most of your general medicine placement: ask questions and absorb as many pearls of wisdom from the consultants as you can.

THE BASICS

1. It's all about the history. As in all specialties history taking is the most important part of the admission, but more so in general medicine where patients are often

complex. A focused, thorough history will mean the patient's problems are identified from the start and appropriately investigated and treated.

2. Knowledge of endless medical minutiae is all very nice but the most important skills on the ward are being efficient, knowing your patients, and recognising if they deteriorate.

3. Most of the things you'll see will be variations of the same common medical themes, but always expect the unexpected. If something doesn't seem quite right, it probably isn't.

4. Hunt radiologists out early and go armed with the facts. Once they've disappeared into a darkened room, they tend to get a bit elusive.

5. Serum rhubarb! Every consultant has one thing he or she always wants to know about. Find out yours before you start and impress them from day one.

6. Deep-vein thrombosis prophylaxis is a hot topic in hospital medicine. Remember to do a risk assessment for every patient. Look up your local protocol or refer to the 2010 National Institute for Health and Care Excellence (NICE) guidance.[1]

7. In the anaemic patient always send haematinics before transfusing. It's important to determine the cause of anaemia and the results can be unreliable after transfusion.

8. Patients should have their statin withheld while taking a macrolide antibiotic – there is a significant risk of severe rhabdomyolysis if taking both.

9. Find some trusted sources on the web. As a general rule the following all have good guidelines:

    › British Thoracic Society – www.brit-thoracic.org.uk
    › British Society of Gastroenterology – www.bsg.org.uk
    › European Society of Cardiology – www.escardio.org
    › British Committee for Standards in Haematology – www.bcshguidelines.com.

10. Learn who your consultant's secretary is. He or she will always be able to track the consultant down and ask that question that has been bugging you.

THE PATIENTS

11. There's no such thing as a typical medical patient – you will see people from all walks of life, of all ages. Ensure that you find out their social history and take it into account when managing their care.

12. Medicine can be very complex. Ensure you take the patient with you and explain to him or her the working diagnosis and the results of investigations carried out.

13. On a general medical ward your patients may feel exposed and vulnerable in addition to being unwell. Bear this in mind; be patient with them. A little kindness goes a long way.

ON-CALL SURVIVAL

14. You will see a lot of acute coronary syndrome (ACS) on-call. Know your local ACS protocol. However, remember that not all chest pain is ACS. The first step is to make the correct diagnosis.

15. Anticipate alcohol withdrawal, but beware over-treatment of those without symptoms. The CIWA-Ar score is a useful tool for assessing the severity of withdrawal and guiding treatment.[2] If your trust has an alcohol nurse specialist, get to know him or her.

16. When asked to write up intravenous fluids always ask why the patient is receiving them and check their most recent U&Es.

17. *Hypernatraemia.* Usually the cause is dehydration and the treatment is fluids. Remember not to drop the sodium too quickly as this can cause cerebral oedema. In a dehydrated hypernatraemic patient the initial fluid of choice is normal saline.

18. *Bilevel positive airway pressure (BPAP)/non-invasive ventilation.* When on ward cover you will frequently be asked to take blood gases from patients with *chronic obstructive pulmonary disease* (COPD) on BPAP. Learn what type of machines your hospital uses and how to adjust the settings. Know how to interpret the blood gas result and adjust settings appropriately.

19. *Insulin sliding scales.* Does the patient really need one? If he or she is eating and drinking and not significantly unwell or ketotic it's better to just adjust the patient's usual diabetic regime.

20. The majority of acute kidney injury (acute renal failure) is due to a pre-renal aetiology. However, a renal ultrasound is essential to rule out a treatable obstructive cause. Remember to dip the urine and stop any nephrotoxic medications.

21. Have a basic framework for managing 'fast atrial fibrillation'. Remember to treat any precipitating causes and ensure the potassium and magnesium are in the normal range. A 15–20 minute crash course from a friendly cardiology registrar is worth its weight in bisoprolol.

22. Never let the sun go down on an empyema. If a patient with pneumonia develops a pleural effusion he or she needs a diagnostic pleural aspiration — frank pus, a positive culture or gram stain or a pH <7.2 equals an empyema and requires a chest drain.[3]

COMMUNICATION AND DOCUMENTATION

23. Problem lists are initially a pain to write but they make your ward rounds flow, your consultants love them, and you'll look super-efficient.

24. When taking referrals on-call, if in doubt ask the referrer to speak to your registrar. Try not to get into a shouting match with the GP/other SHO.

25. If you order a test, remember you are responsible for chasing the result and acting upon it.

26. Try to avoid sedating patients at all costs. Try to work out why a patient is agitated and look for other options. If you absolutely have to sedate someone, be aware of your local guidelines, and clearly document why.

27. If you think a patient should be made 'Do Not Attempt Resuscitation', make sure you pin your seniors down to make a decision. It's you, not them, who has to run to the arrest call.

28. Be proactive when talking to relatives, especially if the patient is sick and there is a chance he or she may not survive. Never assume relatives realise the gravity of the situation. Communication at an early stage can prevent angst later on. Document discussions thoroughly.

MEDICAL EMERGENCIES

29. Revise advanced life support – available on the Resuscitation Council UK website (www.resus.org.uk).

30. Certain conditions have to be treated urgently and aggressively, but to complicate matters there may be variations in guidelines between hospitals. Read through your local ones before your first on-call.

31. If you think there may be ST elevation on the electrocardiogram, don't delay. Show it to your registrar immediately.

32. Treat severe sepsis early and aggressively. Mortality increases by 8% for every hour that passes without antibiotics in a patient with septic shock.[3] Send cultures but do not delay antibiotics while trying to identify a definite source of infection. Ensure the first dose of antibiotics is given in A&E. Refractory hypotension after fluids (for example 2 L crystalloid) should prompt an Intensive Treatment Unit (ITU) referral if appropriate. Read the surviving sepsis guidelines for further details (www.survivingsepsis.org).

33. Neutropenic sepsis is an emergency. As soon as you suspect it, treat it, even before you have any results back.

34. Beware of the young septic patient. From the end of the bed this patient can look well but can deteriorate dramatically.

35. Hypokalaemia can kill in diabetic ketoacidosis. Be vigilant when checking and replacing the potassium in the first few hours, at least until the acidosis has resolved.

COMMUNITY AWARENESS

36. Start planning patient discharge early. If not on day one of admission then soon after. Bear in mind that there is more to discharging a patient than declaring him or her medically fit. Organise physio and occupational therapy (OT) assessments in an organised and planned manner rather then expecting them to happen on the day of discharge. Without these assessments elderly patients will stay on the ward unnecessarily, with an associated increased risk of morbidity.

37. Get to know the availability of the outpatient community teams and resources, from the heart failure nurse specialist to the local 'tea and chat' service.

38. Write good, legible discharge letters. Include a list of changes to medication and the rationale behind them. Write a few lines to let the GP know what happened to your mutual patient. Remember many patients will not recall or understand what has happened to them and the GP may be their first port of call. Discharging patients without details of diagnosis, management and medication changes is unsafe practice.

39. Information can flow both ways. If you don't know if a patient's confusion is acute or chronic, chances are his or her GP will. Give the GP a ring! It is also useful to check a patient's medications and allergies if in doubt.

POTENTIAL PDP POINTERS

› Improve existing skills in the clinical examination, diagnosis and management of common general medical problems.

› Learn to perform tasks expected of the medical junior. If this requires learning new skills, e.g. chest drain insertion, then ensure that skills are learnt in a safe, supervised environment and any local requirements and documentation are satisfied before practising them unsupervised.

› If possible try to observe some common hospital procedures such as endoscopy and angiography.

› Develop upon previous skills to increase confidence in basic ECG and spirometry interpretation.

› Develop simple frameworks for the initial life-saving treatments of common medical emergencies.

› Try to arrange time to visit specialty clinics such as dermatology and rheumatology.

› Experience on-call duties to increase experience in the recognition and management of acutely unwell adults.

› Develop skills in time management, clinical prioritising and delegation to ensure the safe and smooth running of the ward.

› Engage with the related health professionals (e.g. physiotherapists and occupational therapists) who share the ward. Attend multidisciplinary and discharge-planning meetings.

REFERENCES

1. National Institute for Health and Clinical Excellence. *Venous Thromboembolism: reducing the risk* (Clinical Guideline 92). London: NICE, www.nice.org.uk/CG92 [accessed March 2014].

2. Sullivan JT, Sykora K, Schneiderman J, *et al.* Assessment of alcohol withdrawal: the revised clinical institute withdrawal assessment for alcohol scale (CIWA-Ar). *British Journal of Addiction* 1989; **84(11)**: 1353–7.

3. *British Thoracic Society Pleural Disease Guideline 2010*, www.brit-thoracic.org.uk/guidelines-and-quality-standards/pleural-disease-guideline/ [accessed March 2014].

4. Kumar A, Roberts D, Wood KE, *et al.* Duration of hypotension prior to initiation of effective antimicrobial therapy is the critical determinant of survival in human septic shock. *Critical Care Medicine* 2006; **34(6)**: 1589–96.

12

GENERAL SURGERY

Laura Smith, Ross Cruickshank, Neil Cripps and Matt Burkes

General surgery may seem a daunting prospect for many trainees without background experience in its practice. It may also feel alien to your final career path, especially at the sharp end, in theatre itself. On the other hand there are many trainees who develop a taste for 'the cutting' and will go on to run their own minor surgery list in primary care.

Whatever your feelings on the matter, an attachment in general surgery will offer any trainee a wealth of experience across a broad range of skills – be that in the elective theatre, in trauma and resuscitation scenarios in A&E or dealing with post-operative complications. You will become familiar with assessment of the acute abdomen and urology, oncology, vascular, paediatric and endocrine patients. You will see the investigation and management of dozens of chronic conditions in the outpatient clinic.

The most concerning issue is that seniors may not always be able to provide immediate support if they are scrubbed in theatre or in clinic. The key to dealing with any problem is to know what you can do yourself in the interim, and when you need to gatecrash whatever they're up to and call in the cavalry.

THE BASICS

1. Unsurprisingly, surgeons want to know the patient's past surgical history and who did the operation.

2. Even if you hate surgery, the team will appreciate you being the 'medical opinion', so think about the whole patient.

3. Try to get an idea of your registrar's and consultant's timetables early on. Find out when you can call and actually get an answer.

4. You may find that during on-calls you are expected to cover orthopaedics, urology, ear, nose and throat (ENT) and even gynaecology. Find this out in advance and prepare accordingly.

WARD AND THEATRE

5. Try to see everything in theatre at least once; it will give you more insight into what your patients are going through in the community. Prior to an operating list see the patients and know why they need the operation. Obtaining consent from patients is an important skill and should be restricted to those competent to undertake the procedure. Knowledge of individual procedures and their complications will aid you in answering questions on these procedures in primary care.

6. A pyrexia within 24 hours of surgery is most often due to pulmonary atelectasis not sepsis, so think: sit up, humidified oxygen, good analgesia, encourage coughing, and chest physiotherapy before knee-jerk prescribing of antibiotics.

7. Every patient gets deep-vein thrombosis prophylaxis unless he or she is a child or it is contraindicated. For prophylaxis for venous thromboembolism prevention (VTE), remember to check that what you have prescribed has actually been given. Graded compression hosiery only works if it is on the legs!

8. On a ward round think tubes (nasogastric, drain, catheter, IV). What's going in? What's coming out? Which can come out?

9. Post-operative diet used to be increased in a stepwise manner: sips, clear fluid, free fluids, soft diet, full diet. Modern recovery protocols seldom limit oral intake. Consider total parenteral nutrition if patients are unlikely to have oral intake for five days or more. Most elective patients will be on an enhanced recovery programme and be on full diets much earlier – it's best to check local protocol and with your consultant. Establish if an Enhanced Recovery Nurse Facilitator is employed at the trust.

ON-CALL

10. When on-call and assessing (in particular) abdominal pain, remember that the history is the fundamental starting point. Your history informs your physical examination, which informs your investigations; immediate management of the patient flows from this.

11. Do a per rectum (PR) examination. The only exceptions are patient refusal, a child, if it has already been done, or if you can think of a really good reason not to. You can't PR a stoma … but you can per stoma it if required.

12. Always examine for an abdominal aortic aneurysm (AAA) and remember that renal colic is an AAA until proven otherwise.

13. Morphine doesn't mask peritonism. Useful distraction techniques include pressing the abdomen with the stethoscope while auscultating, asking the patient to cough or sit up, and asking kids to hop on the spot.

14. Patients with intestinal perforation need IV access, fluid resuscitation, antibiotics and, if it's possibly an ulcer, IV protein pump inhibitors before theatre.

15. Make all new admissions nil-by-mouth pending senior review.

16. If unsure whether an erect chest X-ray and abdominal X-ray is warranted, check with the local guidelines or the radiologist. If no guidelines exist, suggest jointly writing them.

17. Remember to check amylase if there is even a suggestion of pancreatitis.

18. All females of childbearing age get a beta-human chorionic gonadotropin (βHCG) test.

19. Postpartum females should always be seen by a gynaecologist. Women with low abdominal pain of childbearing age should be jointly managed by surgeon and gynaecologist.

20. On this topic, don't enter into debate with other specialties about the ownership of patients. Discuss it with your senior and let him or her sort it out.

21. If you are worried, do a blood gas – venous is fine initially to establish if there's a problem.

22. Know the local antibiotic policy. The days of 'cef and met' are long gone.

23. Metoclopramide is a prokinetic, therefore don't use it in obstructed patients (there is an increased risk of perforation) but fire away if they have an ileus.

24. Don't give stimulant laxatives or enemas to patients with an anastomosis.

25. *Pancreatitis*: know how to score patients (modified Glasgow or Ransom scales), ensure they've got a catheter and give fluid, fluid, fluid. If they are not responding to the first 2–3 litres, call the high-dependency unit, the intensive treatment unit and a senior.

26. In bowel obstruction remember 'drip and suck': nasogastric tube, fluids and catheter. Small bowel obstruction often presents with abdominal distension and vomiting, while large bowel obstruction as abdominal distension and constipation. Obstruction is painful while ileus is not, even though they both look the same on X-ray.

27. Acute limb ischaemia is an emergency. You have 4–6 hours to intervene. If the patient has no contraindications, heparinise, then call the boss a.s.a.p. If they don't answer, find them!

28. PR bleeds can be investigated as an outpatient if the patient is well. Admission is desirable where bleeding is heavy or there is haemodynamic compromise.

29. Right iliac fossa pain is not always an appendicitis. Think about the differentials and exclude testicular torsion, a septic hip and ectopic pregnancy. A negative βHCG will eliminate this diagnosis.

30. Abscesses need a knife, not antibiotics. However, a groin abscess is a femoral artery aneurysm until proven otherwise.

31. At trauma calls, stand back, let A&E run it, and step in to deal with the abdomen.

32. Pyelonephritis is only a urological condition if the patient has stones.

33. It's amazing how many patients get admitted to hospital with a perfectly normal suprapubic catheter that just needed to be tugged on a bit more to get it out and changed. Try to see this procedure done so you can get confident in doing it.

34. Neither a negative kidney/ureter/bladder X-ray nor absence of haematuria exclude renal calculi — go with the clinical history, discuss with a senior and consider a CT scan of the kidneys (CT KUB).

Remember — if uncertain what to do with a patient with severe abdominal pain get an amylase, liver function tests, a troponin, a βHCG (if female), an electrocardiogram, an arterial blood gas, imaging if appropriate according to local guidelines and do a PR exam … chances are you'll have covered your bases every time. If worried about an unstable patient, request more senior review urgently.

POTENTIAL PDP POINTERS

› Become familiar and proficient with the common surgical clinical examinations.

› Become comfortable with the diagnosis and management of common and serious acute surgical presentations, including appendicitis, pancreatitis, renal colic, PR bleeding, haemorrhoids, bowel cancer, AAA perforation and urinary retention.

› Observe and assist in theatre to gain exposure to the procedures that your future patients will undergo. You should be able to explain what will happen to them by the end of the rotation.

› Try to get some 'hands on' surgical experience in theatre if you are interested, especially in the 'lumps and bumps' day cases.

› Understand the process of pre-operative patient optimisation, a role that is increasingly carried out in primary care.

› Learn how to improve outcome by optimising post-operative care. Seek out local guidelines in the area.

13

GENITOURINARY MEDICINE

Rhianydd McGlone, Ade Adeniyi and Matt Burkes

A genitourinary medicine (GUM) post offers a valuable opportunity to develop skills in an area that is often poorly covered at medical school and elsewhere in the GP training programme. Within your GUM placement you can hope to develop your communication skills, improve your examination and diagnostic abilities, and learn how to recognise, screen, prevent and treat sexually transmitted infections (STIs). You'll also become comfortable in recognising and treating benign genital lumps, non-sexually transmitted genital infections and gain some valuable exposure to HIV diagnosis and management.

If a GUM post is not offered as part of your GP training, strongly consider dedicating a week's study leave to attending GUM clinics or arrange to attend some during an obstetrics and gynaecology (O&G) or GP placement.

Below you will find some useful tips to get you started in GUM and maximise the learning opportunities of your placement.

THE BASICS

1. Review how to take a sexual history and familiarise yourself with both the male and female external genital anatomy in order to recognise the wide spectrum of the normal as well as the abnormal. This will also aid you in the accurate description of your examination findings.

2. Read the information leaflets provided for patients on the common STIs. They are an invaluable source of information, and particularly cover the questions patients are most likely to ask, using appropriate patient-friendly vocabulary.

3. Befriend your GUM department health adviser and spend a few clinic sessions observing him or her. The health adviser is likely to have many pearls of wisdom, particularly in the area of communication skills.

4. For a good initial source of information on STI management, consult the British Association for Sexual Health and HIV (BASHH) guidelines.[1]

5. Be aware of the varied presentations of HIV and the risk factors to look for when conducting a risk assessment.

THE PATIENTS

6. No two patients are alike. There are often complex emotional elements that can accompany physical symptoms. These make the GUM consultation a sensitive event requiring good communication skills.

7. Try not to look shocked by anything a patient tells you! A reassuring, non-judgemental approach will encourage patients to reveal their true sexual history, rather than the version they think you want to hear.

8. Learn the appropriate language to discuss sexual behaviour. It can be embarrassing for the patient and doctor if words such as passive/active/insertive/receptive are used incorrectly. The e-learning for general practice sessions on sexual health will give you a good head start.[2]

GENITAL EXAMINATIONS

9. Where possible, be sensitive to patients' requests for a male or female doctor.

10. Always offer patients a chaperone (regardless of patient and doctor gender). It is an essential habit to get into. Document the outcome of the offer; even if it is declined, and if a chaperone is present, be sure to document his or her name.

11. Most patients are young adults who have never had a genital examination. Take time to describe in detail what will happen: when, by whom, and for what reason. A bad first experience is very likely to deter future inclusion in smear and sexual health screening programmes, while an acceptable one will encourage participation of the patient and his or her confidants.

12. Top tips for a speculum examination are: describe what you will do and why; encourage the patient to resist tensing her pelvic floor and to keep her bottom relaxed on the bed; advise the patient to let you know if the examination is painful; warm the speculum in water but avoid KY Jelly or other lubricant (these may

interfere with sample collection, for example some gels are toxic to *N. gonorrhoea*); if having difficulty visualising the cervix, ask the patient to place her clenched fists beneath her bottom to tilt the pelvis and help bring the cervix into view.

13. It is not unheard of for a male patient to have an involuntary erection during a genital examination. It can be appropriate to complete the examination without acknowledging the erection, but, if required, reassure the patient, offer to leave the room for a few minutes and then return, or continue the examination without interruption if the patient wishes. Document the incident.

14. In certain cases (mainly sex workers and men having sex with men) you may also be required to examine and collect samples from a patient's throat or anus as part of the sexual health screen.

15. Look out for systemic symptoms of STIs such as joint, eye, oral or skin symptoms as patients may not volunteer these routinely.

16. Remember to examine the testicles with a patient both lying down and standing. Genital lumps such as hernias and varicoceles may only be palpable on standing.

GUM CLINICS

COMMUNICATION ISSUES

17. A good prompting question is 'Is there anything else you think I should know?'

18. When breaking bad news try to present the positives as well as the negatives, be sympathetic, and enlist the help of your very experienced health adviser.

19. A useful way to encourage abstinence during STI treatment is to suggest that, like any other injured body part (a cut on the hand), the area 'needs to be kept clean, dry, and rested'.

CLINICAL ISSUES

20. Offer and encourage routine screening tests for HIV, syphilis ± hepatitis, even if low risk. The *UK National Guidelines for HIV Testing* recommend universal HIV testing in all GUM clinics but also provide useful guidance on when to offer HIV screening in other settings (such as general practice).[3]

21. It is unlikely that you will single-handedly review HIV-positive patients, but you will be expected to learn how to conduct a HIV risk assessment, pre-test counselling and deliver a positive HIV diagnosis. When testing moderate- or high-risk patients, a detailed pre-test discussion is required, but in low-risk individuals this discussion can be minimised to the benefits of individual testing and how results will be given.

22. Learn who and how to contact trace.

23. GUM offers a rare captive audience with the teenage population. Use this opportunity to promote safer sex, contraception use, dispel urban myths and educate with regards to safe lifestyle and sexual behaviour.

24. Be on the look out for coercion or sexual abuse and relay any concerns to your supervisor. Familiarise yourself with UK law relating to sexual behaviour, remembering that children under the age of 13 cannot legally consent to any form of sexual activity. Don't shy away from asking if a 'one-off' sexual encounter was consensual, particularly in young patients. Make sure you are familiar with assessing Gillick competency and applying Fraser guidelines. Reassure patients about confidentiality, but acquaint yourself with the conditions under which confidentiality may/should be breeched.

25. Fordyce spots, hirsuties papillaris genitalis (also known as pearly penile papules) and sebaceous cysts are commonly seen in GUM. Be prepared to reassure many anxious teenagers that these lumps are normal! Sexually transmitted molluscum contagiosum is also commonly seen on the genitalia but should raise suspicion of abuse if seen there in children.

26. Samples collected during a GUM consultation may be different from those used in the general practice setting.

27. A bacterial STI screen is only accurate after an incubation period of 7–14 days from the time of unprotected sexual intercourse. Serological tests have much longer 'window periods' of up to 3–6 months.

28. Encourage correct condom use! Challenge the suggestion of 'condom allergy', which is more often a reaction to spermicide, not latex, and often resolved by changing brand. Dissuade patients from using more than one condom at a time, a practice that increases the risk of tears and holes. Similarly encourage the use of marketed lubricants as opposed to substitutes such as 'massage oils or body creams'.

29. Familiarise yourself with the different forms of contraception available as contraceptive advice often forms part of a comprehensive sexual health review. In addition, be aware of how to manage missed pills and the rules for prescribing emergency contraception.

30. Don't underestimate the benefit of lifestyle changes such as avoiding shower gels and wearing cotton underwear in recurrent bacterial vaginosis and thrush.

POTENTIAL PDP POINTERS

Much of what you can hope to learn in a GUM post will be transferable to general practice. Consider, however, that the facilities available to you in general practice will be different from the GUM clinic. Prioritise those skills that can be readily transferred in your personal development plan. Below are a few suggestions.

› Become competent and comfortable at taking a sexual history, putting the patient at ease to encourage accurate history telling.

› Learn to distinguish between common GUM pathologies on clinical grounds.

› Improve speculum and genital examination technique, to aid sample collection and limit patient discomfort.

› Gain experience in cryotherapy.

› Improve knowledge of family planning and encourage its use among patients.

› Learn which conditions require contact tracing and over what time frame.

› Gain experience in dealing with sexual abuse and learn the relevant referral pathways.

› Become skilled at performing HIV risk assessment and pre-test counselling.

› Gain knowledge of Post-Exposure Prophylaxis following Sexual Exposure (PEPSE) indications, regimens and side effects.

REFERENCES

1. British Association for Sexual Health and HIV. BASHH Clinical Effectiveness Group guidelines. www.bashh.org/guidelines [accessed March 2014].

2. Department of Health. *E-Learning for General Practice*. London: DH, www.e-lfh.org.uk/programmes/general-practitioners/ [accessed March 2014].

3. British Association for Sexual Health and HIV. *UK National Guidelines for HIV Testing 2008*. London: BASHH, 2008, www.bashh.org/documents/1838.pdf [accessed March 2014].

14

GERIATRIC MEDICINE

Tom Saunders and Alexandra Pitt Ford

Welcome to the world of geriatric medicine! Your clinical attachment in elderly care will pose many clinical dilemmas and difficult situations but you should find your time not only challenging but also interesting and rewarding. By the time they present to hospital, patients will have lived a full and varied life, and there is much that you'll be able to learn from them. This may be recognising the many different presentations of common pathologies or simply the skill of picking the one salient fact out of a ten minute conversation. Remember that a significant proportion of the elderly still have many years of life in them yet. Although the current UK life expectancy is 79.1 years for a man and 82.9 years for a woman, if a person survives to the age of 65 this climbs to 83.5 years and 86.1 years respectively. [1]

Below are a few tips that will hopefully help you during the next few months.

THE BASICS

1. Try a Fortisip. It'll give you some compassion for the patients you prescribe it to.

2. *Medications*: start low, go slow!

3. Be aware of pressure sores. Learn how to grade and document them.[2]

4. Consider the appropriateness of treatments for your patients. Never allow yourself to feel forced into making decisions. Discuss issues regarding resuscitation, ceilings of treatments and advanced care planning with your seniors and document the outcome.

5. Learn how to do a basic bedside swallow assessment.

6. Be aware of the Driver and Vehicle Licensing Agency (DVLA) guidelines on driving regulations.

THE PATIENTS

7. Take the time to chat to patients. The majority have had interesting and colourful lives.

8. A lot of elderly patients in hospital struggle to reach their food and water. It's the responsibility of *everyone* on the ward to encourage them to eat and drink. Ensure when you do your ward round they can reach their table, and have a glass of water to hand.

9. When speaking to patients and relatives, be realistic. They know you are not going to cure chronic problems and they appreciate honesty.

10. Reassure and orientate confused patients whenever you get the opportunity. You may need to re-introduce yourself every time you speak to a patient.

THE GERIATRIC GIANTS

11. You will be referred many people with falls. The timed get up and go test[3] or the 180 degree turn test[4] are useful screening methods to assess if patients need to be admitted or can be safely managed by a community falls team.

12. Remember polypharmacy! Many elderly patients get started on more and more medications without reviewing/stopping previous ones. The elderly are more prone to side effects/interactions and being on more than four medications is an individual risk factor for falls.[5] The Beers criteria are a useful list to refer to.[6]

13. Consider whether the patient might have hearing impairment, and don't confuse deafness with dementia. Hospitals are noisy environments; patients may have misheard the questions rather than misunderstood them. Every ward should have some form of hearing amplification device.

14. Encourage patients to mobilise as early as possible.

15. Have a vague idea of different walking aids, if for no other reason than it's useful to know what you need to avoid being hit with!

16. Memorise the questions of the Abbreviated Mental Test Score (AMTS).[7] Every patient over the age of 65 should have a baseline assessment of their cognition checked on admission.[8]

17. 'PINCH ME' is a useful acronym for assessing a patient with delirium: **P**ain, **In**fection, **C**onstipation, **H**ydration, **M**edications, **E**nvironment.[9]

18. Think about the 5 Ds – Delirium, Dementia, Deafness, Depression and Drug side effects. All can present in similar ways, but can have very different consequences.

19. Every fall has a cause! All patients who present following a fall (including hip fractures) need to be investigated to determine the reason and ways to diminish further risk.

20. Incontinence can be the cause of many problems including falls and social isolation. Remember simple interventions can make a significant impact.

21. Remember common problems can present in atypical ways, particularly in the elderly. Falls and confusion can be the presenting symptom of a variety of medical conditions.

COMMUNICATION AND DOCUMENTATION

22. Be proactive when speaking to relatives. Often elderly patients are seriously unwell and confused, and therefore unable to tell their relatives what is happening. A quick word of reassurance if you see someone on the ward is often enough to prevent lengthy conversations down the line. Do, however, remember that many patients have the capacity to decide what you tell their relatives, so always check before you divulge their personal information.

23. Consider setting up a weekly relatives clinic, so that if there are issues that need to be discussed they can happen at a time that is convenient to all parties.

24. When discussing resuscitation with patients and relatives, remember decisions should be made on clinical grounds and the best interests of the patient. If the patient has capacity, then he or she should be involved in the decision making. If relatives are involved remember you are not asking them to make a decision for you; you are only trying to obtain information so you can ascertain what the patient's wishes would have been.

25. Collateral histories can be invaluable. The earlier you find out the real reason for the patient's admission, the earlier you'll be able to help him or her and plan for the patient's discharge. It's often the simple things that are missed, but they are the ones that make the most difference.

26. Ensure you document your conversations with patients and relatives. Remember you are working as part of a multidisciplinary team and everyone needs to know what is going on. Even the smaller points, such as who is looking after the patient's dog, are important, so that the patient can be reassured in the middle of the night when you are not there.

27. Discharge planning begins at admission. Remember the sooner you start thinking about issues around the patient's discharge, the sooner these will be resolved. Referrals to therapists and social services can take several days to happen.

28. When clerking in patients ensure you take a comprehensive social history, and think about problems that will arise with discharge planning. If a patient is still driving, think about whether this is appropriate.

29. Do not forget to talk to your patients about discharge planning. Even if some are a little confused they may well still have capacity.

30. Get to know the hospital discharge coordinators; they can be a godsend.

DIAGNOSTIC QUANDARIES

31. Think about constipation. It can actually be the cause of most common presentations, and is easily treatable and preventable. Unfortunately this means that many of your patients will need a rectal examination.

32. There is no such thing as a diagnosis of acopia. A recent review of cases highlighted that over 94% of patients with a supposed diagnosis of acopia actually had an acute medical diagnosis precipitating their inability to cope at home. Not only that, but they have a mortality rate of greater than 20%.[10] A full assessment of these patients is mandatory and neglecting to do this early could be fatal.

33. Forty per cent of elderly patients admitted to hospital may already be suffering from malnutrition. Ensure all patients are assessed using the Malnutrition Universal Screening Tool (MUST).

34. Find out what local admission avoidance services are available. Once admitted, patients can be very hard to discharge.

35. Learn the Bamford (also know as Oxford) classification of stroke.[11] Ensure you document if it is an infarct or haemorrhage.

36. Think about bone protection for all fragility fractures.

THE CONFUSED PATIENT

37. Use sedatives/antipsychotics with caution. Remember side effects, especially Parkinsonian effects. Medications increase the risk of falls and aspiration. The situation can often be calmed by one-to-one nursing, reassurance and the provision of an appropriate environment.

38. Think about night sedation. Not only does a patient actually need it, but delirium is also often caused by the patient's long-term sleeping tablet being missed off their admission clerking.

39. Understand the difference between an enduring power of attorney and a lasting power of attorney.

40. In order to assess somebody's mental capacity, you must first ascertain if he or she has an underlying mental disorder. This includes transient conditions such as delirium or intoxication.

41. Get to know your local psychiatry liaison nurse. He or she can be a help with the escaping patient.

POTENTIAL PDP POINTERS

An elderly care attachment is likely to be busy, but offers great opportunities to gain vital experience that will benefit you throughout your GP career. At the start try to think about what you would like to gain from your time in geriatric medicine, and work with your team to achieve as much as you can. The opportunities are endless, but here are some possible examples.

> Learn how to assess a confused patient and become comfortable with obtaining collateral histories to aid diagnosis.

> Be involved with decisions regarding resuscitation and end-of-life care planning.

> Gain experience in chronic disease management, especially conditions such as Parkinson's disease, dementia and osteoporosis.

> Learn how to perform a basic falls assessment, screening for modifiable risk factors.

> Become confident with secondary prevention for conditions such as stroke and ischaemic heart disease.

> Understand what is meant by the terms admission avoidance, intermediate care and step up/step down beds.

> If possible try to accompany your consultant on a domiciliary visit and visit a community hospital.

> Learn the key features of the Mental Capacity Act, and become confident in assessing a patient's capacity.

REFERENCES

1. Office for National Statistics. Life expectancy at birth and at age 65 for local areas in England and Wales, 2010–2012. Statistical Bulletin, 24 October 2013, www.ons.gov.uk/ons/dcp171778_332904.pdf [accessed March 2014].

2. European Pressure Ulcer Advisory Panel. *Pressure Ulcer Classification.* Oxford: EPUAP, 1998.

3. Podsiadlo D, Richardson S. The timed 'Up & Go' Test: a test of basic functional mobility for frail elderly persons. *Journal of American Geriatrics Society* 1991; **39(2)**: 142–8.

4. Simpson JM, Worsfold C, Reilly E, *et al.* A standard procedure for using TURN180: testing dynamic postural stability among elderly people. *Physiotherapy* 2002; **88(6)**: 342–53.

5. Ziere G, Dieleman JP, Hofman A, *et al.* Polypharmacy and falls in the middle aged and elderly population. *British Journal of Clinical Pharmacology* 1996; **61(2)**: 218–23.

6. American Geriatrics Society. *American Geriatrics Society Updated Beers Criteria for Potentially Inappropriate Medication Use in Older Adults.* New York: AGS, 2012.

7. Hodkinson HM. Evaluation of a mental test score for assessment of mental impairment in the elderly. *Age and Ageing* 1972; **1(4)**: 233–8.

8. British Geriatric Society. *Guidelines for the Prevention, Diagnosis and Management of Delirium in Older People in Hospital.* London: BGS, 2006.

9. Portsmouth Hospitals NHS Trust. *Guidelines for the Diagnosis and Management of Older People with Delirium in a General Hospital Setting.* 2011.

10. Kee YY, Rippingale C. The prevalence and characteristic of patients with 'acopia'. *Age and Ageing* 2009; **38(1)**: 103–5.

11. Bamford J, Sandercock P, Dennis M, *et al.* Classification and natural history of clinically identifiable subtypes of cerebral infarction. *Lancet* 1991; **337(8756)**: 1521–6.

AGE – A STATE OF BEING OR A STATE OF BECOMING?

I saw a 91-year-old man today. He has severe psoriatic arthritis. His hands are crippled and deformed after years with the condition, with every finger dislocated from its joint at the knuckle. He lives alone.

He cannot open a bottle or a jar. But he has a good solution. He lines them up on his kitchen table and invites his friends to undo them. He came to surgery assisted only by public transport (and a walking stick). One could not help but be drawn in by his engaging smile and cheeriness. I had seen him a couple of weeks earlier because he had felt weary – a bit breathless. My enquiries and investigation had turned up nothing at all. I explained to him that I had not really been able to cast any further light on his concerns.

A long, thoughtful pause.

He leaned forward over the corner of my desk and asked, tentatively, in a somewhat hushed voice, as if he really didn't want anyone to hear, 'Do you think I might be getting old?' We both smiled and our eyes met in an understanding kind of way as we pondered as to whether this just might be the case.

I chuckled to myself in my head. But what to say exactly?

He went on to tell me he had just been on a day trip to Manchester with friends to see a wonderful musical, and had to rush off after my appointment as he was on his way to the cinema – 'I just love the cinema.'

Afterwards I wondered, 'When do we get old?'

Perhaps being old is quite different from getting old?

Red Roses *collection curated by Alec Logan and illustrated by Helen Wilson.*

15

HAEMATOLOGY

Simon Glew, Gillian Horne and Paul Ryan

Blood. The fluid carrying oxygen and nutrients to, and waste materials from, all tissues in the body. To most medical postgraduates, however, it is often an area that is poorly understood and considered rather complicated! A rotation through haematology can initially feel daunting: patients can be complex, suffer multiple co-morbidities and rapidly deteriorate. The registrar's bleep goes off continuously. Not only do you have the haematology ward to contend with, but also there is the haematology day unit and referrals from other specialties. It is busy! But you will gain useful insight in to the haematological issues that present in primary care. You should prepare for the rotation by re-reading (or even reading) a concise textbook such as *Essential Haematology*[1] – it will stand you in good stead. Remember you are also surrounded by a wealth of knowledge, whether that is from the pleasant haematology registrar, the approachable consultants, the knowledgeable haematology nurses or the patients. Use them; they want to help you! Make the most of your induction to the unit. Be aware of key policies and where to find them; you'll be grateful for this later.

This attachment is not only about malignancy. You may also become familiar with screening for and the clinical presentation of sickle cell disease and thalassaemia or how to use the diagnostic haematology service in the investigation of anaemia. You will learn lots, while developing good leadership and communication skills. It is a medical specialty and the tips for general medicine[2] apply, but this chapter will provide you with specific tips for getting ahead in haematology.

THE BASICS

1. These are complex patients. Therefore, a focused and comprehensive history and examination is essential when they attend the ward … even if they have been clerked before! Problem lists will simplify your ward round, especially for new patients.

2. It can be helpful to think about history and examination in the context of cell lines. Look for and ask about:

   a) Problems with white cell production
   Leucopenia – Any recent infections? Sore throat? Cough? Urinary symptoms?
   Leucocytosis – Confusion? Priapism?

   b) Problems with red cell production
   Anaemia: Tiredness? Shortness of breath? Pallor? Palpitations?
   Polycythaemia: Headache? Vascular events? Plethora? Pruritus?

   c) Problems with platelet production
   Thrombocytopenia or platelet dysfunction: Easy bruising? Epistaxis? PR bleeding?
   Haematuria? Bleeding gums? Petechiae?
   Thrombocytosis – Vascular events? Pruritus?

   d) Systemic B symptoms
   Night sweats, weight loss, fever.

3. Revise your general systems examination with particular reference to lymphadenopathy and the abdomen – you will feel lots of livers, spleens and nodes! Not only will this provide excellent experience for professional exams but it will also prepare you for primary care.

4. Always check the throat for Candida and treat! Remember, antifungals often interact with other drugs, so ask your pharmacist.

5. Knowing everything about haematological disease and its treatment, including how to read a blood film, is definitely not needed. However, seize every opportunity to attend clinics and the lab.

6. Haematology nurse specialists have vast amounts of knowledge – listen and learn. When they bleep you because they are concerned about a patient … RUN to the ward.

THE PATIENTS

7. Many day unit patients will have become experts on their disease; get to know them and LEARN from them. Often these patients are attending for multi-unit transfusions and will be in the day unit for hours. As a result it can be quite the

social hub (especially for tea and cake!) – make sure you become part of this. You are a GP; you should be able to 'work the room'.

8. Remember that good communication skills involve active listening. As a GP trainee this is an area that you can excel at and really make a difference to patients' experience of their illness.

9. Be proactive when talking to patients and relatives. Communication can prevent angst so never assume they know everything about the disease, especially prognosis. Document these discussions.

10. This is a time where you can learn to discuss difficult prognoses and make medical decisions. If you don't know something, don't make it up – ask your seniors.

11. Know your patients inside and out, and recognise any deterioration. This is the rotation to get into the habit of checking that you've checked!

PRESCRIBING

12. You will prescribe more blood products than you could ever dream of. The governance issues around this are very important and you MUST familiarise yourself with the transfusion policies for both the unit and hospital. For further information about blood components, transfusions and their complications, including the reporting of serious adverse events or reactions, see the Serious Hazards Of Transfusion (SHOT) website.[3]

13. Your haematology unit may look after patients with bleeding disorders such as haemophilia and von Willebrand disease. Familiarise yourself with the appropriate policies and know how to administer treatment.

14. Remember that some patients require irradiated blood products. These include those treated with purine analogue drugs (fludarabine, cladribine and deoxycoformycin), adults and children with Hodgkin's lymphoma. It also includes all recipients of allogenic haemopoietic stem cell transplantation (SCT) from initiation of conditioning chemoradiotherapy and while they receive graft-versus-host disease prophylaxis. Again, there are others so refer to guidelines.

15. Importantly, patients at risk of transfusion-associated graft-versus-host disease should be made aware of their need for irradiated blood products and provided with written information and an alert card. Your blood bank will have a list of these patients.

16. The prescription and administration of chemotherapy are subject to strict regulation and require specific training and certification. You should not be asked to prescribe or administer without this.

17. If you are unsure what a drug or its interactions are – check!

ORAL ANTICOAGULATION

It is important to know what the indication is when prescribing warfarin, and what the target international normalised ratio (INR) should be. Here is a list to help you on your way:

  a) Venous thromboembolism – first episode, target INR 2.5; recurrent – discuss with seniors

  b) Antiphospholipid syndrome – target INR 2.5

  c) Atrial fibrillation – target INR 2.5

  d) Cardioversion – target INR 2.5

  e) Valvular heart disease and prosthetic valves – target INR 2.5–3.5 depending on patient risk factors and valve type.

18. It is good practice to counsel patients prior to discharge. They should know their most recent INRs, the indication for and intended duration of their treatment, as well as when to seek medical help.

19. It is important that the patient's GP knows all this information on the day of discharge; fax him or her a copy of the discharge summary.

20. Most hospitals will have a nurse-led INR clinic. You should familiarise yourself with your hospital's INR services and discharge requirements.

21. The management of high INR in the context of bleeding and non-bleeding patients is useful in all specialties. Here is a quick guide, but be sure to double-check against your local guidelines:

  a) Major bleeding – four-factor prothrombin complex concentrate (e.g. Beriplex, Octaplex) 25–50 u/kg with 5 mg IV vitamin K (fresh frozen plasma produces suboptimal anticoagulation reversal)

  b) Non-major bleeding – 1–3mg IV vitamin K

  c) Patients with an INR >8 who are not bleeding – 1–5 mg oral vitamin K and withhold warfarin

  d) Patients with an INR >5 who are not bleeding – withhold 1–2 doses of warfarin and reduce the maintenance dose.

22. Many drugs interact with warfarin (including herbal or alternative medicines). It is important to ask patients if they take any of these. The most up-to-date information can be found in the BNF. If you are concerned about interactions, repeat an INR 3–5 days after the drug's initiation.

23. For more information on the use of oral anticoagulation, including its management peri-operatively, there is a great review in the *British Journal of Haematology*.[4]

HAEMATOLOGY EMERGENCIES

24. Neutropenic sepsis is a killer. Your department will have a protocol and an audited door-to-needle time. Know both – don't sit and wait for the lab to call you with their count. If you suspect it: TREAT!

25. There are new national guidelines on neutropenic sepsis.[5] It is advisable to revise these prior to starting your attachment so you know what to look out for.

26. Tumour lysis syndrome (TLS) is not as rare as you think! You don't need to know much but here are a few pointers:

    a) TLS can appear before starting treatment as a result of high turnover of the malignant cells or, more commonly, a short time after the beginning of treatment

    b) Risk of developing TLS is influenced by many factors, including tumour type, tumour burden, potential for rapid cell lysis and pre-existing nephropathy. Watch out for lymphomas and acute leukaemias

    c) The prevention and treatment of TLS are based on aggressive hydration, electrolyte corrections and reduction of uric acid levels. For a young adult without co-morbidities as much as 4000 to 5000 mL of IV fluids per 24 hours should be started 24 to 48 hours before induction chemotherapy

    d) Uric acid is reduced with allopurinol over one to three days so isn't much good in these patients. Rasburicase, a recombinant urate oxidase, is becoming increasingly popular. Check with your consultant and your pharmacist.

27. Patients affected by a sickle cell crisis may present with pain and infection but can suddenly deteriorate, so watch them closely. Hydration, analgesia and oxygenation are the cornerstones of treatment.

MOST IMPORTANTLY

Enjoy it!

POTENTIAL PDP POINTERS

There is no specific 'haematology' curriculum statement; however, the post encompasses all six domains of the curriculum. 'End of life care' is a relevant statement and will help to focus a personal development plan. Nevertheless, haematology is clearly not limited to this area alone.

›   Identify and distinguish symptoms, signs and problems associated with the major haematological diagnoses (for example lymphoma, acute and chronic leukaemias, multiple myeloma, sickle cell disease and crisis, anaemias and antiphospholipid disease), their management and prognoses.

› Understand what is involved in treatment with chemotherapy and radiotherapy. Appreciate the common side effects (such as anaemia and fatigue, nausea and vomiting, hair loss, easy bruising, reduced immunity, sleep disturbances, depression and sexual dysfunction) and how to manage them.

› Become familiar with warfarin anticoagulation: its indications, common loading and maintenance regimes, target INRs and the management of raised INR in the bleeding and non-bleeding patient.

› Improve understanding and appreciation of the multidisciplinary input into patients with haematological disease. Shadow the members of the multidisciplinary team (MDT) and ultimately lead the MDT meeting. (If there is not one, consider creating one.)

› Use discharge planning as an opportunity to identify local and national support services that are available to patients and relatives, including hospice care and assisted care at home.

REFERENCES

1. Hoffbrand AV, Pettit JE, Moss PAH. *Essential Haematology* (4th edn). Oxford: Wiley-Blackwell, 2001.

2. Saunders TH, Basford PJ. Tips for GP trainees working in general medicine. *British Journal of General Practice* 2011; **61(593)**: 757–8.

3. Serious Hazards Of Transfusion, www.shotuk.org/.

4. Keeling D, Baglin T, Tait C, *et al*. Guidelines on oral anticoagulation with warfarin – fourth edition. *British Journal of Haematology* 2011; **154(3)**: 311–24, www.bcshguidelines.com/documents/warfarin_4th_ed.pdf [accessed March 2014].

5. National Institute for Health and Clinical Excellence. *Neutropenic Sepsis* (Clinical Guideline 151). London: NICE, 2012, http://guidance.nice.org.uk/CG151/NICEGuidance/pdf/English [accessed March 2014].

16

OBSTETRICS AND GYNAECOLOGY

Alexander Goodman and Matt Burkes

Undertaking a rotation in obstetrics and gynaecology (O&G) can be daunting. Many trainees will not have had any experience of O&G since a short block as a medical student three (or more) years ago. Be reassured that you will not be expected to make decisions regarding methods of delivery. However, you will be expected to assess women at all stages of pregnancy. Safe prioritising and approaching all new cases with history, examination, investigation and senior help as required will enable you to deal with most scenarios. The single most important thing to do before starting is to become familiar with the local management guidelines of women less than 12 weeks' pregnant who present with pain and/or vaginal bleeding. A large (and very useful) component of the rotation is also gynae (e.g. menstrual disorders, ovarian disease, gynae oncology, urogynae).

O&G can be emotionally demanding and pressurised at times. Try to find someone you can share your experiences with. If this is not possible within the O&G department, talk to your educational supervisor. The skills learnt in this rotation will be invaluable for you to safely and effectively manage the women in your care. The following tips aim to help you enjoy your time in this specialty and gain as much useful experience as possible.

THE BASICS

1. All women of childbearing age are pregnant until proven otherwise.

2. Remember to discuss contraception plans with all fertile patients. Remind them that only condoms protect them from sexually transmitted infections.

3. Before the start of your placement revise the signs, symptoms and management of pre-eclampsia.

4. Prioritising is crucial when doing gynae – do not spend time seeing stable Early Pregnancy Assessment Clinic (EPAC) patients if someone is waiting in A&E with a possible ruptured ectopic pregnancy.

5. If you are not happy counselling or performing terminations then let your supervisor know as soon as possible.

6. Try to spend time in the various gynaecology clinics seeing common GP referrals, such as patients with postmenopausal bleeding (PMB clinic), dysmennorhoea, menorrhagia, dyspareunia, prolapse and urinary incontinence (Urogynae clinic).

7. Do not be afraid to ask for help.

THE PATIENTS

8. Remember to remain compassionate. She may be the tenth EPAC patient you have seen that day but the way you handle her miscarriage will stay with her for life.

9. Avoid judging your patients on the basis of their choices or lifestyles.

10. Pregnant patients will often be terrified if they are experiencing bleeding or pain. Empathise with this (but don't get caught up in their fear).

EXAMINING THE PATIENT

11. If it's a long time since you passed a speculum and/or carried out a bimanual examination try to refamiliarise yourself with the procedure in the clinical skills lab prior to starting the attachment. If this is not possible ensure you observe and receive appropriate training prior to unsupervised practice.

12. Always explain clearly to a patient what type of examination you are going to perform and gain informed consent before proceeding. Document this.

13. Always examine the abdomen before conducting a bimanual examination.

14. Always ask a patient to empty her bladder before conducting a bimanual examination.

15. When taking vaginal swabs, always take triple swabs (high vaginal, endocervical and Chlamydia).

16. Never conduct any sort of examination on a woman without offering a chaperone. Ideally the chaperone should be a female member of staff trained in the role. Document the chaperone's identity.

17. Always allow patients to undress and redress in private.

18. Offer to lock the door during an examination.

EARLY PREGNANCY ASSESSMENT CLINIC

19. Give patients who have a pregnancy of unknown location (PUL) clear instructions and EPAC contact details if they are to be managed in the community. These instructions should preferably be written and detail what to look out for and when to return urgently, that is, if there is an increase in pain or heavy bleeding.

20. Beware the patient who has had a scan 'that showed everything was normal' if she doesn't have a copy of the report for you to read.

21. Become familiar and fluent with EPAC management options of the common presentations such as miscarriage, ectopic pregnancy and PUL. At the beginning do not be afraid to ask for senior help.

22. Try to observe an evacuation of retained products of conception (ERPC) early in the rotation as it will make explaining the procedure to patients easier.

23. If you take part in the pre-op assessment or performance of ERPC or termination procedures make sure a 'sensitive disposal of fetal remains' form has been completed and signed by the patient.

ON CALL

24. When you get a referral from A&E, ask them to do observations and a urine dipstick (including βHCG) while you are on your way.

25. Some A&E departments will cannulate and do bloods for you (if you ask nicely). They are more likely to do this if you have not been difficult in the past.

26. Abdominal pain and/or heavy PV bleeding in a woman of childbearing age is a ruptured ectopic pregnancy until proven otherwise.

27. Suspected ruptured ectopic is an emergency requiring cannula, bloods (including Group & Save), prompt senior review and booking for theatre. Remember that these patients can seem well before decompensating rapidly.

28. Postmenopausal bleeding is endometrial cancer until proven otherwise. However, this does not mean the patient needs acute admission unless there is significant haemorrhage.

29. Ensure that patients referred as '?ectopic' have had a positive pregnancy test.

30. Just because a patient is pregnant, it doesn't mean she can't have biliary colic or appendicitis.

OBSTETRICS

31. Try to get on with the midwives as they can make your life much easier or much harder. Ask senior midwives for help – they are very knowledgeable and experienced at managing most obstetric scenarios.

32. When assisting with Caesarean sections, ask the surgeon what he or she expects you to do before the start of the operation.

33. When faced with an obstetric emergency, call for help from the obstetric, anaesthetic and neonatal teams, and then remember airway, breathing and circulation (ABC).

34. Revise the management of the following obstetric emergencies using local trust guidelines before starting:

    › major postpartum haemorrhage
    › eclampsia
    › fetal bradycardia.

35. Learn how to interpret CTGs.[1]

TABLE 16.1: DEFINITION OF NORMAL, SUSPICIOUS AND PATHOLOGICAL FETAL HEART RATE TRACES

CATEGORY	DEFINITION
Normal	All four features are classified as reassuring
Suspicious	One feature classified as non-reassuring and the remaining features classified as reassuring
Pathological	Two or more features classified as non-reassuring or one or more classified as abnormal

Source: National Institute for Health and Clinical Excellence. *Intrapartum Care.*[1]

TABLE 16.2: CLASSIFICATION OF FETAL HEART RATE TRACE FEATURES

FEATURE	BASELINE (BPM)	VARIABILITY (BPM)	DECELERATIONS	ACCELERATIONS
Reassuring	110–160	≥5	None	Present
Non-reassuring	100–109 161–180	<5 for 40–90 minutes	Typical variable decelerations with over 50% of contractions, for over 90 minutes. Single prolonged deceleration for up to 3 minutes	The absence of accelerations with otherwise normal trace of uncertain significance
Abnormal	<100 >180 Sinusoidal pattern ≥10 minutes	<5 for 90 minutes	Either atypical variable decelerations with over 50% of contractions or late decelerations, both for over 30 minutes. Single prolonged deceleration for more than 3 minutes	

Source: National Institute for Health and Clinical Excellence. *Intrapartum Care*.[1]

36. Do not discharge pregnant women with abdominal pain or PV bleeding without consulting a senior colleague first.

37. Remember that pregnancy is not an illness.

38. During the placement become familiar with normal vaginal deliveries.

39. Become confident at examining a pregnant woman's abdomen during your placement.

40. Avoid prescribing non-steroidal anti-inflammatory drugs (NSAIDs) to pregnant women.

41. If unsure always check what you are prescribing is safe for pregnant/breastfeeding women as appropriate. In general it's best to avoid prescribing in pregnancy if possible. Consider sitting the Diploma of the Royal College of Obstetricians and Gynaecologists (DRCOG) and/or the Diploma of the Faculty of Sexual and Reproductive Healthcare (DFSRH) during your placement as this will be the easiest time to sit it.

42. Attend day assessment unit and antenatal clinic in order to observe the management of common GP referrals such as abdominal pain, suspected intrauterine growth restriction, urinary tract infection (UTI), vaginal bleeding, decreased fetal movements and maternal diseases such as diabetes.

POTENTIAL PDP POINTERS

Prior to starting the attachment make a list of things you want to get out of it. Presenting this list to your clinical supervisor at the initial meeting shows you are organised and motivated to learn. Review the list regularly to make sure you are working through it.

> Get Direct Observation of Procedural Skills (DOPS) in bimanual vaginal examination and smear taking.

> Spend time on the labour ward becoming familiar with the management of normal vaginal delivery, instrumental delivery and Caesarean section.

> Spend time in the antenatal clinic to gain familiarity with the management of normal and 'at risk' pregnancies.

> Learn the safe management of problems in early pregnancy, PUL and ectopic pregnancy.

> Learn the management of common obstetric emergencies such as shoulder dystocia and postpartum haemorrhage.

> If possible gain experience of assisted fertility to enable you to offer advice when in primary care.

> Learn the options and appropriate criteria for termination of pregnancy.

> Prescribe appropriately for pregnant and breastfeeding patients.

> Spend time in the outpatient clinic to experience management of common gynaecological presentations such as menorrhagia, amenorrhoea, dyspareunia, postcoital and postmenopausal bleeding.

> Spend time in the day assessment unit and antenatal clinic in order to experience management of common GP referrals such as decreased fetal movements, abdominal pain in pregnancy and vaginal bleeding.

› Observe common operations such as a hysterectomy, marsupialisation of a Bartholin's abscess, ERPC, diagnostic laparoscopy and laparoscopic clip sterilisation.

REFERENCE

1. National Institute for Health and Clinical Excellence. *Intrapartum Care: care of healthy women and their babies during childbirth* (Clinical Guideline 55). London: NICE, 2007.

17

OLD-AGE PSYCHIATRY

Mhairi-Clare Bradshaw

Old-age psychiatry is one of the most interesting rotations available to GP trainees. It encompasses the treatment of functional psychiatric disorders in the elderly along with organic psychiatric disease such as Alzheimer's and vascular dementia. These problems are complicated by co-morbidity, psychosocial factors and challenging therapeutics.

Dementia is common and becoming commoner – people are living longer and therefore developing Alzheimer's disease and vascular dementia. Future GPs will need to become much more involved in the diagnosis and management of dementia as big numbers will swamp secondary care. We shall need to be familiar with the signs, symptoms, diagnosis and management.

Functional disease in old-age psychiatry is particularly fascinating as it allows us to see and explore the natural history of psychiatric disease. Many elderly patients have had psychiatric illnesses from early adulthood and can provide a unique insight into the progression of the illness and its response to treatment. But don't forget that psychiatric illness can have its onset in old age. Think about psychiatric disease as a differential for many common ailments in general practice:

> 'tired all the time' or 'forgetful' – could the patient have depression?

> 'anxious' or 'on edge' – could this be the beginning of a psychotic episode?

> 'hallucinations' – many causes, but a first sign of dementia?

Old-age psychiatry may seem a daunting prospect. How to cut to the chase:

THE BASICS

1. Rapid tranquilisation is different in the elderly. See the National Institute for Health and Care Excellence (NICE) guidance on rapid tranquilisation in patients with dementia.[1]

2. 'Observations' means something completely different in psychiatry. It is the frequency of 'eyes-on' contact that nursing staff will have with each patient, e.g. four-hourly, one-hourly. 'Special obs' means one-to-one constant observation. 'TPR' means temperature, blood pressure, pulse.

3. Make sure you are up to date on managing medical emergencies. You may see myocardial infarction, cerebrovascular accidents (CVAs), acute renal failure, severe pneumonia and acute urinary retention among others. Common general practice ailments on the psychiatric wards include skin disease and infections. Psychiatrists often need our help with common medical problems.

4. Always consider delirium as a cause for acute confusional state. Consider infection, new drugs, renal failure, liver disease, alcohol withdrawal and central nervous system (CNS) disease among others. Also remember that delirium can last for weeks after the initial insult. Try not to accept an acutely medically ill patient to the psychiatric ward – always discuss this with your consultant. The nursing staff on the psychiatric ward may not be trained to manage medical conditions and this must be considered.

5. Alcohol misuse and medication dependency is also a big issue – especially opioid and benzodiazepine abuse. This is not just a problem in younger people!

THE PATIENTS

6. Talk to patients and their families. Mental illness is particularly distressing and difficult to understand. It also still has an unfortunate stigma attached that will only be dispelled by explanation and better understanding by patients, their families, the community and the medical profession.

7. Always obtain a collateral history when dealing with dementia patients. This is the only way to find out the whole story. Ask about day-to-day behaviour, aggression and disinhibition.

8. Disinhibition may need to be treated with medication. Relatives will find this behaviour very distressing and they should be reassured.

9. Remember to make sure you are safe at all times. Don't underestimate the strength of our older patients and take into account that when confused they

will feel vulnerable and threatened – and may lash out. I found this out to my detriment when I was bulldozed out of the ward by an 80-year-old woman!

10. Old people are at higher risk of committing suicide. Do not take risks in any situation you are uncomfortable with. If in doubt discuss with your consultant. Take *any* self-harm attempt in older people very seriously.

LEGAL ISSUES

11. Be aware of key legislation – in England this is the (*inter alia*) Mental Capacity Act 2005 and in Scotland this is the Adults with Incapacity Act (AWI) 2009 – when treating patients who are unable to give consent. What applies where you work? Find out and know how to apply the relevant laws, be that detaining people under section 5:2 in England and Wales or using Short-Term Detention Certificates in Scotland.

12. Although you may not be directly involved, you should know about Sectioning/ Short-Term Detention Certificates, Community Treatment Orders (CTOs), Power of Attorney and Guardianship orders as they will all be relevant during your rotation and certainly later as a GP.

MEDICATIONS AND ELECTROCONVULSIVE THERAPY

13. *Antipsychotics.* You will need to use antipsychotics during your time in old-age psychiatry but use them only if necessary. NICE guidelines suggest only using medications for non-cognitive symptoms of dementia when there is 'severe distress or an immediate risk of harm to the patient or others'.[2] The use of antipsychotic drugs may result in severe adverse reactions in those with Lewy body dementia and increase the risk of CVA and death in those with Alzheimer's, vascular or mixed dementia. Non-pharmacological interventions are suggested as an alternative.[2] Obviously antipsychotics will be necessary in treating psychotic disorders but make sure that the patient has had an ECG prior to commencing these and watch out for common side effects such as sedation, extra-pyramidal side effects, postural hypotension and many others. It may be necessary to change antipsychotics until a suitable one is found. Start at the lowest dose and titrate upwards slowly. Specific drugs are chosen on a patient-specific basis and in line with local Health Board protocols.

14. Sedation is at times necessary but exercise caution and start on a low dose. Remember drug interactions, past medical history and current physical condition. Use benzodiazepines such as lorazepam before antipsychotics.

15. Learn about electroconvulsive therapy (ECT) and try to see it being performed. Unfairly traduced as cruel, aggressive and ineffectual, in reality it can be very effective in medication-refractory depression.[1]

16. Cognitive enhancers are licensed for use in moderate to severe Alzheimer's dementia. Balance of benefit versus risk must be considered. Common side effects include nausea, dizziness, syncope, fatigue, loss of appetite and dyspepsia among others. They may also increase agitation in anxious or agitated patients. Before commencing, patients should have acceptable baseline blood results and ECG. If they are at high risk of falls, then commencing a cognitive enhancer would be contraindicated. If starting a cognitive enhancer, ensure that arrangements are in place to review use after a period – too many patients end up on such medication forever.

17. As in general medicine for the elderly, polypharmacy will be rife. As a generalist it is your duty to protect patients from unnecessary medication.

YOUR TRAINING

18. Take advantage of this post as a training one. It is one of the few specialties that allocates time for teaching on a one-to-one basis. Psychiatry moves along at a much slower pace than other specialties, which is essential for the type of work involved but also allows us to learn much more and more effectively.

19. Enjoy yourself – it's a great post, full of interesting patients, is very rewarding and will be of great benefit in your GP career.

POTENTIAL PDP POINTERS

› Excel at screening for cognitive impairment. Different screening tools can be used and some may be copyrighted, so only use with permission. Find out what test is used in your area and practise this until you can perform it confidently. Assess with a mini-clinical evaluation exercise (mini-CEX) at the beginning of the rotation and another at the end. This is an essential skill for general practice so is a useful learning need to address.

› Remember ethics. The problems and dilemmas surrounding detention of patients are significant and will stimulate learning. Use specific cases as case-based discussions (CBDs) to assess and document your knowledge here.

› You will need to learn about the Mental Health Act so this is perfect for your PDP. Ask your educational supervisor for a tutorial about this and write up specific cases in your learning log.

› Go out on visits with community psychiatric nurses. Speak to social workers. Find out about other services available for patients with psychiatric illness and for those with addiction problems. This often encompasses the 'community orientation' area of the ePortfolio.

REFERENCES

1. National Institute for Health and Clinical Excellence. *Depression: the treatment and management of depression in adults* (Clinical Guideline 90). London: NICE, 2009, www.nice.org.uk/CG90 [accessed March 2014].

2. National Institute for Health and Clinical Excellence. *Dementia: supporting people with dementia and their carers in health and social care* (Clinical Guideline 42). London: NICE, 2011, www.nice.org.uk/CG42 [accessed March 2014].

18

ONCOLOGY

Rob Jones

More than one in three members of the UK population develops some form of cancer in their lifetime[1] so it is something you will be seeing a great deal of throughout your career. The role of a GP in cancer management has traditionally focused on primary prevention, diagnosis and palliative care.[2] In addition to these skills, an attachment in oncology provides an invaluable insight into hospital-based cancer care that will broaden your knowledge base in order that you can confidently manage and advise your patients throughout the entirety of their cancer journey.

While oncological treatments are evolving constantly, the principles of effectively and compassionately managing cancer patients change very little and this is an excellent opportunity to learn them.

THE BASICS

1. When assessing an oncology patient, consider the reason for their treatment:

    ›   neo-adjuvant therapy is given before surgery, normally with the aim of reducing tumour bulk and maximising the chances of a successful operation

    ›   adjuvant therapy is given post-operatively in those patients deemed to have 'high-risk' disease with the aim of reducing the chance of relapse

    ›   palliative treatment aims to improve symptoms (quality of life) and extend life expectancy or both.

2. All oncologists use the World Health Organization performance status[3] as a general measure of patient wellbeing. Familiarise yourself with it and try to include as part of a social history.

3. You will not just encounter purely oncological problems. Cancer patients can (and regularly do) get everything from depression to acute abdomens and you will see a broad range of general medicine. This is an excellent opportunity to develop skills in these areas.

4. Many oncology patients will have steroids and/or opioids prescribed so always consider side effects on ward rounds. *Think bowels, bloods sugars and bone protection.*

5. All are at high risk of blood clots. Be vigilant in prescribing thromboprophylaxis and have a low threshold for investigating suspicious symptoms.

6. Many chemotherapy patients will be immunosuppressed so infection control is paramount. Your patients will not thank you for dragging yourself into work when unwell or passing them *C. difficile* from the neighbouring bay. Immunise yourself against influenza.

7. Some will also have indwelling/permanent venous access for the delivery of chemotherapy. Always include line cultures as part of a septic screen and never access a line unless it is clinically indicated and you are competent to do so.

8. You may well encounter patients on clinical trials, all of which have strict protocols. Do not institute anything other than the most basic resuscitation without seeking advice from seniors or the clinical trials team.

THE PATIENTS

9. Most patients will already have an oncological diagnosis and be known to a consultant team by the time you meet them. It is unusual (but not unheard of) to be diagnosing cancer during your placement.

10. Oncology patients are getting older and the use of chemotherapy becoming more widespread – do not be surprised to be looking after a chemotherapy patient in their nineties!

11. Some inpatients won't have cancer at all! They may be on adjuvant or 'insurance policy' treatment to reduce the risk of relapse – a fact worth remembering if you ever need a surgical or intensive-care review.

12. While surveys have shown most cancer patients would rather die at home, many find themselves in hospital during their palliative phase.[4] Do everything you can to facilitate speedy discharge and for those unable to make it home ensure a

dignified and symptom-free death. Most oncology departments have close links with palliative care teams so involve them early. Sometimes this can be when you make the most difference.

13. Many are long-term patients who will have been though multiple lines of treatment and will understand their diagnosis incredibly well. Listen to and learn from them. It will help you empathise and can shape your future practice.

CHEMOTHERAPY

14. Never prescribe chemotherapy and always seek advice about whether or not it should be given.

15. Remember that (increasingly) not all chemotherapy is intravenous. Tablet chemotherapy can be just as toxic, although patients may not always appreciate that!

16. Always ask exactly when a patient's last dose of chemotherapy was. Blood counts tend to dip seven to ten days post-chemotherapy, which is often when patients are most at risk of neutropenia and other complications. An oncology patient with a temperature is therefore a potential emergency and neutropenic sepsis should always be considered with immediate hospitalisation.

RADIOTHERAPY

17. Only very rarely are radiotherapy patients radioactive! You will be warned about those who are.

18. A course of radiotherapy is ordinarily prescribed as a dose (measured in units of gray) to be given over a number of individual treatments or fractions. Most patients will receive one fraction per day and it is not normally given over weekends. A course of radiotherapy can last anything from one day to over seven weeks.

19. Acute side effects from radiotherapy tend to worsen towards the end of a course and can last for some weeks after treatment has stopped.

20. Many patients develop an acute skin reaction over the radiotherapy field. This is best managed with simple emollients but watch for secondary infection.

NEUTROPENIC SEPSIS

21. *This is a medical emergency.* Seemingly well patients can decompensate rapidly. All hospitals will have their own policy. Know yours inside out. You will be seeing a lot of it.

22. You do not necessarily need to wait for a full blood count and blood cultures result before instituting treatment. If you are worried about the patient, give the intravenous antibiotics while waiting for results. They can always be stopped later.

23. Many trusts are audited on their 'door to needle' time between the patient's arrival in the department and the delivery of antibiotics. Don't just prescribe the drugs but ensure that they are actually *given*.

24. Neutropenic patients often have low haemoglobin and platelet counts too. Take a Group and Save on admission so that you can transfuse blood later as indicated.

SPINAL CORD COMPRESSION

25. Have a low index of suspicion in any oncology patient with suspicious symptoms – particularly those with bone metastases.

26. If there is clinical concern, start dexamethasone according to local protocol and arrange an urgent MRI of the whole spine.

POTENTIAL PDP POINTERS

›   Most oncology patients are not acutely unwell and many see excellent results from their treatments. You will, however, very rarely find them on the ward. For a truly balanced view of the specialty get to the outpatient clinic regularly to see some of the success stories.

›   Research proves that cancer patients have better outcomes when managed by a multidisciplinary team. Spend time with the different professionals and remember that you are unlikely to meet therapeutic radiographers or chemotherapy nurses in any other specialty. They are incredibly knowledgeable.

›   If your hospital has one, go to the radiotherapy department once. Nobody expects a GP to know detailed radiation physics but it could be embarrassing if you don't even know what the machine looks like!

›   Patients entering the palliative phase of their illness provide an excellent prompt for reflective practice. Consider how decisions and discussions made in primary care and at diagnosis can still be impacting a patient towards the end of his or her life. How will this affect your practice?

REFERENCES

1. Cancer Research UK. Cancer statistics key facts: all cancers combined. http://publications. cancerresearchuk.org/downloads/Product/CS_KF_ALLCANCERS.pdf [accessed March 2014].

2. Royal College of General Practitioners. *3.09 The Clinical Example on End-of-Life Care*. London: RCGP, 2010, www.rcgp.org.uk/gp-training-and-exams/~/media/Files/GP-training-and-exams/ Curriculum-2012/RCGP-Curriculum-3-09-End-Of-Life-Care.ashx [accessed March 2014].

3. Oken MM, Creech RH, Tormey DC, *et al*. Toxicity and response criteria of the Eastern Cooperative Oncology Group. *American Journal of Clinical Oncology* 1982; **5(6)**: 649–55.

4. Department of Health. *Improving Outcomes: a strategy for cancer*. London: DH, 2011.

19

OPHTHALMOLOGY

Anna Gruener, Caroline Page and Richard Imonikhe

Medical school does little to prepare future GPs for the relatively large number of patients with ophthalmic complaints they will see in everyday practice, so spending a four-month attachment in ophthalmology is a good way to fill in any gaps in your knowledge. The beauty of ophthalmology is that it bridges medicine and (micro) surgery, so that, even if you know very little about ophthalmology initially, you will be able to integrate a lot of your general medical knowledge when handling ophthalmic presentations (e.g. diabetic retinopathy, thyroid eye disease, retinal vein occlusions and multiple sclerosis).

THE BASICS

1. Read through an ophthalmology textbook prior to starting your attachment and consider looking through some ophthalmic photographs by referring to an ophthalmic atlas or by searching on an appropriate medical website (e.g. www. atlasophthalmology.com/).

BOX 19.1: COMMONLY USED OPHTHALMIC ABBREVIATIONS

AC – anterior chamber

AMD – age-related macular degeneration

CCT – central corneal thickness

CNAG – chronic narrow-angle glaucoma

HRT – Heidelberg Retina Tomograph

IOL – intraocular lens

IOP – intraocular pressure

NPDR – non-proliferative diabetic retinopathy

NTG – normal-tension glaucoma

OCT – ocular coherence tomography

OHT – ocular hypertension

PC – posterior chamber

PDR – proliferative diabetic retinopathy

POAG – primary open-angle glaucoma

PRP – panretinal photocoagulation

VA – visual acuity

VF – visual field

2. Familiarise yourself with the different roles of the staff in the department. There are optometrists, orthoptists and ophthalmic specialist nurses. All of them have their areas of expertise and knowing who to approach with which query can make your life a lot easier.

3. Ask one of the ophthalmologists to demonstrate how to use the slit lamp to its maximum benefit.

4. Familiarise yourself with the four groups of eye drops (steroids, antibiotics, anti-glaucoma drops, tear substitutes/lubricants) that are commonly used in ophthalmology.

5. Ensure you know how to measure and record a patient's visual acuity at different distances. Familiarise yourself with the 'Snellen' and 'LogMAR' charts.

THE PATIENTS

6. A lot of patients are very squeamish when it comes to their eyes, so always be gentle and explain what you are doing as you go along. Tell them beforehand

that most eye drops sting for a few seconds. Remember that fluorescein will stain contact lenses, so ensure they are removed before instillation.

7.   Remember that some patients may have a vagal response to the eye examination. Make sure you know what to do when this happens.

8.   Remember that a patient who cannot see well enough to drive but carries on doing so poses a danger to other people. Explain this to the patient and document that you have done so.

9.   Never tell a patient with poor vision there is nothing else that can be done. Even if there is no active treatment, patients should be given the opportunity to be seen in a low-vision aid (LVA) clinic, where they may at least be given the opportunity to try out different magnifying devices and other reading aids.

OPHTHALMIC EXAM

10. Medico-legally you have no leg to stand on if you have not recorded the patient's visual acuity (VA). It is common practice to measure patients' distance VA but, alternatively, reading vision can be tested with a 'Vocational Near Vision Test Type'. Using a pinhole will largely correct for refractive errors and allow VA to be tested in other circumstances, e.g. when the patient's glasses are not available. A patient's 'corrected VA' refers to his or her VA with glasses or pinhole.

11. Use the slit lamp to examine the anterior segment of the eye systematically. Start with the lids (and never forget to invert the lids if you suspect a foreign body) and then move on to the cornea, conjunctiva/sclera, lens and anterior chamber.

12. Corneal defects are visualised with the help of fluorescein. Bear in mind that most fluorescein eye drops used in clinic contain a local anaesthetic, so if you need to check corneal sensation do so before using any drops.

13. Remember that most dilating drops used in clinic take 15–30 minutes to work and wear off after 3–6 hours. Patients who have had both eyes dilated should not drive until the effect of the drops has worn off and their vision is no longer blurred. Remember that dilating drops can trigger an attack of acute-angle closure in patients with narrow anterior chamber angles.

14. Ophthalmologists specify drops by the annotation 'g' as in *gutta* – which is Latin for drop (e.g. g chloramphenicol). The abbreviation 'oc' (*oculentum*) refers to eye ointment (e.g. oc chloramphenicol).

15. When you start off examining the retina (either with the slit lamp or the ophthalmoscope), always make sure the patient has dilated pupils. Examine the

retina systematically, looking at the disc and the macula first, and then at the vitreous and peripheral retina.

16. When using the slit lamp, you must make sure you are comfortable and that your chair is not too high. Using the slit lamp for several hours in a hunched position can cause severe neck and back pain.

OPHTHALMOLOGY CLINICS AND THEATRE

17. A picture is worth a thousand words and the pathology should be fairly obvious if you know what you are looking for. Draw a large picture of the cornea, optic nerve head or retina and pencil in what you can see. A good drawing of the optic disc and cup is a lot more useful than simply documenting an arbitrary cup–disc ratio. Use a red pen to indicate injection and blood. Use green to indicate corneal staining and yellow to highlight exudate.

18. Lots of patients and some doctors do not take compliance with eye medication seriously enough. Bear in mind that certain eye drops (e.g. timolol) have systemic side effects. Every year, a few severe asthmatics end up in resuscitation because of topically applied beta-blocker drops.

ON-CALLS

19. There are few life- and sight-threatening ophthalmic emergencies. The ones you must not miss are endophthalmitis, giant cell arteritis, acute-angle closure, orbital cellulitis (especially in children), corneal ulcers, third-nerve palsies, a painful Horner's syndrome and retinal tears and detachments. Once a patient has completely lost vision in one eye you probably have missed the boat, but you must bear in mind prophylactic treatment for the remaining eye in cases of giant cell arteritis and acute-angle closure glaucoma. An elderly patient with sudden loss of vision and a headache has giant cell arteritis until proven otherwise.

20. A lot of (neuro)surgical conditions are first diagnosed by the ophthalmologist (e.g. optic neuritis in multiple sclerosis, third-nerve palsies, Horner's syndrome), who will then hand over to the appropriate team (e.g. neurology, neurosurgery, etc.).

21. When assessing patients with posterior vitreous detachments ('flashes and floaters') tell them to return in case of worsening or new symptoms, which may indicate a retinal tear or detachment. Give them a leaflet and record that you have done so.

POTENTIAL PDP POINTERS

Plan what you want to get out of the rotation and let people know. As well as your educational supervisor also tell the rest of the team. Many will help you if they know what you would like to do. Here are a few pointers you might like to consider.

› Become proficient at ophthalmic examination, including being able to record and discuss your findings.

› Gain exposure to common ophthalmic presentations, their diagnosis and management.

› Learn how to diagnose and manage sight-threatening emergencies.

› Spend time in clinic, theatre and on-call to gain as much experience in ophthalmology as possible during the rotation.

› Observe common surgical procedures including cataract surgery.

› Understand the local protocol and procedure for diabetic retinal screening.

› If possible assist/perform supervised minor surgical procedures such as removal of chalazia.

› Discover which local resources are available for the visually impaired.

› Know what benefits are available to visually impaired patients.

20

ORAL AND MAXILLOFACIAL SURGERY

Daniel R. van Gijn

Whether they should or shouldn't, GPs see a lot of dental patients. A grounding in oral and maxillofacial surgery will come in handy. Specialists require a degree in both medicine and dentistry. The scope of the specialty is vast and includes the management of facial trauma, head and neck oncology, orthognathic surgery, facial reconstruction and cleft lip and palate surgery.

The dental element, especially when on-call, cannot be ignored. Many of the clinical procedures that you may be expected to competently carry out involve the oral cavity (a foreign, cavernous black hole to even the well-seasoned medic) and a high degree of manual dexterity. Skills and knowledge learnt in previous rotations are not always transferable. The language is different. Patients will complain of problems with their teeth. Don't let this put you off.

Enter with an open mind. Don't be afraid to ask for help and, first and foremost, learn tooth number and notation. The following tips and tricks are designed to give you both a taster and a head start.

THE BASICS

1. Find and organise the maxillofacial cupboard, and familiarise yourself with the materials within. Get someone to take you through composite, etch and bond, light-curing gun, splinting wire, flat-plastic.

2. The maximum safe dose of lignocaine with and without adrenaline is 7 mg/kg (max 500 mg) and 3 mg/kg (max 200 mg) respectively.

3. Learn to interpret (and pronounce) the orthopantomogram (OPG). It is imperative in suspected mandibular fractures and odontogenic facial infections.

4. Learn to assess a flap. Remember it has an arterial component and a venous component. A good inflow with occluded outflow is of little use. The same is true of the reverse. If you even contemplate calling for senior advice, call. A head and neck surgeon will not be irritated if called to review a patent flap but will rightly be aggrieved if the flap that took him 15 hours to carefully anastomose has died an untimely and potentially reversible death through negligence or uncertainty.

THE PATIENTS

5. Remember that many people get queasy and uneasy when it comes to dental problems. Be sensitive to this. Don't make things worse.

6. People are naturally sensitive about their face – so should you be.

7. Know at what age children have lost all of their deciduous teeth. This saves embarrassment and future teeth when naïvely attempting to re-implant avulsed primary teeth.

FACIAL INFECTIONS

8. Feel the floor of the mouth in ALL dento-facial infections and abscesses. If the surface is firm with swelling raising the tongue, suspect Ludwig's angina – a potentially life-threatening diagnosis.

BOX 20.1: FACIAL INFECTION CASES THAT NEED FURTHER INVESTIGATION AND PROBABLE ADMISSION

- Previous course of antibiotics with little or no success.

- Difficulty eating, drinking, talking, breathing (not in order of importance).

- Erythema approaching the eye … with or without visual disturbance.

- Patients with diabetes.

- Firm floor of mouth.

- Systemic features – pyrexia, tachycardia.

- Obvious abscesses.

- Decreased mouth opening (trismus).

- Drooling.

- Suspected Ludwig's angina.

9. Tap on or manually move suspect teeth. If exquisitely tender, the patient may have a dental abscess.

10. Measure the blood glucose in all facial infections to check for diabetes.

11. Feel for lymphadenopathy.

TRAUMA

12. All lost teeth need to be accounted for. If this is not possible, the patient needs a chest X-ray.

13. Exclude serious head and cervical injury in all cases of maxillofacial trauma.

14. Store avulsed teeth in milk, saline or the patient's saliva. They need to be re-implanted within an hour to maximise chance of survival – ideally within 20 minutes.

15. Assess the facial nerve and trigeminal nerve in facial trauma and lacerations.

16. Look for a septal haematoma in nasal fractures. Consider it a cauliflower ear in the nose and drain accordingly and urgently.

17. Assess eye movement, visual acuity and cheek paraesthesia in suspected orbital fractures. Investigate URGENTLY in children as there is an increased incidence of (permanent) rectus muscle ischaemia.

18. Mandibles are like polo mints. If a mandibular fracture is visualised on X-ray, look for another. Look again.

19. Racoon/panda eyes and Battle's sign, especially when accompanied by cerebrospinal fluid (CSF)/rhinorrhoea/otorrhoea, suggest skull fracture.

20. Beware the intoxicated patient. Not all signs and symptoms can be attributed to alcohol/drugs.

DENTAL

21. Look inside the mouth, even when reluctant to do so. It holds many clues.

22. Recognise and know what a 'dry socket' is. Know the usual suspects: mandibular wisdom teeth; smokers; women on the oral contraceptive pill; history of a difficult extraction requiring lots of local anaesthesia; poor adherence to post-operative instructions; foul taste and smell arising from patient's mouth; and past history of dry socket.

23. Isolated dental pain needn't always be referred to the maxillofacial surgeon. Consider the differentials; you may have missed a myocardial infarction.

POTENTIAL PDP POINTERS

Ensure that you are getting the most from your rotation and not (as a non-dental, non-career surgeon) making up the numbers with regards service provision. This will best be achieved by active management of your PDP and close discussion with your educational supervisor and other members of the department.

› Understand the principles of fracture management and wound healing.

› Feel confident in performing a thorough examination of the head and neck – including neurological examination and assessment of head injury.

› Learn the closure of simple facial lacerations.

› Gain experience in the diagnosis, assessment and surgical management of common dento-alveolar problems and intra-oral soft-tissue lesions.

› Be able to assess the surgical airway.

21

PAEDIATRICS

Matt Burkes and Alexander Goodman

One of the most useful training rotations you can undertake is a stint in paediatrics – it is a rare day in general practice that doesn't involve some paediatrics so it's good to gain experience in an environment where there is senior help at hand. Many start the rotation with some sense of fear, worried that they will have to take responsibility for the health of acutely sick children without help. This is not the norm. Paediatric departments do not expect you to have much knowledge initially but do expect you to assess children thoroughly, safely and sensitively, ideally without getting the parents offside, and to discuss with a senior if you have any questions or doubts. It is probably sensible to discuss all patients you see initially. Access to consultants is usually good compared with other specialties; make the most of this learning environment while you are there.

THE BASICS

1. Before the start of the placement revise the management of common presentations in children (abdominal pain, urinary tract infection, constipation, rash, pyrexia, croup, chest infection, asthma, seizures).

2. Learn from the paediatric nurses. If they say a child 'doesn't look right' take this seriously and see the child *quickly. Don't argue about the observations. Children can decompensate rapidly and the nurses often have a knack for spotting this.*

3. When clerking in a child always ask about family history, social history and immunisations.

4. Ask for a prompt senior review if you have any concerns regarding a child's safety at home/school. If you have concerns, don't ignore them; talk to a senior.

5. Remembering normal values for paediatric vital signs can be difficult in stressful situations. It's often easier to laminate a ready reckoner that fits in your pocket. Some trusts provide this at induction. If yours doesn't, make your own.

THE PATIENTS

6. Try not to be afraid of the kids. They and their parents will sense this. Try to be confident without being cocky. This will become easier with time and experience.

7. Listen to the parents. Listen to the child.

8. Most children love stickers.

9. Try to sit in on outpatient clinics. These are the cases that you will be seeing in your future consulting room.

10. If doing paediatrics on Christmas Eve, ensure that (where culturally appropriate) all admitted children are aware that you have passed on their location and details to Father Christmas and that Rudolph has no problems landing on the roof of the department. This small act can make a very big difference to child and parent.

SKILLS

11. Cannulating a child can be terrifying for all concerned: the child, the parent and the doctor! As in all things, experience improves performance. In time you will pick up this skill. In the mean time, your registrar will probably expect you to have had a go before calling on him or her for help.

12. Always have all equipment ready and distract the child with a helpful member of staff before inserting a cannula/taking blood.

13. Never tell a child you are going to insert a needle – refer to it as a blood test or spaghetti (when cannulating young children).

14. Become confident and competent in delivering intramuscular injections to babies and children as this is a useful skill to have in general practice.

THE NEONATAL UNIT AND NEW BABY CHECKS

15. If covering neonates, ask the registrar to attend the first few 'at-risk' deliveries with you until you feel confident enough to attend by yourself.

16. Try not to panic when you are called to a difficult delivery; neonatal resuscitation is generally easier than adult.

17. When waiting for a Caesarean section to take place on a pre-term baby, use the time to start gathering the required maternal and paternal information for admission to the neonatal unit.

18. Attend a Newborn Life Support (NLS) course as soon as you can after starting your rotation (or even better, before you start).

19. It's probably best to have your first few new baby checks supervised by a senior until you develop a system of examination that you are confident with. Take this opportunity to get it signed off as Direct Observation of Procedural Skills (DOPS).

20. When doing baby checks explain to parents that it is a screening test and be prepared to change a nappy as part of it!

21. During the baby check remember that, no matter how tired or stressed you are, this is a big day for the child and a big day for mum (who has gone through a lot). Don't be the grumpy doctor who spoils it. Be professional and thorough but try also to be bright and positive (even if this is an act).

22. Before you start, make sure you know what hypospadias and talipes looks like (there are lots of pictures on the web).

23. Learn the local pathway for referral of hypospadias, talipes and suspected congenital hip dislocation.

24. Become familiar with the trust protocols for babies with hypoglycaemia, hypothermia, intrauterine growth restriction (IUGR) and maternal diabetes.

25. When admitting a baby from the postnatal ward to the neonatal unit be open and honest with the parents and address any concerns they have. Also make them aware of the visiting times and how and when to raise concerns. Spend your time on the neonatal unit improving your communication skills by talking to the parents. They often feel bewildered and scared yet may be ignored by the doctors who are concentrating on the child.

ON-CALL

26. When taking GP referrals always ask the referring GP how sick the child is and to send very sick babies/children to A&E for you to assess there. All blue-light referrals should be seen in a resuscitation environment rather than on the ward.

27. Don't be rude to GPs referring in from a primary care setting devoid of paediatric nurses, paediatric sats probes and piped oxygen. Bear in mind that you may have more acute paediatric experience than they do and that they do not have the luxury of being able to observe a child for two hours taking regular observations.

28. When you first see a patient, before you do anything else ask yourself if this looks like a sick child.

29. Don't rush in to examine a child in the non-emergency setting; spend a minute chatting to the parents. This will put the parents at ease, which will in turn put the child at ease. It also gives you the opportunity to observe the child, which can be invaluable.

30. If a parent says his or her child has been hot and unwell, then it has been, regardless of observations or presentation now (this isn't just good practice, it's National Institute for Health and Care Excellence (NICE) guidance).[1]

31. Don't discharge a febrile child on antibiotics without finding a source of infection.

32. Don't be too quick to dismiss parental concern as parental over-anxiety.

33. Missing testicular torsion can be a disaster. It's always worth examining the genitals, with parental consent.

34. Check for nappy rash. Know how to treat it.

35. Examining the throat in children can be difficult. The *Oxford Handbook of Emergency Medicine* suggests using 'Dr Stick', a tongue depressor with a face drawn on it.[2] It's amazing how many children will readily let Dr Stick examine their throat, especially if they think they will get to keep him afterwards (sleight of hand may be required to substitute a fresh depressor depending on the throat).

36. Always do (and document) a full examination of children, including ear, nose and throat (ENT), capillary refill time, heart rate, oxygen saturation and respiratory rate.

37. When prescribing, check and recheck all doses in the BNF for Children.

38. Meningococcal sepsis kills quickly. Be prepared to spot it and act quickly, involving senior help. Be suspicious of listless children with abnormal observations.

39. When moving a child into a high-dependency or resuscitation area in the acute setting keep the parents informed of where you are taking their child. This shouldn't get in the way of your medical attention to the patient.

40. If you are doing paediatrics over winter be prepared for bronchiolitis. You will be very busy.

POTENTIAL PDP POINTERS

Generate a useful PDP that covers what you would wish to experience and know before you leave paediatrics. Try to get as much knowledge and skills that will be relevant to your life as a GP as possible. Discuss your educational needs with your clinical supervisor and be sure to let him or her know promptly if you feel they are not being met.

› Gain knowledge of the management of common and serious paediatric presentations such as abdominal pain, urinary tract infection, constipation, rash, pyrexia, croup, chest infection, asthma, seizures and sepsis.

› Learn how to examine and assess an unwell child confidently and competently.

› Develop skills in the management of the acutely sick child.

› Build on existing skills in safe and appropriate prescribing for the paediatric population.

› Have a senior observe some of your clerkings during the placement to aid development and to use as a consultation observation tool (COT) assessment.

› Learn to perform new baby checks.

› Experience community paediatrics and learn about its role and resources.

› Spend some time with the Child and Adolescent Mental Health Services to explore its role in the assessment and management of children with mental health problems.

› Become familiar and confident in handling child protection issues.

REFERENCES

1. National Institute for Health and Clinical Excellence. *Feverish Illness in Children: assessment and initial management in children younger than 5 years* (Clinical Guideline 47). London: NICE, 2007, http://publications.nice.org.uk/feverish-illness-in-children-cg47 [accessed April 2013].

2. Wyatt JP, Illingworth RN, Graham CA, *et al. Oxford Handbook of Emergency Medicine* (3rd edn). Oxford: Oxford University Press, 2006.

CONSULTATION 1

Two remarkable consultations today. One with a splendid and spry 82-year-old lady who is an insulin-dependent diabetic. She has injected insulin at least twice a day since 1965, for over 47 years. Our local diabetologist has discharged her from any further review. What's the point? I started primary school when she started insulin. My dad managed her start in 1965. Now he's not so spry unfortunately.

CONSULTATION 2

A 7-month-old baby called Valentina. Up all night with sniffles. Two worried and haggard parents in attendance. Valentina was well and alert and smiley, then occasionally fractious. Examination was the usual ballet with babies and after a time Valentina's L eardrum was revealed as shiny and pink. Against every ENT stricture, throwing aside NICE guidelines, I decided to prescribe tincture of amoxicillin. Mum handed Valentina back to dad. They spun round to face me. I looked into Valentina's eyes and said, 'This medicine will make you better.' Her tiny hand reached out and clutched the script. Then she put it in her mouth.

All the time she looked at me, eyes widening. I listened carefully. I'm sure I heard a click as Valentina's immune system kicked in.

Red Roses *collection curated by Alec Logan and illustrated by Helen Wilson.*

22

PALLIATIVE CARE

Kieran Tunnicliffe and Alex Mackay

Trainees are faced with dying and death throughout their training. GPs spend a significant amount of their time with patients and their families as they embark on the journey from symptoms to diagnosis and then, ultimately, via more symptoms, to death. Many people, doctors included, find the prospect of hospices a dark and depressing thought. Withhold judgement! Working in palliative medicine can be an overwhelmingly positive experience that will leave you feeling more confident when managing patients in the community, while knowing when to ask for support from the specialist palliative care team.

It is hoped that this advice will prove useful when thinking about palliative medicine whether you are fortunate enough to have a rotation in it or not.

THE BASICS

1. Nausea and vomiting are common and often managed poorly. Think carefully about likely causes and target your treatment. Not all anti-emetics are equal.

2. Understand 'total pain', which encompasses physical, psychosocial, emotional and spiritual domains. Analgesia alone is not always the answer.

3. Bowel dysfunction, not to be confused with bowel obstruction, is a common symptom. Constipation, distension, nausea and vomiting are features. This is a diagnosis of exclusion once other conditions (e.g. opioid-induced constipation, hypercalcaemia and renal failure) have been ruled out.

4. It is acceptable to refer hospice patients to an acute ward. Bowel obstruction, spinal cord compression, superior vena cava (SVC) obstruction and neutropenic sepsis are some conditions that might warrant imaging and acute management.

5. Know what to do in the case of massive haemorrhage. Where are the surgical towels?

6. Differentiate between *getting* and *feeling* better.

THE PATIENTS

7. Examine your patient. Physical contact is reassuring even if just to check a pulse.

8. Spend time with patients. They like to talk about football and gardening as well as their symptoms. Informal chats offer brief periods of respite and have the potential to be valuable therapeutic tools.

9. Leave your sceptical views regarding complementary therapy at home. Whether there is evidence or not, they may leave patients *feeling* better. Spending time with a caring person who is interested in the patient and his or her symptoms may be therapeutic in itself. If not costly and unlikely to do harm, why deny patients this opportunity?

10. Although patients are your primary focus, their friends and relatives need your attention too. Be empathetic to their situation and think about sources of support that could be useful for them, for example the chaplain, psychologist, social worker or GP.

11. Obtain consent to communicate with third parties. Families may not know as much as you hoped. Document these conversations concisely but accurately.

COMMUNICATION

12. Learn how to discuss prognosis. Ask patients what they think; they are often very insightful. It is not helpful to say, 'You have X months to live', as patients and families may take this as gospel and be upset, angry or disappointed if your prediction is incorrect. Consider talking in terms of rate of change. For example, when a patient is deteriorating by the month, his or her prognosis is likely to be measured in months. If the patient is more unwell by the week, his or her prognosis is likely to be weeks. Likewise, if he or she is frailer by the day or hour, the patient's life expectancy is likely to be days or hours. Make sure it is clear that these are estimates.

13. Read the article 'Not TLC but FPI (Friendly Professional Interest)'.[1] It highlights the importance of communication skills in the palliative setting.

14. Do not condemn other professionals for poor communication skills. Patients may say, 'Dr Bloggs never told me I was going to die.' Dr Bloggs may have told them. Did they understand and were they ready to accept this news? Always check the patient's understanding of important information that has been discussed.

15. Do not be afraid to break bad news. Patients have often anticipated that they may have cancer or are dying.

16. Silence is a communication skill. Use it!

PRESCRIBING

17. There is no maximum dose of opioid if the pain is opioid sensitive and side effects are tolerable.

18. Make use of the Palliative Care Formulary.

19. Prescribe modified-release morphine by brand name as different brands may provide varying levels of analgesia.

20. As morphine is renally excreted, patients with impaired renal function require less morphine. Reduce the dose, prolong the interval between doses, or use an alternative such as fentanyl.

21. Obtain a copy of *The Syringe Driver*.[2] It contains information on drugs used in drivers, their indications, dosages and compatibility with other medications.

22. Consult an opioid conversion chart when changing opioids or routes. Do not try to learn conversions and never rush this task. If in doubt, ask.

23. Learn how to prescribe breakthrough analgesia properly. Again, refer to the conversion chart or ask.

24. Check blood sugars of patients taking high-dose steroids.

25. Do not fear morphine or midazolam. Used correctly, they do not hasten death.

26. Medicines are only efficacious if absorbed. If vomited, oral medicines will not work. Patches only work if they adhere.

TEAMWORK AND ORGANISATION

27. Understand the different funding arrangements for patients who require care at home.

28. Listen to the nurses and auxiliaries. They are often very experienced and spend more time with your patients than you do. If they are concerned, there usually *is* something wrong (although it may not always be what they think is wrong).

29. Attend a Gold Standards Framework (GSF) meeting. You will be a fundamental part of these as a GP.

30. Participate in multidisciplinary team (MDT) meetings. Your views really matter (as do those of the nurses, auxiliaries, chaplains, physiotherapists, occupational therapists, complementary therapists and social workers).

31. Become familiar with your hospice's referral criteria. Patients with diagnoses other than cancer may be accepted.

32. Maintain good communication with hospital and GP colleagues. Inform them promptly of discharges and deaths.

33. Do some home visits with another doctor and a clinical nurse specialist.

ETHICS AND LEGAL

34. Remember that mental capacity is decision specific.

35. Complete death certificates and cremation forms promptly.

36. Check patients and their notes for the presence of hazardous implants before completing cremation forms.

37. Focus on ethics. You will come across countless resuscitation, capacity and consent issues, as well as advance decisions to refuse treatment.

38. Not everyone in the hospice is 'DNACPR'. Some patients should still be resuscitated in the event of cardiopulmonary arrest. If in doubt, discuss resuscitation status with your seniors at the time of admission. Also, it is not unheard of for relatives and staff to require resuscitation in the event of an arrest, so know where the defibrillator is!

39. People make eccentric decisions. This does not mean that they lack mental capacity.

40. Advance decisions to refuse treatment (ADRTs), previously known as advance directives, provide a legally binding method for adult patients with mental capacity to refuse treatment in preparation for a time when they may lack capacity. You might be asked to counsel a patient or you might be faced with a dilemma where an advanced directive appears to be in place. Clearly in a palliative care setting these are team decisions but use this as an opportunity to get some practical experience of a challenge that is likely to come up in general practice. There is an NHS website containing a wealth of information relating to ADRTs.[3]

41. Remember … you are the doctor. Nurses may be experienced but do not be persuaded to prescribe or administer medicines unless you can justify it. It does not look good in court when your defence is 'The nurse told me to'!

POTENTIAL PDP POINTERS

Some trainees find writing a PDP to be a difficult task. Try to put yourself in the shoes of a GP managing palliative care patients in the community. What knowledge would make managing those patients easier?

› Become confident in managing symptoms common in palliative care patients. These include pain, nausea and vomiting, and agitation.

› Learn your local palliative care referral criteria.

› Become comfortable discussing prognosis and death with patients and their families.

› Become acquainted with the presentation and management of emergencies in palliative care.

› Learn how to use a syringe driver and some of the drugs that, as a GP, you might be called upon to use in the community.

› Understand fully the valuable role of the clinical nurse specialist.

› Attend some of the secondary care multidisciplinary team (MDT) meetings with one of your palliative care consultants.

› Familiarise yourself with ethical and legal issues frequently encountered in palliative care. For example: DNACPR decisions, mental capacity, consent and advance decisions to refuse treatment.

REFERENCES

1. Brewin T. Not TLC but FPI (Friendly Professional Interest). *Journal of the Royal Society of Medicine* 1990; **83(3)**: 172–5.

2. Dickman A, Schneider J. *The Syringe Driver: continuous subcutaneous infusions in palliative care* (3rd edn). Oxford: Oxford University Press, 2011.

3. Advance Decisions to Refuse Treatment, www.adrt.nhs.uk.

THANK YOU FOR TELLING ME

Today I had to give a patient news of her multiple metastases. This was only a week after her first consultation with me with a rather vague set of symptoms, which she had put down to feeling tired and being just generally under the weather.

At the end of the consultation she thanked me for the way I had explained it to her. I was very touched by this, not least because I could not imagine that anybody would have the mental resources to contemplate this in the light of news that they are dying.

Red Roses *collection curated by Alec Logan and illustrated by Helen Wilson.*

23

PSYCHIATRY

Matt Burkes, Laurine Hanna and James Woollard

Many doctors approach psychiatry with a sense of trepidation and, occasionally, fear. The aim of this chapter is to give some concrete advice to help you relax and enjoy this fascinating rotation. A spell in psychiatry has the potential to be one of the most useful rotations on your training scheme. Much of psychiatry is now managed in the community and when people suffer mental health issues it is often the GP who is their first port of call. A good working knowledge of the field, as well as insight into the mechanisms and frameworks of secondary care, is an asset. During the job, you will also have the opportunities and time to develop your communication skills, occasionally in crisis situations.

As with all rotations, it is imperative that you are organised and clear about what you want to experience and get out of your time. Psychiatry is very different from many of the other jobs on the rotation and requires a different approach, but it should provide you with invaluable experience for your future career.

THE BASICS

1. The psychiatry multidisciplinary team (MDT) is less hierarchical than a standard medical team – respect this. Recognising the skills and knowledge of others will enhance your ability to care for your patients.

2. Listen to the nurses! They spend much, much longer with the patients than you do and have a wealth of knowledge and experience that they are usually happy to share.

3. Most psychiatric units are very different from hospital wards. Remember that many psychiatric nurses are not trained or experienced in spotting medical problems and you should not expect them to – that's your job.

THE PATIENTS

4. Treat patients with dignity at all times. You will never regret it.

5. Try not to be afraid of psychiatry or psychiatric patients. Conflict situations can generally be managed by a calm approach.

6. People with personality disorders can be difficult to manage. They can bring up polarised feelings within you, and between your team (technically known as splitting). Try to get some exposure to Mentalisation-Based Treatment/ Dialectical Behaviour Therapy (MBT/DBT) for borderline personality disorder.

7. Always do a risk assessment and ask about suicidal ideation, thoughts of self-harm and thoughts of harm towards others. Other domains of risk include vulnerability, self-neglect and psychosis. Remember that not all risks are predictable.

8. Mental health stigma and prejudice are real and widespread. Make sure you are not part of the problem.

PSYCHOPHARMACOLOGY

9. Have the local rapid tranquillisation guidelines for managing acutely disturbed patients to hand – especially when on-call. If there is a history of acute behavioural disturbance secondary to psychiatric illness, then consider prescribing rapid tranquillisation on the 'as required' section. Bear in mind this is a treatment of last resort after psychological and behavioural approaches have failed to de-escalate the situation. Discuss with the patient if possible, and check for any advance directives or crisis care plans. Write oral and intramuscular (IM) routes separately and remember that some drugs (e.g. haloperidol) have different 24-hour maximum doses for oral and IM routes.

10. Check if a patient has had antipsychotics before. If so, has the patient had adverse reactions?

11. Know how neuroleptic malignant syndrome presents and how to manage it.

12. Get a good chart to guide you when changing a patient's medications.

13. Try to become familiar with the side effect profile of common or significant psychotropic medications such as lithium, clozapine, the antipsychotics and antidepressants.

14. Learn to spot extra-pyramidal side effects. Write up procyclidine on the 'as required' section for patients who are on antipsychotics.

15. *The Maudsley Prescribing Guidelines* are a fantastic resource.[1]

16. When starting patients on serotonin-specific reuptake inhibitors (SSRIs) warn them that anxiety can get worse in the initial period. Also warn them that positive effects generally take at least two weeks, and often a month, to kick in.

17. 1 mg lorazepam = 5–10 mg diazepam.[2]

18. Always warn patients that benzodiazepines are addictive (and antidepressants aren't). Remember that SSRIs may have a discontinuation syndrome if stopped abruptly.

CONFLICT AND DIFFICULT SITUATIONS

19. Attend a breakaway training course that shows you physical techniques to remove yourself from violent encounters. Hopefully you will never have to use the skills, but you won't regret having them, even when you have finished psychiatry and doing other jobs.

20. Remember that disinhibited elderly patients with dementia can also assault staff.

21. Direct confrontation and shouting at agitated patients rarely calm the situation or lead to a favourable result. Always try to de-escalate tense situations. Offer oral medication before resorting to the IM route.

22. Learn the process, and become familiar with the paperwork, of detaining patients under section 5:2 of the Mental Health Act. When you need to do this you don't want to be learning on the job and paperwork errors cause great headaches for the entire trust.

23. Try to de-escalate situations before resorting to the Mental Health Act. If patients feel they have been listened to they can often be persuaded informally to stay.

24. Get in the habit of carrying a personal alarm. Know how to use it. Know how to provide assistance to others who need it.

25. Do not get involved in restraint unless you have proper training. Without training restraint is very dangerous for the patient (and for you).

ON-CALL

26. Become fluent in the performance and recording of the mental state examination. You'll be doing a lot of it! Take a crib sheet with the headings on for the first few on-calls and clinics till it becomes second nature (as it will).

27. Take drug charts and all admission forms to A&E when on-call in case you need to admit a patient. That way you can take care of all the paperwork at once.

28. Make sure you know which consultant is on-call and his or her contact details. Find this out at the start of the shift rather than after hours when you need to speak to the consultant urgently.

29. Initially you should be discussing all patients you see with a senior.

30. Think about any child protection issues.

31. If you ever think you need to call the consultant, do so. But, before you do, make a formulation using the biopsychosocial precipitating/predisposing/maintaining matrix. Be clear what the main areas of risk are, and how likely you think they are to happen.

32. Always do a physical exam and bloods when admitting a patient unless he or she really is too agitated. Try not to leave it for someone else to do the next day. It would be awful to miss a medical problem and this could result in significant harm to the patient.

GENERAL MANAGEMENT AND PERSONAL DEVELOPMENT

33. Learn some cognitive behavioural therapy (CBT). If you can't attend a course get some teaching from your team psychologist. GPs pay good money to go on courses to get this experience! Make sure this training finds its way onto your CV!

34. Try to do some home visits with the community psychiatric nurses (CPNs) if appropriate.

35. Let it be known that you are interested in seeing some mental health assessments performed by the consultants. The insight into the process that you will gain will be useful when you are a GP.

36. Don't let your physical medicine slip – some psychiatrists have been out of the general hospital long enough to feel deskilled in managing physical (i.e. non-mental) problems. Your team will often be looking for your leadership in this area. Remember to consider organic causes of psychiatric presentations.

37. Patients with alcohol issues are difficult. Accept that you won't cure them until they become motivated to change.

38. Make sure you laugh. Psychiatry is emotionally demanding and without this release you will really struggle.

39. Attend a Balint group; engage with the Balint group; write about the Balint group in your ePortfolio (educational supervisors love it!). If there is no Balint group then create one.

40. Regardless of your placement try to sit in on or get experience of child and adolescent, working-age and older-persons' mental health. Try to experience liaison psychiatry, forensic psychiatry, eating disorder services, learning disability and any other specialist clinics that you think will be useful or interesting.

POTENTIAL PDP POINTERS

Try to sit down with your clinical supervisor to formulate a PDP early in the rotation. This meeting will be more useful if you have prepared a few ideas to discuss. Your plan should be tailored to your individual needs and interests. However, the following examples may prove useful.

› Become proficient in the assessment of a patient's mental state, including risk assessment.

› Gain skills in the management of common mental health problems and presentations including depression, schizophrenia and bipolar disorder.

› Become familiar with community mental health resources and how to access them.

› Develop and consolidate knowledge of the Mental Health Act, with particular reference to general practice and the acute psychiatric setting.

› Recognise that mental health uses a multidisciplinary approach, and that this approach relies on mutual respect and support for team members. Develop awareness of the roles of other team members within the Community Mental Health Team (CMHT), including CPNs, social workers, crisis team, psychology and therapists. Also gain more understanding of allied professionals in mental health, e.g. police, solicitors, advocates. etc.

› Find out about counselling and talking therapies that are available and the techniques that they employ and teach.

› Become familiar with the use, safe prescription and monitoring of common psychotropic medications, including antipsychotics, mood stabilisers and antidepressants. Gain experience in altering medications and the precautions and regimes used in transition.

› Offer to take the (supervised) lead in a ward round to facilitate obtaining consultation observation tools (COTs).

REFERENCES

1. Taylor D, Paton C, Kapur S. *The Maudsley Prescribing Guidelines in Psychiatry* (10th edn). London: Informa Healthcare, 2010.

2. Joint Formulary Committee. *British National Formulary* (60th edn). London: BMA and RPS, 2010.

24

PUBLIC HEALTH

Yolande Knight

Public health is a specialty in which few of us have practical experience. It's generally poorly covered at medical school but, believe me, there's more to this stuff than statistics and John Snow's pump handle!

Until 2013, the typical GP placement involved working in the local Primary Care Trust (PCT), primarily in the Department of Public Health, and working within the local Health Protection Unit (HPU) covering disease outbreak response work and its on-call service. Under the reforms of the Health and Social Care Act of 2012 both agencies no longer exist.

From April 2013 public health placements will be with Public Health England (PHE), encompassing the work formerly conducted with the Health Protection Agency (HPA) and some of the work of the former PCT. This could be in the national PHE office or with the regional PHE units.

Your involvement with the assessment and planning of population health will be within the Local Government Association (LGA), that is, local authority. Here you will have a chance to work with the Commissioning Support Service (CSS) and the Health and Wellbeing Board (HWB) on health needs assessments and strategic planning of local health care. A summary of the new public health system and its organisations is available on the PHE[1] and local.gov[2] websites.

As a medic, your clinical knowledge and training in communication skills will be invaluable in helping to coordinate responses to outbreaks and events.

WORKING IN THE LOCAL GOVERNMENT AUTHORITY (FORMERLY PCT AND DEPARTMENT OF PUBLIC HEALTH)

Your managerial, fact-finding and analytical skills will be utilised here. You will be involved in the planning and provision of the myriad health services for your local area. This is where the slow burn of long-term healthcare provision is stoked.

1. Local authorities can be opaque when it comes to finding out who does what. Read a copy of the department structure and obtain a telephone list. Make friends with the PA to one of the Public Health Consultants – the PAs know everything – and introduce yourself to all of the team members.

2. Befriend the departmental statistician/data analyst. Make an attempt at analysis but remember that this is not medical school: these calculations determine service provision! An online textbook of statistics for public health is available at healthknowledge.[3]

3. The departmental annual report may seem dry, but it will provide you with a guide to local priorities, spending areas and recent achievements. Read it in your first week with a strong coffee to hand.

4. If you're writing an exceptional-circumstances panel report (used to decide if a patient should receive a particular treatment when he or she doesn't meet the local criteria), be focused and limit the document to six pages including references. Panel members have many cases to consider and rely on your report for important decisions. Be aware that National Institute for Health and Care Excellence's (NICE) cost-effectiveness threshold is £30,000 per Quality Adjusted Life Year (QALY) gained.

5. If you are preparing a media statement, ensure your consultant has proofread it before you send it to the Communications Department. This will hopefully avoid red faces on the *News at Ten*.

6. Different reports often follow specific formats – always look at similar reports so you know what's expected. You may suffer culture shock on first working in project management. Don't be intimidated by project management speak and the abundance of acronyms. Try to pick up some project management skills – it will help your CV in a world of GP commissioning!

7. When in doubt, always ask a public health senior for help or advice. Along with GPs and paediatricians they are the friendliest of specialties.

8. Beware the rush of offers for projects and reports when you start as the department's fresh blood; don't just say yes. Find out first if it's achievable within your placement period and *agree a timeline*.

WORKING IN THE PHE UNIT (FORMERLY HPU)

Your clinical knowledge will come to the fore here, where the majority of your work will involve taking calls from GPs and other health professionals. Most calls relate to notifiable diseases, disease outbreaks or health hazards in your area.

9. Before your first on-call, familiarise yourself with the local software, your local unit's on-call pack and the PHE/HPA website.[4] Do a practice call with a colleague.

10. Know how to use the phone. It sounds stupid but your callers will not thank you for accidentally cutting them off when you think you're putting them on hold.

11. When you take a call, always start by recording the caller's name, address, phone number and job title before launching into the reason for the call. You will regret it if you haven't and you later need to retrieve information from them. Most units have a pro forma; use it.

12. Revise the clinical presentation and health protection approach to common calls such as seasonal flu, measles, mumps, meningitis, tuberculosis, enteric fevers, gastroenteritis outbreaks in institutions such as schools and nursing homes, and Panton-Valentine Leukocidin (PVL) *Staphylococcus aureus*. Also remind yourself of the notifiable diseases.

13. Revise childhood immunisations before your first on-call, and always refer to the Green Book for queries.[5]

14. When investigating your first outbreak, ensure you have a clear plan for data collection (questionnaire), data analysis (software such as STATA, usually chi-squared test) and reporting. Ask your consultant to show you an example report.

15. Get on with the Environmental Health Officers. They're invaluable colleagues on the ground during illness outbreaks.

16. Know the difference between seasonal flu and swine flu. Be prepared to answer questions about the vaccines and who should be receiving them. Policies change as flu trends evolve; the onus is on you to keep updated.

17. You will often be speaking with tuberculosis nurses. Appreciate that they have a difficult job, so time your phone calls accordingly (i.e. not every day!).

18. When you have to complete long, trawling questionnaires over the phone with a patient (such as in cases of *Listeria* or PVL *Staphylococcus aureus*) be patient with the patient; remember that he or she is unwell.

19. When a GP calls you, remember that you will be one yourself one day. He or she may not always have all the information you require, and the GP will often not manage to call you back. Be realistic.

20. *Remember*: It's okay to say you'll call back if you don't know the answer. GPs and practice nurses may have the patient there in front of them and may pressure you, but it is better to give the right information after a delay rather than the wrong information immediately.

POTENTIAL PDP POINTERS

Domain 5 of curriculum statement 3.01 *Healthy People: promoting health and preventing disease* is the main section covering public health. There is an emphasis on population health, statistics surrounding this, health promotion, disease prevention and surveillance.

> Spend time observing a Public Health Specialist at work and learn as a GP how to access his or her advice.

> Identify the top ten most important local health promotion and disease prevention strategies in place.

> Gain confidence in interpreting epidemiological studies and health surveillance data with the local Health Observation Unit.

> Spend time in the local Health Protection Unit undertaking on-calls and disease outbreak investigations.

> Gain knowledge of UK immunisations and vaccinations, and the problems encountered with them in primary care.

REFERENCES

1. http://webarchive.nationalarchives.gov.uk/20130107105354/http://www.dh.gov.uk/health/tag/public-health-england/.

2. Local Government Association, www.local.gov.uk/health.

3. Health Knowledge, www.healthknowledge.org.uk.

4. Health Protection Agency, www.hpa.org.uk.

5. Salisbury D, Ramsay M, Noakes K. *Immunisation against Infectious Disease* ('the Green Book'). London: DH, 2006, http://immunisation.dh.gov.uk/category/the-green-book/ [accessed March 2014].

HUG

In 17 years of general practice only one patient has ever asked me to be hugged. She was younger than me, in her thirties, and had end-stage alcoholic liver disease. Her abdomen was distended with fluid. I thought that she might die, and for the first time she had realised that she might die. Her mother had been my father's patient and my babysitter. I needed to admit her. She was frightened, and as she left my consulting room, admission letter in hand, she asked for a hug. I obliged. I still hope not too stiffly.

A week later my partner was called to an unexpected death. My patient. She had spent four hours in A&E waiting for her bed, become tremulous, and discharged herself. She died alone in her flat later that weekend.

Our new PFI-funded hospital has elaborate shrubberies but too few beds. This enrages me.

(From *Foreword*, Secrets from the Black Bag, *RCGP 2005, with permission.*)

Red Roses *collection curated by Alec Logan and illustrated by Helen Wilson.*

25

RESPIRATORY MEDICINE

Tim Martindale, Katie Pink and Jim Pink

Respiratory medicine has a lot to offer for the GP trainee. It is a great mixture of both acute and chronic illnesses, from the young with asthma and pneumonia to the more elderly with chronic obstructive pulmonary disease (COPD) and lung cancer. There are practical procedures aplenty, and you will get very good at arterial blood gas (ABG) sampling and interpretation, and get the chance to perform invasive procedures such as chest drains. There are a lot of social issues too, such as dealing with relatives, the emotion that goes with a new diagnosis of cancer, or just a patient's realisation that he or she will never be able to return home due to a decline in lung function.

As with every new job, take time at the beginning to ask what you want to achieve from the job and how it will benefit you. If you don't do this early, you'll find yourself halfway through the job before you realise it. The chronic aspects of respiratory disease such as symptom management and prognosis are perhaps the most important thing for GP trainees to take out of the attachment, and these are best learnt by clerking people in clinic and presenting to the consultants. Of course, at the time there are so many other things that need doing on the ward, but remember that you are a GP trainee not a Foundation Year doctor any more, and clinic is a very valuable part of your education!

THE BASICS

1. Respiratory is very busy but if your team is organised then you can usually be home on time. If you leave everything to the new Foundation Year doctor then be prepared to stay late!

2. Lung cancer accounts for a large number of respiratory inpatients. Involve the clinical nurse specialists or palliative care nurses as appropriate. Be aware

of the oncological emergencies in these patients: hypercalcaemia, spinal cord compression and superior vena cava compression.

3. Spend some time with the asthma nurse – he or she is an invaluable source of advice.

4. Learn the British Thoracic Society asthma guidelines – not only will they ensure you are following best practice, but they may also come up in your MRCGP exams.

5. Learn the colour of inhalers! Patients seldom know what they contain. If they don't know the colours then suspect non-compliance!

6. The CURB-65 score[1] is only applicable to community-acquired pneumonia.

7. Beware of asthma. Patients can deteriorate rapidly. Remember that a normal or rising CO_2 level in an acute exacerbation is a sign of a patient getting tired. Involve the Intensive Care Unit (ICU) and your senior. This time, don't wait for the consultant ward round!

8. Oxygen should be prescribed according to the target oxygen saturations you are trying to achieve. In acutely unwell patients this should be 94–8%; in patients at risk of hypercapnic respiratory failure this should be 88–92%.[2]

9. Ask radiologists for 'their opinion' on a clinical case rather than demanding a scan be done. Generally this means you get what you wanted in the first place, only quicker and without any tears. If you don't know why you are requesting a scan, check with your senior first.

10. Chest physiotherapists are absolutely invaluable. Get to know them early and enlist their expertise for sputum retention and dyspnoea.

11. Get to know this graph (Fletcher Peto) – it provides good evidence for the value of stopping smoking and is a useful tool when trying to persuade patients to quit.

FIGURE 25.1: SMOKERS WITH AIRWAY OBSTRUCTION

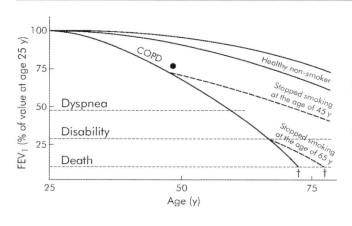

Source: Reproduced from Bednarek M, Gorecka D, Wielgomas J, *et al*. Smokers with airway obstruction are more likely to quit smoking. *Thorax* 2006; **61**(10): 869–73 with permission from BMJ Publishing Group Ltd. [3]

THE PATIENTS

12. Many of your patients will be scared, in pain and in considerable distress (physical and psychological). Be aware of this and act appropriately.

13. If you take the time to have a family conversation, take the time to document it properly.

14. Watch an elderly person with rheumatoid arthritis trying to use an inhaler, and then go and read up about different types of inhaler and the devices to aid their use!

COMMUNICATION AND DOCUMENTATION

15. You will be busy. Make sure you are organised; this will help. An up-to-date patient list with a diagnosis and notes of any outstanding investigations/jobs to do is essential.

16. Have a 'board round' early afternoon to review patients' progress and delegate jobs.

17. Cancer isn't cancer until it is under the microscope; however, if clinical suspicion is high, introduce the possibility to the patient early.

18. Communication is key in non-invasive ventilation – try a mask on and experience the claustrophobia.

19. Get your specialty registrar/consultant to make Do Not Attempt Resuscitation (DNAR) decisions on patients early – it's unfair (for patients, relatives and doctors) to leave it to the on-call team when the patient is peri-arrest at the weekend.

20. Make sure you know the ceiling of care for patients started on non-invasive ventilation. If they do not improve, should they be for intubation and ventilation or is palliative care more appropriate?

SKILLS AND MANAGEMENT

21. Consider venous thromboembolism prophylaxis in everyone. Dehydration, asthma/COPD + pulmonary embolism (PE) don't go very well together, and in-hospital PEs are largely preventable.

22. Unless in extremis, use 2.5 mg of nebulised salbutamol only – you can always give two nebulisers but it is easy to become horribly tachycardic and hypokalaemic with repeated doses of 5 mg.

23. Chest drains should only be inserted by a clinician who is skilled in the technique. Nowadays they are inserted under ultrasound scan (USS) guidance when used to drain pleural effusions. There is no organ in the abdomen that has not been perforated with a chest drain trochar.

24. Pain felt during chest drain insertion comes from the pleura – anaesthetise generously (max 3 mg/kg lidocaine or 2 mg/kg bupivacaine). Ensure adequate oral analgesia.

25. Never clamp a bubbling chest drain – you could give the patient a tension pneumothorax.

26. If you insert a chest drain for drainage of an effusion, stay with the patient until you see how quickly it drains. If a significant amount comes out or the bottle starts filling up quickly it will need clamping or the patient may develop rebound pulmonary oedema and subsequent cardiac arrest.

27. Use local anaesthetic for ABGs – they're horrible if you don't.

28. Try to get a 'well' ABG prior to discharge – this is useful information to have on subsequent admissions.

29. Escalate to Intensive Therapy Unit early if appropriate. This decision should be led by a consultant.

30. Reviewing previous sputum culture results is always useful before starting antibiotics in patients with chronic respiratory conditions. This is particularly the case for bronchiectasis and cystic fibrosis. Treatment can be tailored to treat whichever organisms are colonising the patient.

31. If in doubt, ask!

POTENTIAL PDP POINTERS

› Achieve competency in managing acute exacerbations of COPD and asthma.

› Learn how to manage community-acquired pneumonia and acute PE.

› Improve knowledge of the management of chronic respiratory conditions by attending outpatient clinics.

› Attend multidisciplinary team (MDT) meetings and clinics to gain experience in the management of patients with lung cancer.

› Develop working relationships within the multidisciplinary respiratory team including physiotherapists, nurse specialists and smoking cessation counsellors.

› Develop skills in time management.

› Consolidate existing skills in chest X-ray and arterial blood gas interpretation.

› Learn how to perform and interpret peak flow accurately.

› Learn how to perform and interpret spirometry.

› Consolidate skills in the assessment and management of acutely unwell patients.

› Take the opportunity to observe pulmonary rehabilitation, sleep clinics and the use of non-invasive ventilation.

REFERENCES

1. British Thoracic Society Standards of Care Committee. BTS guidelines for the management of community acquired pneumonia in adults. *Thorax* 2001; **56(Suppl 4)**: iv1–64.

2. O'Driscoll BR, Howard LS, Davison AG. BTS guideline for emergency oxygen use in adult patients: *Thorax* 2008; **63(Suppl 6)**: vi1–68.

3. Bednarek M, Gorecka D, Wielgomas J, *et al.* Smokers with airway obstruction are more likely to quit smoking. *Thorax* 2006; **61(10)**: 869–73, doi: 10.1136/thx.2006.059071.

26

RHEUMATOLOGY

Victoria Welsh

INTRODUCTION

One in four people registered with a GP will consult for a musculoskeletal problem over a 12-month period; this accounts for one in seven GP consultations.[1] Musculoskeletal conditions significantly impact daily life through pain, disability and psychological ill-health.[2,3] A rheumatology rotation is therefore a relevant and practical rotation for GP trainees to undertake.

The key learning points from a rheumatology rotation include: the early recognition of inflammatory arthritis to enable timely secondary care referral; the identification of the red flags of joint sepsis and development of an understanding of the social and psychological consequences of chronic musculoskeletal conditions; and becoming familiar with disease-modifying anti-rheumatic drugs (DMARDs).

THE BASICS

1. Before your first day, read current guidelines relating to common rheumatological conditions in both primary and secondary care, for example the National Institute for Health and Care Excellence (NICE) guidelines for osteoarthritis (OA) and rheumatoid arthritis.[4,5]

2. Practise your examination skills. Although you are likely to be an experienced junior doctor, asking a friendly registrar to demonstrate his or her slick examination style and asking for tips will save you a lot of time.

3. Learn the monitoring requirements and side effects of the commonly used DMARDs. Seek advice on how to manage borderline results.

4. Practise joint injections at every opportunity. Ask your unit if it is planning to run a course or look online for your nearest one.

5. Find out about local and national support services for your patients. Knowing and sharing information about such systems, including 24-hour advice lines and patient support groups, really does make a difference.

6. Read some patient information leaflets for tips on the less-discussed aspects of chronic musculoskeletal disease, for example sex. Arthritis Research UK is an excellent resource for patients and clinicians.[6]

THE PATIENTS

7. People with rheumatological diseases span a wide range of age groups, socioeconomic backgrounds and ethnicities. Treat each person as an individual and avoid stereotyping patients. All people have fears and concerns that are personal to them so don't be afraid to ask.

8. Common concerns relate to fitness for work. Be supportive and realistic. Remember there is multidisciplinary team input to support employment for patients of working age.

9. Chronic pain, both current pain and the potential for future suffering, is a real issue. Remember the psychosocial aspects of chronic pain. Analgesia isn't just about medications; don't forget other physical treatments and development of coping strategies. Learn from specialist pain teams, sit in clinics and ask patients about their own pain management techniques.

INPATIENTS AND ON-CALL

10. Clerking rheumatology patients can take a significant amount of time. Factor this into your day and make the effort. The insights gained from really listening to the patient – considering his or her full case, co-morbidities, medications, home circumstances, social aspects and psychological health – will be invaluable.

11. Rheumatology inpatients are often very complex to manage. Multi-system disease involvement, the presence of unrelated co-morbidities and conditions resulting from medical treatment all add to the challenge of clinical management. Accept that you can't know everything.

12. You may be covering day case admissions for immunosuppressant or bisphosphonate infusions. Learn what goes on from a health professional and patient viewpoint. This will help you appreciate your patient's experience and assist you in answering patient questions.

13. Remember, a patient with active synovitis from an inflammatory arthritis can also have septic arthritis.

14. Don't forget that access to certain investigations may not be possible in the rheumatology ward, for example arterial blood gases. You may need to refer the patient to an acute medical ward, so don't be afraid to do this if necessary.

OUTPATIENTS

15. Outpatient clinics are highly relevant to GP work. Seeing new patients and instigating management plans is particularly beneficial. Listen to the patient stories, particularly around how the disease initially presented. This will stick in your mind when you see similar cases in primary care and help your decision making.

16. You may be working in a unit that supports research into new drugs. Take the opportunity to learn more about research in health care. At the very least, this will give you an appreciation of research participation and may even spark your interest in research.

THE MULTIDISCIPLINARY TEAM

17. Get to grips with the different roles of each team member, including physiotherapists, occupational therapists, specialist rheumatology nurses and the pain team.

18. Spend time with the occupational therapists and a few hours talking to patients about their daily functioning and the assistive devices available. You'll be amazed at the array of implements available, including tin openers, tap handles, jar openers, cutlery and writing tools. Knowing about these devices and how to arrange their acquisition will help your future patients.

19. Shadow a physiotherapist in the outpatient department. Watching him or her at work will provide you with some gems of practical advice for patients that simply are not available from any other learning resource.

POTENTIAL PDP POINTERS

› Revise current guidelines and management of OA in primary care by reading NICE guidelines[4] and complete relevant e-learning modules. You should be able to counsel patients with OA or a fear of developing OA about diet, exercise and other lifestyle aspects according to current evidence base and guidelines.

› Learn about the side effects of commonly used DMARDs and monitoring requirements. Learn how to prescribe these drugs safely.

› Increase awareness of resources available to support patients with rheumatological diseases, including electronic and community-based resources. Be able to signpost patients in primary and secondary care towards accurate information and support networks.

REFERENCES

1. Jordan KP, Kadam UT, Haywood R, *et al*. Annual consultation prevalence of regional musculoskeletal problems in primary care: an observational study. *BMC Musculoskeletal Disorders* 2010; **11**: 144.

2. Mottram S, Peat G, Thomas E, *et al*. Patterns of pain and mobility limitation in older people: cross-sectional findings from a population survey of 18,497 adults aged 50 years and over. *Quality of Life Research* 2008; **17(4)**: 529–39.

3. Mallen C, Peat G. Screening older people with musculoskeletal pain for depressive symptoms in primary care. *British Journal of General Practice* 2008; **58(555)**: 688–93.

4. National Collaborating Centre for Chronic Conditions. *Osteoarthritis: the care and management of osteoarthritis in adults* (Clinical Guideline 59). London: NICE, 2008.

5. National Collaborating Centre for Chronic Conditions. *Rheumatoid Arthritis: the management of rheumatoid arthritis in adults* (Clinical Guideline 79). London: NICE, 2009.

6. Arthritis Research UK, www.arthritisresearchuk.org/.

27

STROKE MEDICINE

Matthew Yates and Ottilia Speirs

Stroke units make a massive difference to the lives of your patients and their families, following what is generally an earth-shattering event. While working on a stroke unit you will see a vast spectrum of patients. Some of these patients will make a full recovery from their stroke while others will subsequently deteriorate, and the majority will fall somewhere between. You may work on a Hyperacute Stroke Unit, a Stroke Rehabilitation Unit or an Integrated Unit (which combines both).

Stroke medicine is a sub-specialty of geriatric medicine. However, stroke is not just a condition of the elderly. The practice of stroke medicine relies on a good core working knowledge of general medicine and neurology.

You will have heard of multidisciplinary teams (MDTs) before. In no other field of hospital medicine will you have the opportunity to work so closely as a member of an MDT and see what a positive effect they can have. This chapter provides a guide to prepare you for a job on a Stroke Unit. This will allow you to feel more prepared for the days ahead and the expectations on you as well as covering your educational needs.

THE BASICS

1. Understand how stroke presentation relates to neuroanatomy.

2. Revise how to conduct a full neurological examination: testing cranial nerves, peripheral nerves, speech and cerebellar function.

3. Learn about the Face Arms Speech Test (FAST) tool, Recognition of Stroke in the Emergency Room (ROSIER) and the ABCD2 score (as a risk stratification tool for transient ischaemic attack [TIA]).

4. Learn about the National Institutes of Health Stroke Scale (NIHSS) and its use in assessment of an acute stroke prior to thrombolysis.

5. Make sure you know the indications and local protocol for urgent CT scanning, how to organise one – whatever the time of day or night – and how to get it reported.

6. Understand the role that thrombolysis, antiplatelet and anticoagulation therapy play in acute stroke. Find out about local arrangements for stopping them prior to percutaneous endoscopic gastrostomy (PEG) insertion and carotid endarterectomy.

7. Think homeostasis – stroke can knock the body severely off balance, so monitoring of BMs, BPs, pulse and Sats are all important.

8. Familiarise yourself with the helpful stroke guidelines produced by the National Institute for Health and Care Excellence (NICE),[1] Scottish Intercollegiate Guidelines Network (SIGN)[2] and the Royal College of Physicians (RCP).[3]

9. Get used to writing up medicine as PO/NG rather than simply PO. This will make sure that the patient gets his or her medicine on time as well as saving you time.

10. Think about the role of palliative care teams.

11. Don't neglect your wider medical and surgical skills – they may be required on the ward or on the general take when you are on-call. Stroke patients often have co-morbidities.

12. Remember that chronic disease causes depression. Screen for depression using the Hospital Anxiety and Depression Scale (HADS) and Geriatric Depression Scale (GDS) so that you can involve the clinical psychologists where appropriate.

13. It would also be useful to have a working knowledge of the Modified Rankin Score, Barthel Scale and cognitive screening tools such as the mini-mental state examination (MMSE) and Montreal Cognitive Assessment.

14. Plan your discharges early. Get writing those discharge summaries early so that, on the day of going home, you only have to check and make some small amendments. Most units will have an MDT approach for discharge, so work closely with colleagues.

THE PATIENTS

15. Just because a patient is unable to speak does not mean that he or she lacks capacity. Communication underpins stroke medicine – failure to communicate well with patients and within the MDT will result in poor outcomes for your patients.

16. Stroke is a life-changing condition, so be sensitive to this. No one expects a stroke to happen. Be aware of the impact that the stroke will have on all aspects of your patient's life – and that of his or her loved ones.

17. Remember a stroke patient must be nil by mouth until he or she has passed a swallow screen performed by a trained member of staff. If the patient is nil by mouth, don't forget his or her hydration and nutritional needs.

18. Try a thickened drink yourself – it will help you to empathise.

19. Patients and their families will want to discuss what's happened and what the plan is. Take time to do this. Familiarise yourself with the notes in advance. Find an appropriate location. If the patient is not present, do you have his or her consent to talk to the family?

20. Do not be drawn on a prognosis by the family. Strokes can lead an unpredictable course; answering questions about what the future holds is firmly the territory of career stroke physicians.

21. Get used to discussing lifestyle change with your patients. A little exercise, a healthier diet and stopping smoking have incremental and significant benefits for stroke patients. But don't lecture patients: it doesn't work.

REFERRALS AND TEAMWORK

22. Get to know the radiographers in CT, MR and ultrasound.

23. Get to know the gastroenterology registrar who will be responsible for inserting PEGs, as well as the vascular team who will be carrying out carotid endarterectomies.

24. Get on good terms with your physiologists/clinical investigations team – you will be providing them with copious requests for echocardiograms and 24-hour tapes.

25. Put yourself in the position of the GP receiving the discharge summary of a patient who has been in hospital for six weeks. What is important? Medication changes, functional ability, capacity and social needs are a good start. Be sure to document what follow-up is planned – even if a clinic date has not been finalised.

26. Make sure you know how to set up anticoagulation clinic appointments – otherwise discharges can be delayed.

SKILLS AND DEVELOPMENT

27. For MMSEs, give your patients every opportunity to score as well as they can.

28. Familiarise yourself with the Oxford Community Stroke Project (OCSP) classification.[4]

29. Understand the stroke and TIA pathways (both as inpatient and outpatient) where you work.

POTENTIAL PDP POINTERS

› Learn to prioritise clinically and investigate patients as they are admitted to the stroke unit.

› Learn to delegate tasks appropriately and to work with the wider MDT.

› Build on existing skills in CT, echocardiogram and ECG interpretation.

› Develop skills in MRI interpretation.

› Build diagnostic skill and confidence by exposure to the acute medical take.

› Improve knowledge of the management of common acute stroke presentations including crescendo TIA and stroke (including those affecting the posterior circulation).

› Improve knowledge of the management of common acute stroke presentations and chronic complications.

REFERENCES

1. National Institute for Health and Clinical Excellence. *Stroke: diagnosis and initial management of acute stroke and transient ischaemic attack (TIA)* (Clinical Guideline 68). London: NICE, http://publications.nice.org.uk/stroke-cg68 [accessed March 2014].

2. Scottish Intercollegiate Guidelines Network. *Management of Patients with Stroke or TIA: assessment, investigation, immediate management and secondary prevention.* Edinburgh: SIGN, www.sign.ac.uk/guidelines/fulltext/108/index.html [accessed March 2014].

3. Royal College of Physicians Intercollegiate Stroke Working Party. *National Clinical Guideline for Stroke* (4th edn). London: RCP, 2012, www.rcplondon.ac.uk/sites/default/files/national-clinical-guidelines-for-stroke-fourth-edition.pdf [accessed March 2014].

4. Bamford J, Sandercock P, Dennis M, *et al.* Classification and natural history of clinically identifiable subtypes of cerebral infarction. *Lancet* 1991; **337(8756)**: 1521–6.

28

TRAUMA AND ORTHOPAEDICS

Edward Dawe and William Reeve

Be prepared to learn! Trauma and orthopaedics is a huge subject that is only sparsely taught at medical school. You may initially be confused by the terminology (see Table 28.1). Time on-call in orthopaedics can be stressful due to a high demand for decisions on the many different referrals to the specialty. We present brief guidance on how to avoid major pitfalls and get the most benefit from your time in this specialty as a GP trainee.

THE BASICS

Orthopaedics, like many medical specialties, suffers from jargon. Here is a beginner's guide to some of the common terms used:

TABLE 28.1: GLOSSARY OF TERMS

DHS	Dynamic hip screw.
IM nail	Intra-medullary nail.
K-wire	Kirschner wire. A pointed wire that can be passed through the skin to hold a fracture in position.
Mal-union	Bones have healed in an incorrect position.

MUA	Manipulation under anaesthetic. The patient is anaesthetised and then the fracture is reduced, usually under X-ray guidance. This may avert the need for more invasive surgery.
Non-union	Bones have not healed.
NOF	Neck of femur.
ORIF	Open reduction and internal fixation. This is an operation to fix a fracture, where a cut is made in the skin, the bone ends reduced directly (OR) and then held in place using a device such as a plate and screws (IF).
POP	Plaster of Paris.
SUFE	Slipped upper femoral epiphysis.

1. Ensure that each injury you see has been appropriately visualised on X-rays:

    ›   two views are essential, usually antero-posterior (AP) and lateral

    ›   patients in plaster should have views in plaster regardless of whether there has been further manipulation

    ›   to assess if a shoulder is in joint then a third view should be used. If the patient cannot abduct his or her arm for an axial view (as with a proximal humeral fracture) then this should be a modified axial or Velpeau view

    ›   a painful hip in a child should be imaged with both an AP and frog lateral view

    ›   the cervical spine should be visualised with AP and lateral as well as open-mouth peg views.

2. Go to clinic. The Elective Clinic and, to a lesser extent, the Fracture Clinic will be the destination for the many patients you refer over your career. Spending some time in each clinic will give you a valuable understanding of assessment of these problems.

3. For injuries to hands and wrists always document the dominant hand and employment/activities that involve the hands.

4. Learn how to document neurovascular status. Most trainees' knowledge of the course of peripheral nerves is hazy and should be brushed up. Where you are unsure, ask your senior which nerves to test and how to document your findings. All peripheral injuries should have distal sensory and motor function as well as circulatory function (capillary refill time and specific pulses) documented. This is essential both for deciding management and from a medico-legal perspective.

5. Be familiar with assessing patients for compartment syndrome. Do not confuse these with features of an ischaemic limb, as these symptoms mostly occur far too late (such as paralysis and pulselessness). Appropriate early features to look for are: pain out of proportion to the injury despite analgesia; pain on passive movement of toes (or fingers in the upper limb); and paraesthesiae. If you are left in any doubt after assessing the patient then ask a senior urgently to assess the patient.

THE PATIENTS

6. Your patients will often be in pain, so make sure you address this early. Many will be scared and traumatised by their injuries, so be sensitive to this and remain patient with your patients.

7. You will see a lot of paediatric patients. See Chapter 21 for tips on working with this group (and, just as importantly, their parents).

8. For many of your patients, especially the elderly, rehabilitation goes much further than the surgery alone. View them as the individuals they are and take an active role in this. Remember that a fractured neck of femur (NOF) may be commonplace to you but is a life-changing event to the patient.

FRACTURES: DESCRIPTION AND MANAGEMENT

9. The most common presentation to the majority of trauma departments is a fractured NOF in older people. These patients are potentially the most unwell and frail group in the hospital and you must take care to ensure they are seen early, fully investigated, and have sufficient intravenous (IV) fluids and analgesia. Patients who have this injury under the age of 65 years should be quickly referred to a senior as they may require urgent fixation.

10. Remind yourself how to describe fractures before starting. Try using the following order:

    ›   open/closed fracture (avoid compound)

    ›   the location of the fracture in the bone (for example, midshaft/proximal/distal)

    ›   which bone and what side

    ›   describe the appearance of the fracture (transverse/oblique/spiral/multifrag-mentory)

    ›   describe displacement in terms of angulation (the angle the **distal** fragment makes with the proximal), translation (the percentage that the bones have slipped off one another [0–100% and off ended]), shortening and rotation.

11. All obvious fractures should be splinted and the patient given adequate analgesia before any X-rays are taken. Your patients will thank you for this. These simple interventions are too often forgotten in the haste to get an X-ray.

12. Open fractures should be washed out and debrided in theatre at the earliest possible stage. When faced with an open fracture make sure you follow the essential steps as set out in Box 28.1.

BOX 28.1: ESSENTIAL STEPS WHEN DEALING WITH OPEN FRACTURES

- Assess the patient using an ABC approach, document and treat any other injuries.

- Take a photo of the fracture.

- Ensure the patient has adequate tetanus cover.

- Give intravenous antibiotics according to local protocol.

- Document the distal neurovascular status of the limb.

- Apply saline-soaked dressing and splint the limb.

- Take a series of X-rays and ring your senior once these are well underway. (He or she will prefer it if there is an X-ray to look at.)

13. If you are concerned that a plaster cast is too tight then split it using a plaster saw or plaster scissors. Ensure that you have also cut all layers of cotton wool as these often hold unexpected amounts of tension.

14. Patients with femoral shaft fractures or subtrochanteric fractures will be considerably more comfortable once they are placed in skin traction. 'Five lbs please' is usually the correct answer to the question of 'How much?' Tables are readily available to calculate appropriate values in children.

ON-CALL

15. As an orthopaedic junior, regardless of your interest, when on-call you invariably cannot make the final decision as to the best course of action. This is perfectly normal. Good documentation and asking for help are the way forward.

16. Keep a clear list of the patients you have been referred during your on-call, not just the ones you have accepted. When you need to ask someone about a referral, take full details of the patient and the referrer so you can get back in contact when necessary.

17. Many things will be referred to you erroneously. Open skull fractures, fractured jaws and fractured penises are neither trauma nor orthopaedics. Do not accept them!

18. *Cauda equina* syndrome is an emergency that must not be missed. There should be evidence of saddle anaesthesia, reduced anal tone, and altered bladder or bowel function. If you detect abnormal findings during your examination then discuss the case with your registrar and consider imaging. Give these patients high priority and go to see them early. You may prevent lifelong urinary or faecal incontinence in a young person. Discuss any concerns you have with your senior.

19. Children with painful joints need careful assessment. You will speed their assessment by asking if the child could have topical local anaesthetic applied as early as possible and blood taken to help exclude septic arthritis. Be aware that pain in the knee may be coming from the hip and examine both carefully.

20. Ensure that all patients admitted have their regular medications properly prescribed before leaving the emergency department, and leave clear instructions in the notes about what is to be given. Most patients admitted under you will have been made 'nil by mouth' from the moment the ambulance arrives. This may be unnecessary if they are not listed for imminent theatre and patients should not be prevented from having their medication. Common groups particularly at risk are patients on anti-epileptic drugs, Parkinson's drugs, anti-anginals, diuretics or insulin.

21. Learn how to aspirate knees, ankles, shoulders, wrists and elbows. This will be useful for diagnosis in patients with possible septic arthritis, and will also be good practice for joint injections in the surgery for many years to come.

22. Do not aspirate prosthetic joints in the Emergency Department and do not start these patients on antibiotics without discussion with the on-call team. If the joint is infected then antibiotic therapy should be planned in discussion with the microbiologists and after aspiration, with or without tissue samples taken in theatre.

23. Patients who require IV antibiotics for any extended duration should have long-term access such as a peripherally inserted central catheter line arranged at the earliest possible juncture. This will prevent both painful and increasingly difficult attempts at IV access for your patient and will also save you large amounts of time.

24. On-call and at night you may be required to cover other surgical specialties. Clarify your responsibilities in advance of your first on-call shift.

POTENTIAL PDP POINTERS

› Make your time in trauma and orthopaedics work for you and your training. The understanding of how to fix each fracture is only really useful within hospital orthopaedics and you may never need it again. The understanding and assessment of joint problems, back pain and soft-tissue injuries, as well as practical procedures such as joint aspiration, may be invaluable in your career and will be useful on a daily basis. Take in as much as you can!

› Become proficient at the musculoskeletal clinical examinations and use them to inform appropriate diagnosis of musculoskeletal problems.

› Learn the acute management of common orthopaedic presentations, including open fractures, fracture dislocations and fractured NOF.

› Attend the Outpatient Clinic to gain knowledge of the management of common primary care referrals.

› Learn to inject and aspirate joints, initially under supervision.

29

UROLOGY

Thomas Renninson and Laura Smith

Urology is a relatively small specialty with a large number of patients, and a very useful placement for GP trainees. It is full of bite-sized procedures and manageable protocols so you can become relatively independent at dealing with referrals, giving advice, treating people and diverting referrals to outpatient services as appropriate.

You will be asked to see countless patients who others have been unable to catheterise. With a few tricks of the trade you will consistently be able to help these patients and they will be amazingly grateful for it.

Most of these tips would as useful in the primary care setting as they are to anyone doing a job in urology.

THE BASICS

1. Urological complaints are common. Prostate cancer accounts for almost 25% of all male cancers and approximately two-thirds of men and women report having lower urinary tract symptoms (LUTS).

2. There are very few actual urological emergencies and they are uncommon; testicular torsion, priapism, an infected obstructed kidney and severe renal trauma are the only things that will legitimately wake a consultant overnight.

3. To minimise time spent doing intimate examinations set up beforehand, expose the patient at the last moment and do the examination properly once. The last thing any patient wants is to have to be re-examined for the sake of a rushed job.

4. Urological procedures are generally uncomfortable. Be honest with the patient about this. A good warning about the level of discomfort doesn't normally put patients off and may conversely lead to praise when it isn't as bad as they expected.

5. Instillagel doesn't 'numb' anything – it only takes the edge off at most. Leave it for a good minute to work. This is longer than you think!

THE PATIENTS

6. Always offer a chaperone. Don't get complacent, even for examinations on patients of your own gender.

7. Patients coming into urology for the first time will be very nervous. A lot of what we do is very embarrassing and uncomfortable. Don't mistake bravado, which is common, for a lack of nerves.

8. Patients generally like confidence. If you know what you are doing and go about a task as if you do it every day you will inspire confidence and normalise very foreign situations for the patient.

9. Cancer is always in the patient's mind even if it is not in yours. Appropriate reassurance on this point is something that causes great relief.

CATHETERS

10. You are not a catheter service!

11. If someone has previously failed to catheterise a patient, go prepared with a bigger catheter.

12. For difficult or three-way catheters use two Instillagels.

13. Inflate the balloons with sterile water, not saline. Saline crystallises within the balloon, and then it can't be deflated.

14. Three-way catheters can have 30–40 ml in the balloon. Make sure it is all aspirated before removing it.

15. If the catheter balloon doesn't deflate, cut the end of the port off.

16. Large prostates do not shrink the lumen of the urethra; they kink its path, thereby changing the angle of the urethra leaving the prostate. Coudé tip catheters have a curved end that helps the passage through the kinked prostatic urethra. The same is true for introducers, but they are only for the registrars or consultants.

17. With prostatic obstruction, you will feel the catheter coiling in the bulbar urethra. Try:

    a) Two Instillagels

    b) Using a larger catheter, preferably long term as they are stiffer

    c) Straighten the penis vertically

    d) Insert till resistance is hit, before dropping the angle of the penis towards the bed

    e) Push further, and hopefully you'll be successful

    f) If you are not convinced, insert to the hilt, and wait (up to 30 seconds!). The catheter sometimes seems to find its own way in!

    g) A Coudé tip catheter is the next step

    h) If you have still failed, stop and seek help. You may be damaging the urethra.

18. If you have the opportunity, get involved with some flexible cystoscopies. This will give you a much better understanding of urethral anatomy, and hence helps with your catheterisation skills.

19. In an uncircumcised man always replace the foreskin.

20. Penile tip pain in catheterised patients is due to bladder spasm onto the catheter balloon and usually responds to oxybutynin.

21. If you can't find a female urethra, it's probably on the anterior vaginal wall.

22. Obstruction from a urethral stricture feels like hitting a brick wall after going in only a short distance. Try using the smallest catheter but stop if you are still not succeeding. They may require urethral dilation, or a suprapubic catheter.

23. Suprapubic catheters are just normal catheters in a different anatomical location. They should be inserted (as an unplanned procedure) when:

    a) You have failed with a urethral catheter

    b) There is a palpable bladder, i.e. the patient is in retention

    c) There are no concerns about bladder cancer. In these cases there is a risk of the tumour spreading down the catheter track, so always ask a senior.

24. Be very wary of putting a suprapubic catheter in someone with previous abdominal surgery due to the risk of hitting the bowel. If you are not confident in placing a suprapubic catheter, aspirating the bladder is a safe way to buy some time.

25. When changing a suprapubic catheter, clamp the existing one for 30 minutes. It's always reassuring to get urine out of the new catheter.

URINARY RETENTION

26. Urinary retention doesn't necessarily require hospital admission.

27. Retention with a residual volume of >600 ml usually warrants observing for 6–12 hours for diuresis, which may require fluid replacement and renal function tests for high-pressure chronic retention.

28. Retention with a residual volume of <600 ml can be discharged once catheterised, for a trial without catheter (TWOC) in the community when the cause has been treated.

29. There is no point measuring a prostate-specific antigen (PSA) in the acute phase because it will be falsely high. In patients for whom you have a clinical suspicion of prostate cancer, arrange for it to be taken while awaiting outpatient appointments.

30. Nocturnal enuresis is a cardinal sign of high-pressure retention. The catheter should always be left on free drainage. Never TWOC the patient before he or she has had definitive treatment for the cause of the retention.

NEPHROSTOMIES AND STENTS

31. Bilateral hydronephrosis and renal failure unresponsive to catheterisation are caused by ureteric obstruction and will require a nephrostomy/ies.

32. An infected obstructed kidney is an emergency, and requires a nephrostomy or retrograde stent a.s.a.p.

33. Retrograde stents are near impossible in hydronephrotic prostate cancer patients; request antegrade stents.

UROLOGICAL CANCER

34. Ninety per cent of bladder masses are cancer. Intravesical BCG prevents recurrence, while intravesical mitomycin prevents recurrence, and an increase in grade.

35. Finasteride decreases the size and vascularity of the prostate, hence reducing intra- and post-operative bleeding at transurethral resection of the prostate (TURP). However, if you suspect prostate cancer or are actively monitoring beware because it interferes with PSA results.

36. PSA can be low in prostate cancer. This is generally bad, since the tumours tend to be a higher grade.

37. Palliative radiotherapy is very good at treating haematuria secondary to prostate cancer.

38. Prostate cancer has a high affinity for bone. If suspicious, think about a bone scan. In prostate cancer and back pain, worry about metastasis and always consider cord compression.

39. To treat prolonged bleeding post-TURP, inflate the three-way catheter balloon so it contains 40 ml of water, and hang over the end of the bed with a small amount of tension for a couple of hours. This helps tamponade the 'raw' area.

HAEMATURIA

40. People rarely haemorrhage significantly from haematuria; it also rarely needs treatment to stop the bleeding.

41. Haematuria is a symptom, not a diagnosis. The underlying cause may be most appropriately treated in another specialty, e.g. an excessively elevated international normalised ratio (INR) in a warfarinised patient.

42. Three-way catheters are for haematuria or, explicitly, clot retention.

43. Catheter irrigation doesn't clear clots; it just stops new ones forming.

44. Bladder washouts break up clots. They are not gentle. You have to aspirate back hard to suck out the clots.

45. Microscopic haematuria after renal trauma doesn't require investigation; however, macroscopic does.

RENAL STONES

46. If <6 mm or in the lower third of the ureter renal stones will likely pass spontaneously.

47. Not all renal stones are associated with haematuria.

48. Tamsulosin causes ureteric smooth-muscle relaxation, which eases pain, and sometimes helps the passage of a stone. Note, this is off-label use, so check your local protocol.

49. You only need to admit renal colic if:

    a) Pain is uncontrollable

    b) There are signs of infection

    c) Renal function is deranged

    d) You are concerned about severe hydronephrosis.

50. Unless you already have radiolucent stones diagnosed, a CT KUB is the imaging of choice, not a plain KUB X-ray.

TESTICULAR TORSION

51. Torsion in someone over 30 is very rare. The diagnosis is more likely to be epididymitis/epididymo-orchitis, so get a urine dip and a sexual history.

52. There is only a six-hour window to save the testicle.

53. A normal ultrasound doesn't rule out torsion, but can falsely reassure you.

54. A torted hydatid doesn't need surgery, although it can mimic a torted testicle. When in doubt, explore the scrotum.

POTENTIAL PDP POINTERS

› Learn to manage the treatment and investigation of urinary retention.

› Learn to catheterise patients confidently and competently, and deal with the common problems associated with failed catheterisation.

› Become familiar in the investigation and subsequent management of haematuria.

› Become comfortable with the diagnosis and management of prostate and bladder cancer.

30

VASCULAR SURGERY

Laura Smith, Ross Cruickshank, David Beattie and Matt Burkes

Vascular surgery as a specialty involves the investigation and surgical management of patients suffering disease of their arterial, venous or lymphatic circulations. While the presentation of a patient with a ruptured abdominal aortic aneurysm (AAA) or acutely ischaemic limb is certainly frightening and stressful, your first actions are always the same – get senior help now! On the other hand elective vascular patients tend to be elderly with multiple co-morbidities and the management of their chronic illness is fraught with difficulties. Experience in vascular surgery can be useful not only in terms of learning to manage emergency presentations and acutely unwell patients, but also to practise the skills of risk–benefit analysis, effective communication and the multifactorial issues that arise in the management of any chronic disease process.

The following tips hopefully will offer some useful advice, whether you happen to find yourself caught up in the A&E Department or scratching your head in clinic:

THE BASICS

1. Vascular patients have multiple co-morbidities. Do not forget this.

2. Risk factors for vascular disease, and the disease processes, are the same as for coronary artery disease; the arteries are just in a different location.

3. Address the risk factors – advise smoking cessation, control blood pressure to 140/90, start Simvastatin 40 mg/day even if cholesterol levels are normal unless contraindicated. Patients should also be commenced on clopidogrel

or aspirin unless contraindicated. A caveat is that new guidance from the National Institute for Health and Care Excellence (NICE) is expected shortly, so this may change.

THE PATIENTS

4. AAA may be common in a vascular clinic, but it is still a scary diagnosis for the patient. This is particularly true when your management plan is 'surveillance'. Pre-empt their concerns and thoroughly explain the risk–benefit balance to allay their fears.

5. It is easy to become embroiled with the pathology and degree of stenosis as a cut-off for treatment. Try to avoid this and focus on patient symptoms and the impact they have on their lifestyle. The patients' concerns need to be heard.

6. Vascular patients are all 'high risk'. As debilitated as they are by their disease, any intervention comes with the risk of loss of life or limb. Sometimes, conservative management is the best course of action.

7. Patients with ulcers/ischaemia who need debridement and possible amputation can find this hard to accept, particularly if they are diabetic and don't have any pain. Painting a bleak picture, with the utmost honesty, is sometimes the only way to convey the importance of treatment.

CHRONIC PERIPHERAL ARTERIAL DISEASE

8. Revise the vascular examination and ankle-brachial pressure index (ABPI) procedure and interpretation.

9. Be sure to document colour and appearance of skin (pale, shiny, hairless in peripheral arterial disease [PAD]) and presence of any ulcers or necrosis, warmth, capillary refill time and pulses. If you cannot palpate a pulse always listen for it with a Doppler. Examine pulses from proximal to distal and compare the sides.

10. Key details in the history of chronic limb ischaemia consist of claudication distance, distribution of pain and presence of rest pain or tissue loss/ulceration.

11. Remember that claudication can also be neurogenic in origin, for example from spinal canal stenosis as a result of prolapsed disc or osteophyte formation. Generally this pain will be slower to resolve on resting and is especially relieved by sitting (which makes the spinal canal broader, thus relieving pressure).

12. The interventional treatment of limb ischaemia can be thought of in straightforward terms of first finding the level of the blockage (duplex or angiography), then either unblocking it (angioplasty, endarterectomy or thrombolysis), bypassing it *or* (as a last resort) removing the ischaemic tissue, i.e. amputation.

13. Beware diabetic patients. They can suffer microvascular disease such that, despite normal large vessels, they may progress through to end-stage PAD with resulting tissue loss and ulceration. Clinical examination can be misleading with elevated ABPIs and palpable pulses despite critical lesions.

14. Don't give compression stockings to patients with PAD!

15. Chronic limb ischaemia is not an emergency. It needs a potentially urgent clinic referral, not an on-call assessment.

ACUTE ARTERIAL DISEASE

16. Remember that the 6 Ps (pain, pallor, pulseless, paraesthesia, paralysis and punishingly cold) equate to acute limb ischaemia. This is an emergency and senior help should be *immediately* sought; you have only 4–6 hours to save the limb so don't wait for them to finish clinic or their theatre list.

17. If acute ischaemia could be due to embolism, heparinise. Once the problem is resolved, find the embolic source. This is often the heart so obtain an echocardiogram, but do not forget about AAA.

18. If you suspect a transient ischaemic attack [TIA] then patients should be promptly referred to TIA clinic, having been scored using the ABCD2 system.

ANEURYSMS AND DISSECTIONS

19. Examine leg pulses in known AAAs – other distal aneurysms (popliteal) or PAD can coexist.

20. Always consider a ruptured AAA in any patient with sudden-onset abdominal pain. This is especially the case in any patient over the age of 50 with first-presentation 'renal colic'.

21. A patient with a ruptured AAA should not be resuscitated to a BP of greater than 90 mmHg systolic as this will only exacerbate bleeding and prevent tamponade.

22. A major post-operative risk after AAA is abdominal compartment syndrome. A quick bedside test for this is to raise the patient's catheter above the level of the bed. If it doesn't drain back down into the bladder this may indicate raised pressures.

23. A dissecting aorta can present in many different ways from a pain in the chest (ascending aorta), jaw (aortic arch) and the interscapular area (descending aorta), down to the abdomen and even the groin. A dissection that involves the aortic root may also cause ECG changes, so beware the patient who is suffering an 'MI' who just happens to have an ischaemic limb!

VENOUS DISEASE

24. Varicose veins can only be operated on if the deep veins are competent – a history of deep-vein thrombosis (DVT) or lower-limb/pelvic fractures *may* contraindicate surgery.

25. Skin changes in venous insufficiency follow the sequence of – varicose veins, bleeding/phlebitis, haemosiderin deposition, lipodermatosclerosis and finally venous ulcers.

26. Patients should always be warned that any varicose vein operation may result in a poor aesthetic result. If this is your patient's main reason for wanting surgery then his or her expectations should be managed accordingly.

OTHER CONDITIONS

27. Remember to consider acute mesenteric ischaemia in patients who are suffering severe abdominal pain with a relatively normal abdominal exam and very high white cell counts. Chronic mesenteric ischaemia often presents vaguely with weight loss and post-prandial abdominal pain.

28. Treatment of lymphoedema should focus on advising patients to keep their legs elevated, pay attention to skin hygiene (common complication of bacterial/fungal skin infections), lose weight and strictly comply with wearing compression garments. Diuretics have no place in the management of lymphoedema!

POTENTIAL PDP POINTERS

› Become familiar and proficient with the common vascular clinical examinations – including examination of pulses and aneurysms, and use of the hand-held Doppler probe.

› Attend outpatient clinics to familiarise yourself with the diagnosis and management of patients with chronic vascular conditions, their attendant co-morbidities and the decision-making processes involved.

›   In the consideration of primary and secondary prevention become familiar with the risk factors for the development of peripheral arterial disease and the steps that can be taken to negate these.

›   Become familiar with the different surgical and non-surgical interventions carried out in the treatment of varicose veins and the associated advantages and disadvantages of both.

›   Learn principles and approaches to wound and ulcer care.

PART II

TIPS FOR TRAINEES WORKING IN THE GP SETTING

31

YOUR FIRST GP ROTATION

Matt Burkes

Starting your first GP job as a GP specialist trainee is a momentous occasion. You may have done general practice as a Foundation Year 2 doctor (FY2) or this could be your first taste of being a primary care provider since medical school. Regardless, there will be a certain amount of anxiety attached to the job. This is now your chosen career path and you will have many questions:

› Will you like it?
› Will you be any good?
› Will they like you?
› Will you like them?

These feelings are compounded if you intend to work in the locality after you finish training. If this is the case then it's especially important that you make a good impression. GPs are a close-knit bunch and do chat about trainees.

So, no pressure there then.

As well as this, there is the *mélange* that is the typical GP surgery. Packed to the brim with stuff that you never covered in medical school and never saw in hospital. Then there's all the stuff that you DID see in hospital but palmed off by sagely advising the patient to 'go see your GP about that'. Well, it's your bag now. Much like life, there's no substitute for experience. Get stuck in and be prepared to learn a lot, quickly. If you were hoping that general practice was going to be an easy ride, then I truly hope you find it that way. I must confess that I never did (and still don't).

The following list of basic survival tips is largely derived from mistakes that I made in FY2 and Specialist Trainee Year 1 (ST1) GP rotations and the wise words from those with more experience than I, whom I pestered. I hope you find them as useful as I did.

THE BASICS

Find out where the practice is and how to get to it in advance of your start day.

Call the practice manager to touch base well in advance and see what paperwork he or she is expecting you to bring, e.g. you will need a completed Form R7 to make sure that you get paid and that you are on a Primary Care Organisation Performers List.

If you know someone who has worked at the practice before, have a cuppa with him or her and get some pointers.

Don't be late.

If you are going to be off sick, let the practice know EARLY. Most practices don't cancel appointments but carry the extra load between those doctors who are there. It is better to know you are not coming before the phone lines open so they can block your available slots.

Unlike in FY2, the practice is not obliged to provide you with any equipment. See Chapter 34 to find out what you will need.

The *Oxford Handbook of General Practice* (or equivalent) is worth owning. Not to mention this book, I humbly suggest.

HOME VISITS

This is likely to be the part of general practice that will make you the most uncomfortable. There's no help at hand. There's no oxygen. There's not even an examination couch. However, the medicine is the same, regardless of the venue.

Try to do some home visits with other doctors; watching their style and approach will be very useful and you will rarely get an opportunity to do this ever again. They will probably appreciate the company too!

Anyone who feels he or she is poorly enough for a home visit should have vital signs recorded.

Appreciate the opportunity to see how the patient is functioning, or not, in his or her own home environment rather than your practice room.

Get to know the local residential/nursing/care homes. It will come in handy.

Never accept tea on a home visit. It will be awful and you'll be there all day.

THE PRACTICE

All practices are different, so make the most of your time learning what they do well and what they do less well – this will be invaluable when you are running your own practice in the future.

Familiarise yourself with the IT systems. Try to ensure that your orientation has a session early on to cover this.

Be careful about offering medical advice to receptionists etc. If you're not careful you will end up running a clinic with no notes and questionable legal cover (and the partners won't like it).

Know how to get help urgently.

Know how to provide help to other staff urgently.

Take in cake on your first and last day.

Find out the practice telephone number that bypasses the recorded stuff and gets you through to a receptionist straight away.

Get your supervisor's mobile number.

If the practice manager is up for tutorials on the business side of general practice, go for it!

PAEDIATRICS

Always do a full examination of infants and record their vital signs (including capillary refill time and respiratory rate) regardless of what they are presenting with.

If your practice has a paediatric sats probe, know where it is and how to use it.

Revise bronchiolitis.

If you are uncertain or worried about either diagnosis or what to do next – SEEK HELP.

Revise Gillick competencies and Fraser guidelines.

Find out how to get in touch with the local school nurse. Also, many towns have an 'info shop' that is a great port of call for young adults who are upset/agitated/distressed/normal.

Buy a thermometer that measures temperature in the ear or spend time wrestling with paediatric patients. It's your choice.

Don't ignore child protection issues but do get help, advice and support and attend a course.

OBSTETRICS AND GYNAECOLOGY

There's a lot of gynaecology in primary care. If you are female, some days it can feel like you are running a gynaecology clinic. You will need to be up to speed with both the examination and management of common conditions.

Make sure you know how and where to refer for a termination of pregnancy, as learning on the job isn't ideal.

When a patient tells you she is pregnant don't say congratulations till you know she is happy about it.

The Royal College of Obstetricians and Gynaecologists' (RCOG) latest advice about antibiotics is that oral contraceptive pill (OCP) users only need to take extra precautions if taking enzyme-inducing antibiotics like rifampicin or rifabutin.[1] If you find you are prescribing a lot of rifampicin, have a word with one of the partners! The guidelines do caution that any antibiotic (or illness) that causes vomiting or diarrhoea could decrease the efficacy of oral contraception and additional precautions should be used.

Find out how to obtain a smear-taking number and get qualified after gaining supervised competency in this essential skill.

REFERRALS

The process of acute referral to secondary care varies across the country, so find out your local protocol before you need to use it. It is often possible to speak to a medical consultant or registrar to obtain advice about patients, which might avoid an admission. Many hospitals have a GP-oriented website that lists local referral criteria. The Primary Care Organisation or Health Board that you work in will be available on your intranet together with templates for different referrals.

Make any non-acute referrals promptly; don't save them up till the end of the week and do them all then. Ideally dictate as you go along if you can. Try at least to do them on the same day. This is obviously especially true of urgent and two-week rule referrals.

On the subject of two-week rule referrals, most hospital departments expect you to have discussed the potential diagnosis with the patient – seek guidance on this.

If your practice is using Choose & Book, find out how they implement it.

When referring acutely to a junior hospital doctor, remember what it was like to be on the receiving end and try to be sympathetic.

TRAINING

Hit the ePortfolio hard in GP placements. You are seeing a lot and are sat at a computer. It's much harder in hospital jobs.

Remember to organise your leave in advance to fit in with the surgery rota. Book holiday early. Book holiday for your next job now.

Schedule your consultation observation tool (COT) and case-based discussion (CbD) assessments in advance to ensure you get them done. This rotation is actually quite an easy one to get Workplace-Based Assessments (WPBAs) completed, unlike some hospital jobs, so make the most of it.

'GP STUFF'

Offer a chaperone if indicated!

Ask all doctors at your practice to let you know whenever they have any dermatology cases. Make sure you know how to spot common skin problems and important diagnoses, e.g. a malignant melanoma.

If a patient makes you feel scared, threatened or bad about yourself then talk to someone else about him or her.

Most practices have an attached community psychiatric nurse (CPN). Get to know him or her.

If the practice nurse asks you to review one of his or her patients, then review the patient.

When your Friday afternoon list is over-running and is challenging, remind yourself that you are not working Saturday.

Sometimes you will have to say 'no'. Learn to do this with grace but unequivocally. If you are dealing with an acutely unwell patient, you cannot 'have a quick look at this ingrowing toenail'.

If your patient does becomes acutely unwell during the consultation, ask for assistance promptly.

Never skip lunch. Your afternoon patients will suffer and so will you.

Find out how to get an urgent ECG done at your practice. Also make sure that YOU know how to perform one with the practice's equipment. You never know when this skill will be required.

When someone says, 'I've got a list', it's best to flush it all out first and negotiate what will and won't be covered in the consultation. Don't be surprised to find that your priorities are different from your patients' priorities. You may discover central crushing chest pain is the last item on the list, below a fungal toenail. When an older gentleman presents with mechanical back pain, make sure he has had recent bloods including PSA.

Learn the prescribing criteria for sildenafil. Men often seek out the new registrar.

Beware the patient you don't like. This patient sometimes really does have something wrong with him or her!

Have a laugh. It's a long day without one.

REFERENCES

1. Faculty of Sexual and Reproductive Healthcare. Clinical Effectiveness Unit. *Drug Interactions with Hormonal Contraception*. London: RCOG, 2011, www.fsrh.org/pdfs/CEUGuidanceDrugInteractionsHormonal.pdf [accessed March 2014].

SHORT AND SWEET

I was in the middle of a busy morning surgery. My next appointment was a 'telephone consultation'. A patient had booked a slot and asked me to ring back.

The patient was someone I had seen in surgery only once before, for a minor illness almost a year earlier.

After the initial niceties and introductions she explained that in 20 years of bee-keeping her bees had produced the best honeycomb ever this season and asked me if I would like some. I was a bit taken aback, but remembered that she had given me some honeycomb the previous year, after that first consultation. It was delicious. Of course I protested … said she shouldn't really … all those things, but she was quite insistent. So I agreed. She arranged to leave some at reception for me the following week.

After that was arranged, I enquired, 'Well Mrs X, how can I help you today anyway?'

She sounded rather surprised and replied, 'Well … nothing … no … that was it.'

If only all consultations were so short and sweet.

Red Roses collection curated by Alec Logan and illustrated by Helen Wilson.

32

INTRODUCTION TO THE REGISTRAR YEAR

Matt Burkes

Congratulations! You survived your hospital placements! Although you are required to fulfil some out-of-hours (OOH) experience during your registrar year, it is unlikely to be as onerous as the on-call rota you have left behind. You are now free to wallow in all the experiences and delights that full-time general practice has to offer. Ah the bliss!

At the risk of shattering this golden moment, there are a few things that you need to be aware of: exams, assessments, expenses and the like. These will be covered in more detail in the following chapters.

As well as these specifics there are a few more general points that are covered here to allow you to better hit the ground running.

Remember to enjoy yourself!

THE PRACTICE

Make a point of being friendly to the practice staff. You are going to be there for a year, rather than the usual four months that you are used to. You will need them; they will need you.

You will inevitably have to go through a period where you have to 'prove your value' to at least one member of staff. I have always found being positive and getting stuck in makes this transition period shorter and easier.

If you find you have finished early (this can happen, especially with your early long slots) offer to help the duty doc. General practice is a team game, so learning how to play early will pay dividends down the line.

Offer to help sign the huge piles of repeat scripts that accumulate daily.

Hopefully the practice will offer you an induction period where you will get to see how the practice works and who does what. If you are hopeless with names, make notes.

If the practice doesn't have an induction pack that contains all the useful local numbers and referral forms, then offer to create one. It will be good for you and good for them.

You will often be asked to see extras or review patients by the practice staff and nursing team. Registrars are often singled out as they tend to be seen as an easier target. Always try to help out, but if this is becoming problematic then you may need to discuss this with your trainer.

Some practices are friendlier than others. If you are feeling lonely in your room, find the time to have a cup of tea with the staff. If this isn't working, meeting with other registrars local to you can be a great informal lunchtime Balint group.

YOUR TRAINER

You will have met your trainer (educational supervisor) over the course of your hospital jobs for reviews but you will now be under a period of more intense mentorship. Find out what makes him or her tick. Even if your personalities are very different try to build a friendly rapport. It will make the year better for you both.

Work out what you want and need from the year. Discuss this with your trainer. If you want exposure to minor surgery or family planning clinics then tell your trainer. He or she won't know if you don't.

Sit in with your trainer and observe his or her style and consultation skills. If you can, sit in with all the GPs in the practice. You will NEVER have another opportunity to observe another primary care physician in practice again. Treat this as the golden opportunity it is.

Remember – your trainer will write a reference for you. It will be the reference that is most keenly read by potential future employers.

If you are really not getting on with your trainer – seek help. A good start is an informal discussion with your local programme directors.

TIMINGS

You will probably start initially on long appointment slots. Some practices even start on 30 minutes. Enjoy this while you can. You will however need to increase your speed. Don't make this the Holy Grail though; you must get good BEFORE you get quick. You will consult at ten minutes for the rest of your working career so you don't need to rush to it too soon.

If you feel you are being pressurised to cut your timings too soon, then say something. This can be a tricky conversation to have, so feel free to discuss with your programme director to get his or her advice.

When you are on 15-minute appointment slots and aiming to go down to ten minutes, spend a few weeks aiming to complete by ten minutes but with the safety net of the longer appointment blocked.

By the end of the year, but ideally sooner, you will need to be confidently consulting in ten minutes. This is vital to be successful at the Clinical Skills Assessment (CSA).

TRAINING COMMITMENTS

Read well the following chapters on the ePortfolio and assessments. They are not optional and will not go away. Not engaging will upset your trainer.

Be proactive in your group vocational training scheme (VTS) teaching. Get involved. If they are not providing what you need, let them know early. Don't wait till the end of the year.

Appreciate your organised protected teaching and study leave. Book time off for it early and as required. Once you have left your registrar year it will be up to you to organise your own education.

Get stuck into whatever OOH commitment you have early. Leaving it to the last minute will lead you to driving long distances to cover the shifts no one else wanted.

THE FUTURE

Use the year to start building your CV in earnest. You will want to get a job at the end of it.

It is acceptable to ask your trainer if there is likely to be work available there beyond the training year. This will help you plan.

Look around the practice. What do you like? What don't you like? File this information away for the future when you settle in your own place.

33

LESS THAN FULL TIME
A PERSONAL VIEW WITH PRACTICAL ADVICE

Sam Sewell

If you are a doctor in training who has been overtaken by life events, then part-time training (properly, less than full time or LTFT training) may be for you.

The criteria for LTFT training approval are caring for small children (youngest under six years at time of my application but this has now been relaxed) or other family members, personal ill health and being involved in sports training at a high level.

If you are thinking of going LTFT, you need to contact the LTFT team at your deanery early on and apply for LTFT training approval. Do this before you tell your trainer, your royal college, anybody, as approval is the only thing that counts. Approval is not an automatic right but has to be granted and this process can take time. Approval will not last for the whole of your training either and needs to periodically be reapplied for, although subsequent approval should be automatic and the process of re-applying should be less arduous than the first time.

The preferred structure of LTFT is 'slot share'. Supernumerary posts are no longer available. Slot share should in theory be more flexible than a 'job share' but in reality is not. Firms are, unsurprisingly, not that keen to have two trainees for three days a week and none for the remaining two days, i.e. they expect the job to be truly shared. In order to do this, you will need a slot share partner. If you already know someone, then great, but finding him or her is in fact a trust/deanery issue. If one cannot be found, you will be offered the last resort: 'reduced hours in a full-time slot'. In theory, this situation permits the funding for you to share the post with a locum. In reality, when my slot share partner left a post part way through on maternity leave, a locum was only found for the on-call commitment and the team was left a senior house officer (SHO) down for two days a week. The reduced-hours option therefore leaves firms short-staffed and the LTFT trainee feeling guilty and stressed. I am asked daily by juniors and seniors alike whether I will be in tomorrow, as though my work pattern were so profoundly random it could never be understood; my work pattern is Monday, Tuesday, Wednesday.

The final drawback is that on the reduced-hours scheme you have to do on-call pro rata, whereas with a slot share partner you split it 50:50. This point is moot if you are training at 50% but you will feel the difference at 60% and over.

You will need to be super-organised because the Goddess of LTFT is Chaos. By definition, LTFT trainees have Life Issues and slot share partners will come and go. Try not to worry about this as it is the trust/deanery's job to sort out your posts, whether reduced hours or slot share. You won't ever be left jobless, although you may well be left with the last job in the trust (which in my case currently means a different hospital from where I am officially training) and no one will care that you have done that job before and didn't get the rota till the day the job started. In fact, the whole concept of 'choice' in LTFT training posts is set to be phased out and trainees will have to make the most of what they are given, much as Foundation doctors have to do. Inevitably the posts with a significant service commitment are likely to feature heavily and trainees will have to work hard and use study leave to cover the curriculum.

Overall, your posts, assessments, ePortfolio, reviews and general progress will be far more complicated than those of the average trainee and often only you will have sight of all the pieces in the puzzle at any one time. Be prepared to know more about LTFT than the particular deanery sub-manager whom you are emailing at any one time. They rarely reply to trainee queries anyway. Deaneries are huge, unwieldy beasts and the different departments do not seem to communicate efficiently with each other. Get a reliable web connection and email address, as the deanery emails all the time from different departments to repeatedly ask you the same things. Keep copies of everything and keep them to hand. Do not let your British Medical Association (BMA) membership lapse and check what pay scale you are on for every new post. If you are really banging your head against the wall, ask your educational supervisor to intervene; often his or her senior voice is heard a little more readily than yours.

Be prepared for the Little Mermaid aspects of LTFT. Yes, you really do need to complete the same number of log entries as your full-time colleagues in considerably less time. Junior colleagues will leapfrog you because you will be an SHO forever and your self-directed learning time will be expected to come out of your family time. Your hospital colleagues will say, 'See you tomorrow!' every Wednesday and you will have to say, 'No, see you next week!' and they will hate you. Male consultants will say, 'Part time, eh? I've got five children and never went part time' and it will be your job to bite your tongue and not say, 'True but you weren't their mother.' Female consultants who were not offered LTFT training will decline your annual leave request at half-term because 'cover is thin' (answer: call the BMA; parental leave may be unpaid but is always an option).

There is some long-overdue good news, though: as of 2012, LTFT trainees are no longer required to complete the same number of Workplace-Based Assessments (WPBAs) as their full-time colleagues. This issue has been a *bête noire* of LTFT trainees for years but we were previously told it was legal as it pertained to our education. It seems someone has at last looked more deeply into this logic! The requirement is now pro rata. The Multi-Source Feedback (MSF) and Patient Satisfaction Questionnaires (PSQs) in years 1 and 3 also only need to be completed for the mid- and end-point reviews, which decreases the overall number for those at 50%, but possibly not at 60% and over. Still, it is a step in the right direction and many LTFT trainees will be heaving sighs of relief.

Keep your eyes on the prize. You will need to develop strategies to remind yourself why you are putting yourself through such a long haul. I relish every minute of daft tasks like doing the school run.

If this all sounds hard then good, because thinking LTFT is an easy option is a big mistake. Huge. It is, in fact, a great option if you want to continue your training but have commitments outside of work and it is, for a significant minority, the only option. Kent, Surrey and Sussex Deanery runs an annual seminar in November where LTFT trainees can gather, access information and network. You may not find your dream slot share partner but I did (for a year!) and it's a great place to start. Good luck!

34

HOW MUCH DOES IT COST TO BE A GP TRAINEE?

Fiona Robbie

Once you accept your offer to become a GP trainee you also become an Associate-in-Training (AiT) of the Royal College of General Practitioners (RCGP). Having 'done your time' and passed all of the appropriate exams you become a member of the RCGP.

All trainees are encouraged to join the AiT programme. This link provides details why: www.rcgp.org.uk/membership/join-rcgp-trainee-gps.

There is a fee for becoming an AiT but in return you will receive a highly rated and handy journal for AiTs (*InnovAiT*) each month, receive the BJGP, have free access to the ePortfolio and various educational events put on by the RCGP plus a 10% discount at the RCGP online book shop.

For a Specialist Trainee Year 1 (ST1) the costs of being an AiT at the time of writing include an initial subscription fee of £163 and an annual retention fee of £369. This totals £1270 over a three-year training scheme.

The fees mentioned above and some of the professional expenses discussed below may be considered 'allowable expenses' and therefore could be subject to tax relief. Up-to-date information can be sought by contacting the HMRC.

MEDICAL INDEMNITY INSURANCE

This often comes as a bit of a shock after paying around £40 a year as a hospital monkey. The basic fact is, when you are a GP you are responsible for your decision making! Hence protection is imperative and costs! Luckily for us the postgraduate deaneries have taken pity on this and kindly reimburse insurance costs while you are practising as a GP trainee in general practice. Be sure to check if your deanery has made arrangements to pre-purchase your insurance through a particular indemnity company. Some deaneries will guarantee full payment towards one indemnity insurance company but not another. Also bear in mind that you will need to pay for your insurance initially while you wait for reimbursement. This may be done either as a lump sum or on a monthly basis. Last year the average insurance cost was approximately £900 for an ST3.

DOCTOR'S BAG

Some of you may already have the essentials sorted (stethoscope, thermometer, lubricant …), but for those of you who don't here is a comprehensive list of what you need.

› A bag (who'd have thought!).
› Stethoscope.
› Sphygmomanometer.
› Oro/ophthalmoscope.
› Thermometer.
› Pulse oximeter.
› Glucometer.
› Urinalysis sticks.
› Gloves.
› Prescription pad.
› Cuddly toy.

Each practice will vary according to how generous they are with equipment. Some of you will be lucky and have a GP bag lent to you for the year, but this goes practice by practice. You will of course need your own bag by the time you qualify. The majority of practices will give you all of the consumable elements such as tongue depressors, thermometer covers and gloves.

As you guessed this all mounts up. This is your financial responsibility so be savvy, get together with local trainees to see if you can get discounts for bulk buys and trawl the internet.

EXAMS

These are non-debatable and non refundable. Therefore my tip would be start saving from your first pay packet and pass first time!

› Applied Knowledge Test (AKT) – £517.
› Clinical Skills Assessment (CSA) – £1737.

TRAVEL

CAR MAINTENANCE AND MILEAGE

You will be able to claim mileage for certain journeys. For example, if you travel to work and do a home visit you will be able to claim not only the travel to the visit but also your travel to work that day. Day-to-day journeys without home visits or likewise are not covered. It is worth noting that most deaneries will have a maximum distance for travel reimbursement.

If you own a car you may also be entitled to a lump payment called the 'motorised vehicle allowance'. This should help with the necessary costs of your vehicle.

Having a driver's licence is required as part of the RCGP selection criteria. If you do not own a car you may have to pay for other forms of transport, which may not always be covered.

CYCLE TO WORK SCHEME

For those of you feeling green ask your practice if they are involved in the cycle to work scheme.

Take a look at the catchment area of your practice before you commit. A 20-mile round trip for a home visit may impact seriously on your time management and leave you a bit sweaty for your afternoon surgery. The payment system works over a 12-month minimum period so you will have to be organised from day one.

STUDY BUDGET

You will be entitled to a small study leave budget. Your programme directors will be able to advise how much when you start. You cannot request funding for the exams.

Each course/educational event you request reimbursement for will need to be approved by your trainer and the training programme directors. It is therefore worth running this by your trainer before you part with your money and choosing courses that you really feel will be beneficial. Again you will be required to pay upfront, with the money being reimbursed from the available budget sent to you at a later date.

RELOCATION

If you have had to relocate because of your GP training you may be entitled to funding for essential relocation costs, such as removal costs and house purchase costs. There are of course certain criteria that will need to be fulfilled but this is definitely worth a look into if you are moving from Aberdeen to Southampton. Contact your new deanery for more advice.

GENERAL MEDICAL COUNCIL

You will need a full registration with a licence to practise from the General Medical Council (GMC) to take part in your GP training. This is a universal charge for all doctors and currently costs £390 per annum.

CERTIFICATE OF COMPLETION OF TRAINING

After you've passed your exams and are coming towards the end of your ST3/4 year, you now need to apply for your Certificate of Completion of Training from the GMC in order to practise as a GP. This cost £800 in 2009, £500 in 2010 and dropped to £390 in 2011. Let's hope the trend continues!

FORMS THAT YOU SHOULD BE AWARE OF ON YOUR DEANERY WEBSITE

GPSTR payment form. You will need to fill this in a couple of months before your placements starts in order to get paid.

Travel claim form. Every time you do a home visit remember to write down where you went, what you were doing and how many miles you travelled.

Authorised vehicle user application form. This will detail how much you are entitled to for the safe running of your vehicle. This will vary according to the size of your engine!

Relocation eligibility form. This details how to initiate a request for relocation funding.

All fees are correct as of March 2014. Check the RCGP website for the latest figures.

35

THE EPORTFOLIO

Matt Burkes

I'm faced with a difficult task.

I must convince you that the ePortfolio is not a tool designed by the Royal College of General Practitioners (RCGP) to upset and frustrate registrars. I must try to get you to engage with your nemesis and use it to your advantage.

Here goes.

Many registrars find the ePortfolio frustrating. Accept this point and rise above it. You need to master the ePortfolio if you are to become a qualified GP. It's worth it.

Build the ePortfolio into your working day. This involves having a notebook by your side, on your desk during every consultation. And using it. Jot down the details of every interesting case IMMEDIATELY, preferably before the door closes behind the patient, no matter how late you are running. If you wait until the end of the surgery, you will have forgotten the name of the patient. A week later you will have forgotten what day you saw him or her on. A month later you will only be able to dredge the details up by opening and rereading all the consultations you have done over a two-week period. This will take time that you don't have and don't need to spend.

Know the curriculum statements and competencies. Print them out and stick them to your wall. 'Spot' patients during your consultations, match them to the statements and document them. You need to ensure you can demonstrate that you are experiencing a good coverage of the skills needed to be a complete GP. In the future, you will need to do this via another web-based portfolio for revalidation, so there really is no ducking this.

Become familiar with navigating the ePortfolio. It's not always intuitive, but hidden in the nooks and crannies of the website are interesting backwaters. Be aware that the ePortfolio is constantly being redeveloped so things change, hopefully for the better. However, like Hogwarts, when the staircases move it can be hard to find your way. Pooled knowledge with your peer group of fellow registrars will save you time and tears.

Consider word processing your entries first, especially long/cathartic or meaningful ones. Then copy and paste them into the ePortfolio. All websites can crash, and it's gutting to lose a good reflective piece. You have been warned.

Don't ignore the ePortfolio until the night before a review and then spend all night writing 60 poor-quality entries. This will antagonise your trainer (educational supervisor). He or she will have better things to do than read those 60 entries all at once in the hour before your review. Do you really want to go into a review having just annoyed your trainer? I would suggest not.

Many deaneries and localities are so annoyed with the above practice that they are considering not counting any entries written during the week prior to the review.

Think about 'reflective learning'. Most doctors do this several times a day, every day of their working life and even occasionally at weekends. When you talk about a patient with your mate, spouse, trainer or dog you are engaging in reflective learning. You are reflecting on a case and working out what you learnt, what you would do differently (maybe nothing) and how the case made you feel. This is what the ePortfolio is after. The only difference is that they want it in written form. This naturally throws most of us, who are more used to talking than writing. Don't let it. It's *your* ePortfolio; your reflections can be as informal as you are.

Remember: THE EPORTFOLIO IS NOT A COLLECTION OF CASE REPORTS IN A JOURNAL. Most of us start, not unreasonably, at the first box in a learning log entry that asks 'what happened'. We generally get a bit bogged down here and blow all our time and energy creating a wonderfully medically accurate handover of the patient. We then run out of steam with the sections asking about what we learnt, what we would do differently, how we felt, what learning needs we have highlighted and how we will address them. This is EXACTLY THE WRONG APPROACH. Remember this is reflective learning, not just reflection. I've heard it advocated that the form should be filled in from the bottom up so that one's best work is put into recognising the learning that has occurred (or needs to occur). The 'what happened' section should be a couple of lines to set the scene.

It's no wonder that we all fall into this mistake – we have been trained to think this from day one of medical school. In your hospital jobs, imagine starting the post-take ward round saying, 'This patient highlighted the following areas of deficiency in my medical knowledge and here are my plans to put this right.' You wouldn't last long. However, the ePortfolio is NOT a post-take ward round, and you need to change gear.

Good-quality vs. poor-quality reflection is a Big Deal with the RCGP. It produces a short, helpful document to support you entitled 'Hallmarks of good practice in information recording in the ePortfolio', which is available on the RCGP website.[1]

Putting aside a few minutes to read and digest this document will pay dividends. What they are looking for is evidence of critical thinking and analysis, openness and honesty, in evaluating one's performance and feelings and some evidence of learning. Bear this in mind when you're writing. Copying and pasting from GPnotebook will not cut it. Neither will a few lines about a case that show none of the above qualities. Learn to write in the style they are looking for.

The 'industry standard' requirement seems to be two quality reflective entries per week, but this may change and remember this is regarded as a bare minimum. There is presently marked inter-deanery variation in how many entries are required.

Write often. You will improve. The deanery doesn't expect perfection but does expect effort.

The PDP should not be ignored! The deaneries are especially keen on this. Again it shows that you are proactively planning your career development, something we wholeheartedly advocate in this book. You can send entries in the learning log straight to the PDP after saving them. Ensure that you review it occasionally to update what you have learned, add new challenges and make sure you are not missing things. The PDPs from your hospital rotations should all be in there as springboards. Entries should be SMART (specific, measurable, attainable, realistic and time bound). This will be expected by Annual Review of Competency Progression (ARCP) panels and deaneries.

Use the ePortfolio as a repository for good bits of info you find. They can be stored in the Personal Library. Next time you find that excellent patient information leaflet, make sure you store it. It's the same with that presentation that you did at the locality teaching group!

I am not suggesting that you will learn to love the ePortfolio (though you may). However, you must engage with it if you wish to become a member of the RCGP. Not engaging is simply not an option. Make it easy on yourself. The registrar year is busy and stressful enough without your trainer and deanery on your back about a paucity of quality entries.

REFERENCES

1. RCGP Workplace-Based Assessment (WPBA) Standards Group. Hallmarks of good practice in information recording in the ePortfolio. www.rcgp.org.uk/gp-training-and-exams/~/Fmedia/Files/GP-training-and-exams/WPBA/GPST-learning-log-resource-June-10.ashx [accessed March 2014].

36

WORKPLACE-BASED ASSESSMENTS IN THE REGISTRAR YEAR

Matt Burkes

To successfully complete your training you will have to pass each of three separate assessments: the Applied Knowledge Test (AKT), the Clinical Skills Assessment (CSA) and the Workplace-Based Assessment (WPBA). The purpose of the last is to accumulate evidence in the ePortfolio of your competency to practise in the 12 key areas outlined in Box 36.1.

BOX 36.1: THE COMPETENCY FRAMEWORK[1]

1. *Communication and consultation skills*: this competency is about communication with patients, and the use of recognised consultation techniques.

2. *Practising holistically*: the ability of the doctor to operate in physical, psychological, socioeconomic and cultural dimensions, taking into account feelings as well as thoughts.

3. *Data gathering and interpretation*: the gathering and use of data for clinical judgement, the choice of physical examination and investigations, and their interpretation.

4. *Making a diagnosis/making decisions*: this competency is about a conscious, structured approach to decision making.

5. *Clinical management*: the recognition and management of common medical conditions in primary care.

6. *Managing medical complexity and promoting health*: aspects of care beyond managing straightforward problems, including the management of co-morbidity, uncertainty, risk and the approach to health rather than just illness.

7. *Primary care administration and IMT*: the appropriate use of primary care administration systems, effective record keeping and information technology for the benefit of patient care.

8. *Working with colleagues and in teams*: working effectively with other professionals to ensure patient care, including the sharing of information with colleagues.

9. *Community orientation*: the management of the health and social care of the practice population and local community.

10. *Maintaining performance, learning and teaching*: maintaining the performance and effective continuing professional development of oneself and others.

11. *Maintaining an ethical approach to practice*: practising ethically with integrity and a respect for diversity.

12. *Fitness to practise*: the doctor's awareness of when his or her own performance, conduct or health, or that of others, might put patients at risk and the action taken to protect patients.

Whereas the AKT and CSA are short, furious 'exam' tests of your competency, the WPBA offers more of a 'continual assessment' approach. Possibly as a result, it's tempting to be less organised in your approach to them. *Resist this temptation.* It will be annoying (to say the least) to have trained for three (or four) years and have passed the expensive and challenging College exams and then miss out on MRCGP for the want of a team member signing off your Direct Observation of Procedural Skills (DOPS) in applying a simple dressing.

So, best to just do them, then.

This will best be achieved with an organised approach that will see you complete the assessments early. NB the assessments have to be done WELL IN ADVANCE of the end of your training. You really need them finished by May, giving you ten months rather than 12 to do them. Also remember that the Annual Review of Competency Progression (ARCP) panel will wish to see evidence of engagement in advance of the six-month review.

GENERAL POINTS

The good news is that actually most of the assessments are quite easy to get done. In your early meetings with your trainer, highlight the need to get them done promptly. This will be music to their ears and they will enjoy bragging about their wonderful new registrar at trainers' groups. Get your diaries out and write out the dates that you will complete the assessments (typically, but not always) during tutorials. By doing this you will push yourself (and occasionally your trainer) into actually doing the things rather than putting them off.

THE ASSESSMENTS

During your registrar year you will be expected to perform the following assessments:

› case-based discussion (CbD)

› consultation observation tool (COT)

› Multi-Source Feedback (MSF)

› Patient Satisfaction Questionnaire (PSQ)

› DOPS.

MARKING

In COTs and CbDs in primary care each of the 12 areas of competency are assessed and graded as per Box 36.2.

BOX 36.2: MARKING SCHEME FOR WBPA[1]

I – INSUFFICIENT EVIDENCE

From the available evidence, the doctor's performance cannot be placed on a higher point of this developmental scale.

N – NEEDS FURTHER DEVELOPMENT

Rigid adherence to taught rules or plans. Superficial grasp of unconnected facts. Unable to apply knowledge. Little situational perception or discretionary judgement.

C – COMPETENT

Accesses and applies coherent and appropriate chunks of knowledge. Able to see actions as part of longer-term goals. Demonstrates conscious and deliberate planning with increased level of efficiency. Copes with crowdedness and is able to prioritise.

E – EXCELLENT

Intuitive and holistic grasp of situations. No longer relies on rules or maxims. Identifies underlying principles and patterns to define and solve problems. Relates recalled information to the goals of the present situation and is aware of the conditions for application of that knowledge.

Each of the 12 competency areas has a slightly different take on the grades in Box 36.2 and can be viewed in more detail in the ePortfolio. It's tempting to do nothing for a couple of months to 'get in the swing of things'. DO NOT DO THIS. This will cut you down to eight months and will make getting them done that much harder. People often do this because they feel they will not be good enough initially. DON'T

WORRY about this. The point of the WPBA is to show continued development over the year. Put crudely, you're supposed to be a bit iffy to begin with, gradually climbing in your scores over the year to the dizzying heights of excellence towards the end.

CASE-BASED DISCUSSION

The most highbrow of assessments is the CbD. This is your opportunity to grapple with a clinical scenario with your trainer, to unpick the consultation and have a discussion in depth about the issues arising. The College recommends that these should last around 30 minutes. They advise preparing for them by selecting four suitable cases and submitting them to your trainer a week prior to the tutorial. From these, your trainer will select one or two to cover as CbDs – NB the RCGP is happy for two to be covered if time allows. It's not cheating![1] I found these sessions some of the most useful parts of my training. The key to 'doing a good CbD' is picking good cases – something with some 'meat', preferably an ethical dilemma or two, complex issues and some new knowledge. DO NOT PICK EASY CASES WHERE YOU KNEW ALL THE ANSWERS. This will not make for a good CbD! Remember this is about illustrating your thought process and learning. Some good guidance is available from the RCGP.[2]

Some of my CbDs were based around consults that I genuinely wanted to explore with my trainer in almost a therapeutic manner, including those where I felt I had made errors. I found the process helpful and enlightening! So keep your eyes open during your surgeries and scribble down those names so you don't forget.

Remember, you will be unlikely to address all 12 competency areas in each CbD. This is fine. Just make sure that over the year you cover all the bases.

You will be required to carry out 12 CbDs in your registrar year, six prior to the six-monthly review, and six following.

CONSULTATION OBSERVATION TOOL

This is a primary care version of the hospital mini-clinical evaluation exercise (mini-CEX). It is designed to provide your trainer with a quantifiable evidence-based tool to observe and comment on you holistically. The assessment is based on you and your trainer either watching a videotaped consult, or with your trainer directly observing you consult with a patient. Many people find videoing their consults enormously stressful. However, it's a good skill to get under your belt. And it is a skill. You get better and more comfortable with the set-up the more times you do it. Remember in CSA you will have an examiner directly observing you (and indeed you may be in one of the rooms that videotapes the exam for standardisation purposes). Being comfortable consulting with an audience is therefore a skill you need.

Despite the stress, watching a video of one's consultations is an enormously valuable thing to do. Likely you will be much more critical of your performance than any observer. It is an excellent way to work on body language, pace and nuance. These are all things you need to master. As time progresses you may wish to consult with the competencies stuck to your wall and ensure that you are 'showing your workings'. The College provides a useful guide to the marking criteria, which will help.[3] You may find watching the consultations back to be an uncomfortable affair. Good. This is completely normal. I would be more worried if you didn't! I found this a great way to iron out the consultation structure and erase the bad habits – 'I didn't know I did THAT', 'I can't believe I said that', 'I looked SO defensive there', 'That shirt doesn't go with those trousers', etc. are all useful things that best be discovered on video and should be discovered BEFORE sitting the CSA. Again, don't expect to achieve excellence initially. This is about you learning to consult, so don't be afraid to show your less successful tapes, especially if you have learned something from them.

Getting your trainer to directly observe you is also useful, but probably won't provide the same instant and irrefutable visual feedback of the video. One popular approach is to run a joint clinic with your trainer during a tutorial. He or she sees one and you watch; you see one and he or she watches. These are long slots with plenty of time to discuss the cases.

COTs are also popularly performed in out-of-hours (OOH) sessions with the lead doctor. These cases can give exposure to previously uncovered areas of the competencies, so go to OOH sessions prepared to ask and help the lead doc to assist you.

Again, you need to have six done prior to the six-monthly review and six following. The RCGP recommends you have at least one paediatric (under ten years) COT, one featuring a patient over 75 years and one mental health COT.[1] It also recommends they are done one at a time, unlike CbDs (see above).

MULTI-SOURCE FEEDBACK

This is a 360 degree questionnaire[4] that must be performed twice in your registrar year. You should select (at least) five clinicians, mostly GPs for obvious reasons and five non-clinicians. In practice, it's best to ask as many of both as you can because completing the MSF involves completing an online questionnaire and you always lose a few who don't manage to do it. Your peers will rate you on your performance and will also be given free-text spaces to comment directly about you. Your trainer will arrange a time to go through the feedback score and comments with you. Hopefully this will be a session in which you bask in the rosy glow of praise, but if not, or you have trouble getting people to agree to complete your MSF (people are reluctant to put the boot in and would often rather not get involved), then have a good look in the mirror and talk through the specific criticisms with your trainer. If they seem fair then make a plan to address them and get back on track.

PATIENT SATISFACTION QUESTIONNAIRE

The PSQ should be completed once or twice in the registrar year, depending on whether you have completed one in primary care previously to your Specialist Trainee Year 3 (ST3) year.[1] You will need to print out a stack of questionnaires[1] and hand them out to the patients you have seen. Inform your practice manager that you are about to start doing this because he or she needs to input the data into the ePortfolio from the completed questionnaires. You need 40 completed questionnaires so the whole process may take a while. Make it easy for your patients by getting a box of pens to hand out as they leave. Again your trainer will have a tutorial with you to go through the feedback. You can't please all the people all the time but 40 is a reasonable number. If you are consistently scoring poorly, make the required changes to your practising style while you can. This is IMPORTANT – if you upset all your patients in the exam, you will fail. If you upset all your patients as a locum, you will go hungry.

Both MSF and PSQs will form the supporting information required for GP revalidation so this will be good practice for when you enter the GP specialist register.

DIRECT OBSERVATION OF PROCEDURAL SKILLS

You will likely remember these from Foundation years, hospital jobs or, these days, even medical school. Someone considered to be qualified to do so will watch you perform a procedure, offer critique and, if appropriate, sign you off as competent to perform it unsupervised. There are eight mandatory procedures and eleven optional procedures.

They are listed below, though may be subject to change.

MANDATORY

> Application of simple dressing.

> Breast examination.

> Cervical cytology.

> Female genital examination.

> Male genital examination.

> Prostate examination.

> Rectal examination.

> Testing for blood glucose.

OPTIONAL

> Aspiration of effusion.

> Cauterisation.

> Cryotherapy.

> Curettage/shave excision.

> Excision of skin lesions.

> Incision and drainage of abscess.

> Joint and peri-articular injections.

> Hormone replacement implants.

> Proctoscopy.

> Suturing of skin wound.

> Taking skin surface specimens for mycology.

The intimate examinations can most easily be done by the good practice of always having a chaperone. Ensure that your chaperone is qualified to sign you off and knows that you want to be assessed. If you don't let him or her know this the chaperone may not be observing you closely enough to feel able to sign you off. Some DOPS can be combined, e.g. prostate and rectal examination in male patients, so being aware of what you need to cover will help. NB male (and reluctant female) registrars – cervical cytology is NOT optional! Find out about your local smear takers' course and get the skills and accreditation, then ask the practice nurse to let you sit in and do some to get it signed off. This is harder as a male so it's important to make an effort early.

SUMMARY

No one likes assessments but being aware of what you have to do, the rationale behind them and the scoring criteria will hopefully make the process less stressful. Try not to be one of the trainees who is running around trying to get six DOPS signed off, while doing three CbDs and two COTs the week before your review. You just don't need the stress!

REFERENCES

1. MRCGP Workplace-Based Assessment, www.rcgp.org.uk/gp-training-and-exams/mrcgp-work-place-based-assessment-wpba.aspx [accessed March 2014].

2. Case-based discussion, www.rcgp.org.uk/gp-training-and-exams/mrcgp-workplace-based-assessment-wpba/cbd-for-mrcgp-workplace-based-assessment.aspx [accessed March 2014].

3. Consultation observation tool, www.rcgp.org.uk/gp-training-and-exams/mrcgp-workplace-based-assessment-wpba/cot-for-mrcgp-workplace-based-assessment.aspx [accessed March 2014].

4. Multi-Source Feedback, www.rcgp.org.uk/gp-training-and-exams/mrcgp-workplace-based-assessment-wpba/msf-for-workplace-based-assessment.aspx [accessed March 2014].

37

THE APPLIED KNOWLEDGE TEST

Michael Banna and Matt Burkes

The Applied Knowledge Test (AKT) is a slightly unusual exam in many ways. We suppose any exam that is intended to test your knowledge of a subject as vast as general practice is going to be. It's a bit like ePortfolio, broccoli, exercise and all other exams in the sense that nobody actually wants to do it, but it is good for you, and if you want to grow up to be a big strong GP you have no choice. There is no particular secret or trick to passing the exam but here are a few tips that should see you on your way to another big green tick in your ePortfolio.

WHAT'S IT ALL ABOUT?

The AKT is a computer-delivered test of clinical knowledge that is designed to ensure that the passing candidate has the knowledge required for independent practice.[1] It lasts three hours and consists of 200 questions taken from a bank of over 3000. The composition of each exam is designed so that all areas of the curriculum are covered. The exam consists of 160 questions (80%) on clinical medicine, 20 questions (10%) on research and statistics, and 20 questions (10%) on administration, legal matters and ethics.[2] It is offered three times a year and is sat at a nationwide network of venues, so hopefully you will be able to sit it locally, unlike the Clinical Skills Assessment (CSA). The RCGP website has a PowerPoint presentation that goes into more detail about what is and isn't covered in the questions.[2] This is especially useful with regards the stuff you have never been examined on before like prescribing controlled drugs, the GP contract and Driver and Vehicle Licensing Agency (DVLA) guidelines.

THE QUESTIONS

Unlike exams you may have sat before, the AKT is a truly multimedia experience. A mix of single-best answer (SBA) and extended matching questions (EMQ) make up the majority of the exam, although more innovative question styles are increasingly used. These include algorithm questions (in which the correct step in a treatment algorithm must be selected), picture questions, video questions and data interpretation questions (which typically involve interpreting a statistical figure). Another new challenge is the inclusion of free-text answers – these are particularly tricky as there is no list of potential answers to choose from, just a blank box for you to type your answer in, making guessing that much harder.

Each question carries an equal weighting (1 mark) and there is no negative marking. In 2012 the three sittings had pass marks between 68% and 69.5%. In October 2013 76.1% of candidates passed. First-time takers generally fare better than those repeating and have pass rates of 87.4% (ST2) and 83% (ST3).[2]

PRACTICE MAKES PERFECT

For most of us this is the first exam that we will have done in quite some time. If you follow any of the advice in this chapter, it should be to do as much AKT practice as is humanly possible. Websites like passmedicine.com have literally thousands of questions that are very similar to the real thing. They also have great answers to go with the answers that contain a lot of the stuff you need to learn, so don't be tempted (as one author of this chapter often was) to skip to the next question in order to comfort yourself by actually getting one right.

Also available, and free, are 50 sample AKT questions (though no answers) provided by the RCGP that, for obvious reasons, should not be missed.[3] The Associates-in-Training journal *InnovAiT* also features sample AKT questions in each issue and these are also collected online.[4]

When you get to the point where you absolutely cannot face doing any more questions, do another few hundred and you should be ready.

IT'S ALL IN THE TIMING

The AKT has many similarities to comedy in general, one of which is the importance of timing. It is a fast-paced exam with little margin for error in time management, so try to time your practice questions so you know you are doing them at the right pace. In the exam you have approximately 54 seconds to read, ponder and answer each question. You will not have an awful lot of time in the exam to redo questions, or even think too much about your answers, so getting into the habit of answering them fast and going with your instincts will help. Questions can be skipped and returned to later and those you're unsure of can also be flagged up. Try not to get into the habit of relying on this though, because time is tight and an unanswered question is a lost mark.

IT'S STILL ALL IN THE TIMING

Another important thing to decide is when you want to do the AKT. It does help to have done some general practice. The exam can be sat in either ST2 or ST3 years. A GP rotation in ST2 can be a perfect opportunity to get it out of the way. Unfortunately this is also a perfect opportunity to make the most of not having to do nights or on-calls, and to try your hand at baking, knitting, etc. Trainees who started training after August 2010 can have a maximum of four attempts at AKT, while those whose training started before August 2010 can have an unlimited number of attempts providing they are still on a training programme.

THE YEAR OF THE PARROT

There are a lot of small facts that make up decent AKT knowledge – this isn't for everyone, but one author found it very helpful to write down random facts he learnt (by getting practice questions wrong) to revise from at the end of the day. He is certain that at least 5–10% of his points were gained from reading this on the way to the exam, and there is nothing he loves more than being jammy.

EIGHTY PER CENT OF STATISTICS ARE MADE UP ON THE SPOT

Stats are quite important for AKT, which can be a problem because for many they make no sense whatsoever. It's worth trying to learn the important formulas, because you can guarantee that these questions will come up. Try to get someone who understands stats (they do exist) to go through the basics with you if you are really struggling. A useful and approachable guide can be found in the *InnovAiT* archives.[5] The e-GP website contains a module on evidence-based medicine and a web search will reveal a wealth of good-quality but more informal resources that are emerging from locality groups around the country. Bother your programme directors for some good teaching. Ditto with the 10% of management-type questions. These two areas count for 20% of the final score – you ignore them at your peril!

DON'T BE AN IDIOT

Finally, after all the preparation, why not allow yourself the chance to actually sit the exam? There is a list of items you must have with you, and a list of items that you should leave at home.[2] Your ID must match the details you submitted at the time of application (so if you have changed your name, be aware of this). If they don't, or you forget your ID or you arrive late … then you're not sitting the exam. End of story. These tests are run at centres that are used to running the driving theory test, so they have heard every sob story in the book and your pleas will have no impact. I forgot my passport and had to return home to get it, much to my inconvenience and that of my friend who I was travelling with. Luckily my propensity for doing stupid things like this also meant we'd left an hour early, which also helped when I couldn't find the passport when I got home. Also, had it not been for the fact that I was topless under my hoodie, I would have been forced to surrender it at the door. So … actually take the time to read the info for candidates!

REFERENCES

1. GP curriculum: overview, www.rcgp.org.uk/GP-training-and-exams/GP-curriculum-overview. aspx [accessed March 2014].

2. MRCGP Applied Knowledge Test (AKT), www.rcgp.org.uk/gp-training-and-exams/mrcgp-exam-overview/mrcgp-applied-knowledge-test-akt.aspx [accessed March 2014].

3. MRCGP Applied Knowledge Test: 50 sample questions, www.rcgp.org.uk/gp-training-and-exams/mrcgp-exam-overview/~/media/Files/GP-training-and-exams/AKT%20page/AKT-sample-paper-final-November-11.ashx [accessed March 2014].

4. *InnovAiT*, www.rcgp.org.uk/publications/innovait.aspx [March 2014].

5. Irving G. Goodbye to gobbledegook: an introduction to basic statistics in primary care. *InnovAiT* 2009; **2(6)**: 372–83. doi: 10.1093/innovait/inp057.

38

HOW TO PASS AND FAIL THE CLINICAL SKILLS ASSESSMENT

Michael Banna

The Clinical Skills Assessment (CSA) is a treacherous exam, and don't let anybody tell you any different. I have both passed and failed the CSA (not in that order), and there is only one outcome I would recommend. Prior to my first CSA attempt, a lot of the advice I was given (or at least that which I listened to) varied around themes of you'll be fine/everybody passes the CSA/smile lots and be nice/just remember ideas, concerns and expectations (ICE). We all know about ICE, shared management plans and hidden agendas, but it was only after I failed that I really found out through experience, deanery revision courses and the awesome power of cheesy inspirational 80s music, what I really needed to do to pass. Ultimately, failing the CSA once, twice or even three times is not the end of the world, but no matter how you dress it up each attempt is more than £1500 that will be missing from your bank account FOR THE REST OF YOUR LIFE. So hopefully these top tips will help you avoid financial woe and having to listen to 'Livin' on a Prayer' more times than is healthy.

PREPARING IN THE PRACTICE

Seeing patients is the best revision you can do, so make sure you are putting in the time at your practice. Use the consults to experiment with and develop your consultation model. Write down your model and stick it on the wall. Practise your set pieces – PSA testing, smoking advice and healthy lifestyle modifications are all areas that you should have a well-rehearsed script for. If you are not getting access to a particular type of patient at your practice due to the demographics of the area then discuss this with your trainer and programme directors, as you need good exposure. If you feel that you are being worked too hard at your practice and this is getting in the way of your exam preparation then, again, seek to discuss this early, but bear in mind the opening sentence of this paragraph. The dreaded video consultations are a good way to discover unpleasant habits that you might have picked up.

PREPARING AT HOME

Getting together in groups to regularly role-play consultations is another rite of passage for the registrar. Many books are available that contain cases for you to use in these sessions, and you may even be able to pick up some freebies from the year above if you ask nicely. In these sessions make sure you get involved rather than sit on the sidelines. It will feel weird at first but become second nature over time. If you are observing a role-play ensure you provide useful criticism at the end. Be honest in your critique but not unkind. Telling someone they were brilliant when they weren't is easy but not helpful. Similarly, trashing someone who has had difficulty is likely to be counterproductive. Remember that exposing yourself, your consulting style and your knowledge gaps to your peers in these role-plays takes a leap of trust. Do not abuse this when giving feedback to others.

WHAT TO TAKE TO THE EXAM

A useful guide to this can be found on the Royal College of General Practitioners (RCGP) website.[1] Take your normal bag; it will be a comfort blanket as you walk to the exam centre. In it put *British National Formulary* (BNF), stethoscope, ophthalmoscope, otoscope, thermometer, patella hammer, tape measure, peak flow meter with disposable mouthpieces and SPARE BATTERIES. Don't leave it on the train. There is no spare equipment at the exam centre. You are allowed to 'role-play' lost/missing equipment but why put yourself through it? You currently do not need to take a sphygmomanometer, but check this is still the case prior to your exam (see the College website). Check travel details minutely and if in doubt or prone to tardiness/anxiety consider a nearby hotel for the night before. There are places for every budget within walking distance of the exam centre and you can now stay in the College.

WHAT TO EXPECT

You need to know what is going to happen on the day. Check the College website and find this out before you arrive. You don't need to be learning new information on the day. Chat to some of the people in the year above to get an idea but remember the RCGP views discussing previous CSA cases as a breach of probity.

You have been warned. The RCGP website describes the basics of the exam,[1] which was formally held in a specialist exam centre in Croydon, though this has now moved to the new RCGP headquarters in Euston. Check this and make sure that you attend the right venue. You will be installed in a room set out like a typical GP's consulting room but with less art.

THE BELLS, THE BELLS

The 'patients' will rotate around you; you will stay put. Each patient has an accompanying vignette, as in medical school OSCEs. You will have two minutes to read and contemplate on this before a bell rings and the patient is at the door. Bring the patient in and get going; you've got ten minutes to save the world. After this another bell rings and he or she will leave. The patient will not wait for one more *bon mot* from you. You cannot chase him or her down the corridor to complete the consult. If you are finished early you can get the patient to leave; you don't have to pad things out to ten minutes. The room contains all the usual things: request forms, prescription pad, blood forms, pen and paper, etc. Anything you give to the patient will be looked at by the examiners and marked. You can of course tell the patient to pick up the forms/script later. The 'patients' are highly skilled actors who will be accompanied by an examiner. The examiners generally keep out of your line of sight while they make notes that will determine your future happiness. Be prepared to examine the patient and initiate this by explaining to the patient the examination you are about to carry out. Occasionally the examiner will provide the findings, e.g. observations, examination findings, etc., if you say what you are looking for. In other cases the examiner will observe your examination technique, so don't bank on getting the info for free … and make sure you have practised your examination technique. You may be asked to change rooms to simulate a telephone consultation or a home visit.

WHAT ARE THEY GETTING AT?

The CSA is designed to test primary care management, problem-solving skills, comprehensive approach, person-centred care, attitudinal aspects and clinical practical skills.[1] You will be marked on your performance in the domains of data gathering, clinical management and interpersonal skills. In each domain you will be awarded a Clear Pass, Pass, Fail or Clear Fail. Definitions of these can be found on the RCGP website.[1] It also gives you some sample cases with rationales that you would be foolish not to look at.[1] The method of calculating the pass mark is complex and beyond the scope of this article, but may be of interest to those with a keen interest in statistics.[2]

ARE YOU A MODEL?

During your revision you should have developed a solid structure to your consultations, which you should stick to in the exam. Under pressure it's very easy for the 'Golden Minute' to become the 'Golden Ten Seconds' or to offer the patient only two treatment options – my way or the highway. Remember there are ALWAYS options, even if one is to do nothing. Your consultation model is there to help you in times of stress and panic – use it.

TIME IS RUNNING OUT

Time management is key; there will be a clock in the room. Use it. It is important that you get as close to the end of the case as possible. You don't have to finish, but if you don't show them the goods, they won't give you the points. You should not take the CSA until you are consulting in ten minutes. This doesn't mean you need to be on ten-minute appointments, but the consultation part of the process (i.e. without printing scripts, writing up, etc.) should be taking you ten minutes. The best way to get to this point is simply to see as many patients as possible. Also remember that as many marks are gained for your management plan as for your data gathering, so give it the time it deserves. You should almost always devote the last five of your ten minutes to the management plan, which may seem a bit excessive but really isn't in reality. Which brings me to my next point.

IT'S GOOD TO SHARE

We are often led to believe that the way to a shared management plan is giving the patient a list of options and choosing the most appropriate together, but your management plan should be just as much of a dialogue as your data gathering. After suggesting a diagnosis, ask the patient what he or she knows about what might normally happen next. The patient could either do the classic 'I dunno, you're the doctor', which gives you go-ahead to provide him or her with options, or the patient might mention a couple of options he or she has heard of, and may also express a preference. You can find all sorts of ICE and hidden agendas through this (and this is why you need five minutes), but ultimately it saves time that you might otherwise spend going on about pills when all they want is yoga and crystals. Also remember to always consider lifestyle options and other more holistic methods.

I WOULD RATHER STICK NEEDLES IN MY FACE

I would really advise spending some time on Wikipedia or patient.co.uk finding out what things like acupuncture, osteopathy and chiropractic therapy actually are.

The same goes for podiatry, chiropody, etc. You may be asked questions about these things by the patient, and it only takes a matter of minutes to learn information that could mean the difference between you looking like a holistic, open-minded practitioner, and a total idiot.

DRESS TO NOT KILL

Every examiner I have ever spoken to has a story about a candidate who dressed inappropriately. You need to look like a professional, or at least somebody taking a professional exam. What you wear is up to you, and the jury is out on suits, but at the very least you must wear something appropriate for work. Equally, do remember that you are not being examined by Vivienne Westwood, you are being examined by GPs who probably think that Ralph Lauren is a jockey. They don't care if your belt matches your shoes, as long as it stops your trousers from falling down, and if you look too trendy they may well find it threatening. I tell myself that this is what happened to me the first time round. Jeans and exposed flesh should be avoided. Gentlemen, remember your fly. Ladies, remember your neckline.

HELP YOURSELF

There are lots of ways you can do this from within the exam. Write down your bullet-pointed consultation model (which you have of course been using on a daily basis in practice) with the stationery provided. You are allowed to do this. This crib sheet can be massively useful when you are having one of those panic moments – simply refer back to your model and go back to basics. You can take your BNF into the exam. Colour-coded BNF bookmark tags will save you fumbling around like a lunatic for the Viagra prescribing rules at nine and a half minutes. Do remember that the BNF is full of amazing information that you can use to cheat. And it's not cheating if it's legal (NB writing notes in your BNF *is* cheating and you *will* get busted). Read the intro section of each chapter in the BNF before the exam. You will see that they have lots of National Institute for Health and Care Excellence (NICE) guidelines outlined for you to fall back on when your mind goes blank.

YOU'RE NOT IN KANSAS ANYMORE

Remember you are working in a FAKE surgery, where the possibilities are almost endless. As long as you don't tell the patient that you'll arrange for an alien to use a sonic probe to remove their sebaceous cyst without leaving a scar, you pretty much have *carte blanche* to decide what services you offer. You will undoubtedly have a physiotherapist attached to the practice, as well as a counsellor and probably many others, all of whom will be able to see the patient within a couple of days. You will also, of course, be able to bring a patient back at any time for a double appointment to discuss his or her diagnosis in more detail. Given this wonderful level of access make sure that you have safety-netted appropriately.

TALK PROPER

Take some time to think about how you talk to patients – watch videos of your consultations and try to work on not saying really annoying things. Common culprits are starting sentences with 'obviously' or 'basically' – there is little that should be considered obvious or basic to a patient, and it can come across much more patronising than you realise. Another big bugbear is referring to the medical profession as 'we', for example 'We would normally advise you to take this medication.' We is fine only when talking about you and the patient.

IT'S ALL ABOUT THE CONFIDENCE

This is NOT true. Confidence is really important, and never underestimate the power of a positive attitude when taking the CSA, but equally you need to know your stuff or admit that you don't. Over-confidence is a big no-no, and there is no shame in saying that you will look something up/talk to your trainer/discuss with the GP in the practice who is a specialist in that area and get back to the patient. You should still offer what you do know, but back it up with the promise to make sure of the knowledge if you're not. This is not a watertight rule – remember you will lose more marks for not knowing how to treat a chest infection than not knowing the genetics of Tay–Sachs Disease. And on the subject, when you find a case that involves describing the genetics of Tay–Sachs Disease, don't panic. Most people will not know this stuff. The examiners are looking at how you handle this situation. Go back to basics, look at your consultation model and go to work. You will find that there is plenty that you CAN do to pass this station.

KNOWLEDGE IS POWER

Notwithstanding the above advice, you do need to know something. You can practise cases till you are blue in the face and have the best consultation style on the planet, but if you don't know anything you will still fail. Make sure to do plenty of actual study as well as practice. Learn the guidelines, two-week rule criteria and management of common conditions. Over-investigating or inappropriate referrals will be marked down. Doing three two-week rules and an emergency admission in my first CSA attempt taught me this.

DO AS YOU'RE TOLD

If you are going off on the wrong tangent, the actor will usually try to steer you back to the right road. Do not make the mistake, as I did, of always thinking that the patient is trying to trick you. By the same token, don't waste time digging too hard for a hidden agenda – if there isn't one by the time you've asked twice, accept that he or she may just have a cold and move on. However, if the patient says something twice, explore it. He or she is trying to help you.

AND FINALLY ...

Good luck. You can do it.

REFERENCES

1. Clinical Skills Assessment (CSA), www.rcgp.org.uk/gp-training-and-exams/mrcgp-exam-overview/mrcgp-clinical-skills-assessment-csa.aspx [accessed March 2014].

2. The new CSA standard-setting system, www.rcgp.org.uk/gp-training-and-exams/mrcgp-exam-overview/~/media/Files/GP-training-and-exams/Standard-Setting-the-CSA-from-September-2010-onwards.ashx [accessed March 2014].

39

AUDIT FOR IMPROVEMENT

Paul Bowie, John McKay and Murray Lough

Demonstrating the ability to improve patient care by applying audit method is a lifelong expectation for all GPs. Audit is a mainstay of *Good Medical Practice* and a key part of clinical governance, GP appraisal and revalidation. Beyond fulfilling these professional obligations, you might even find that audit – when done properly – can help to make your clinical practice much more effective and efficient, and also enhance your patients' experiences of the care they receive. It makes perfect sense, therefore, that related knowledge and experience are gained during GP training rather than afterwards.

We know in general practice that audit can be an effective tool when it is applied robustly and with a strong mix of leadership and team involvement. Research involving GP principals and trainees strongly suggests that small, highly focused audits often lead to a much better chance of meaningful improvements in patient care being implemented.

THE AUDIT CYCLE

The audit cycle or loop is the traditional theory behind the method we follow when carrying out an audit project (Figure 39.1, opposite). There are a number of different stages to the audit cycle and all of them must be closely followed to enable a successful audit outcome. Failure to do so invariably leads to an audit project being left incomplete or abandoned altogether.

FIGURE 39.1: THE AUDIT CYCLE

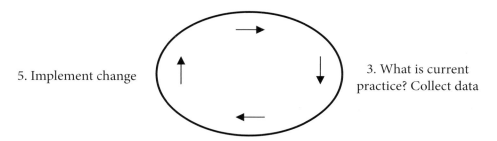

1. Choose an audit topic

2. Define criteria and set standards to be measured

[REPEAT THE AUDIT CYCLE]

5. Implement change

3. What is current practice? Collect data

4. Compare current practice against standards

CHOOSING AN AUDIT TOPIC

› This is a very important first step. Aim to achieve consensus within the practice that the chosen topic for audit is a worthwhile area to study, i.e. you are unsure of current practice in that area or there is agreement that this is an area where practice could be greatly improved.

› Undertaking an audit project in isolation from colleagues will potentially lead to a number of difficulties and should be avoided at all costs, e.g. staff or colleagues may not be as keen to help with data collection if they feel uninvolved or suspect that the audit has been imposed on them.

› You may experience difficulty or even hostility in getting others to change practice in light of your audit findings if they have not been informed or involved since the start.

› It is extremely important that all relevant staff are aware of what you intend to do, how you intend to do it, and are agreed at the outset that it is a worthwhile exercise and are willing to support you.

› We cannot stress highly enough that keeping your audit projects short, simple and easily manageable is critical to success.

EFFECTIVE AUDIT PRACTICE

We recommend following the eight-stage process outlined below when undertaking and reporting a completed audit cycle for these very specific reasons:

›   it naturally follows the aforementioned audit cycle

›   it is validated as a 'best practice' method to not only conduct an audit in general practice, but also to assess the standard of the audit project undertaken (under the previous UK GP training system)

›   each stage becomes one of eight very obvious headings to be included in a full written report of a completed audit cycle, which allows for consistent and coherent reporting of audit findings for appraisal and other purposes.

1. REASON FOR THE AUDIT

›   The opening section of the report should clearly explain why the audit topic was chosen. As a result of this choice there is the potential for improvement to be introduced that is relevant to the practice or you as an individual practitioner.

2. CRITERIA TO BE MEASURED

›   Criteria are very precise, logical statements that are used to describe a definable and measurable item of health care, which describes quality and can be used to assess it.

›   Criteria and standards are often cited as the most confusing terms associated with audit. Both cause doctors and others the greatest difficulty in understanding and putting into practice. We like to think that if you can understand and differentiate between an audit 'criterion' and a 'standard' then you are well on your way to grasping basic audit method.

BOX 39.1: EXAMPLES OF AUDIT CRITERIA

- Patients with a previous myocardial infarction should be prescribed aspirin, unless contraindicated.

- Patients with chronic asthma should be assessed at least every 52 weeks.

- Patients should wait no longer than 20 minutes in the surgery before consultation.

- The GP's medicine bag should contain a supply of in-date adrenaline.

- Surgeries should start within five minutes of their allotted time.

- The blood pressure of known hypertensive patients should be <140/85.

> It is best to restrict the number of criteria to be measured for any given audit.

> Focusing on one or two criteria makes data collection much more manageable and the introduction of small changes to practice much less challenging. Overall it offers a better chance of the audit being completed successfully within a reasonable time span.

> It is important that audit criteria should be backed up with quoted evidence (e.g. from a clinical guideline or a review of the relevant literature).

> However, depending on the topic, suitable evidence is not always readily available. In this case simply explain this, but also stress that there is agreement amongst your colleagues on the importance of the topic and the chosen criteria.

3. SETTING STANDARDS

> An audit standard quite simply describes the measurable level of care to be achieved for any particular criterion.

> It is unlikely that you will find actual percentage standards quoted in the literature or in clinical guidelines. You should arrive at the desired level of care (standard) by discussing and agreeing the appropriate figure(s) with colleagues.

> There is no hard rule about standard setting – the agreed level is based on professional judgement and this will obviously vary between practices for a variety of medical and social reasons.

BOX 39.2: EXAMPLES OF AUDIT STANDARDS

1. 90% of patients with a previous myocardial infarction should be prescribed aspirin, unless contraindicated.

2. 80% of patients with chronic asthma should be assessed at least every 52 weeks.

3. 75% of patients should wait no longer than 20 minutes after their allotted appointment time.

4. 100% of GPs' medicine bags should contain a supply of in-date adrenaline.

5. 95% of surgeries should start within their allotted times.

6. 70% of blood pressure measurements of known hypertensive patients should be <140/85.

> Agree on a standard that you all believe to be an ideal or desired level of care and briefly explain why each standard was chosen (remember that different standards can be applied to each criterion).

› The standard(s) set should be outlined together with a time scale as to when you expect it to be achieved (e.g. within three months if that is how long you envisage to complete the audit project).

› In some cases you might require to set realistic targets and a time scale towards the desired standard over a longer period of time (e.g. 50% of asthmatic patients should have a management plan within 16 weeks, rising to 70% in 52 weeks, and surpassing 80% within 104 weeks).

4. PREPARATION AND PLANNING

› This is an important section that is often overlooked when compiling an audit report.

› As explained, audit should not be undertaken in isolation. Teamwork is essential to audit success and this must be demonstrated during the audit with related evidence provided in the report.

› Quite simply explain in one paragraph who was involved in discussing and planning the audit, how the data were identified, collected, analysed and disseminated, and who gave you assistance at any stage of the project (e.g. with a literature review or with collecting or analysing data) if this was required.

5. INITIAL DATA COLLECTION (1)

› The initial data collected should be presented using simple descriptive statistics in table format or using graphs (bar charts, pie charts, etc.). Remember to quote actual numbers (n) as well as the percentage (%). Do not quote irrelevant data (for example on age, gender or past medical history) if it bears no relation to your chosen audit criteria.

TABLE 39.1: EXAMPLE OF DATA COLLECTION (1) PRESENTATION

Criterion	Number of MI patients (n)	Number contraindicated (n)	Number of patients on aspirin		Standard (%)
Patients with a previous MI should be prescribed aspirin, unless contraindicated	53	3	30/50	60%	80%

› In the above example the initial audit shows that current practice is below the set standard. It is important to comment on the difference between the first collection of data (current practice in this area) and the standard previously set (the desired level of care).

6. DESCRIPTION OF CHANGE FOR IMPROVEMENT

› The essence of audit is to change practice in order to improve patient care and services. This section should adequately describe any changes that were discussed, agreed and introduced to practice by the team and how you believe this will lead to improved care. The role of others involved in this process should also be described.

› An explicit example of the change(s) that was introduced should be attached in evidence as an appendix to the report, where this is possible. Examples could include a new or amended protocol, guideline or flow chart that is introduced to practice, or a letter that is sent to a group of patients inviting them in for a medical review.

7. DATA COLLECTION (2)

› After change has been agreed and implemented, and a reasonable period of time has elapsed to allow any new practices or systems to take effect, then you must complete the audit cycle.

› The failure to complete the audit cycle is arguably the single most common reason why many audit projects are left incomplete. As well as being a waste of time and resources, this leads to frustration for those involved as well as many missed opportunities to improve patient care.

› Completion of the audit cycle is achieved by carrying out a second data collection in order to measure and evaluate what impact the newly introduced change has had on improving practice in the area being audited.

› If no change has been introduced or it has not been given enough time to take effect then there is no point in undertaking a second data collection – the findings are unlikely to show any improvement in the time that has elapsed because there has been no intervention.

› Data from the second data collection should be presented in a similar way to the first round of data, but also include the results from data collection (1) alongside your desired standard as well so that comparisons can be easily made.

TABLE 39.2: EXAMPLE OF DATA COLLECTION (2) PRESENTATION

Audit	Number of MI patients (n)	Number contraindicated (n)	Number of patients on aspirin		Standard (%)
Data collection (1) – March 2011	53	3	30/50	60%	80%
Data collection (2) – June 2012	56	3	48/53	94%	80%

Note: criterion = patients with a previous MI should be prescribed aspirin, unless contraindicated.

› Remember to comment on the comparison between data collections (1) and (2), and the desired standard to be achieved. If the standard is not attained or surpassed, explain why you think this is the case and how you would propose to reach it in future.

CONCLUSIONS

› The final section of the audit report should conclude by briefly summarising what the audit achieved in terms of improvement and learning. In doing this, the benefits achieved through the audit should be discussed along with any problems encountered with the process or findings.

› Consideration should also be given as to how improvements in care will be sustained and whether the audit will be repeated in future and if so when and by whom.

40

LEARNING FROM ERROR

Paul Bowie and Elaine McNaughton

INTRODUCTION

Significant event analysis (SEA) is the most frequently applied approach to learning from error in general practice.[1] The requirement for SEA in the Quality and Outcomes Framework (QOF), GP appraisal and medical revalidation – as well as specialty training – reflects the importance of participating in such activity. In your trainee role, identifying and analysing a significant event as part of the team and leading on related learning and improvement is important for professional development, a key safety skill to acquire and a core attribute of good medical practice.

Taking part in SEA prompts the care team to hold regular structured meetings to prioritise and reflect on events that are recognised as being 'significant' and helps them to identify learning needs and plan effective action. Importantly, when undertaken constructively, it provides an opportunity for meaningful reflection, discussion and analysis in what should be a non-threatening and empathic environment. If done well, SEA can enhance teamworking and morale, and improve communication and understanding between team members, all of which helps to build a more positive safety culture in GP surgeries.[2]

However, the evidence suggests that we often struggle to engage with and apply SEA effectively for a range of reasons. Involvement in significant events challenges the quality of our own performance and, similar to receiving negative feedback, may result in an emotional response that can impede constructive investigation of the event.[3] Also, a failure to apply an objectively structured systems-based approach results in a superficial analysis with no measurable improvement. There is therefore a need to consider the emotional barriers faced by the individual when raising a significant event, and to apply an integrated team-based human factors approach (Box 40.1)[4] to the analysis of errors (Box 40.2). Reflecting on and incorporating these concepts offer the practice team a means to differentiate between the personal and systems-level factors at play and also deflect the potential to 'blame' individuals.

BOX 40.1: TAKING A HUMAN FACTORS APPROACH TO SEA[4,5]

Human factors are those factors (e.g. personal characteristics, job tasks and complexity, environmental issues, and workplace culture) that combine to influence people and their behaviour in the working environment.

In summary some of the common human factors that can increase risks and contribute to significant events include:

- mental workload
- distractions
- the physical environment
- physical demands of the job
- design of equipment and products
- teamworking
- design of processes and procedures.

BOX 40.2: EXAMPLES OF ERRORS AND SYSTEM FAILURES

- Disease diagnosis and disease management *(e.g. missed or delayed diagnosis of cancer, terminal care pain management).*

- Prescribing, dispensing and other drug issues *(e.g. wrong/inappropriate drug prescribed/administered, warfarin issue).*

- Patient and relatives *(e.g. patient behaviour, anger or upset).*

- Investigations and results *(e.g. incorrect results given to patient, results not acted upon).*

- Communication *(e.g. lack of communication, unsuccessful communication, inadequate communication).*

- Administration *(e.g. complaint, breach of protocol).*

- Medical records and confidentiality *(e.g. breach of confidentiality, wrong records accessed).*

- Home visits and external care *(e.g. delay in arrival, visit request not done).*

- Equipment *(e.g. computer search facility ineffective, difficulty accessing cupboard containing medical supplies).*

GOOD PRACTICE IN ANALYSING A SIGNIFICANT EVENT

A key step in applying SEA is the investigative process and a less than rigorous approach can be non-productive – see recently published national guidance for more detail.[5] Different formats for reporting SEAs exist, including the MRCGP ePortfolio Template, but regardless of the report format used the analytical (and writing-up process) should be guided by in-depth consideration of four key questions.

Before addressing these questions, stop and reflect on your reaction to the event and on how other members of the team might feel about their involvement. Consider discussing this with a colleague in order to help you gain a better understanding of any potential emotional barriers to exploring the event in depth. The aim of this is to facilitate your readiness to undertake the following analysis objectively.

1. WHAT HAPPENED AND HOW?

› Establish what happened and how in detailed, chronological order.

› Collect as much factual information as possible from written and electronic records, as well as from personal testimony from those directly and indirectly involved. Include patients, relatives and colleagues from other NHS bodies, where appropriate.

› Determine what the consequences were or could have been, e.g. clinically/emotionally for the patient, the team members involved, or the liability of the practice.

2. WHY DID IT HAPPEN?

› Establish the *main* and *underlying* reasons contributing to why the event happened.

› Consider, for instance, the professionalism of the team, the lack of a system or a failing in a system, lack of knowledge or the complexity and uncertainty associated with the event.

› Try to avoid simply focusing on superficial causes of events (for example, 'I forgot to pass on an important message about the condition of an elderly diabetic patient to the practice nurse'). Use simple problem-solving techniques such as Toyoda's Five Whys or the Fishbone Diagram (visit the quality tools section at www.institute.nhs.uk/) in order to focus discussions and analysis on practice systems, rather than on individual team members.

› Alternatively, if it is a positive event, what were the underlying factors that contributed to a successful outcome?

3. WHAT HAS BEEN LEARNED?

› Outline the learning needs identified from the event.

› Demonstrate that reflection and learning have taken place on an individual or team basis.

› Consider, for instance:

- a lack of knowledge and training
- the need for, or to follow, systems or procedures
- the vital importance of teamworking or effective communication.

4. WHAT HAS BEEN CHANGED OR ACTIONED FOR IMPROVEMENT?

› Outline the action(s) agreed and implemented (where this is relevant or feasible).

› Action is not always necessary – particularly for 'positive' and 'purely reflective' events – but should always be considered and justifiably ruled out if not required. Outlining the specifics of good practice is important in reinforcing and consolidating current systems.

› Consider, for instance, if a protocol has been amended, updated or introduced, how this was done and who was involved, and how will this change was monitored.

POSSIBLE OUTCOMES OF A SIGNIFICANT EVENT MEETING

› *Celebration* – exemplary care, e.g. the team-based effort in successfully resuscitating a man who collapsed in the surgery waiting room.

› *No action* – event is an accepted part of everyday practice or is so unlikely to ever happen again that it would not be an effective use of time and resources putting preventive measures in place.

› *A learning need* – a patient's sudden collapse in the surgery revealed that the nurse and doctor who attended needed refresher training in cardio-pulmonary resuscitation (CPR).

› *A learning point* – a discharge summary was received in the practice, but the patient's repeat medication record wasn't updated, i.e. there is no robust system in place to ensure this happens.

› *A conventional audit* – a problem is revealed, but the team is unsure how common it is, e.g. a 49-year-old overweight patient and smoker is admitted to the local hospital with a myocardial infarction (MI). Review of his records shows that he was at risk, but was not on appropriate medication.

› *Immediate change* – a child was given an out-of-date vaccination, prompting a complaint from the parents. A formal protocol was introduced immediately to ensure regular checking of vaccinations and refrigerator temperatures by designated staff.

> *Improvement plan* – a new system is developed whereby discharge summaries all follow a clear administrative pathway via a member(s) of the team with designated responsibility for ensuring all repeat medications are updated in the patient record.

WRITING UP THE SEA REPORT

It is important to document the event analysis, particularly for QOF, appraisal and revalidation purposes. It is also good practice to attach any additional evidence of action (e.g. a copy of a letter of apology or an amended protocol) to the report. The report should be written up by the individual who has the greatest knowledge of the event or who led on the event analysis. It is also good practice to keep the report anonymous so that individuals and other organisations cannot be identified. The report should reflect an in-depth account of each of the four areas of analysis previously outlined, rather than a superficial attempt to simply describe the event.

BARRIERS IMPEDING SUCCESS

The following issues may hinder potential success and need to be borne in mind:

> sensitive events may provoke a barrier of defensiveness and be too uncomfortable, threatening and emotionally demanding

> the focus is often on the role of individuals rather than the weak, inadequate or missing systems and processes within the practice to minimise risks

> employed staff may feel low in the hierarchy, find it difficult to act confidently as equals and feel vulnerable in speaking out

> medical domination of meetings is possible without strong leadership and facilitation

> the process may be destructive for poorly established teams – the team dynamic may militate against the critical appraisal of care delivered

> inadequate leadership can hinder the non-threatening environment, the appropriateness of topics and the uncovering of hidden agendas

> prioritisation may focus on 'safe' events rather than on complex or serious ones to minimise embarrassment, conflict or concerns about confidentiality and litigation

> 'positive' events are rarely chosen because care teams perceive a greater challenge in resolving 'negative' events, which are more likely to initiate change.

CONCLUSION

At its core, SEA is based on sound educational principles. It is one key element amongst others in a 'learning organisation' that promotes an effective safety culture within the practice team and facilitates change. Importantly, SEA encourages a culture of honesty in the team as well as both individual and team-based reflection. However, to make SEA a much more meaningful experience we need a deeper consideration of the emotional demands involved in raising a significant event (at the individual level) and the most professionally appropriate and effective way to analyse the event (at the team level). Guiding the analysis using a basic human factors framework depersonalises the incident and focuses attention on the 'true' contributory issues, i.e. how processes, systems and the complexity of tasks can interact with the human element in the practice to increase the risk of errors.

REFERENCES

1. Pringle M, Bradley C, Carmichael C, *et al. Significant Event Auditing: a study of the feasibility and potential of case-based auditing in primary medical care* (Occasional Paper No. 70). London: RCGP, 1995.

2. Bowie P, Pope L, Lough M. A review of the current evidence base for significant event analysis. *Journal of Evaluation in Clinical Practice* 2008; **14(4)**: 520–36.

3. Sargeant J, Mann K, Sinclair D, *et al.* Understanding the influence of emotions and reflection upon multi-source feedback acceptance and use. *Advances in Health Sciences Education* 2008; **13(3)**: 275–88.

4. Patient Safety First. *Implementing Human Factors in Healthcare: 'how to' guide.*

   www.patientsafetyfirst.nhs.uk/ashx/Asset.ashx?path=/Intervention-support/Human%20 Factors%20How-to%20Guide%20v1.2.pdf [accessed March 2014].

5. Bowie P, Pringle M. *Significant Event Audit: guidance for primary care teams.* London: NPSA, 2008, www.nrls.npsa.nhs.uk/resources/?entryid45=61500 [accessed March 2014].

IMMEDIATE DISCHARGE LETTER

An elderly burnt-out patient with schizophrenia discharged into the community after over 20 years in our local asylum, now thankfully closed. On shed loads of powerful drugs, complex multidisciplinary arrangements for follow-up, multiple co-morbidities. But none of this on the crumpled carbon copy of his Immediate Discharge Letter. No, a model of brevity, Less is More – no name, no address, no list of medication. In the box for Diagnosis, 'Dougie, the door has fallen off the tumble dryer.'

Red Roses *collection curated by Alec Logan and illustrated by Helen Wilson.*

41

THE HOME VISIT

Anne T. Thompson and Alec Logan

Visiting a patient in his or her own home gives the doctor a unique opportunity to assess the patient in his or her own environment. The patient's home can give us a lot of information about a patient and his or her illness. Obviously house calls do not represent an efficient use of a doctor's time so should be carefully monitored. With an increasingly elderly population the majority of house calls will be to this group. Being out and about in the community on your own may make you feel exposed and vulnerable. You are away from the safety of the surgery and the support of your fellow colleagues.

A few sensible guidelines will enable you to make the most of this experience. Your best anecdotes to bore your own registrars with in the future will probably come from your experiences on house calls. One of the author's occurred in the East End of Glasgow. While taking her shiny new doctor's bag out of the boot of her Mini Metro a muzzled greyhound dog jumped past her and sat elegantly to attention in the back of my car. A wheezing portly man called to the author, 'Sorry, hen, she thinks it's time to go racing. Just pull her muzzle and she'll come out.' She opted for bribery with dog biscuits instead. Then there was the couple with flu-like symptoms who were becoming more unwell. After two visits to the surgery they requested a house call, which was unusual for them. A colleague was able to admit them to hospital as cases of psittacosis after bumping into a bird cage containing a sickly looking parrot on the way upstairs.

As GPs we are in a privileged position in being invited into our patients' homes when they are at their most vulnerable. Increasingly patients are languishing at home with chronic disease. Most patients want to die at home. This is very challenging. Follow best palliative care practice. Remember that continuity of care is no longer a slogan. This time it really counts.

Most patients are very grateful for your attention and treat you with respect. This may not always be the case and you must assess the situation carefully and usually put your safety first. If you are at all uncomfortable, leave and discuss this with your colleagues back at the surgery.

A FEW GUIDELINES

> *Urgent calls should be done first.*

> You will take your turn on the rota to be on house calls.

> This may be for part or all of the day. Make sure you arrive in good time, especially if you start at 8 a.m. Make sure you know when your surgery starts and be back on time. Inform the practice staff if you are genuinely delayed.

> Be flexible and be prepared to do your fair share of the house calls. (Or more than your fair share – some practices seem to ask too much of their trainees and this is an issue that should be discussed with your trainer or training programme director.)

> Others will help you out at first but you have to learn to manage a day on-call to be fit to practise independently.

> Check your bag. This should contain equipment, essential drugs and paperwork, including a prescription pad.

> Ensure your car is fully serviced and has enough fuel. It is your office and mobile surgery.

> Consider a sensible car, one that is reliable and economical. This should perhaps be a small car but also a car that you can drive safely should there be snow or ice. Avoid silly BMWs and Mercs with rear-wheel drive. Chelsea Tractors only in Chelsea.

> A local map or A–Z may be useful. Make use of local knowledge from staff, especially in rural areas. Sat navs are increasingly good, but not infallible. Remember to download updates regularly.

> Local radio and Radio 5 Live are useful for traffic information.

> Check addresses assiduously. Wrong postcodes cause havoc. Find out if there are there any details regarding Key Safe codes or contact telephone numbers to let you in.

> Plan your route before you leave so that you can do calls geographically close together. Obviously this plan must be fluid to accommodate emergency calls. Leave outlying areas till later in the day unless the call is urgent. Consulting Google Maps before you leave the surgery can be useful.

› Ensure your mobile is charged and the staff know how to contact you. To ensure your safety the staff should know where you are going.

› Take notes as you go along on the patient's summary. Update the record as quickly as you can.

› Ensure you have supplies of water and fruit in case you are very busy. Seasonally appropriate footwear is essential, e.g. boots/wellies/gloves. And a snow shovel.

› Be aware of personal safety. Carry a personal alarm when appropriate. Do not allow yourself to be locked into a patient's home – it can happen.

› If in any doubt contact the police. They are usually very quick, responsive, supportive and psychologically astute. They are skilled at defusing tense situations.

LASTLY

› BEWARE OF DOGS and other livestock.

› Ask for dogs to be removed from the room before you enter the house. Don't believe the statement 'They won't touch you, doctor!'

› Google Iain Bamforth, Chekhov, Bulgakov and William Carlos Williams.

PORK CHOP?

Oh dear!

I visited a lady with dementia at home today. She was wearing three skirts all at the same time.

Now she has accused me of pinching a pork chop out of her fridge.

Why would I want a pork chop?

Lots of reasons I suppose.

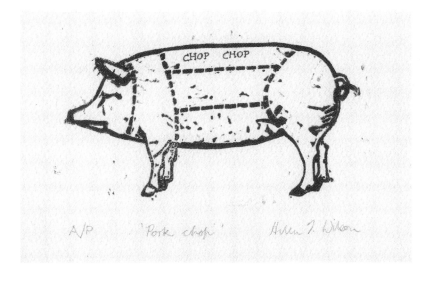

A/P   'Pork chop'   Helen J. Wilson

Red Roses *collection curated by Alec Logan and illustrated by Helen Wilson.*

42

OUT-OF-HOURS CARE

Max Inwood

Out-of-hours work or unscheduled care is similar to but not the same as daytime general practice. Although no longer a standard part of the GP contract, GP registrars coming through the system do need to complete a certain number of sessions to demonstrate competency in the area.

You may like to continue this work after vocational training. It can be rewarding and make a refreshing contrast to daytime NHS general practice. Skills and confidence once lost can be difficult to recover. New IT systems and referral pathways can be difficult to master after a long break. The pay is superannuable.

Arrive on time for your shift. The traffic was heavy or I could not find a parking space are excuses for patients, not professionals. Others who get paid less than you will notice. Lead by example.

At the end of the session, be careful about taking a complex psychiatric case ten minutes before the end of the shift. Clinical priority is of course paramount but remember that you are human too and need to get home. If you are unavoidably kept late more than a few minutes, it is worth asking for additional payment.

Watch your weekly working hours and don't overdo it. It should be self-evident that an overnight shift should not be followed by a normal day in the surgery. Being self-employed, we are not under immediate management scrutiny but ask what guidance operates in your area.

Dress appropriately. What image are you trying to project to anxious, confused or frightened patients who have never met you? If there is a dress code, find it and read it. For those who wish to dress down, there are many ways to look smart without formality. Find one of them.

Work well and hard for the full duration of the shift. Unlike general practice, a manager will have easy access to your work profile. Most centres will have a skill-mixed staff. Doctors are expected to be quicker than their nursing colleagues. Make sure that your higher pay also brings added value.

If you think that a case is not an emergency and should have waited for the GP in the morning, you should say so nicely with a smile but do not allow that feeling to affect the consultation. The patient does not have a medical degree and his or her social circumstances may not be conducive to patience.

Familiarise yourself early on with the equipment that you are required to use. Many managed services will insist that you use the supplied doctor's bag. Check it at the start of the session to make sure that your colleague going off shift has not used the last urine dipstick. Always keep a note of what you use and replace it.

The IT will not give you all the support that you have become accustomed to in the day job. The patient's interpretation of what is important to pass on may not be the same as yours. Check and check again if it is important.

You will not know the patients. Some will be deaf and agree with all that you say. Some may have dementia and give you a false impression of the problem. Use your sixth sense to pick up on inconsistencies in the story and check with a relative or carer on issues of competency.

If calling patients from a waiting area, take a moment to establish that you have the right patient. Anxiety, deafness or similar names may cause the wrong patient to respond to your call.

Frail elderly patients in nursing homes on house visits can be difficult to assess and manage. Think very carefully and consult as widely as you can before making your decision. Look for a Do Not Attempt Resuscitation (DNAR) form or anticipatory care plan as evidence of family and GP intentions. In general, masterly inactivity and confining yourself to symptom relief is a good starting point.

Revise the regulations surrounding the prescription of controlled drugs. Palliative care involving opioids is a common reason for contact and the chemist has no discretion in this area. Remember that a prescriber must be identifiable by name and a simple signature may not be enough. Print your name clearly at the bottom of the script.

There will be a policy on how to handle patients requiring drugs of abuse or dependence. Read it and stick to it absolutely. The answer will almost always be no. Issuing a script to cases that seem particularly deserving to you just makes the job of colleagues more difficult in the future.

Your job will be easier if you limit yourself to the acute problem that led to the call being made that day. The back story may be relevant but avoid being part of a saga. It will take a long time and may lead you into conflict with the GP's long-term plan.

Some patients must be dealt with immediately, usually by a speedy referral to secondary care. A history or examination suggestive of central cord compression or cerebrovascular accident (CVA) would be appropriate for an emergency admission.

Others should be helped with symptom relief. If doing that includes a diagnosis, it is satisfying but it is not essential. Bloods and ECGs will rarely be necessary and, if your thoughts go in these directions, it may be best to involve secondary care.

If your local laboratory allows access to laboratory results on computer, try to get a password allowing you access to the whole database. Being able to access last week's urine result or INR can be a great help in making a plan on a Saturday morning.

Be clear about any plans for follow-up. Most organisations will email your consultations overnight for GP attention in the morning. GPs may however not read them as quickly as you expect. If you want urgent action the next day, try to get the patient or a relative to contact the GP the next day as well.

43

HOW TO GET THE MOST OUT OF THE RADIOLOGY DEPARTMENT

Alexander C. Maclennan

Increasingly, medical undergraduates learn anatomy by cross-sectional imaging, not by dissection. Unfortunately, they usually do not learn more about radiology. Radiology departments are busy places full of expensive 'high tech' equipment. Every service wants a piece of this action and all clinicians would like their patients examined or scanned promptly. Managing waiting times by giving priority according to clinical history is routine. The access to radiology, available to you as a GP trainee, will depend on whether you are in a hospital or GP training post. The following tips should help you to get the best from your local radiology department.

THE REQUEST

Visit the department, or speak to a senior clinician, to find out the range of tests available to you. Trainees generally ask for more tests than established GPs.

1. The Ionising Radiation (Medical Exposures) Regulations 2000 mandates that you, the referrer, give sufficient clinical details to allow the examination to be justified and then performed.

2. *iRefer* is the seventh edition of the Royal College of Radiologists guidance, published in 2011, and lists hundreds of clinical scenarios with advice on appropriate imaging. It is available electronically to all NHS health professionals. The portal for viewing *iRefer* depends on the country where you work within the UK. Ask your IT department if you cannot find it.

3. Write legibly, if electronic requesting is not available, and give a succinct relevant history. The report is often tailored to your history. Remember, 'Garbage In (may) = Garbage Out.'

4. Date and type of previous exams is useful especially if performed in a different hospital.

5. Try to avoid abbreviations.

6. Most radiology departments offer 9-to-5 access for plain radiographs. Usually, you give the request to the patient who then attends at his or her convenience.

7. In hospital, it is useful to detail likely problems for the department on request cards. Immobility, drips and oxygen impacts on transporting the patient and time taken for examination. Abnormal renal function impacts on use of contrast in CT and MRI.

THE REPORT

8. *Treat the patient not the test result.* As examples, septic arthritis and stress fractures are not shown on initial plain films and radiological improvement of pneumonias lags behind clinical improvement.

9. Knowing the turnaround time from request to exam to report can help you plan when to see the patient.

10. Always wait for the final report. It may suggest follow-up, another test or hospital referral.

SPECIFIC DO'S AND DON'TS

11. Some patients cannot have a test. It is impossible to perform a barium enema on an incontinent, immobile patient. Very overweight patients may not fit into the bore of scanners or exceed the weight limit for the scan table. Both plain films and ultrasound are also limited by obesity.

12. In hospital, do not be insulted if the first question is 'Who has seen this patient?' See the next point.

13. Faced with a diagnostic dilemma, senior review is a better diagnostic strategy than fishing with radiology tests.

14. Still faced with a diagnostic dilemma, discussing with a radiologist which tests and in what sequence is a better diagnostic strategy than fishing.

15. Do not order a test if you don't want to know the result. It is your responsibility to read, then act on, the result of a test that you have requested.

16. Do not order a test if it does not alter management.

17. Radiology is often used to rule in or rule out important diagnoses. Be clear what you are looking for from the test. A normal CT brain does not rule in early stroke but does rule out a bleed.

18. Know the limitations of tests. A normal chest X-ray (CXR) in a smoker with haemoptysis can hide small hilar cancers and even sizeable lymphadenopathy. The patient will still need respiratory referral.

19. Know low-yield examinations. A lumbar spine radiograph in chronic back pain is almost never useful but does involve a significant radiation dose to the patient.

20. Some radiology departments have GP direct access to CT or MRI, usually by following a lengthy protocol. It may not be worth following through the protocol if you are going to refer the patient, irrespective of the result.

THE SERVICE

21. Radiology imaging targets, to speed up cancer diagnosis, concentrate on cross-sectional imaging so can have a detrimental effect on other aspects of the service, such as plain film reporting.

22. Review the turnaround of reports. If the service is slow or slowing, then discuss with the department. There may be a good reason, but an underlying resource issue such as lack of typists can be improved if GPs complain.

23. Radiology advice should be available to all GPs. There is usually one point of contact, such as a duty radiologist, during working hours.

AND FINALLY ...

Befriend a local radiologist. Having a point of contact in your local radiology department is useful for advice and for short-cuts when you want something done quickly. A useful opportunity is when a radiology report is caustic and requests further information. You, as the requesting clinician, are not handled as respectfully as perhaps some eminent consultant. Contact the department and bond with an individual. A quick chat will warm him or her up and supply a point of contact for decades to come.

44

HOW TO GET THE MOST OUT OF THE BIOCHEMISTRY DEPARTMENT

Anne M. Cruickshank

Biochemistry departments across the UK are merging to form larger laboratories, which may deal with thousands of samples per day. Moreover, some biochemistry departments have merged with haematology to form departments of 'blood sciences'. Whatever the nature of your biochemistry service, there should be a 'duty biochemist', usually a clinical scientist, immediately available to deal with any queries you have. There may be different contact numbers for getting results or asking for tests to be added retrospectively. Laboratories should also have a consultant medical biochemist, a.k.a. chemical pathologist, to provide clinical advice if necessary. Make sure you know how to contact your laboratory and make sure you have an up-to-date laboratory handbook, or, even better, can access this online.

SAMPLES AND REQUESTING TESTS

Do be familiar with sample pick-up arrangements for your surgery. Try to minimise the time samples lie around before pick-up. If your samples are not centrifuged within a few hours of venepuncture, you may get problems with spuriously high potassium results. Other tests may also be affected.

Don't take an FBC sample before the U&Es sample. The FBC bottle contains potassium EDTA as an anticoagulant and cross-contamination can occur, increasing the potassium concentration in the sample for U&Es.

Do be specific about which tests you require. Biochemistry departments often provide a vast range of tests and you cannot expect the unqualified staff manning laboratory reception areas to know what you mean by requests such as 'hormone profile'. If *you* don't know what you want, they certainly won't. If you're not sure which tests to ask for, get advice – contact the laboratory. Alternatively, www.labtestsonline. org is an excellent online resource.

Do check sample requirements if unsure. It is important that you are aware of any relevant patient preparation, correct sample timings, the right container to use and transport considerations, e.g. a drug concentration on a mistimed sample is unhelpful and potentially misleading. Sample requirements should all be detailed in the laboratory handbook but, if in doubt, contact the laboratory.

Do give relevant and accurate clinical information when requesting a test. This helps the duty biochemist to decide if further tests are required or to provide interpretive comments on reports. Accuracy is also important because, increasingly, results are transmitted to large electronic databases accessible to many other healthcare professionals. You may know the 'fasting' glucose is high because the patient wasn't actually fasting but another doctor may not. For the same reason, if you know there has been a sample mix-up at your end, let the laboratory know.

Do phone the laboratory if you have an urgent sample. The laboratory needs to know how and when the sample will be delivered and the contact details for phoning the results. Writing 'urgent' or 'please phone' on a request form buried among hundreds of others is unlikely to be effective.

Don't ask for lots of tests just because you can. Quality and Outcomes Framework (QOF) aside, only ask for tests if there is some clinical indication and don't repeat tests unnecessarily. You'll be saving the taxpayer money, but more importantly diagnostic tests are far more useful if used selectively, i.e. when the pre-test probability of a disease process is higher. The more tests you do, the more likely you are to find an 'abnormal' result, which is actually normal for that particular patient. The problem is that you won't know if it's significant or not.

RESULT REPORTING

Most laboratories still issue paper reports to GP surgeries although paper reports should increasingly be replaced by electronic download of results directly into GP systems.

Laboratories will analyse most samples either on the day of receipt or the following day and GPs should receive paper reports in most cases within 72 hours. Results may be available electronically earlier than this. If you don't think you are getting reports back quickly enough, contact someone senior in the lab, either a consultant or the laboratory manager.

Laboratories will phone abnormal results requiring urgent action. They will not phone for all abnormal results.

Most laboratories will provide some interpretive comments, particularly for more specialised tests. They can't do this if you don't supply relevant clinical information. All laboratories should have a medical consultant or a clinical scientist you can contact if you're not sure what results mean or what you should do about them.

All laboratories make mistakes. If you get a result that seems odd or doesn't fit with the clinical picture, either contact the lab and query it, or send a repeat. If you think the lab has made a mistake, let them know so they can take preventive action for the future.

AND FINALLY ...

All NHS clinical laboratories are obliged to deal effectively with complaints as a condition of accreditation. If you are not happy with aspects of your biochemistry service, you should get in touch, preferably by email, with a consultant or the laboratory manager.

POTASSIUM SUPPLEMENTS

Miss J's U&Es are on my desk and K is 3.4. A zealous younger partner has not ticked the Tell Patient Normal box and suggested telephone consultation.

Morning Miss J, about your blood test, your potassium level very slightly down, nothing to worry about. ... Probably your bendroflumethiazide, for blood pressure. Do you like bananas? *I love bananas!* Good. How many bananas do you eat per day? *One, usually.*

Well, lots of potassium in bananas, so I suggest two or three per day over the Christmas period. How do you fancy that? *That would be great!* Enjoy your bananas.

She laughs. I smile. I press the Next Patient button.

Addendum. Just six weeks later Miss J's potassium is 5.2. Yikes! Maybe she'll have to cut back a little, maybe to single small fair-trade banana b.d. How shall I break the news?

Red Roses collection curated by Alec Logan and illustrated by Helen Wilson.

45

HOW TO GET THE MOST OUT OF THE MICROBIOLOGY DEPARTMENT

Marjory Greig

The years when medical undergraduates spent several terms studying microbiology are long past. Learning the new language of bacteria was difficult enough then, but the GP trainees of today will have learned almost all they know of the subject during their Foundation Year(s) and consequently will enter general practice with a patchy and variable level of understanding. This situation is unlikely to change in the near future, but fortunately pathology services have evolved to ensure there is help available in the form of policies tailored for use in the local community. More detailed and patient-specific advice is available from your microbiologist. Most are still local, but the era of mega-labs is fast approaching and, while the service will continue to be available, no one can predict how local it will be. The following tips are compiled in an attempt to help get the best out of the service.

THE REQUEST

It's easy for microbiologists to identify new trainees: they almost always act as they did in hospital and send more test requests than established GPs. Learning when a test isn't necessary is something that will come with experience. However, it can be speeded up by reviewing the value of the result at the time of receipt compared with when you requested it and how you managed your patient at that time.

1. Know your practice specimen pick-up time(s). If it has been missed, consider whether it's worth asking the patient to deliver the specimen directly to the lab, or come in with/for a fresh specimen the next day. All specimens start to deteriorate from the time of collection.

2. Please write legibly if electronic requesting isn't available. Try to avoid anything other than the most common abbreviations. Microbiologists use the information you provide in order to try to tailor your report.

3. If you have a specific thought or query, tell/ask us so we can address it.

4. Let us know what your patient is allergic to.

5. Also say where they've travelled to recently and if any other contacts have already received a specific diagnosis.

THE REPORT

6. *Treat the patient not the result.* Just because something is there doesn't necessarily mean it's significant. Also, just because we've given you sensitivities doesn't mean you always need to give the patient antibiotics.

7. Conversely, if we don't give you sensitivities it's usually because what has grown is rarely considered a pathogen requiring antibiotics, but we are not always correct.

8. If we haven't answered your question, check if it's a final or just an interim report before chasing it up.

9. With a few exceptions, it is rarely appropriate to act on a bacteriology report a week or more after the specimen was taken. The infection will either have resolved or changed.

SPECIFIC SPECIMEN-RELATED ISSUES

10. Look at urine microscopy to assess the quality of the specimen. If there is a lot of epithelial cells (particularly in excess of white cells) then it wasn't a good mid-stream specimen and the growth probably reflects urethral contamination. Re-teach your patient the collection technique and repeat if clinically indicated.

11. Urinary dip-stick tests are a waste of time for microbiological purposes in catheterised patients. Within three days of catheter insertion the dip-stick will be positive in most patients, making the result completely uninterpretable.

12. Treatment of asymptomatic bacteriuria in the elderly can cause more harm than good. Only send specimens if the patient is symptomatic. NB Smelly urine doesn't count as a symptom.

13. Three-day therapy for a urinary tract infection (UTI) is only appropriate for non-pregnant young adult women with lower-tract symptoms only. Otherwise seven-days therapy is recommended.

14. Leg ulcers are heavily colonised. The wetter they are the more likely they will have *Pseudomonas spp.* or coliforms. Only send specimens if there is spreading cellulitis.

15. Antibiotics don't make chronic wounds/ulcers heal any faster. There is no substitute for good wound care and sorting out the underlying problem (e.g. vascular insufficiency).

16. *Gastroenteritis.* It takes several days to identify faecal pathogens from the primordial soup of bowel flora. By the time we have done so, the patient is usually well on the road to recovery. It is still worth sending specimens for epidemiological purposes though antibiotics are usually only needed if the patient has systemic symptoms.

17. Sputum samples deteriorate very rapidly and are hardly worth sending unless they can be delivered to the lab during working hours within a few hours of collection.

18. If you're requesting something unusual and can't get hold of us to ask what tube to use, 99 times out of 100, the answer will be a clotted blood sample.

THE SERVICE

19. Review the turnaround times of reports. If it's consistently slow then it needs to be discussed with the lab. For example, most urine samples should have a useful (if not a definitive) report issued within one working day of receipt. There may be good scientific reasons for a delay, but it may be a resource issue and having a customer raise it as a problem can often unlock the resources! NB This should probably be a whole GP practice rather than an individual approach.

20. Microbiology advice should be available to all GPs. We may not be immediately available but there should be the means to leave a message letting us know when is a good time to get back to you (we don't like interrupting you in surgery unless it's urgent). Please leave a contact number that bypasses the need to listen to your seasonal flu advice message.

21. Don't try to use hospital antibiotic guidelines in the community, but do remember that we often use higher doses in hospital practice than we recommend for routine use in the community. So rather than prescribing serial courses of different antibiotics in a definitely infected patient who has failed primary therapy, think about using higher doses.

22. Don't use community antibiotic policies drawn up elsewhere. Resistance patterns vary from place to place.

Finally, a word about infection control: With the increasing devolution of healthcare delivery to the community, we are seeing more infections that were previously considered 'hospital acquired' arising clearly from community practice. External scrutiny of your practice and practices will increase so keep a close eye on your aseptic technique and hand and equipment hygiene, and make sure it is impeccable at all times.

46

ON BEING A 'GOOD' GP TRAINEE
AN ETHICO-LEGAL LEXICON

Deborah Bowman

Experiences of ethico-legal education differ. You may have been trained somewhere that roped in a consultant to tell a couple of anecdotes or somewhere that replaced anatomy demonstrators with philosophers.

Whatever your experience and knowledge, ethico-legal issues are experienced differently in general practice. This lexicon offers thoughts on those differences and how to survive them.

A IS FOR AUTONOMY

Autonomy is pre-eminent amongst the four principles (see 'F is for the "four principles"') and the preoccupation of Western ethics. Meaningful autonomy is informed and facilitated by an effective therapeutic relationship. Getting to know patients in general practice means that you are better placed to foster and respect autonomy than anyone else. Well, anyone else apart from ethicists, who usually only do it in theory. Go forth and facilitate autonomy.

B IS FOR BURNOUT

It happens and you have a duty to look after yourself. Ethical practice is too often understood in relation to doctor–patient interactions, but it extends to how you treat yourself (and your colleagues).

C IS FOR CONSENT

Many ethical words begin with 'C': capacity, confidentiality, conflict of interest, consequentialism. Yet it is 'consent' that secures the slot.

Ongoing relationships with patients can be both help and hindrance when it comes to consent. Does familiarity breed consent? The ways in which familiarity might inform consent differ. First, there is familiarity with obtaining consent. Most practitioners seek consent in a way that is familiar, e.g. particular words to explain a diagnosis. Yet, a 'routine appointment' is rarely part of a patient's routine. Second, a history of working with a patient can be an asset, but can lead to short-cuts. Consent is about sharing perspectives, without unduly privileging expertise. Feeling that one knows the patient's priorities may compromise both consent and the consultation. It is easy to assume and anticipate, rather than to ask and explore. Does familiarity breed consent? Perhaps, but it may be a suboptimal version.

D IS FOR DUTY OF CARE

Put simply, a duty may arise from morality, professional guidance or the law and creates an obligation. The notion of duty as an obligation refers to another ethical word beginning with 'D': deontology. Failing to fulfil the legal duty of care renders a GP vulnerable to complaint and potentially a negligence action. Many GPs worry about duties of care when they are off-duty. The expectation is that an off-duty doctor will help according to expertise and the appropriateness of the intervention, e.g. Are you sober? Are you confident doing scary things with coat-hangers on planes?

E IS FOR EUTHANASIA

Euthanasia remains illegal and much-debated. The debate risks becoming 'stuck' and views so entrenched that arguments are rehearsed but rarely reflected upon. The first step to a mature discussion is to listen. To hear the words spoken, rather than the words imagined, and to do so without preconceived perceptions of those with whom we disagree. Reflect on your own views with reference to some of the fallacies that detract from the quality of ethical analysis. Maurice Bernstein used his blog (http://bioethicsdiscussion.blogspot.com) to explore how common fallacies hinder discussion.

F IS FOR THE 'FOUR PRINCIPLES'

First proposed by Tom Beauchamp and James Childress, this approach took the world of ethics by storm. It identifies four tenets of ethical practice: autonomy, beneficence, non-maleficence and justice. There is ethical life beyond the four principles – go find it.

G IS FOR GIFTS

'Thank you' cards and chocolates are familiar sights in surgeries. Such presents might appear to threaten little more than waistlines, but gifts can be ethically problematic. Therapeutic relationships depend on boundaries. Patients must believe that the GP practises without bias or favour. That the doctor–patient relationship is not one of friendship allows for the sharing of confidences, disinterested assessment and fair response. GPs use talk as much as tablets with the potential for transference and counter-transference. Of course, a gift may be an innocent expression of thanks, but it is impossible to know whether a gift is a token of appreciation or a sign that expectations are compromised. There is an ethical line to be drawn regarding presents. The challenge is when, how and by whom that line should be drawn. A 'yes' or 'no' to gifts is clear but is neither grounded in reflective practice nor practicable. A more nuanced approach involves considering the nature of the gift, its value, the donor and its impact on the therapeutic relationship. Surgeries could agree that all gifts will be declared, which facilitates collective consideration and minimises the potential for flattery to impede judgement.

H IS FOR HONESTY

Honesty is non-negotiable. Deceit compromises trust. Clinical teams depend on trust and patients assume that they can trust GPs. Dishonesty can become a default defence. It may be tempting to try to save your skin, but it is never acceptable and dysfunctional responses can become habitual.

I IS FOR INFALLIBLE

You aren't, so be kind to yourself. Sometimes you are more vulnerable to fallibility. Watch out for those times. There are some excellent services specialising in supporting clinicians including the Practitioner Health Programme, MedNet and the British Medical Association's (BMA) confidential counselling service.

J IS FOR JUSTICE

The requirement to treat people fairly and with proper regard for entitlements and desserts, i.e. needs differ and that should be acknowledged.

K IS FOR KINDNESS

You know it makes sense.

L IS FOR LASTING POWER OF ATTORNEY

Patients may nominate a proxy to make decisions on their behalf via a lasting power of attorney. The proxy must decide what is in the patient's best interests and life-sustaining treatment can be refused only if expressly provided in writing.

M IS FOR THE MENTAL CAPACITY ACT 2005

The statute that applies where there are questions about an individual's ability to make decisions. The nuts and bolts of capacity assessment (comprehension, retention and weighing of information and communication) derive from this act. Less well known are the ethical principles on which it is based and the requirements for involving advocacy services. As capacity is the door to self-determination, it is worth spending a bit of thinking time on.

N IS FOR NEGLIGENCE

More feared than experienced in general practice. It comprises three elements:

1. A duty of care
2. A breach, by an act or omission, falling below the standard of care expected
3. Causation, i.e. the breach resulted in loss or damage.

Neither are the courts concerned with best practice. GPs aren't 'super doctors' who never make mistakes. What is expected is that a practitioner behaves as a reasonable doctor – who is not perfect.

O IS FOR OPENNESS

Openness is valuable, particularly when something has gone wrong. The General Medical Council (GMC) expects doctors to apologise and explain when errors occur. You are not compromising your position by apologising and/or explaining. Indeed, you may prevent complaints and/or litigation.

P IS FOR PARTNERSHIP

A big question for all would-be and newly qualified GPs. The ties that bind GPs in partnership can influence care both positively and otherwise. Personal loyalty and financial conflicts of interest can arise. Practices are small businesses and the effects of disrupting the partnership are considerable. The impact of dissolving partnership is even greater. These factors will influence working lives.

Choose your partners carefully.

Q IS FOR THE QUALITY AND OUTCOMES FRAMEWORK

Who could object to quality? And linked to outcomes? Yet, the Quality and Outcomes Framework (QOF) is one of the most ethically problematic policies since, well, the last ethically problematic policy. The QOF alters the consultation and therefore the interaction between doctor and patient. That is not to say that external accountability is undesirable, but it raises questions about what is prioritised, why and by whom.

When priorities are linked to payment and reputation, one doesn't need to be an ethicist to see the potential for conflicts of interest and diversion of resources. Applied unthinkingly, the QOF may compromise 'quality'. Helping the vulnerable, who do not fit under any QOF category, may be providing a lifeline to a patient, but as far as the QOF is concerned it is invisible work. What's more, it privileges those that are already pretty privileged. The practices that serve marginalised and hard-to-engage populations suffer. Those who cannot afford to invest in 'buffing' records because they are too busy providing health care also suffer. QOF is an ethical issue. How the profession engages with it is a moral question for all GPs. How individuals respond when the computer butts in to another sensitive consultation is a daily ethical challenge. What is your response?

Incidentally, the ethical issues relating to the QOF are not dissimilar to those that arise in relation to the Quality Adjusted Life Year (QALY). QALYs, much-loved by the National Institute for Health and Care Excellence (NICE), weigh the effect of an intervention on a life. Many will spot ethical difficulties. QALYs assume that quality of life can and should be measured objectively. They may be ageist in that life expectancy is prioritised. Many interventions do not have a QALY value. QALYs work at a population level, generalising about patients, diseases and interventions. Pre-existing disabilities influence QALY assessments leading to 'double jeopardy' for some. Finally, QALYs focus on outcome rather than need: those who are likely best to benefit are treated instead of those who most need treatment.

Apart from that, they're great.

R IS FOR RESOURCES

Where 'first come first served' is not appropriate, access to treatment may be rationed according to need or quality of life. Alas, that is easy to write and hard to do. GPs are increasingly involved in decisions about resources – don't forget the ethical dimension.

S IS FOR SUPEREROGATION

An action that goes beyond what is required by duty: an ethical super-hero if you will.

T IS FOR TRUST

It is essential. It is earned. It is easily compromised or lost.

U IS FOR UNCERTAINTY

Any discussion of general practice will address uncertainty. Renée Fox argued that there are two types of uncertainty. The first refers to the limitations of an individual GP's knowledge; the second describes the intrinsically limited nature of medical knowledge itself. Uncertainty is inherent in the 'risk sink' of medicine. You are not alone in the sink. Seek the experience and wisdom of others as you take your first steps in an uncertain world. It will become more comfortable.

V IS FOR VALUES AND VIRTUES

Fed up with the four principles? Try these approaches to ethics instead.

W IS FOR WHISTLEBLOWER

Whistleblowers are protected under the Public Interest Disclosure Act 1998. The GMC states that a doctor who has concerns must act to protect patients. Yet, the experience of whistleblowing can be painful and difficult. Know the process for raising concerns in your area and seek advice early. The organisation Public Concern at Work is a great resource.

X IS FOR XENICAL

And other drugs that raise fundamental questions about what the NHS exists to do and how it should do it. Talk to your colleagues. You'll be surprised at the range of responses.

Y IS FOR YOUNG

The basics are often overlooked. For example, most GPs understand the significance of Gillick competency as a functional not chronological assessment, but continue to have policies about the age at which young people can be seen alone. Likewise, consent forms for teenagers having vaccinations routinely seek parental consent. Does your practice reflect what you learnt to pass exams?

Z IS FOR ZEALOT

Enthusiasm, spirit and passion can be helpful in ethico-legal decision making; zealotry rarely is. Keep it for the football team/musical tastes/*Strictly Come Dancing* contestants.

47

RASH DECISIONS
DERMATOLOGY IN GENERAL PRACTICE

Tony Foley

From your very first day as a GP you will encounter skin disease.

It may be the patient's primary reason for attending, or may be the customary parting shot of, 'Oh by the way, doc, will you have a quick look at this?' You will be the privileged purveyor of a vast array of lesions and rashes as you commence your apprenticeship in itch-craft.

Dermatology consultations constitute up to 15% of a GP's workload, so a degree of proficiency is preferable, if not essential.

Some describe the dermatology marmite-factor – you either love it or hate it. Others disparagingly bemoan, 'If they're not on a steroid cream, put them on it; if they are, then take them off it. If it's wet make it dry; if it's dry make it wet.'

However, dermatology can be fascinating, even rewarding.

Sleuth-like, one can piece together the clues. They're all there.

Dermatology has its own proud language and it's well worth learning to speak that tongue. Using the correct terminology will direct you to a diagnosis and will improve your referral letters.

Dermatology is important. Skin cancers are increasing in frequency. Litigation for missed melanomas is increasing too. Skin disease can weigh heavily on patients, most especially on vulnerable young shoulders. What is mild acne to you may not be mild acne to them.

Acne may leave indelible scars, physically and psychologically.

Some of the following tips should help you to avoid making inappropriate rash decisions. I have made many.

› 'Wear sunscreen. If I could offer you only one tip for the future sunscreen would be it.'[1] Your dermatological credibility will be destroyed by your luminous glow.

› Take a detailed skin history. Years spent in the Tropics will raise your suspicion of a skin cancer. Be nosy about what the patient does at work.

› Seek out patterns: the Christmas tree distribution of pityriasis rosea, the symmetry of psoriasis, and the linear belt of shingles. The history of the herald spot harks the diagnosis of misnomered pityriasis versicolor plaque.

› Debunk the myths. Acne is not caused by a poor diet. Scabies is not caused by dirt. Psoriasis is not contagious. Scarlatina isn't scarlet fever. Ringworm has nothing to do with worms.

› Be discerning when choosing lotions and potions. Creams dry the skin. Ointments moisturise the skin.

› To confirm psoriasis on examination, hum 'Head, elbows, knees and nails, knees and nails …'. Remember to ask about groins too as some patients are a little shy.

› Lichen simplex is characterised by well-defined itchy plaques, with increased skin markings on the occiput, ankles, elbows and genitalia. Choose your words carefully when explaining the cause of this: scratching by the patient him or herself. This is easier said than done.

› Don't ponderously observe a suspected keratoacanthoma, waiting for it to regress. Refer. It may be an aggressive squamous cell carcinoma.

› For itchy elbows, knees and sacrum, with papules and plaques, check bloods for coeliac antibodies. It may be dermatitis herpetiformis.

› Consider psoriasis for a non-resolving groin rash treated as tinea cruris. Cue, 'Head, elbows, knees and nails …'.

› Malodorous sweaty feet with pitted heels and forefeet in a trainer-wearing teenager may be pitted keratolysis – especially if they've already tried antifungal creams and powders with no success. Keep the feet dry. Discourage trainers and nylon or cotton socks. Encourage bringing spare socks to school and sandal-wearing. Good luck with that! Prescribe topical Fucidin, clindamycin lotion or oral erythromycin.[2,3]

› For unilateral nipple 'eczema', not responding to moisturisers and topical steroid, think Paget's disease of the nipple. Refer to a breast surgeon.

› Eczematous or blistered shins on an older person may be varicose or discoid eczema. However, remember to consider bullous pemphigoid.

› Avoid patient anger and poor compliance. Explain that actinic keratoses will look worse before they look better when prescribing topical 3% diclofenac gel, 5FU or imiquimod.

> What lies beneath? Don't monitor a cutaneous horn. A squamous cell carcinoma may lurk at its base.

> *Facial rashes.* For papules and pustules, with no comedones, consider rosacea instead of acne vulgaris. Tiny red papules and pustules around the mouth, sparing of the skin immediately around the lips, indicate perioral dermatitis. Ask, but don't accuse, regarding injudicious topical steroid use.

> You've been unsuccessfully treating a psoriasis plaque on the lower leg of an older lady with calcipotriol. Reassess. Is it Bowen's disease?

> *Fungal toenails; onychomycosis.* Don't prescribe oral agents unless you have mycological confirmation. Let the nails grow out and then enjoy scraping and scooping the moist debris from underneath the nails. Advise that it may take a second sample to confirm the fungus. Consider whether you need to treat at all. Could the crumbling dystrophic nails be psoriatic?

> *Topical steroids.* Know the strengths and choose according to diagnosis and skin location. The flexures absorb the most. With atopic dermatitis, avoid frightening already wary parents by advising sparing hydrocortisone use. The more common mistake is to under-treat.

> Learn to punch-biopsy, but use it sparingly. Don't biopsy a pigmented lesion. Have a system for following up on biopsy results.

> Never worry about a funny looking mole. Refer now; don't wait and review.

> Impetigo is very contagious. Look for the glazed honey-crusted lesions. It's probably wise not to send your own impetiginised child to crèche. It's never good to be the source of an outbreak. (For your own entertainment, explore the etymology of *Staphylococcus aureus*.)

> Scalp ringworm is mostly seen in children. Send plucked hair and scale for mycology. Remember to explain first that you're going to pull their hair. Ask about a pet and get the vet involved.

> *Facial shingles.* If there are lesions on the side of the nose (Hutchinson's sign) then the eye is likely to become involved and you should arrange ophthalmology referral. Be clear on the shingles–chickenpox axis. Learn to explain it clearly. You will be asked and challenged.

> *Atopic eczema.* Moisturise, moisturise, moisturise. Choose a moisturiser the patient likes. Then he or she will use it. Advise application 30 times a day! Ban soap.

> Cryotherapy is a useful weapon, but don't mass-destruct. Warts, seborrhoeic keratoses and actinic keratoses are ideal targets. Never aim at anything pigmented. Be extra-careful with shins that are prone to ulceration.

› *Mea culpa*. Remember iatrogenic rashes from your well-intentioned prescription.

› No, it's not the washing-powder! Discard that question in your interrogation.

› Have http://dermnetnz.org/ and http://emedicine.medscape.com/dermatology in your favourites menu. Seek National Institute for Health and Care Excellence (NICE) guidance. Use www.bad.org.uk for patient information leaflets and encourage self-help groups, such as www.psoriasis-association.org.uk.

› Invest in a camera and magnifying glass. Consider dermatoscopy – go on a course. You're a skin detective now.

But, above all, remember the sunscreen!

REFERENCES

1. Schmich M. Advice, like youth, probably just wasted on the young. *Chicago Tribune*. 1 June 1997.

2. Pitted keratolysis. www.dermnetnz.org/bacterial/pitted-keratolysis.html [accessed March 2014].

3. English JC, III. Pitted keratolysis. http://emedicine.medscape.com/article/1053078-overview [accessed March 2014].

RINGWORM

'I have a rash', said my patient, a thirty-something accountant. And she had, anterior chest wall, patchy itchy red rings, three or four centimetres in diameter. The diagnosis was obvious – a fungal infection, tinea corporis, popularly known as ringworm. Nothing to do with worms – 'ringworm' on account of appearance, not cause. I love diagnosing ringworm. It's easy to spot, treatment is simple, and invariably effective.

'This is …' I began, then paused. I remembered an earlier consultation, over 20 years previously, at our branch surgery some miles away. Another case of ringworm, this time a young girl, with her anxious mum. 'That's ringworm!' I pronounced, with insufficiently disguised relish. And my poor young patient burst into tears. A lesson learned.

Back to the present.

'This is', I began again, 'a fungal infection. A bit like athlete's foot. Sometimes we call it ringworm. Nothing to do with worms of course. It's the ring-like appearance. But I've always been wary of calling it ringworm since I upset a patient many years ago. …'

'That was me', said my patient.

An epiphany. I had hoped for 20 years to see that girl again. I was able to apologise for my gaucheness, to tell her how much I'd learned from my mistake, how many times I'd recounted the story whilst teaching medical students and trainee GPs. We shook hands warmly and off she went with her prescription.

(From *Foreword*, Black Bag Moon, *Radcliffe Medical Press 2012, with permission.*)

Red Roses *collection curated by Alec Logan and illustrated by Helen Wilson.*

48

EVERYTHING YOU EVER WANTED TO KNOW ABOUT NEUROLOGY BUT WERE AFRAID TO ASK

Kingsley Poole

Neurological problems in general practice can cause much anxiety.

As a GP you have less than ten minutes to sort out the problem and the patient usually has three other things he or she wants to talk to you about, the practice nurse needs you to check an ear, reception needs a script signed and more often than not you've missed coffee. Here are some tips to help you assess the neurological problem within a few minutes and get the basics right.

As any neurologist will tell you, 'It's all in the history.' Don't get too worried about the finer points of neurological examination technique – as long as you can take a decent history you can get nearly everything.

The basic symptoms that you will come across as a GP are: *headache, fits and faints, tremor* and *dizziness*.

HEADACHE

The most common neurological conditions are migraine and tension or 'chronic daily' headache (see Table 48.1, below).

TABLE 48.1: HOW TO TELL THE DIFFERENCE IN YOUR TEN-MINUTE SLOT

Chronic daily	Migraine
No aura	Can have aura (20%)
>50% days	Variable frequency
Usually both sides	Hemicranial in 60%
Usually doesn't vomit	Nausea and may vomit

Note: there can be overlap between these two types of headache – 'chronic daily headache/migraine overlap'.

Men with tension headache often say things like 'Ibuprofen doesn't touch it', 'It needs sorting' and 'I need a brain scan'. Check their fundi to be on the safe side but in my neurology colleague's 15 years as a consultant he had *never* seen a brain tumour presenting as a chronic daily headache alone. That is not to say that it doesn't happen – just that it is rare. Interestingly, scans are abnormal in about a third of cases anyway. Radiologists seem to write what appears to be a teasing sentence about these incidental artefactual findings.

You can look up migraine prophylaxis in your local guidelines, but amitriptyline (10 mg nocte) tends to be a good starter for either type of headache. If need be you can slowly notch up the dose. I also issue them with a set of relaxation exercises to try. Other things to discuss would be taking a careful drug history – lots can give headaches and watch out for codeine headaches. Look for and treat any depression.

DANGEROUS HEADACHES

Meningitis. Temperature? Unwell? Exhibiting the classic signs? Make sure you know what to do!

Temporal arteritis. They say never in anyone under 50 years' old; ESR is over 50; it can be occipital; there can be jaw claudication; the patient can have systemic malaise. Check your local protocol but if there are no visual symptoms it will likely involve steroids and a temporal artery biopsy within a week. If there are visual symptoms, use higher-dose steroids and consider talking to the ophthalmologist/rheumatologist on-call.

Subarachnoid haemorrhage. This can be indicated by any severe headache that presents suddenly. If it literally wasn't there a moment ago and the next moment it was, you send the patient to A&E or the medics and that's it. Don't spend ten minutes examining and agonising – with that history no one can argue that the patient doesn't need a scan. The pick-up rate is about 1 in 20 but it's worth it. The medical defence people would want to know why you didn't refer.

Subdural haematoma. The signs and symptoms are: usually elderly post-fall; headache; worse on straining; drowsiness; and subacute decline in cognition. Gait can be affected but often there are no focal signs.

FITS AND FAINTS

The bit they told you in medical school, about taking an accurate history, was in fact correct. The best test for epilepsy is an eyewitness account ('and whenever the spirit seizes him, it convulses him, and he foams at the mouth and grinds his teeth', Mark 9:18).

If a fit is suspected, tell the patient to stop driving, document it in the notes and tell him or her to inform the Driver and Vehicle Licensing Agency (DVLA). A very helpful document is the DVLA's *At a Glance Guide* (available at www.dft.gov.uk/dvla/medical/aag.aspx). And refer.

Most importantly, tell the patient to either take a witness with him or her to the outpatient appointment or bring in a written description of what the witness saw. The patient may be about to lose his or her job because of having to stop driving – the best way that epilepsy can be diagnosed with any degree of accuracy is from the eyewitness.

TABLE 48.2: FIT VERSUS FAINT

Fit	Faint
Often no warning	Usually a warning
Not postural	Usually postural
Can be prolonged	Usually short (less than one minute)
Post ictal	Quick recovery

PARKINSON'S DISEASE

I have a prized possession – an autographed picture of Muhammad Ali standing over a defeated, prostrate opponent. People look at it and say, 'Where's the signature?' I point to a tiny jagged scrawl and they look incredulous. The signature is tiny – 'micrographic' – one of the classic signs. Before it gets to this stage, the writing can look shaky and erratic; the patient will often have trouble drawing an inward spiral. The other give-away features of Parkinson's are:

› decreased arm swing, which is often overlooked. Watch the patient's arms as he or she walks up and down the corridor. One will swing less than the other and it can be very obvious

› bradykinesia – best tested with finger taps (biting movements between the fingers and thumb)

› rigidity – best tested at the wrist

› tremor – you can get the patient to close his or her eyes and count backwards to bring it out.

TABLE 48.3: DISTINGUISHING PARKINSON'S FROM ESSENTIAL TREMOR

Parkinson's	Essential tremor
Unilateral	Usually bilateral
Resting tremor	Usually postural
Short history	Gradual
Idiopathic	Autosomal dominant – you can draw fancy family trees
Refer	Reassure, beta-blockers

DIZZINESS

This is often benign paroxysmal positional vertigo (BPPV). The patient will typically tell you that he or she becomes dizzy when turning over in bed or looking up. You need to know the Hallpike test and the Epley manoeuvre. The Epley manoeuvre, by which I mean a simple twist and turn sequence, can cure someone dramatically and rapidly.

Useful video clips can be found on the web to learn the manoeuvre. Or ask your trainer to show you. If your trainer doesn't know how to perform it, then learn it yourself and teach him or her. It will save lots of referrals and can be very satisfying (for you and the patient)!

FINAL WORD

Good luck. Remember it's really not that important to know how to do a perfect neurology exam. However, if you are having trouble with the ankle jerks get the patient to kneel on the chair with his or her feet dangling down – then tap the patient's Achilles tendons. This works nine times out of ten.

Remember: If in doubt, ask someone. You never stop learning.

49

CHILD AND ADOLESCENT MENTAL HEALTH (CAMHS) IN A TEN-MINUTE CONSULTATION

James Woollard and Matt Burkes

It's the stuff of GPs' nightmares. You're actually running to time and then see on the screen the name of a teenager you don't know. The admin staff have annotated 'depressed' next to the patient's name. You have ten minutes to resolve this complex situation. Half an hour later, the waiting room is stacking up, you've got the beginnings of a stress ulcer, the child's parent is crying or angry (occasionally both) and the patient still hasn't said anything.

CAMHS in a ten-minute consultation?

Can't be done.

However, you need to pick up some skills to handle this increasingly common presentation. Remember that CAMHS is an underfunded specialty, so help through referral may take a long time to arrive. Here are some things to consider while you wait.

SEEING A YOUNG PERSON

First, don't panic. It won't help. The young person will be highly anxious and he or she needs you to be able to provide help.

If the young person comes with his or her parent and doesn't seem to be talking much, suggest that the parent leaves the room. This may make the young person more comfortable and able to disclose vital information, including the possibility of abuse, which may significantly alter your management plan and prevent harm. Overall you will save time even if it appears to take longer.

Sometimes it can be difficult for young people to answer 'Why'-type questions. These are often questions they get asked repeatedly by anxious parents. A 'Why' question can often result in an 'I don't know', which gets no one anywhere and is generally frustrating for all. Instead ask 'How' questions. Imagine that 'Why' might involve disclosing that the patient's parents are hitting each other or that the patient has had a harmful sexual experience – this could be too painful or embarrassing to talk about. 'Why' can also feel blaming.

BOX 49.1: EXAMPLES OF 'HOW' QUESTIONS

- How are you feeling? How is this affecting you?
- How are you coping at home? At school?
- How do you think I/your mum/your dad/the school can help?
- How is life outside of school? Friends? Any interests?

MAPPING SYMPTOMS AND EFFECTS ON FUNCTION

- How does your anxiety/mood affect you at school?
- How do your parents help you manage your anxiety/mood?
- How does your family life make it hard for you to manage your mood/anxiety/voices?

LOOKING FOR RESILIENCE

- How does self-harm help? How is it a problem?
- How could you manage without self-harm?
- On a day when you choose not to self-harm, how do you manage that?
- How do you look after yourself?

Your job is to establish an initial sense of how affected the young person's mental health is. Get young people to rate their mood, anxiety and energy levels out of 10 (10 being the best/highest and 1 being the lowest/worst), both currently and in the past when they were well. This is a quick way of establishing the change in their health and it is readily accessible to young people. Again it doesn't involve 'Why' questions. The vital things to establish are:

1. Risk to self – cutting is frequently a coping or relief mechanism in young people. Have their thoughts changed or escalated to more suicidal/dangerous behaviour including drug use

2. Are they at risk from someone else: their parents; other family members; other young people? Child protection is paramount.

Are their parents aware of their needs or risks? Remember that asking questions doesn't kill young people; not asking questions does. Your own embarrassment or awkwardness should not get in the way of asking questions. It wouldn't if you were asking them about their defecation so it shouldn't with exploring their cutting. Get over yourself; young people need us to be braver than that.

Using 'problem-free talk' can also be useful in establishing dialogue with a young person who is finding it difficult to talk about his or her problems. Although this may take a few minutes it might help everyone to relax enough to be able to talk and prevent prolonged staring at the floor in mute silence, and the young person not saying anything either. Problem-free talking is an example of a technique from solution-focused therapy and you may wish to read more about this (www.brief.org.uk).

LOCAL SERVICES FOR POSSIBLE REFERRALS

There will be a CAMHS team that has responsibility for caring for young people in your area. Some of them will only go up to 16 years' old, while others will see young people until they are 18. There may also be other more specific local arrangements about referral criteria. Get hold of your local CAMHS team's phone number. This can generally be found on the website of the overarching mental health trust, or you can check the letters of another patient who is being seen by the CAMHS team.

Phone the local team and establish its referral criteria for age, GP, address and school. Establish whether there is a referral form you need to fill in and get the team to send you one for your file.

Commonly a CAMHS team will have a duty worker for each working day. He or she will be able to discuss referrals with you.

Establish whether there are Tier 2 services. Sometimes known as early-intervention services, these are often psychology and nursing led. They often work through schools and see young people who do not necessarily have the mental health needs for the Tier 3 CAMHS service but who still require supportive psychological input. Table 49.1 (below) describes the different tiers.

TABLE 49.1: THE FOUR TIERS OF CAMHS

Tier 1	Universal services consisting of all primary care agencies, e.g. general medical practice, school nursing, health visiting
Tier 2	A combination of some specialist CAMHS and some community-based services including primary mental health workers
Tier 3	Specialist multidisciplinary outpatient CAMHS teams
Tier 4	Highly specialised inpatient CAMHS units and intensive community treatment services

Source: adapted from Integrated Care Pathways for Mental Health.[1]

Make a note of all this information and keep it in your desk drawer or make a note on your phone (in case you are on an emergency call or using another office).

If you are going to be working in an area for a prolonged period then it may be worth establishing a relationship with the senior staff of the local CAMHS team. This can help to facilitate the care of the often complex cases found in child and adolescent mental health.

Knowing the contact details of the local social services team for children and families is also important.

Get to know the local schools and school nurses. Understand the Common Assessment Framework (CAF) and Team Around the Child (TAC) frameworks. Know how these systems work and how to instigate them. They are there to make your life easier by involving a multidisciplinary team in the care of children. Find out when the key meetings take place. You may not have time to attend but it would be useful to know what the outcomes are.

Get to know the local counselling services and drop-in centres. These can provide excellent support for troubled teens. They do this on a daily basis, have more experience and time than you, and are almost certainly 'cooler' to adolescents than you. Use them.

LINKING PATIENTS TO THE APPROPRIATE SERVICES

There are a number of possible outcomes to your consultation:

1. Emergency assessment in A&E for medical treatment and/or psychiatric assessment out of hours. If sending to A&E, contact the paediatric team for under-16s. Local arrangements for 16–18-year-olds may vary

2. Phone call to local CAMHS service to discuss/arrange urgent referral

3. Urgent paper referral to local CAMHS service

4. Non-urgent referral to local CAMHS service

5. Referral to Tier 2 service if available and appropriate

6. Suggestion to self-refer to local youth counselling service if available

7. Wait and review – arrange to see young person again

8. Referral to social services, particularly in the case of child protection concerns.

Generally, in working hours phone the local CAMHS service first. In out of hours phone the local mental health trust or acute hospital and ask for the duty psychiatry worker covering the local A&E.

NAUGHTY CHILDREN

You will often be asked to refer/'cure' naughty children. Parents have often checked on Google and will have a range of diagnoses already covered. It should be obvious, but do not refer these children to CAMHS unless you think they have mental health problems.

There are many reasons for children to appear as if they are difficult to manage. Poor or insufficient parenting could be a significant factor. Explore whether the difficulties exist at school or at home. Explore whether the difficulties are only with certain people.

Know about your local provision for parenting classes. This may be the solution to many cases.

Their 'naughtiness' may reflect a problem within the family system – divorce, separation, drug use, abuse, domestic violence, sibling difficulties, ill health … it could go on. Be aware that the child can be just a 'scapegoat'.

EATING DISORDER

Anorexia is lethal; never forget that. Any young person should be asked about his or her eating and if you suspect an eating disorder you may wish to consider urgent medical assessment. The patient could present with more medical problems such as dizziness. BUT the patient could also have a medical problem that is causing him or her to lose weight. It's worth arranging a comprehensive screen of blood tests and ECG to rule this out and to check for indications of biochemical disturbances associated with eating disorders.

QUESTIONNAIRE AND SCALES

These can be useful for young people and parents to take away and complete. They could help you get a clearer picture of a young person's difficulties, particularly for a patient who finds it hard to articulate his or her problems and the parents aren't aware. A commonly used scale is the Strengths and Difficulties Questionnaire (SDQ).[2]

It gives an overall probability for any disorder and a breakdown to emotional, hyperactive/inattention, conduct, peer relations problems, and prosocial behaviour. This will help your referral, clarifying the difficulties for you and the CAMHS team receiving it. It is available in many languages and online at www.sdqinfo.org.

FINAL THOUGHTS

Is the patient in a gang? Is he or she being exploited by the gang, or used as a honey trap to draw in other young people to the gang via social media networks?

IN ALL CASES consider the young person's digital worlds: social media use, involvement in immersive, virtual game worlds, use of text and instant messaging in personal relationships, and research on the web in terms of self-harm and suicide. The sending of indecent self-images to partners and peers is increasingly common and often a source of bullying and distress if the images are distributed through a social network, which can happen very rapidly.

BUT remember that the internet and social networks can also be a significant source of readily available support. Familiarise yourself with the appropriate resources that young people can access online and via their phone. Moderated use is the key. Have the list pinned to your surgery room wall for quick reference.

Is the patient taking drugs, including legal highs? Has he or she bought any medication on the web?

Remember: Sometimes a tricky first consultation is a bridgehead to more useful sessions further down the line.

BOX 49.2: RESOURCES FOR SUPPORTING YOUNG PEOPLE WITH MENTAL HEALTH DIFFICULTIES

TRAINING AROUND FIRST AID FOR MENTAL HEALTH PROBLEMS

- Youth Mental Health First Aid England, www.mhfaengland.org/first-aid-courses/first-aid-youth.

CRISIS, SUICIDE AND SELF-HARM

- Papyrus, www.papyrus-uk.org, 0800 068 41 41.
- Samaritans, www.samaritans.org, 0845 790 90 90.
- ChildLine, www.childline.org.uk, 0800 1111.

GENERAL INFORMATION

- Royal College of Psychiatrists, www.rcpsych.ac.uk.
- YoungMinds, www.youngminds.org.uk.
- Medicines for Children, www.medicinesforchildren.org.uk.
- MindFull, www.mindfull.org.

PARENT SUPPORT

- Family Lives provides general support for families. See http://familylives.org.uk/.
- YoungMinds also has a parent helpline. See address above.

SPECIFIC DISORDERS AND PROBLEMS

- OCD action, www.ocdaction.org.uk.
- Beat (eating disorders), www.b-eat.co.uk.
- Anxiety UK, www.anxietyuk.org.uk.
- National Autistic Society, www.autism.org.uk.
- Hearing Voices, www.hearing-voices.org. Hearing Voices Network provides support and information specifically for young people.

BULLYING

- Cyber bullying, www.beatbullying.org.
- Kidscape, www.kidscape.org.uk/.

CONCERNS ABOUT ABUSE

- National Society for the Prevention of Cruelty to Children, http://www.nspcc.org.uk/help, 0808 800 5000.

ANTI-STIGMA CAMPAIGN

- Time to Change, www.time-to-change.org.uk/youngpeople.

REFERENCES

1. Integrated Care Pathways for Mental Health. CAMH service tiers. www.icptoolkit.org/child_and_adolescent_pathways/about_icps/camh_service_tiers.aspx [accessed March 2014].
2. Goodman R. The Strengths and Difficulties Questionnaire: a research note. *Journal of Child Psychology and Psychiatry* 1997; **38(5)**: 581–6.

50

REMOTE AND RURAL MEDICINE

David Hogg and Simon van Lieshout

Over a fifth of the UK's population lives in rural or remote areas, which cover 95% of the UK's landmass. Unique opportunities exist across this spectrum of rurality to practise generalism at the very core. From farming areas and the need to consider zoonoses such as orf and brucellosis, to remote island practice meaning that 'you are it' – at least until a helicopter can get to you – rural and remote practice is the best kept secret of general practice. It is one that the majority of trainees find rewarding and enjoyable.

Of course, to a large extent rural general practice is general practice. There's no knowing what will come in the door next, and this makes it continually fun and interesting. However, there are specific challenges and peculiarities in rural practice, and it helps to understand these before ordering the leather elbow-pads and the border collie.

YOUR COMMUNITY

You'll quickly become known as the local doctor, which carries certain privileges and expectations. This will be similar to the way in which the community also knows its nurses, vet, dentist and mechanic. Take the time to get to know how your community works, and put aside any frustrations until you understand why certain idiosyncrasies exist. Personalities shine out from small communities, and there will be plenty of local history with which you won't be familiar. Local people will want to trust you, as a skilled practitioner as well as a confidant. If you can offer that trust, you will find much support and reward in return. Maintaining personal and professional boundaries can be challenging, but this is the case for many other people living in a close-knit community. Take advice from friends and senior colleagues, but don't feel that you need to become a nomad to avoid seeing patients in a social context – that is inevitable.

THE MEDICINE

You can't know everything, so keep this in mind. However, rural practice demands an extended generalist knowledge, and nowhere is this more apparent than emergency care. Good preparation can yield confidence and competency in managing even the most complex of emergencies. Develop a competent ABCDE approach to medical emergencies – including paediatrics, trauma and obstetrics. Thinking laterally becomes part of the job, and treatment decisions are heavily influenced by your own skills, transport availability (ambulance, ferry, helicopter, etc.) and patients' wishes.

Your training may include dispensing medication, working in the community hospital and travelling to more remote branch surgeries. At these points, reflect on how lucky you are to be able to use *all* your training experience, of course while working within your limitations. If you still have some hospital training to go through, use rural practice as a 'passport' to get extra experience – whether it's aspirating pleural effusions, carrying out minor surgery, assisting with childbirths or setting up syringe drivers. Consider attending a British Association for Immediate Care (BASICS) course, especially if pre-hospital care is part of your on-call commitment.

ON-CALL

Inevitably, many rural areas still rely on local GPs to provide out-of-hours care. Many different models exist. Discuss with your trainer what equipment and drugs are required for this: ultimately it is up to you to decide if you need to keep Syntometrine, a defibrillator or intravenous fluids in your car.

› Find out what mobile network works best – and switch if you can. Rural areas are notorious for poor reception, so at least ensure that you have a good landline connection early on. Make sure people know how to contact you if there are interesting things happening.

› Get to know your paramedics and community nurses as they can be incredibly helpful and useful when things get busy.

› Find out about other emergency services in case you need their help. Mountain rescue, coastguard and lifeboat teams are often keen to get local medical input. If you feel competent to do so, this can also be a useful way of getting to know people.

› Establish good links with your local receiving hospital (you may have already worked with senior colleagues there). They can be very useful for phone advice, and being able to put names to faces is great when calling about worrying presentations.

› Remember that, as a trainee, you shouldn't be working without back-up. Once your trainer is happy for you to work alone, make sure that you know the contact details of colleagues who can assist if necessary.

TRAINING IN A RURAL AREA

Rural practice offers superb GP experience for students and trainees. It is usually easy to find material for case discussions and patients who are willing to be videoed. However, it can be difficult to maintain contact with your peers, especially if they are situated in urban practices and have easier access to events such as study days. Make the most of physical trips to these events, for example socialising or doing Clinical Skills Assessment (CSA) practice with colleagues while you are all together.

› Get to know what Skype/videoconferencing (VC) networks are available. If it's difficult to get away for any study days, try to encourage the use of VC to keep you involved remotely. Your trainer will be able to tell you what has worked for previous trainees.

› Keep focused on the RCGP curriculum. Ensure that you are covering the core elements such as consultation skills, reflective practice and good chronic disease management. It's easy to become distracted with so many other things going on.

› RuralGP.com offers information and access to email groups.

THE REST

Rural areas are usually outstanding places in which to live and work. Get to know your local area, be it on foot, on a bike, in a canoe or from a hang-glider. Be prepared for the interest from friends and family in visiting – even more so if you have a room or two to spare! If you're on an island and dependent on ferries, get to know the best websites for weather forecasts and travel information. Take time to relax, and keep in touch with friends and family regularly in order to maintain a sense of perspective.

FANCY MAKING IT A CAREER?

Rural practice is one area that continues to attract newly qualified GPs for a whole range of reasons. Some like the ability to maintain elements of hospital work, as the community hospital is a core part of some rural jobs. Others like the easy access to the outdoors: mountain bike tracks, sailing centres, lochs to canoe or hills to climb. Others might find it easier to practise the 'continuity of care' that attracted them to general practice in the first place; smaller list sizes (not necessarily with a reduced workload) mean that getting to know your patients is not only easier, but also more important.

A number of options exist for life after the Certificate of Completion of Training (CCT). Locums can be an excellent way of seeing many different rural practices, with stunning scenery to match. There are some schemes such as the Rural Fellowship in Scotland, which offer time to acquire additional skills. Ask your trainer for advice and keep an eye on sources such as BMJ Careers.

FURTHER READING

> Baird AG. Why should I become a rural GP? *InnovAiT* 2008; **1(12)**: 820–5.

> Gillies JCM. Remote and rural practice. *British Medical Journal* 1998; **317**: S2–7166.

> Hogg D, Lunan R. The medical bag. *InnovAiT* 2010; **3(8)**: 479–82.

> Sparrow M. *Country Doctor: tales of a rural GP*. London: Robinson, 2002.

RESOURCES

> BASICS England, www.basics.org.uk/.

> BASICS Scotland, www.basics-scotland.org.uk/.

> Centre for Rural Health, www.abdn.ac.uk/crh.

> Dispensing Doctors' Association, www.dispensingdoctor.org/.

> Institute of Rural Health, www.irh.org.uk/.

> RCGP Rural Forum, www.rcgp.org.uk/rcgp_rural_forum.aspx.

> Remote Practitioners Association of Scotland, www.ruralgp.com/wp/rpas.

> Rural Fellowships (Scotland), www.ruralgp.com/wp/prepare/fellowship/.

> RuralGP Blog, www.ruralgp.com/.

> RuralGP Network, http://groups.google.co.uk/group/ruralgp.

THE GAELIC? THE GAZA

From Germany originally, I fell in love with the wild west of Scotland and did my trainee post on Mull. A few words of Gaelic went a long way. *Fliuch* (wet) gave you some street credibility and described the weather on an almost daily basis. Thawing out in front of the fire of a remote cottage with a hot cup of tea I realised that I must have been picking up the singing lilt of my native Gaelic-speaking patient when he asked me, 'Doctor, are you having the Gaelic?' 'No,' I replied, 'but I am having the German!' 'Aye, aye,' he nodded slowly, 'that would do.'

Then I worked as an anaesthetist in Gaza. Arabic was a wee problem, but as my patients spent most of the time asleep I could usually keep it very simple.

During recovery almost all problems could be solved with two commands:

Chud nefes! (Take a deep breath!)

Ifta tumak! (Open your mouth!)

On my first *Chud nefes!* nothing happened. I asked Mohammed, the anaesthetic nurse, for help. So he shouts *CHUD NEFES!* at a hundred decibels. What a big breath!

The British are right about foreign languages. If anyone doesn't understand you, Shout Louder!!!

Red Roses *collection curated by Alec Logan and illustrated by Helen Wilson.*

51

THE NEW THERAPEUTICS
TEN COMMANDMENTS

John S. Yudkin

› Thou shalt treat according to level of risk rather than level of risk factor.

› Thou shalt exercise caution when adding drugs to existing polypharmacy.

› Thou shalt consider benefits of drugs as proven only by hard endpoint studies.

› Thou shalt not bow down to surrogate endpoints, for these are but graven images.

› Thou shalt not worship Treatment Targets, for these are but the creations of committees.

› Thou shalt apply a pinch of salt to Relative Risk Reductions, regardless of *P*-values, for the population of their provenance may bear little relationship to thy daily clientele.

› Thou shalt honour the Numbers Needed to Treat, for therein rest the clues to patient-relevant information and to treatment costs.

› Thou shalt not see drug reps or covet an Educational Symposium in a luxury setting.

› Thou shalt share decisions on treatment options with the patient in the light of estimates of the individual's likely risks and benefits.

› Honour the elderly patient, for although this is where the greatest levels of risk reside, so do the greatest hazards of many treatments.

52

TEN COMMANDMENTS FOR TESTING

Michael Power and Greg Fell

SCOPE

'Test' includes questions in history taking, physical examination, laboratory tests, imaging investigations, diagnostic procedures and therapeutic trials.

Tests can be used to rule in/rule out a diagnosis (*in people with symptoms*), screen for a disease or risk factor (*in people without symptoms*), assess risk or prognosis, or monitor treated people for adverse effects, disease activity or response to treatment.

TEN COMMANDMENTS FOR HIGH-QUALITY, HIGH-VALUE TESTING

1. *Thou shalt be a faithful advocate for your patient and a dutiful steward of NHS resources. Remember: If it is not sustainable, it is not equitable*

Thou shalt not bow down before marketing representatives, even those bearing unrestricted educational grants.

Thou shalt ensure that each test contributes to the quality of the care you provide and services you manage. Thou shalt consider if each test has a positive net value and if it is affordable. When assessing value, thou shalt not overlook 'downstream' benefits and harms that take a while to become manifest.

If a cheaper test would be as useful, thou shalt use it. Thou shalt not covet thy neighbour's graven images (i.e. PET scanner, fMRI scanner, high-resolution ultrasound scanner), nor his micro-array genetic tests, nor his direct-to-consumer testing business, nor his yacht, nor any thing that is thy neighbour's – unless it provide greater value than thy old-fashioned test.

2. Thou shalt not take the evidence in vain

Thou shalt labour to find the whole body of relevant evidence with the following three questions.

› Does this testing practice improve patient outcomes? (Your first question.)

› Does using the test improve on information provided by the history, examination and other cheaper or more readily available tests? (Your second question.)

› How accurate is the test? (Your third question.)

Thou shalt follow an efficient strategy for searching. Look first for evidence-based guidelines, then for meta-analyses, systematic reviews and health technology appraisals, and finally, if no one else has done the work for you, primary studies.
   And then, thou shalt labour to critically appraise the evidence.

› Was the research methodology appropriate?

› Were effect sizes clinically important?

› Were the confidence intervals wide?

› Is there a significant risk of bias or error in the results?

› Was there worrisome heterogeneity in the studies and results?

› Is the evidence indirect in any respect? (Use the PICOTS acronym to remind you to check for indirectness with respect to Population, Intervention (i.e. the test), Comparison, Outcome measures, Time, and Setting.)

3. Thou shalt apply the evidence with careful judgement

There is no certainty in a test's results, even if generated by a computer.
   With most tests, uncertainty can only be reduced, not removed, by testing.
   The probability threshold for action depends on the clinical stakes – when the stakes are high, the threshold of probability for action is correspondingly low.
   Prevalence critically affects predictive values – the lower the pre-test probability, the lower the predictive values.
   If you want to rule a diagnosis in, you need a highly specific test (SpIn).
   If you want to rule a diagnosis out, you need a highly sensitive test (SnOut).

4. Thou shalt test efficiently

Thou shalt test only when the results could influence your management, and never only because it is (thought to be) the custom.

5. Thou shalt follow a patient-centred approach when testing

Thou shalt remember Lance-Corporal Jones's advice to General Kitchener: 'They don't like it up 'em, sir. They don't like it'. Explain what is involved in the procedures you expect your patients to undergo, what the management options are for a positive, or inconclusive, or negative result, and what support is available should the result be distressing.

Honour thy elderly patients, for although this is where the greatest levels of risk and temptation to test reside, so does the greatest need to avoid useless and harmful testing.

6. Thou shalt test ethically

Thou shalt not use testing solely as a defence against legal action, or as a placebo, or as a delaying tactic while nature takes its course, or to avoid confronting the limitations of curative medicine and thus not providing appropriate care, support or palliation.

7. Gnothi seauton

[If you don't read Greek, this is Socrates' commandment: 'Thou shalt know thyself.']

Thou shalt be aware of the normal human biases that cause diagnostic errors.

Thou shalt not overly rely on test results, but shalt apply your clinical judgement after clinically assessing your patient.

Thou shalt never assume that all abnormal results are important, or that an abnormal result is sufficient to explain thy patient's symptoms.

Thou shalt consider the whole picture, and the differential diagnosis, and the possibility that tests bear false witness against thy patient.

8. Thou shalt not commit over-diagnosis

Thou shalt remember the downsides and drivers of over-diagnosis.

Downsides of over-diagnosis include waste, harmful labelling and adverse effects from procedures and false positive or false negative results.

Drivers of over-diagnosis include culture (e.g. belief that more is better), improved technology and more sensitive tests finding more 'incidentalomas', conflicts of interests, and perverse incentives that penalise under-diagnosis while rewarding over-diagnosis.

9. *Thou shalt help thy patient confront the many uncertainties that he or she (and you) will face*

Diseases are gradual and progressive. They are analogue processes, not digital events.

Limits, thresholds and categories are chosen for convenience, not to reflect nature.

Test results are never certain. Nature guarantees statistical variation. People guarantee bias and error.

The average is not the message. Focus on the confidence interval for diagnosis, and the long tail of the survival curve for prognosis.

10. *Thou shalt consider how emotions, especially hope and fear, bias decision making*

In the clinician, fear of failure to cover every possibility of disease promotes risk aversion and over-testing.

In the patient, fear of missing a remote possibility of cure promotes risk seeking and requests for risky or expensive testing.

PROVENANCE

These commandments were developed by Michael Power and Greg Fell who were inspired by John Yudkin's 'Ten commandments for prescribing', and much helped and somewhat provoked by members of the Evidence-Based Healthcare Discussion list.

The commandments summarise an article published in the journal *Evidence-Based Medicine*.[1]

The visual metaphors in this chapter should help you to think intuitively about testing, and the reference at the end of the chapter should provide good starting points for further reading on each commandment.

Our ten commandments pay homage to those in Exodus 20: 1–17 and Deuteronomy 5: 4–21. Like Moses, we would hope that they be taken seriously.

REFERENCE

1.   Power M, Fell G, Wright M. Principles for high-quality, high-value testing. *Evidence-Based Medicine* 2012; **18(1):** 5–10.

53

A LA CARTE BLANCHE
LEAVING GP TRAINING

James Woollard

It is a common experience that when you are out for dinner with friends and your food arrives, other people's choices look far more appetising than yours. Perhaps if they let you have a forkful of theirs, you even realise that it tastes better too. In medical training your career choice could seem a bit like this, except there might be the added feeling that you decided to have 'general practice' for every dinner for your working life and not just for this particular mid-week friends' reunion.

If you are reading this maybe you are thinking about leaving general practice or maybe you are quite comfortable and you just like to be reassured you know where the exits are at all times. Maybe you haven't thought about it until reading this. Whatever position you are in, this article is not going to give you the answer that you are looking for – i.e. what should I do? Hopefully it will help you think.

The changes that occurred through Modernising Medical Careers (MMC) appeared to straighten out the careers pathways of doctors. Training schemes were to become escalators of highly driven consultants-in-waiting, with divergence or detouring being made to seem impossible and certainly unwanted.

MMC ostensibly removed the possibility of a senior house officer (SHO) having a taster in any number of specialties before deciding what to do. It was argued that this prevented 'a lost tribe' of junior doctors who never made it to the just desserts of a registrar scheme. Some expressed the fear that this would prevent trainees from gathering a wide range of experiences that would have made them 'more rounded' doctors. Arguably, because we are all human and fallible, the reality of MMC has been a little messier and perhaps we should be glad of this as it makes the thought of leaving a training scheme not only possible but also far from catastrophic.

Why would you want to leave GP training? What has changed to make you think about leaving? Your choice to do general practice as your specialty could have been based on a myriad of factors, but generally it would have involved some thought about lifestyle and personal circumstances, as well as what particular kind of medicine you wanted to practice.

So is it your personal circumstances or lifestyle that have changed to make you think about leaving? If it has, it is important to think about the permanence of these changes. Are there going to be potentially more changes down the line? There are always things that you will have difficulty predicting but what I would say is that nearly all other specialties have training schemes that are far less predictable than general practice. You might have to move hospitals across quite large geographical areas every six months to a year for up to six years. You might not know where each rotation will be until a few months before and then it could still change depending on what NHS trusts require.

Spouses, children and, financially, houses are all going to come into play if you are changing specialty, not least because if you are set on switching to a particularly competitive specialty you might not get a job in your current area. It may be that the change in your personal circumstances may have made this less of a problem or even an advantage. You need to think these through with some care and attention, and consult with as many people as you need to.

Talk to your trainer (educational supervisor) and programme director. Ensure that the placements are the problem, rather than the specialty of general practice.

If general practice is no longer the particular kind of medicine you want to do, then first congratulate yourself on beating the system and getting a longer period of broader experience than most. You will never lose this experience and it will come in handy when you least expect it. Where do you want to go from here? Have you worked in the specialty you want to move to already? What is it about this other specialty that is pulling you towards it?

Looking through rose-tinted glasses at ophthalmology as an alternative and actually spending the rest of your life looking into people's red eyes are two different realities. If you haven't experienced the specialty 'on the job', then getting some experience of what the reality of clinical practice is like is a must. Even if you have this already, you should speak to the senior trainees and consultants in the specialty. Meet the local training programme director or college tutor and discuss it with him or her. He or she will probably know about competitiveness both in the local deanery and nationally, as well as upcoming spaces on training schemes and when applications are happening. A programme director may also be on an interview panel so making a good impression might help later.

In discussion with your educational supervisor and programme director, as well as with senior clinicians in the specialty you want to move to, the critical things to think about are whether you have the right skills and aptitudes for the specialty you want to move to. Honestly look at Workplace-Based Assessments (WPBAs) you have done and see if you can provide evidence for the core skills that the specialty requires. If you can't, you are going to need to see if you have them prior to going through an application. Enthusiasm and politeness open a lot of doors, so see if you can get a clinician to let you sit in on a clinic and to test your skills. It would be even better if he or she can put any feedback on a WPBA for you to use as evidence in your application. If the feedback does not have a positive core, be honest with yourself about what you would have to do to change that and whether you want to do it in order to move to the new specialty.

Being careful and thoughtful should not get in the way of you actually applying to change specialty. It does take a little courage. Hopefully you are in a position where you already have a training scheme job and therefore it is not a stark reality between unemployment and the new specialty.

Waiting should never be overlooked as an option: waiting to see how changes in your own life settle down; waiting to see if this is just a blip period or as a result of a particularly bad run of patients or colleagues; waiting until the end of your GP training and the completion of your Certificate of Completion of Training (CCT) before changing. If you take this last option you have 'banked' the training you have done to get something that you can call upon to pay the bills at least (doing locum work while having a shadowing experience with a colleague in another specialty is an example of this). However, if you finish your training you would have to go back to a lower rung on the ladder, and stomach the potential pay cut.

For me it was a change in my personal circumstances that led me to reappraise the original reasons for choosing general practice in the first place. Now I would say that luckily this happened at a time when I was working in psychiatry as a GPST1. My supervisor, who was also the college tutor, was highly influential in persuading me not only that it was practically possible but also that I could have the courage to do it. I should say that I had long been interested in psychiatry throughout medical school and had done an F2 rotation in it. While in my GPST1 year, I applied for psychiatry in Round 2 of applications that year and got a run-through core training post. I haven't looked back but my time as a GP trainee helped me mature. I gained confidence and experience as a clinician, which has helped me every day in my work as a psychiatrist. See www.medicalcareers.nhs.uk for more advice and links.

54

MINOR SURGERY

Matt Knapman

So now you're all grown up. You've passed your AKT and your CSA, your ePortfolio has been buffed and polished to within an inch of its life and now you are officially a fully qualified, certified GP – congratulations! Now what are you going to do with the remaining 30 or so years of your working life? A daunting/depressing thought? Well it needn't be, because you have chosen one of *the* most flexible career paths in medicine – one that you can mould to create a bespoke and ultimately exciting occupation. If you are of the more practical mindset, minor surgery may be the field for you.

Esteemed surgical consultants may once have said 'There's no such thing as minor surgery, just minor surgeons!' – not true – because, as the NHS is constantly evolving, increasing amounts of work are filtering through to primary care and this is where *you* can make a difference.

WHY DEVELOP AN INTEREST IN MINOR SURGERY?

While there is clearly nothing wrong with being a career GP who is content to manage the day-to-day challenges of 'normal' general practice, the majority of us tend to choose a 'hobby' or sub-specialty to help break up the working day or week. Depending on the structure of your practice you could devote a whole session to procedures – imagine spending a pleasant Friday afternoon excising Alfred's sebaceous cyst while discussing the merits of the referral system for the last Ashes tour! Or you could make time in between regular appointments, during which you can often come up with a plan for that patient who is TATT or has itchy teeth. In other words it provides a good break for the mind and soul.

Without such an option some people may simply succumb to the 'use it or lose it' principle and the hard-earned practical procedures of your earlier career could soon be lost. By retaining these skills you arm yourself to cope with the walking wounded with lacerations requiring closure, and you could also become a GP who enjoys the occasional shift in A&E. At a later date some people also choose to formalise their qualifications as a GP with a Special Interest (GPwSI).

At the end of the day, being able to provide this service is good for the patient. They get to see their GP, who diagnoses their lesion, performs an excisional or punch biopsy as appropriate and can then see the patient for follow-up with the histology result, all without a trip to hospital. You also start to develop relationships with your patients. Aside from discussing sporting controversies, you may also uncover other pathology as part of the wider consultation.

For any skin lesion, treat appropriately where you are confident you know what it is, e.g. cryotherapy for a plantar wart. If a skin cancer is suspected, e.g. a basal cell carcinoma (BCC), and you are fairly sure of your diagnosis, remove and send for histology, outlining your clinical suspicions.

For a melanocytic lesion you should always completely excise if you have the necessary skill and experience to do so and not take a biopsy. The punch biopsy needs to be used with care. Use it if you have a good idea of what the lesion is and punch it to confirm, e.g. suspected lichen planus. If in doubt about any skin lesion, ask a senior and consider referring.

It is important to check with your Primary Care Organisation (Clinical Commissioning Group or Health Board) regarding any local regulations and minor surgery. Some insist that GPs undertaking minor surgery demonstrate experience in this area, have attended a course or even have a formal qualification.

Lastly, apologies for lowering the tone, but it can also be good for business, generating a supplementary income for your practice and also making you more employable as a skilled GP.

HOW TO GAIN THE EXPERIENCE/SKILLS?

If you are an MRCS-qualified surgeon who has chosen late in his or her career to convert to the joys of general practice, this section need not apply to you. For everyone else – get involved early. Treasure your hospital jobs, since each may be the last opportunity for you to pick up specific practical skills. A&E and surgical posts are obvious examples, but even in general medical jobs there are plenty of practical procedures suitable to refine your technique.

Let your boss know early. Once he or she is aware that you are a GP and not a surgical trainee, you hopefully may not get so many questions on the course of the left renal artery and instead may get some time-handling tissues, getting used to equipment and gaining experience in closure of skin. Once you are in the community as a trainee, let your tutor know a.s.a.p. and spend some time with the practice specialist GP.

Depending on your deanery you may have some spare time during the week agreed with your clinical or educational supervisor. You could become acquainted with your local surgeon (maybe even your old boss) and scrub-in on a list, or maybe negotiate a supervised list of your own.

You can also practise at home. Reps tend to have non-sterile practice suture packs available; just be responsible with your sharps. Pork belly is good – it mimics human skin reasonably well and you can practise excisions, closure and sutures to your heart's content. Just remember to remove the Ethilon before cooking!

Whatever you do … keep a log book. It needs to be confidential and secure. It is an essential means of recording your procedures and acts as an evidence base for the effectiveness of your work. It could even be used for audit purposes for continuing professional development (CPD).

COURSES

The RCGP-endorsed Minor Surgery Courses are an excellent way of being introduced to basic surgical techniques or even brushing up/developing on previously learnt skills.

They are usually run by plastic surgeons and/or dermatologists. The more basic courses run through equipment needed, basic excisions and closure techniques. The more advanced introduce more complex procedures such as flaps and grafts.

Some courses focus purely on surgical skills, while others incorporate joint injections and cryo-surgery.

Such events are not just informative; they also form the foundation of experience upon which you may have to rely in a medico-legal defence situation. If you are performing minor surgery, make sure you let your medical defence organisation know.

LEARN SOME DERMATOLOGY AND HISTOPATHOLOGY!

Having a good idea of what you are cutting out before you get the pathology report back is probably a sensible principle. This will hopefully keep to a minimum any nasty surprises and awkward phone calls to your local consultant to explain why the 'solar keratosis' you curetted came back as a melanoma!

It can be useful making friends with your local dermatologist, so sit in on their clinics and get involved. You'll find you can learn more in an afternoon than you did for the entirety of your rather hazy medical school career. These specialists will also become rather useful sources of information and, with the advent of email advice, a quick snapshot of a lesion could speedily aid your further management plan.

Some regions advocate and others insist on attendance to multidisciplinary team (MDT) meetings. This may only need to be a few times each year, but they do actually place the histo-pathology into clinical context and provide an invaluable learning opportunity.

Dermoscopy (or dermatoscopy depending on your preference) can be a useful adjunct to any aspiring skin surgeon. There are several simple methods taught on courses that can help you to pick up those lesions that are safe for you to remove in-house and more importantly the potential 'nasties' that are better referred on to our colleagues in secondary care. Some practices may have a dermatoscope that you can experiment with. Once again, the more you see, the more you learn and try to correlate your dermascopic findings with the final histology report – a secure photographic database of the lesions examined can be useful here.

Regarding dermoscopy, remember, 'If you look at a lesion for more than 5 seconds and you don't know what it is then get out the dermatoscope. If you look for more than 5 seconds at it under the dermatoscope then you need to re-think.'

At the end of the day the usefulness of a dermatoscope is operator dependent, and if there is any doubt in your mind – always seek a further opinion/refer.

THE BORING (BUT POTENTIALLY CAREER PRESERVING) MEDICO-LEGAL BIT

No one likes being sued … fact! You needn't go through your career obsessing about it – in reality that could be quite detrimental to the way you practise – but with some basic principles risk can be minimised. For a comprehensive but not easily digestible guide there is a 45-page publication by the Department of Health.[1]

One needs to be sure when consent is required, who can obtain it and in what form. Consideration should be given to what information needs to be provided – consent is not considered valid under English law unless it is truly informed. Finally, special attention should be paid to situations when minors (or non-competent adults) are being treated and establishing who has parental responsibility.

It is also a sensible idea to inform your medical indemnity company as to what you are up to – most do cover minor surgical procedures without adding to your premium.

A NOTE ON JOINT INJECTIONS

Minor surgery and joint injections are often regarded under the same umbrella. Being able to confidently deliver a steroid/local anaesthetic injection into a joint, a carpal tunnel or an inflamed bursa/tendon can bring about prompt symptomatic relief for the patient, while again avoiding a referral to hospital.

Injection techniques are often held as part of a wider minor surgery course where you can practise on models, before being unleashed on the general public.

If such a skill appeals to you, once again let your boss know early and make the most of the opportunities presented in your hospital training posts. If you are lucky enough to have an in-house physiotherapist make them a friend – their anatomy knowledge is second to none and many are expert with a needle!

SUMMARY POINTS

› Get to know your local guidelines – both National Institute for Health and Care Excellence (NICE)[2] and local variations.

› Get qualified – courses endorsed by the Royal College of General Practitioners (RCGP).

› Practise, practise, practise.

› Make use of your hospital experiences.

› Learn some dermatology.

› Maintain good documentation including consent.

› Be aware of your limitations – deciding when not to operate can be a clinician's best tool.

RESOURCES

- Minor surgery RCGP webpage:
  www.rcgp.org.uk/clinical-and-research/clinical-resources/minor-surgery.aspx
  [accessed March 2014].

- Minor surgery courses: www.rcgp.org.uk/courses-and-events/minor-surgery-courses.aspx
  [accessed March 2014].

REFERENCES

1. Department of Health. *Reference Guide to Consent for Examination or Treatment* (2nd edn). London: DH, 2009.

2. National Institute for Health and Clinical Excellence. *Improving Outcomes for People with Skin Tumours Including Melanoma*. London: NICE, 2009, www.nice.org.uk/csgstim [accessed March 2014].

PART III

BEYOND
TRAINING

55

ACADEMIC GENERAL PRACTICE
OFF ALL SUMMER

Tom O'Dowd

Academic GPs get used to being asked by envious or mischievous colleagues, 'I suppose you will be off all summer?' The cartoon image is of the highly tuned academic mind needing to recuperate from the common room sherry and frightful university politics.

Almost every GP who has graduated in last 30 years will have been taught by an academic GP. What those graduates will remember most, however, is not the time they spent in seminars but in their undergraduate practice where for the first time doctors seemed to know their patients well and the sheer variety of medicine was on display every day, all the time. It is hardly surprising then that most young doctors think of teaching when they think of academic general practice. 'Know something about something. Don't just present your wonderful self to the world. Amass knowledge and offer it around.' This was the advice that Richard Holbrook, the late US polymath and diplomat, gave to young diplomats. It seems that after ten or 12 years of amassing knowledge in medicine young GPs feel compelled to offer it around and perhaps the only ones who will listen are medical students. It is a good place to start.

Students talk about 'my GP' more often than they talk about the 'good GP'. This shows a personal attachment and many students may be using their GP teacher as a role model. GP teachers are being called to profess their discipline – to show an underlying belief in their work. Students are attracted by the often unselfconscious humanity of the doctor in the face of the drama that often presents itself in the consultation. A sick child, drug addiction, depression, palliative care, anger, sadness, madness. Medicine at its best and quite a responsibility.

The medical student mind has been characterised 'as a cerebral shoe box containing a vast anatomical index in which you can find the name of every nerve ending and every follicle and also, in an unswept and unvisited corner, a small withering organ called common humanity' by Kevin Myers, a former *Irish Times* columnist. GPs often concern themselves with trying to teach common humanity or at least trying to shore it up from withering. It is a vital part of the hidden curriculum for any GP who is interested in teaching and it is a noble task for medical schools to find good role models full of common humanity.

General practice is at its best when it sees itself as David rather than Goliath, and the academic analysis is vastly more entertaining. Take Julian Tudor Hart, on medical education: 'our system of medical education is still designed to produce community clinicians only as a by-product, an afterthought following a core curriculum designed by, and for, specialists'. If a young GP shares this analysis then it is inevitable that someone who believes in what he or she does will want to try to redress this imbalance, to produce doctors that match the needs of patients. Julian's conclusion on medical education is delicious: 'its central aim remains the production of specialist excellence, unsullied by prior contact with the society it serves'. This eloquent allegation of elitism is again irresistible and inspirational for doctors who want to change things.

Only a minority of young GPs, who express an interest in academic general practice, come in via the research door, yet research is the bedrock of an academic career. Getting an appointment as a clinical fellow and pursuing a masters or PhD in an organised, mentored and funded manner improves the odds for success. More experienced GPs get involved in research because of a desire to do an MD. Universities and funders prefer PhDs because it commits both student and supervisor to deliver. Adding to knowledge is a powerful reason to engage in research. The critical thinking involved in refining a good research question is a transferable skill that is of use in clinical practice, teaching and life in general. Like any endeavour, whether it be clinical or teaching, knowledge of research methods is necessary. Clinicians often feel an affinity with qualitative methods because it involves talking to participants and themes fall out of it that make connections with patients. Many successful researchers are increasingly adopting a quantitative approach, mainly using epidemiological techniques in primary care. An ability to ask good research questions of the increasing number of large databases often means the researcher is off to a flying start. Having a good grounding in epidemiology, statistics and their associated analysis packages are an essential part of the kitbag for future researchers.

Academic GPs always worry about the relevance and impact of their research. Marshall Marinker said, 'my fear for academic general practice is that it may develop along lines laid down by fashionable research which is neither consonant with the clinical experience of GPs nor central to their concerns'. This of course has not happened as GPs have been involved in groundbreaking research on conditions such as meningococcal meningitis, Bell's palsy and incentives in general practice. Graham Watt, Professor of General Practice in Glasgow, worries that academic general practice has not influenced so-called ordinary service GPs. Much of the stuff done by academic departments at local or regional levels has more impact than stuff done at national or international levels because it responds to local need.

There is an emerging gap in GP research that is in the area of genetics. It is puzzling to note that the family, which is the smallest unit of population where the gene and the environment can interact at will and is the key determinant of so many diseases, is passing GP researchers by. This is a wide open area for a future Nobel Prize winner in general practice.

Whether you spend a year or a lifetime in academic general practice, and in particular in research, you will learn a variety of transferable skills that can be used in teaching, research, advocacy and patient care. Over a lifetime such skills combined with clinical experience give the modern GP an unbeatable and authoritative voice in health care.

For a GP looking at an academic career I would advise on the following:

1. You need a good contract that ensures your freedom to speak

2. You need good data and politicised senior colleagues who understand the implications of your findings in relation to creating local and national change

3. You need to maintain strong roots in general practice as the combination of the evidence base and clinical experience is unbeatable

4. You need a good ear for the voice of patients and the public

5. You need to know how the media works, as they will use your research to get a message across to a wider audience than you could ever dream of

6. Most importantly, you need a good mentor/advocate in an increasingly competitive arena.

But most of all you need patience and persistence, and the discipline to take the long view. In return you get a rich and varied life but don't expect the summer off.

56

ACADEMIC GENERAL PRACTICE
A CODA

David Blane and Bhautesh Jani

A CAREER LADDER FOR ACADEMIC GPs[1]

› Academic Foundation Year 2 (F2) placements in general practice – four-month placements in F2.

› Academic Clinical Fellowships (ACFs) for GP specialist trainees – extend current training to four years.

› Academic In-Practice Fellowships (IPFs) for fully trained GPs – two years' part-time training (see below).

› Training fellowships – Department of Health, Medical Research Council, Wellcome Trust and other charities (e.g. Arthritis Research UK, British Heart Foundation) – three years' full-time equivalent, leading to a doctorate.

› Clinical lectureships – for postdoctoral GPs, half-time for up to four years.

› Clinical senior lectureships – university, NHS or joint funding, leading to a professorial post.

ALTERNATIVE ROUTES INTO GP RESEARCH[2]

Individual GPs or GP trainees can approach their local academic department for advice initially and the following may be recommended.

> National Institute for Health Research (NIHR).

> ACFs.

> IPFs.

[Information on both is available at www.nihrtcc.nhs.uk/intetacatrain/.]

> In Scotland, there are ACFs available in each of the university departments of general practice, which are for those who have completed their GP training. There are also Scottish Clinical Research Excellence Development Scheme (SCREDS) posts. More details are available via www.scotmt.scot.nhs.uk/specialty/scottish-academic-training-%28screds%29.

> RCGP Research Ready Scheme, www.rcgp.org.uk/researchready.

Links to departments can be found through the Society for Academic Primary Care (SAPC) at www.sapc.ac.uk.

USEFUL MEETINGS TO ATTEND

> SAPC.

> RCGP Annual Conference.

> Scottish School of Primary Care Conference.

> North American Primary Care Research Group Annual Meeting.

USEFUL COURSES TO ATTEND

[These formal courses are usually run throughout the country by different universities.]

> Introduction to research methodologies.

> Introduction to medical statistics.

> Paper appraisal skills.

> Presentation skills.

REFERENCES

1. Modernising Medical Careers. *Medically- and Dentally-Qualified Academic Staff: recommendations for training the researchers and educators of the future.* London: Modernising Medical Careers, 2005, www.nihrtcc.nhs.uk/intetacatrain/copy_of_Medically_and_Dentally-qualified_Academic_Staff_Report.pdf [accessed March 2014].

2. Walton L. A Jester joins the Gatekeeper and Wizard: working as an academic GP. *British Journal of General Practice* 2011; **61(593)**: 744–5.

57

COMMISSIONING

Peter Davies and Mayur Lakhani

WHAT IS COMMISSIONING?

Commissioning in the NHS is the process by which a health service commissioner specifies what services it needs from its healthcare service providers. Done well it is based on both understanding the historical patterns of service usage and on detailed needs assessment of what local people need now and in the future, from their local healthcare system. It is a process of alignment whereby the activity of the healthcare providers is matched with the capacity of the commissioner to pay for them to an agreed standard of quality. Done even better it is visionary in that it actually looks at what health care is needed and sets contracts based on clinical pathways so that what is needed gets delivered, and what is unhelpful or needless goes by the wayside. But it is not really about contracts. This is a big turn-off for most GPs. Instead, think of commissioning as a way of improving clinical outcomes in a collaborative way between primary and secondary care, and often with council colleagues in social care. The patient will benefit from an overall better-planned system of care.

WHY IS IT NEEDED?

Patricia Hewitt, the former Secretary of State for Health, described commissioning as the neglected function of the NHS. She was right. The history of the NHS and the Department of Health (DH)[1,2] has been one of its battle against 'producer capture'. The NHS has always struggled to articulate what it wants and so achieve it. Instead it has been largely run reactively trying to keep up with the activities of its doctors. It has always left politicians and DH civil servants vulnerable to 'shroud waving' by doctors. Examples here include apparent shortages such as waiting lists or failure to fund expensive cancer drugs. The doctor then says, 'Something must be done about this' and the press picks up the story and the politicians then have to be seen to go and badger the Treasury for some extra funds.

Producer capture occurs when the activity of a system is dictated by what is available, or by what the producers want to do, rather than by what is actually needed. For example, at various times in both the UK and USA it has been shown that the number of tonsillectomies performed in an area is as much a function of the number of ear, nose and throat (ENT) surgeons in the area as any difference in actual clinical need for the operations.[3,4]

Commissioning is an attempt to bring the wide clinical knowledge of primary care clinicians (principally its GPs) together with its management (the finance teams) and the business intelligence teams and public health teams. Collectively it is hoped that this will enable better analysis of existing patterns of activity, and better direction of these flows in future. With better direction of the flows comes smoother systems,[5] fewer gaps at the interfaces,[6] and actually less cost – it is cheaper to do an activity right first time and once only, than to have endless glitches that take time and energy to sort out later. You do not have to spend long in your consulting room to see many glitches in action.[7] Commissioning is a chance for us as GPs to start sorting these out, and our knowledge is crucial to this happening. The managers do not see them – we do.

It is predicated on a reification of each GP referral decision into a commissioning decision.[8] As GPs we have always accepted that we are the beginning of the process, not the end of it, and that we will regularly need help from specialist colleagues. The referral system is how the NHS has managed this process for many years.[9,10]

Outcomes for commissioning have been defined. The NHS clinical outcomes set these out in five domains.[11]

1. Preventing people from dying prematurely.

2. Enhancing quality of life for people with long-term conditions.

3. Helping people to recover from episodes of ill health or following injury.

4. Ensuring that people have a positive experience of care.

5. Treating and caring for people in a safe environment and protecting them from avoidable harm.

The current reforms can be summarised as providing an opportunity to create a clinically led NHS, focused on delivering improved clinical outcomes and an improved clinical experience.

EVERYTHING IS BOTH CLINICAL AND FINANCIAL – CARE COSTS

We need to realise that every decision we make as doctors is both a clinical and a financial decision.[8] Every decision we make has a cost that is paid by the NHS on behalf of patients. Every time we talk about something being 'of value' we are making a statement that is in part measured financially. We are implicitly making a statement that it is worth spending money on a particular activity such as an operation.

As we own this NHS expenditure that we drive, we realise that nothing is 'purely clinical'. The NHS has done a good job in protecting doctors from commerce, but it has kindly allowed us as health professionals to be a little naïve about the financial implications of our work and activity. At a similar senior level in any other profession or industry no one would be talking about activity flows separately from money flows – the two are inextricably linked, and part of your seniority would be based on your ability to manage these flows sensibly and reliably. This reality is now becoming starkly visible to UK GPs, some of whom are recoiling from it in horror.[12]

We need to acknowledge opportunity costs – that money is finite and that a pound spent here cannot then be spent there. Every decision to do one thing is in part a decision against doing something else. The wise use of resources is an important duty on doctors. One of the central tasks of commissioning is to tackle inappropriate, and probably unwarranted and ineffective, clinical variation.

We need to be wary of historical patterns of activity. They may not have been needs assessed even at first, and may now be archaic or irrelevant. We do know that current NHS spending patterns result in significant areas of unmet need and hidden morbidity.[13]

Overall there is a significant opportunity in NHS commissioning for primary care to assert its rightful place as the leader of the NHS, and as the system navigators for patients and as pilots for the NHS system itself.

COMMISSIONING AND PRIMARY CARE

The new commissioning work is major new work for primary care and it carries with it interest and opportunity. Primary care is in an anomalous position with regard to commissioning. In primary care we both provide medical services and commission secondary care activity. If commissioning is seen as a crude tactic done by primary care against secondary care then it will be resisted, and will deservedly fail.

If it can be done in such a way as to specify clearly what health care is needed in an area then it will be very good, and may well bring primary and secondary care closer together. Currently in our localities in Calderdale and Leicestershire commissioning is bringing together managerial and clinical knowledge in primary care, promoting better collaboration between primary and secondary care, and tackling health inequalities.

Commissioning is best thought of as a specialised specification and purchasing function, which allows the local NHS bodies to achieve their duty to obtain best value in services for the patients in their area.

One issue in all this move to system-wide thinking is that primary care also needs to be commissioned to play its proper part in local service developments. One of the authors (PD) of an article in the *British Medical Journal*[14] wrote in 2003: 'Perhaps the territory crossed by medicine in 2003 has not been mapped clearly enough for doctors' and managers' maps of reality to align comfortably with each other, or with the ground itself.'

This mapping process is if anything even less precise in 2014, although there are helpful hints about what is needed from a good primary care service from the King's Fund,[13] the Health Foundation[15] and the RCGP. We may need better ways of supporting our work as GPs, and the current contractual arrangements may need to be revisited.

Commissioning is a major new function for GPs and it creates many opportunities for us as GPs to work both in and on the NHS system. In part it rewrites our understanding of our role, bringing clinical and cost-effectiveness together. We see this as a necessary if uncomfortable adjustment for GPs.

HOW DO I GET INVOLVED?

As a GP you are already involved in this – your practice has to become part of a Clinical Commissioning Group (CCG). Opportunities for leadership development abound. We have never known a better time for GPs to become involved in improving standards by transforming care. It is essential that trainees become engaged with the issue and take up opportunities for leadership training and development. Grasp the opportunity early. More positively, commissioning is a spur to us all to think about what we do, why we do it and whether we are cost-effective in our activities. Over time this will lead to us looking at our activities carefully and critically, and seeing what adds value and what takes it away.

The more you can learn about commissioning, and the more you can help the local CCGs to develop, the better for you, the better for the local NHS systems, and the better for your patients.

Commissioning is one of the biggest opportunities we have had as GPs to make the system work better, both so that we have fewer glitches to sort out, and so that our patients can receive a better service. In terms of the RCGP's *Roadmap*[16] it provides the forum within which GPs can realise the vision:

We urge that GPs organise themselves into a force to be reckoned within their local health economies. We hope that this document will be used by GPs and others as a basis for declaring an ambition to improve their local NHS.

In conclusion, when you hear the word commissioning, do not think 'contracts'. Instead think: clinical leadership, improved clinical outcomes and better patient experience!

REFERENCES

1.   Webster C. *National Health Service: a political history* (2nd rev. edn). Oxford: Oxford University Press, 2002.

2.   Klein R. *The New Politics of the NHS: from creation to reinvention* (5th rev. edn). Oxford: Radcliffe Publishing, 2006.

3.   Glover JA. The incidence of tonsillectomy in school children. *Proceedings of the Royal Society of Medicine* 1938; **31**: 1219–36. (Reprinted in: *International Journal of Epidemiology* 2008; **37(1)**: 9–19.)

4.   Wennberg J. Time to tackle unwarranted variations in practice. *British Medical Journal* 2011; **342**. doi: http://dx.doi.org/10.1136/bmj.d1513.

5.   Seddon J. *Systems Thinking in the Public Sector: the failure of the reform regime … and a manifesto for a better way.* Axminster: Triarchy Press, 2008.

6.   Lakhani M, Baker M. Good general practitioners will continue to be essential. *British Medical Journal* 2006; **332(7532)**: 41–3.

7.   Davies P. The great NHS communication breakdown. *British Medical Journal* 2008; **337**. doi: 10.1136/bmj.a664.

8.   Davies P, Garbutt G. Should the practice of medicine be a deontological or utilitarian enterprise? *Journal of Medical Ethics* 2011; **37(5)**: 267–70. doi: 10.1136/jme.2010.036111.

9.   Davies P, Pool R, Smelt G. What do we actually know about the referral process? *British Journal of General Practice* 2011; **61(593)**: 752–3.

10. Loudon I. The principle of referral: the gatekeeping role of the GP. *British Journal of General Practice* 2008; **58(547)**: 128–30.

11. NHS Commissioning Board. *CCG Outcomes Indicator Set 2013/14: technical guidance*, 2012, www.england.nhs.uk/wp-content/uploads/2012/12/ccg-ois-tech-guide.pdf [accessed March 2014].

12. Gerada C. From patient advocate to gatekeeper: understanding the effects of the NHS reforms. *British Journal of General Practice* 2011; **61(592)**: 655–6.

13. King's Fund. *Improving the Quality of Care in General Practice*. London: King's Fund, 2011, www.kingsfund.org.uk/publications/gp_inquiry_report.html [accessed March 2014].

14. Davies P, Glasspool J. Patients and the new contracts. *British Medical Journal* 2003; **326(7399)**: 1099.

15. NHS Leadership Academy, www.leadershipacademy.nhs.uk/.

16. Royal College of General Practitioners. *The Future Direction of General Practice: a roadmap.* London: RCGP, 2007, www.rcgp.org.uk/policy/rcgp-policy-areas/future-direction-of-general-practice-a-roadmap.aspx [accessed March 2014].

DOG'S LIFE

One of my patients seemed a little harassed today. I was running 20 minutes late.

He apologised for seeming a bit hurried – but it was Tuesday.

And on Tuesday he takes his dog for acupuncture.

Red Roses *collection curated by Alec Logan and illustrated by Helen Wilson.*

58

ON DIAGNOSIS

Cliff Godley

My patient's left hand was much warmer than her right. She complained of left periscapular discomfort, but did not agree with my suggestion that her left upper lid drooped a little. She was otherwise well but I knew she had discontinued tamoxifen earlier that year after five years' disease-free treatment for breast cancer. I already had a working diagnosis, but neither of us believed it would take three scans, four different specialty opinions and six months to confirm it. Reliance on tests and specialisation left the patient and her non-diagnosis firmly within primary care.

These days of process-driven medicine, where algorithms and tests replace critical thinking and reflective practice, have produced a world in which 50% of working diagnoses in A&E are clinical symptoms (chest pain, collapse, 'off-legs', confusion, etc.).[1] Working and differential diagnoses are rarely encouraged and there is even less time for the contemplation of difficult problems and reflection.

However, although no two patients present in exactly the same manner, most physicians will on average interrupt a patient describing symptoms within 18 seconds,[2] often having already decided on diagnosis and treatment by then. They are frequently right but at critical times can be wrong.

Although experienced physicians form better hypotheses and diagnostic plans more rapidly than novices, 10–20% of diagnoses are still incorrect.[3] There are ways to perform better and, although many patients return from A&E and outpatient departments with worrying conditions such as coronary insufficiency or cancer excluded, you will still be left with their undiagnosed presenting symptoms.

The roles of hospitals and specialists have changed from the days when I considered myself an inadequate medical registrar when I could not dream up more erudite tests for difficult clinical conundrums. Now you will be faced with patients whose undiagnosed symptoms persist after specialist assessment.

Fortunately, primary care has never had greater access to investigations (though still inadequate and inconsistent in their availability). You do not therefore have to stick to tests, which may have the in-built confirmation bias of many clinical algorithms that do not search for the unusual. Indeed, guidelines by their nature are the antithesis of the Art of Medicine.[4] And good diagnosticians require expansive and often 'eccentric thought'.

Careful and adequate history taking can produce a diagnosis in 85% of cases, with clinical examination contributing a further 5–7%,[5] but no tests provide 100% specificity or sensitivity.

You will make diagnoses both intuitively and analytically; experience will help with pattern recognition and categorisation. 'Thin-slicing' will provide you with the diagnosis with one glance – enough to provide instant recall of the condition.

['Thin-slicing' – *using one's ability to gauge what is really important from a narrow period of experience. It is the use of rapid intuitive judgement, usually by immediate pattern recognition of a particular feature that the diagnostician has previously recognised as being important and indeed 'diagnostic'. Such a diagnostic technique has always to be prefaced by immediately constructing a differential diagnostic list to test the hypothesis by applying critical thinking to your 'thin-slice' diagnosis.*]

There is therefore no substitute for seeing as much interesting pathology as you can and for two-way sharing of this with your colleagues. However, even intuitive diagnoses must be subject to reflection and analysis since diagnosis is most often heuristic (best fit) and rarely are all the boxes ticked.

› Be prepared to live with uncertainty.

› Collect and share diagnostic stories.

› Recount them after morning surgery, at the dinner-table, at postgraduate meetings, on the cable car, in the cockpit of a yacht on passage across the Sea of the Hebrides.

› Share knowledge and offer your opinion. It might sometimes be correct.

Although British GPs are recognised as being globally the best at managing co-morbidity and complexity[6] you may now need to take on a more diagnostic role.

Of course, common conditions are common, but doctors can misunderstand, misinterpret or be selective in their analysis of test results. Unravelling the patient's story may be complicated but always satisfying – the epitome of good detective work. When things are opaque, employ the methods of Sherlock Holmes by 'considering the improbable when you have excluded the impossible'.[7]

Knowledge is not static but adaptive and active. Diagnosis is the continuous generation and then testing (and re-testing) of hypotheses.

Experience helps us with decision making but it should be augmented by teaching and by encouraging critical thinking, which some of you will have experienced in undergraduate courses.

You will amass a huge amount of knowledge about your patients, enabling you (with the aid of comprehensive records) to avoid making diagnoses in isolation. By communicating your thoughts to your patients you can empower them to be their own advocates. Teach them to enlighten any attending doctor to significant past history and current problems. Especially out of hours. An 'expert' asthmatic, for example, should know his or her normal PFR or O_2 sats.

Use *Occam's razor* (the principle of parsimony whereby an attempt is made to provide one unifying diagnosis) to identify the simplest explanation for a constellation of symptoms[8] but remember *Hickam's dictum* that a patient can indeed have more than one common ailment, rather than a complicated unifying diagnosis.[9] A probability approach to diagnosis (*Murtagh's process*)[10] is vital but textbooks often fail to include probability in their lists of differential diagnoses.

Nevertheless unusual conditions do exist. (Three phaeochromocytomas in our practice of 6100.) [*And one plum-sized phaeo in this book's contributors, Ed.*] So do not be afraid to look for them.

Doctors still outperform computer-aided diagnosis. However, to improve performance, doctors must:

› practise reflectively

› use memory aids such as mnemonics

› use decision support software, e.g. ISABEL (www.isabelhealthcare.com)

› ensure a pathway for follow-up by making the patient your partner

› pass on problems so that colleagues can identify if you are normalising any deviations

› use technology such as graphic displays to identify trends that you might otherwise miss

› always strive to improve your communication skills.

Despite this you will still make mistakes. Always acknowledge them at least to yourself and you will learn much more from these than your successes. Patients will usually forgive diagnostic and management errors. But they will never forgive you if they think you have abandoned them.

Finally, my patient.

She is currently remarkably well – her left hand is less warm and her Horner's has not progressed. She has partially responded to rescue chemotherapy for the recurrent breast cancer that caused the thoracic sympathetic chain problems and Pancoast syndrome, which ultimately took her from the puzzled breast and vascular surgeons to the ENT specialist who confirmed her left recurrent laryngeal nerve palsy, and then the respiratory consultant who still insisted on bronchoscopy after her second thoracic CT scan showed a left phrenic nerve palsy and by then the left apical lesions that undoubtedly were there when I made my initial diagnosis. Unfortunately each negative investigation returned the patient to general practice symptomatic and unsupported without a specialist diagnosis.

FURTHER READING

- Doyle AC. *A Study in Scarlet*. London: Penguin, 1981 [1887].

REFERENCES

1. Bhadrani S. A single-centre audit of junior doctors' diagnostic activity in medical admissions. *Journal of the Royal College of Physicians of Edinburgh* 2009; **39(4)**: 307–12 doi: 10.4997/JRCPE.2009.423.

2. Groopman JE. *How Doctors Think*. New York: Houghton Mifflin & Co., 2007.

3. Shojania KG, Burton EC, McDonald KM, *et al.* Changes in rates of autopsy-detected diagnostic errors over time: a systematic review. *Journal of the American Medical Association* 2003; **289(21)**: 2849–56. doi:10.1001/jama.289.21.2849.

4. Toft AD. How about some courage? *Journal of the Royal College of Physicians of Edinburgh* 2006; **36(3)**: 194–5.

5. Hampton JR, Harrison MJ, Mitchell JR, *et al.* Relative contributions of history-taking, physical examination, and laboratory investigation to diagnosis and management of medical outpatients. *British Medical Journal* 1975; **2(5969)**: 486–9. doi: 10.1136/bmj.2.5969.486.

6. Schoen C, Osborn R, Squires D, *et al.* New 2011 survey of patients with complex care needs in eleven countries finds that care is often poorly coordinated. *Health Affairs* 2011; **30(12)**: 2437–48

7. Doyle AC. *The Sign of the Four*. In: *Sherlock Holmes: The Complete Stories*. Ware, Herts: Wordsworth, 1989 [1890], ch. 6, p. 122.

8. Thorburn WM. The myth of Occam's razor. *Mind* 1918; **27(3)**: 345–53. doi: 10.1093/mind/XXVII.3.345.

9. Noble JD. Noble J. David, MD, reminisces. *Journal of Neuro-ophthalmology* 2002; **22(3)**: 240–6.

10. Murtagh J. Common problems: a safe diagnostic strategy. *Australian Family Physician* 1990; **19(5)**: 733–42.

NOTHING

Just before Christmas. I fetch my next patient from the waiting room. We exchange pleasantries. 'So, what can I do for you?' I asked. She smiled. 'Nothing', she said. 'I've come to give you ten minutes off. You work too hard and you could do with a break.'

You know what? She was right.

There are many doctors who would have been annoyed, affronted, insulted. I was deeply touched. These curious interactions we have with our patients involve two human beings, not one. We sometimes forget that.

Red Roses *collection curated by Alec Logan and illustrated by Helen Wilson.*

59

INTERACTING WITH THE DEPARTMENT FOR WORK AND PENSIONS

Max Inwood

The Department for Work and Pensions (DWP) is responsible for out-of-work benefits, usually Jobseeker's Allowance (JSA). This would rarely involve primary care.

GPs, as certifying medical practitioners, have a statutory obligation to provide certain statements of incapacity to patients on their list. That is a Med 3 generated by a GP or an ESA 113 requested by the DWP. No fee is payable.

If a patient is medically unfit to work and signed off by the GP, Employment and Support Allowance (ESA) may be awarded. This allows the patient to receive benefit but exempts him or her from the need to attend job interviews. Unless the patient is very severely disabled, he or she is expected to attend some meetings to keep in touch with the world of work. Disability Living Allowance (DLA) for the under-65s and Attendance Allowance (AA) for the over-65s may be awarded when illness leads to a level of disability so high that the patient needs help with his or her personal care or getting around. It is possible to work and receive DLA.

Our patients bump into the DWP in several different ways. Sometimes their contact is brief and satisfactory. At other times it is difficult and confrontational. In a minority of cases it becomes a personal crusade against perceived injustice. In all cases it means a great deal more to them than to you, so try to ensure that you give this area of work due priority and try to be truthful and accurate.

Decisions on illness and disability benefits are based on a claim form completed by the patient along with the results of a medical examination conducted by a health professional trained in disability analysis. Be aware that this may be a doctor, a nurse or a physiotherapist.

A GP certificate may be revoked by the DWP when a medical is performed. The client may then appeal and turn to primary care to provide evidence in support of his or her case. If DWP or the Appeals Service consider that further, more detailed medical evidence is necessary, they will seek it. They will be responsible for paying any fee to the doctor providing the report. NHS GPs are under no obligation to provide such evidence to their patients nor to provide it free of charge. If a GP does not agree to provide additional evidence for his or her patient, then it is a private matter to be resolved between the GP and the patient. Find out your practice policy and stick to it. A united front from all clinicians is essential.

Be careful what you write. Decision makers and tribunals pay particular regard to a supportive GP letter. However, they understand that our long-term relationship with claimants can pose problems in framing replies. They are also good at picking up the coded message in a letter starting, 'He tells me that ...'.

Do not extrapolate or speculate in response to questions from the DWP about the Activities of Daily Living of which you have no knowledge. Say what you know or observe and decline to comment further.

Be aware that your patient will see a copy of your report or letter. Although you do not need to see a signed consent form for DWP reports, you may wish to phone the patient to discuss the terms of your proposed reply.

At the risk of stating the obvious, any reply should be legible and avoid unduly technical language.

Welfare rights organisations may write seeking support for their client's appeal tribunal. You are not obliged to provide such reports. Check if there is a practice policy about them. A fee is generally not available.

You may be tempted to provide a summary printout from your computer system. Don't. This may give more information than is requested, including contact details about third parties, and may lead you into regulatory difficulties.

Opportunities exist for employment in the Tribunal Service, hearing appeals against a disallowance of benefit. This is generally sessional. This seems to suit doctors towards the end of their careers, perhaps even retired from active practice.

ATOS Origin, a commercial company that does the disability analysis, also employs doctors as part of the skill-mixed team. These opportunities would be salaried and require a more regular commitment.

DLA is to be phased out from 2013 in favour of the new Personal Independence Payment (PIP). The conversion process was started in June 2013 with fresh claimants being assessed under the new rules. Over the next four years the 3.2 million current claimants of DLA will be migrated across to the new benefit. The paperwork and processes have yet to be finalised but GP engagement with the new benefit will follow similar principles as before. Keep it factual. Say what you know and do not speculate. And yes, you did read right, there are 3.2 million claimants of DLA. It will be a big and hotly contested migration process and we will be involved.

The DWP website (www.gov.uk/government/organisations/department-for-work-pensions) should be consulted for up-to-date information.

60

HOW TO WRITE A PAPER

Tony Foley

The prospect of writing a paper may seem a little overwhelming at first. Usually loquacious GPs may be rendered temporarily mute by the thought of writing a paper for publication. The paralysing frustration of attempting to transfer clinical reflections or innovative research into legible sentences may trigger white-page terror and writer's block. Yet, it doesn't have to be so.

Writing can be fun. It can be strangely cathartic and can force you to pause for timely reflection on the complexities of life as a GP. While the 'publish or perish' ethos may not predominate as much as in other specialties, publication may advance a GP's academic career and may be a source of immense personal and professional satisfaction.

A life in general practice offers a wealth of writing opportunities. You are witness to ethical dilemmas, clinical conundrums and all the drama that life and death brings. Daily surgeries supply you with abundant material for personal reflections, opinion pieces, case studies and clinical reports. You may choose to research qualitatively your patients and colleagues or to number crunch quantitatively your endless data. Regardless of taste there's a menu on offer to suit the pickiest of palates.

However, before you get started it is advisable to know the rules of the writing and publishing game. Below are a few useful tips.

1. Have a digital camera on stand-by for ready shots of notable cases. You may not see the lesions of juvenile spring eruption again for a while.

2. Become a reflective practitioner. Reflective practice helps us to look critically at our own practice systematically and rigorously so that we can learn from our experiences. Thought-provoking essays can spring from this fount of internal debate.

3. Write what you know about, or what you want to get to know about. It's going to take time and effort; you may as well enjoy it. Genuine interest will stimulate and motivate you.

4. Be clear from the outset exactly who the author of the paper is and whether there are co-authors. You may find you've become incredibly popular when your paper is finally ready for submission. All listed authors need to sign off on the final draft. Give credit where credit is due; acknowledge appropriately in the text those who have given a helping hand.

5. Identify your target audience and write for them. Your message must mean something to them.

6. Target an appropriate journal and know who reads it. Peruse back issues for content and style. The 'advice for the authors section' gives exactly that. Heed it carefully. Know the word count that's permitted for your type of paper.

7. Consider the journal's prestige and impact factor, but be realistic. Be ambitious but be grounded.

8. Consider investing in citation-managing software such as EndNote or Zotero to manage your references. Valuable time spent learning how to use them is time well spent.

9. Search the literature. What is known, what's new and what gaps in current knowledge can you fill? Ascertain the originality and need of your intended work. Databases like PubMed, CINAHL, Embase, Web of Knowledge, SCOPUS and Google Scholar may all help you navigate the dizzying milieu. Cast a critical eye over your findings. Don't forget to scour the grey literature of unpublished sources, such as government papers, conference proceedings and works-in-progress (PhD studies). Librarians are nice and helpful people; get to know them.

10. Think about ethical approval. If you're performing research you may need to seek permission to proceed. This may take many months so plan in advance. You will need to state whether informed consent was requested and received from study participants. Highlight your strict adherence to participant confidentiality.

11. Create the mood. You will need precious me-time, uncluttered space and an uninterrupted focus to write. You don't, however, need a month in Provence.

12. Have a plan. Complete a Gantt chart or bar graph with a feasible and achievable project schedule. This will guide you and speed you on your way. Try breaking down your opus into multiple attainable goals, remembering you have a family, hobbies and a day-job too.

13. Avoid over-reading, revising and revisiting. Get writing. Don't procrastinate or obfuscate but write little and often.

14. Don't surrender to writer's block. Fight back by brainstorming, mind-mapping, walking or just having a coffee. Choose a time when you know you're most industrious. There are no absolutes; you can start with your conclusions or abstract if that's easier. You may need to cut yourself some slack. The most prolific of authors can have a barren spell too.

15. Choose your words carefully, aiming for clarity and brevity of expression. If it can be described in fewer words then do so. Avoid slang, unexplained acronyms and stock phrases. Needless to say, omit phrases like 'needless to say'.

16. Avoid cutting and pasting yourself into a plagiarism controversy. If you quote it, reference it.

17. Each paragraph should have a dedicated theme and paragraphs should flow logically from one to the next.

18. Remember, the first draft is just that. You can work afterwards on crafting the masterpiece. Take advice from those you know, trust and respect.

19. Start with a working title that describes what you are writing about. A catchy, concise, unambiguous title will come to you when you least expect it. The publisher may suggest the final title.

20. By convention most medical papers follow the format of introduction, methodology, results, discussion and conclusions. Unless there is a strong reason to be otherwise, be conventional.

21. Your introduction should explain why the topic you've chosen is interesting and important. The reader needs to appreciate the true value of your work. Contextualise your research question by reviewing the relevant literature and giving background subject information. Clearly state the purpose of your study, outlining your specific objectives.

22. The methodology section should explain each step of your research journey so that your study can be replicated. Inform the reader who participated in the study, why they were chosen and your sample size. Justify your research strategy in light of your research question. Detail all procedures followed, avoiding use of any patient identifiers. Describe how you collected your data and how you went about analysing it. Document what statistical techniques were used. Clarify that ethics approval was granted.

23. Your results should be presented in a logical sequence without interpretation. Use graphs and tables judiciously and don't replicate in text what is demonstrated in picture-form. Avoid using the words 'normal' or 'significant' unless in the technical, statistical sense.

24. The discussion section should be a deliberation on your results, interpreting their meaning and putting them into perspective. Comparison with previous studies should be made to support or refute what light you have shed on current thinking. Here you need to acknowledge the strengths, weaknesses and limitations of your study. Success lies in recognising and admitting one's perceived failures.

25. Your conclusion should be closely linked to your opening objectives. Summarise your findings and make appropriate recommendations. Proudly flag how you have contributed to the existing body of evidence. We all stand on the shoulders of giants.

26. Write up your abstract. This is a synopsis of your work, capturing the essence of your study. Keep it brief and structured.

27. Take advice from a learned friend or join a medical writing group. Collaboration can facilitate the process and make it a whole lot easier and more enjoyable.

28. Proofread your manuscript and ask a friend to do likewise. Remember that spellcheck is your (American) friend.

29. Ensure your referencing style matches that of your chosen journal.

30. Compose a courteous covering letter to the editor explaining why you have written this paper and highlight why it suits his or her particular journal. Submit to only one journal. Courting other journals simultaneously may lead to unseemly literary polygamy.

31. Be ever optimistic, but be prepared for disappointment. The editor may reject your paper outright or may offer helpful, constructive suggestions for revision prior to acceptance. Should you agree with these revisions then make the necessary changes and re-submit as soon as possible, highlighting and justifying the changes that you have made. Outright unconditional acceptance is a rare but joyous treat.

32. You may need to revise and re-format your paper for another journal. Take time over this and carefully adhere to the new journal's style and referencing requirements, otherwise they'll sense that they were your second choice. *[And especially if you forget to change addressee in the covering letter. Ed.]*

Becoming an author can be a challenge. Obstacles and excuses can impede your progress but can be overcome. Thoughtful planning, meticulous implementation and diligence in following the rules of the game can yield gratifying results. Writing skills can be honed with practice and persistence. So come on and get writing; you have a story to tell.

61

EVENTS MEDICINE

Mary-Jo Sommerville

I'm a GP. Twenty years ago I provided medical cover for a Bruce Spingsteen concert in Glasgow. The medicine was good, though Bruce possibly better.

Twenty years on I am a key medical player at T in the Park, a fixture in the summer festival diary. Should GPs do this sort of stuff? Absolutely!

THE SUB-SPECIALTY

The sub-specialty of event medicine first started in the wake of the Hillsborough Disaster in 1989 where a total of 96 fans lost their lives.

After a public inquiry, new safety measures were introduced at football grounds around the UK.

These have been developed and distilled into the *Guide to Safety at Sports Grounds* – 'The Green Guide'. Also available are *The Event Safety Guide* ('The Purple Guide') and the *Technical Standards for Places of Entertainment* ('The Yellow Guide'). These are all available online, and give guidance as to the level of multi-agency cover recommended, and to risk assessment of events.

The guides are not legally binding as such, but rather provide a guide to levels of cover required at events, for local councils, licensing boards, and other interested parties including event promoters, ambulance services and voluntary agencies. In some Health Boards there is also representation from public health or from civil contingencies, although this is by no means universal.

THE EVENTS

There are a small number of GPs and hospital doctors who provide cover for these events, and who are happy to advise and support each other (and you). The level of medical cover will vary depending on crowd size and demographics. Events vary in size and in risk from 5000 at Disney on Ice (well-equipped purpose-built arena, minutes from a major hospital) to Scotland's jewel in the crown – T in the Park, with 85,000 visitors (open fields in Kinross, for three days the third largest town in Scotland, 40 minutes by road from the nearest hospital). You find yourself liaising with police intelligence regarding illicit drugs, with environmental health and public health regarding suspected food poisoning and swine flu, and with the Fire Service.

THE SET-UP

This varies from a Portakabin or tent, to a purpose-built medical suite in arenas/sports stadia, to a field hospital with a five-bed resus facility and a campsite branch surgery (at T in the Park).

THE CROWD

Most revellers are well-behaved and responsible. But a small number of people can be determined to cause as much mayhem as possible.

We need to be aware that our role also involves the pastoral aspect of ensuring that vulnerable patrons, particularly if they are under-age, are only discharged into the care of a responsible adult. (Remember that 'responsible' and 'adult' are not always interchangeable.)

TOP TIPS

For any aspiring event doc these would be as follows.

1. *Get involved* – ask around and cut your teeth on low-volume, low-risk events before diving into the big gigs.

2. *Ask for advice from colleagues* – doctors, nurses and paramedics. All will have more experience than you during your initial outings. 'The Team' in event medicine is multi-professional, much like our Primary Care Team.

3. *Be respectful and considerate – of patients.* This should go without saying. Patients at events may have waited all year for this event, and be deeply disappointed if their experience is marred by illness or injury. They will not always thank you if you send them home or to hospital.

4. *Be respectful and considerate – of colleagues.* Our voluntary agency colleagues work long hours for no financial gain. Be supportive. Be generous with your knowledge and share it graciously. Our colleagues from the Security Services do a very difficult job, maintaining crowd (and your) safety and dealing with potential conflict. So never underestimate their vital role.

5. *Be respectful and considerate – of artists.* Many promoters will have a dedicated 'production doctor' to look after the artists. If, however, you are unexpectedly called upon to treat a performer, remember to be discreet and professional. And to remove any obvious external identifiers of your profession. It is hard to preserve patient confidentiality if you stride in with a stethoscope around your neck. Remember that the performers are in some respects similar to elite athletes, and that for them to cancel a performance because of illness or injury would be enormously stressful. And potentially eye-wateringly expensive.

6. *Be professional* – remember there is a world of difference between 'informal' and 'unprofessional'. You are not wearing your Doctor Disguise, so always introduce yourself and seek the patient's consent for examinations and procedures.

7. *Be prepared* – from equipment malfunction to colleague absence, always have a Plan B.

8. *Be adaptable* – auscultation is not always an option at a loud concert, so look to other recordable parameters for patient assessment in these circumstances, e.g. pulse oximetry, heart rate, blood pressure.

9. *Be thorough* – with your examination, taking care not to miss potentially serious illness by failing to check simple things such as blood glucose and temperature.

10. *Be legible* – keep good notes. These should be legible to you and your colleagues. And the fiscal/coroner.

11. *Be indemnified* – see above, and be sure to let your Defence Organisation know of your events in advance.

12. *Check everything. Twice.*

13. A Good Place to discover that your glucometer sticks are incompatible with your glucometers is in your local pharmacy. A Bad Place is in a field 40 miles from nowhere.

14. *Use local knowledge* – at T in the Park many of our nursing colleagues are from local hospitals. They are invaluable in making things run smoothly and keeping us right with respect to referral protocols etc. They also have access to a wide variety of supplies and equipment in the rare event that our on-site supplies are running low. Similarly, the local Scottish Ambulance Service at events have excellent local geographical knowledge, not just of transit times to hospitals.

15. *Be aware* – of local services and distances/transit times to local hospitals/pharmacies. Liaise in advance.

16. *Be aware* – of the local Major Incident procedure, and of what your role and responsibility would be in this circumstance. Ask your most senior medical or Scottish Ambulance Service colleague.

17. *Be aware* – that in these days of mobile phone cameras, you are only one click away from starring in The Most Incompetent Resuscitation Ever on YouTube. So ….

18. *Be educated* – ideally through courses run by the Advanced Life Support Group (ALSG), e.g. MIMMS, ATLS, ALS and ALSO. The British Association for Immediate Care also runs courses designed specifically for GPs and nurses, e.g. BASICS + PHEC. These are pitched at a more achievable level and are very suitable as initial qualifications. They are infinitely more impressive than an exhaustive knowledge of the Arctic Monkeys back catalogue.

19. *Be appropriately dressed* – embrace the fleece and Gore-Tex collections. For a woman whose main form of exercise is running upstairs in Harvey Nicks, I have an impressive range of extreme-weather gear!

In the main, death and serious injury are the exception rather than the rule in event medicine. But minimise risk from start to finish.

If you enjoy working with enthusiastic and like-minded colleagues, and practising off-*piste* medicine in a variety of challenging environments, then events medicine is the best thing ever.

> › *Key tip* – get yourself some Really Excellent Wellies!

62

FIRST5

Clare J. Taylor

> While standing on top of Everest, I looked across the valley, towards the other great peak, Makalu, and mentally worked out a route about how it could be climbed … it showed me that, even though I was standing on top of the world, it wasn't the end of everything for me, by any means. I was still looking beyond to other interesting challenges.
>
> (Sir Edmund Hilary, mountaineer and explorer)

The general practice training years can feel like climbing a mountain. The new trainee sets out from base camp with a group of peers, everyone both excited and nervous about the challenge ahead, and all keen to reach the summit. The trainee has a guide with each step of the way and knows that there are other more senior guides back at Deanery HQ tracking the journey to make sure that they are staying on course. There are highs and lows along the way. As each acronym hurdle is overcome – the Applied Knowledge Test (AKT), the Clinical Skills Assessment (CSA), the Annual Review of Competency Progression (ARCP) panel – the sense of achievement increases and the trainee starts to feel that he or she might reach the summit. The day arrives when the summit is reached. The hard work and determination of the three-year climb have been rewarded by a sense of great achievement and pride. The new GP stands on the edge of the summit looking out over the whole world of general practice. What an amazing view! A lifetime of opportunity and fulfilment awaits.

But now at the summit, it's a long way down and which direction to take anyway? There's the rocky road of the locum, the apparently smoother road of the salaried GP or the perceived rich fields of the partnership. The new GP has many skills learnt during the climb, but there are still things not known, and areas where confidence will only grow with experience. And who will be there to help and to guide? The guides have new climbers to take care of now. And the group of fellow trainees have all gone their different ways, embarking on new journeys of their own. The senior guides at Deanery HQ who tracked progress during the climb no longer have responsibility for wellbeing. Instead there is a new observer called 'the appraiser' to whom you are suddenly accountable. Scary! The journey ahead is suddenly rather daunting.

The Associates-in-Training (AiT) committee 2008–9 of the Royal College of General Practitioners (RCGP) recognised the excitement and fear of trainees as they approached the summit at the end of training and embark on a new career, alone in the world of general practice for the first time. They realised that the College was well placed to support this important career stage and developed the First5® concept. The First5 initiative began in 2009 and aims to support new GPs from completion of training through the first five years of independent practice. The initiative has five pillars and each pillar can help the new GP in different ways to smooth the transition from the summit to the new world that lies before him or her. Here's how:

PILLAR 1:

CONNECTING WITH COLLEGE – PROMOTING A SENSE OF BELONGING AND APPROPRIATE REPRESENTATION FOR THE FIRST5 COHORT WITHIN THE COLLEGE

The new GP is aware of the RCGP from the climb to the summit. The RCGP set the path for the climb with the curriculum and organised the trainee journal *InnovAiT*, and discounted access to the BJGP as well. The College represents trainee views through the trainees (or AiT) committee, and AiTs now have a representative on UK Council with full voting rights. But now venturing from the summit, the new GP will still find the College supportive. The College will be responsible for improving quality and standards in the world of general practice in which the new GP lives and works. Fortunately, there is now a First5 local lead in every College faculty who will arrange networking events and provide new GPs with a voice at faculty level. The College will hear and respond to views of new GPs for the first time. The new GP should attend the RCGP Annual Conference – there are workshops and social events specifically for new GPs, and a sense of belonging to a vibrant group of like-minded individuals. Afterwards the new GP can join the First5 Facebook group and follow First5 on Twitter. The new GP can then read the monthly First5 e-newsletter, and then participate!

PILLAR 2:

FACILITATING NETWORKS – ENCOURAGING PEER SUPPORT AND MENTORING THROUGH THE DEVELOPMENT OF LOCAL NETWORKS USING THE RCGP FACULTY STRUCTURE

The First5 local lead organises a networking event where the new GP is able to meet with fellow new GPs and forms a First5 Continuing Professional Development (CPD) Group. The groups now meet every 6–8 weeks to discuss difficult cases, learn from each other and provide the support that the new GP enjoyed from fellow trainees on the climb to the summit. The new GP also has the opportunity to have a mentor: a wise colleague not connected to everyday work available for a chat and rumination.

PILLAR 3:

SUPPORTING REVALIDATION – OFFERING SUPPORT THROUGH REVALIDATION

The new GP is more likely to be in a sessional role than more senior colleagues. Revalidation is more challenging for sessional, particularly locum, doctors who may find themselves working across different practices or on short-term contracts, which can make patient feedback difficult to collect and an audit cycle difficult to complete. The College offers support to the new GP through the revalidation ePortfolio. It is also aware of the challenges faced by new GPs and takes these into account in negotiations with the General Medical Council about the exact requirements of revalidation.

PILLAR 4:

CAREER MENTORSHIP – HIGHLIGHTING THE OPPORTUNITIES A CAREER IN GENERAL PRACTICE OFFERS AND HELPING NEW GPs GET THE MOST OUT OF BEING A GP

The new GP has many career paths to choose. The RCGP has much expertise in different areas of general practice and can provide information on the opportunities available from prison medicine to international work, medical education to research activity. The College also focuses on the importance of being a generalist through the Commission on Generalism report.[1]

PILLAR 5:

CPD – IDENTIFYING AREAS OF CPD THAT MEMBERS IN THE FIRST FIVE YEARS FEEL ARE NOT WELL PROVIDED AND DEVELOPING MATERIALS THAT WILL ADDRESS THEIR LEARNING NEEDS

The new GP is keen to keep on learning, to meet outstanding learning needs and keep up to date in the rapidly changing world of modern general practice. There are several courses on the RCGP website that have been developed specifically for new GPs. Of note the 'First5 Leadership' course provides an insight into key leadership attributes and the importance of being an effective clinical leader in a modern healthcare system like the NHS. The First5 CPD group guide (downloadable from the First5 website) helps new GPs run sessions, and explains how to document educational activity (and CPD points) using the forms at the back of the guide. Before long the new GP should be reading then contributing to the BJGP and BMJ.

After a couple of years, a new GP is more comfortable in the world gazed at from the summit of the mountain. There is still much to learn, and a lifetime of doing so, but support and guidance are available. The path ahead is bright and is filled with opportunity and excitement. Enjoy every step of the way!

Full details of the First5 initiative are available at www.rcgp.org.uk/first5 or by emailing first5@rcgp.org.uk. Please join us on Facebook (RCGP First5) and follow us on Twitter (@rcgpfirst5). First5 is a copyright of the RCGP.

REFERENCE

1.   Commission on Generalism. *Guiding Patients through Complexity: modern medical generalism* (report of an independent commission for the Royal College of General Practitioners and the Health Foundation). London: Health Foundation, 2011.

63

TIPS FOR TEACHING

Polly Duncan and Veronica Boon

INTRODUCTION

Teaching is a fantastic way to add variety to your job and to brush up on your own knowledge and skills – you have to have a good understanding of something to be able to teach it. It is also part of the RCGP curriculum and a requirement of the General Medical Council (GMC). Most doctors will have had some experience of teaching but many will not have put much thought into how they teach or how they could improve their teaching. This article will provide some simple tips on planning, delivering and evaluating a teaching session, and will also highlight some of the teaching opportunities available.

PLANNING

1. *Who? Know your audience.* It is important to have an understanding of what your students already know and what is expected of them so that you can pitch the session at the right level. Make it relevant to their professional and learning needs. For example, if you are teaching medical students, *Tomorrow's Doctors*[1] outlines the GMC-recommended learning outcomes for all undergraduates and can be used to tailor your teaching appropriately.

2. *What? Identify aims and objectives.* Aims are broad statements that describe what you want to achieve during the session. Objectives are more precise statements

of what you hope the students will learn. A good acronym to use when writing objectives is 'SMART'. Each objective should be specific, measurable, achievable, realistic and time-bound. Use the phrase 'by the end of the session the students should be able to...'. This puts the emphasis on the student's learning rather than your teaching. It is important that your aims and objectives and corresponding teaching activities are devised to match the intended learning outcomes. This is known as constructive alignment and is based on the theory that providing the student with a clearly specified goal will enhance learning by enabling him or her to understand the relevance of the new material.[2]

3. *Where?* Check whether your teaching venue has the resources you need (e.g. flip charts and pens) or whether you need to bring them with you. Think about things like toilets and tea-making facilities. It sounds simple but concentration spans can wane if these physiological needs are not met.

4. *How? Be creative.* We have all sat through countless PowerPoint presentations. Try something different. Think about balancing teacher and student activity; you should not be doing all the work.

5. *Plan. Use a lesson plan* (see Table 63.1). This is a great way to work through the who, what, where and how. It will also help you to be realistic about how much you can fit into the session in the allocated time.

TABLE 63.1: EXAMPLE OF A SIMPLE LESSON PLAN

Date: 17 January 2013	Venue: GP surgery	No. of students: Four	Level of students: Third-year undergraduate medical students
Aim: To improve the student's knowledge of diabetes		**Objectives:** By the end of the session the student should be able to: – take a history from a patient with diabetes in a systematic way – give three examples of how the diabetes has affected the patient from a psychosocial point of view – list five complications of diabetes – list five other risk factors for cardiovascular disease	
Opening activity: Students to be split into pairs and asked to find out one interesting fact about the person they have been paired with and to share this with the group		**Closing activity:** Students to be given a Post-it note and asked to write down one thing they have enjoyed about the session and one thing that could have been done better	

Time:	Teacher activity:	Student activity:	Resources:
9:00–09:15	Introduction. Set out the aims and objectives of the session	Opening activity. Invited to add any other topics relating to diabetes they would like to cover	Flip chart, pens
9:15–10:00	Facilitate discussion about diabetes	Students split into pairs and asked to make mind maps of what they know about diabetes	Paper from flip chart, pens
10:00–10:15	Break	Break	
10:15–11:00	Observe students taking a history from the patient	Students take it in turns to take different parts of the history	Patient with diabetes. Consultation room with no interruptions
11:00–11:15	Break	Break	
11:15–12:00	Give feedback to the students and facilitate discussion about what they have learned	Students to be involved in the feedback process. Students to be tested against the objectives. Closing activity	Flip chart and pens

Source: adapted with permission from the Bristol Teaching and Learning for Health Professionals session *pro forma*.

DELIVERING

6. *Consider different learning styles.* There are several models describing different learning preferences. VARK outlines four main learning styles: visual, aural, read/write and kinaesthetic.[3] Students will have individual preferences for each of the learning styles. Learning the same topic with different styles can improve learning, so you should endeavour to include a mixture of all of the learning styles in your teaching. Examples include videos, group discussions and practical exercises. The Myers–Briggs personality-type indicator is another model that can be used to inform a learner about his or her learning style and approach to learning.[4]

7. *Engage the students from the start using an 'ice breaker'.* This is a short introductory activity that can be used to establish prior knowledge or familiarise the students with each other. The opening activity in Table 63.1 is an example of this.

8. *Use interactive methods.* Most people's concentration spans range from 5–15 minutes so try to avoid long lectures and instead vary your teaching style, for example using role-play, quizzes and brainstorming exercises.[5] Observing other teachers is a good way to pick up new teaching techniques.

9. *Give constructive feedback.* Reflecting on a student's performance has been shown to have one of the biggest impacts on learning. Kolb's learning cycle can be used to enhance student learning and reflective practice (see Figure 63.1). There are four stages: concrete experience (a practical activity), reflective observation (reflect and review what happened), abstract conceptualisation (draw up a list of rules based on the reflection) and active experimentation (apply the rules to a new activity).[6] For example, a student is observed taking a social history from a patient; the student and teacher discuss what went well, what went less well and what could be improved; the student and teacher draw up a list of consultation skills that can be used when taking a social history; the student and teacher role-play a similar situation to practise the consultation skills (see Figure 63.1).

FIGURE 63.1: FOUR-STAGE LEARNING CYCLE

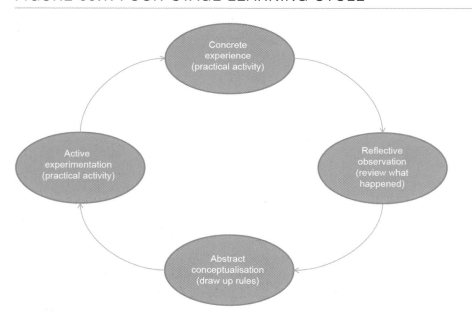

Source: Reece I, Walker S. *Teaching, Training and Learning.*[7]

EVALUATING

10. *Reflect on your teaching session.* Good teachers learn from both their successes and mistakes. Use your lesson plan to record comments on each of the different aspects of your session. Did you meet your aims and objectives? What was it about a particular activity that the students liked? What would you do differently next time?

11. *Get feedback from students.* Rather than using a standard individual feedback form, encourage more meaningful responses by using novel methods. For example, ask students to write one strength and one weakness of the session on differently coloured Post-it notes, or ask the group to discuss the session and give collective feedback.

12. *Ask someone to observe you teaching or video a session.* This can offer an invaluable insight into your interaction with the students.

HOW DO I GET INVOLVED?

13. *Teach your colleagues.* Vocational training scheme (VTS) teaching sessions are a brilliant non-threatening environment to try out new teaching methods. There is often scope to teach during hospital and GP posts too, for example at journal clubs or clinical meetings.

14. *Teach medical students.* There are often opportunities to help facilitate problem-based learning groups or communication skills sessions, or to run small-group teaching sessions with medical students attached to your GP practice. Contact the head of primary care teaching at your local medical school and check the university websites. Your local GP deanery and GP trainer are a useful source of knowledge too.

15. *Examine medical students.* This can be a useful way to find out what level of knowledge is required of students.

16. *Apply for study leave* so that teaching sessions are protected and free from clinical distractions.

17. *Go on a teaching course.* Many universities offer teaching courses for health professionals. These can range from short workshop courses to programmes leading to a postgraduate certificate, diploma, masters degree or PhD. The University of Dundee is one example and offers both taught courses and distance learning courses (http://medicine.dundee.ac.uk/).

18. *Attend a conference.* The Association for the Study of Medical Education (ASME) has an annual UK conference (www.asme.org.uk). There is also a trainee branch of ASME called TASME – both have regional divisions and these are another great source of information about medical teaching opportunities. The Association

for Medical Education in Europe (AMEE) is an international organisation that has an annual conference offering an opportunity to find out about teaching methods in other countries. The Society for Academic Primary Care (SAPC), UK Conference of Postgraduate Educational Advisors in General Practice (UKCEA) and Committee of General Practice Education Directors (COGPED) are all organisations that specifically relate to general practice teaching.

19. *Apply for an education fellow post.* If you enjoy teaching this can be a great way to make teaching part of your career as well as developing your skills.

20. *Teach.* The best way to become an effective teacher is to get lots of practice. If you have had a bad experience of teaching do not let it put you off. We all have bad days and some types of teaching will be better suited to you than others.

RESOURCES

› Association for the Study of Medical Education, www.asme.org.uk.

› Postgraduate Certificate in Medical Education, University of Dundee [online], http://medicine.dundee.ac.uk/course/pg-certificate-med-ed [accessed March 2014].

› Teach the Teachers Course, www.medical-interviews.co.uk/p-220-teach-the-teacher-course.aspx [accessed March 2014].

› Teaching and Learning for Health Professionals [online], www.bris.ac.uk/medical-education/tlhp/tlhp-programme/ [accessed March 2014].

REFERENCES

1. General Medical Council. *Tomorrow's Doctors.* London: GMC, 2009.

2. Biggs J, Tang C. *Teaching for Quality Learning at University.* Maidenhead: McGraw-Hill and Open University Press, 2011.

3. Fleming ND, Mills C. Not another inventory, rather a catalyst for reflection. *To Improve the Academy* 1992; **11**: 137–55, www.vark-learn.com/documents/not_another_inventory.pdf [accessed March 2014].

4. Briggs-Myers I, Briggs-Myers P. *Gifts Differing: understanding personality type.* Mountain View, CA: Davies-Black Publishing, 1995.

5. Steinert Y, Snell L. Interactive lecturing: strategies for increasing participation in large group presentations. *Medical Teacher* 1999; **21(1)**: 37–42.

6. Dennick R. Twelve tips for incorporating educational theory into teaching practices. *Medical Teacher* 2012; **34(8)**: 618–24.

7. Reece I, Walker S. *Teaching, Training and Learning.* Sunderland: Business Education Publishers, 2007.

64

GETTING A JOB

David Matthews and Matt Burkes

Towards the end of your registrar year you will hopefully have the horror of exams behind you and thoughts will turn to your next challenge: supporting yourself financially after your training ends. This will be especially pressing if you have a family to support. It may come as something of an unpleasant surprise to discover that the last few years of training slog were actually the easy bit. During those heady days you were cosseted in a world of secure income with people who cared about your education and wellbeing. This is no longer the case – you are now on your own.

If you are lucky you may walk into a job at your training practice, although you may not consider this to be lucky.

More likely in the present economic climate you will have to find work elsewhere. If this is the case, it's worth having a think about what type of work you want and how far you are prepared to go to get it.

You may decide that you will only apply for partnerships. If so, good luck – the opportunities seem to be few and far between at present and most likely you will be competing against an internal candidate. Don't necessarily let this put you off but consider the safety net of a Plan B. That said, with the increase in superannuation costs for locums, it is possible that more partnerships and salaried jobs may be on the horizon.

If you decide that you are going to opt out of the UK altogether then do read the chapter on working overseas (Chapter 75) and start planning EARLY. You can't just get off the plane and start seeing patients.

Salaried work is a common model and has a number of advantages over partnership: the work and administrative load is typically significantly less than that of a partner, you will not have to make a financial commitment to the practice, and your pay will be fixed, which will allow you a greater degree of financial security – something that many find very attractive after the security of a training position. These days, many salaried doctors are positively encouraged to have a say in the policy direction of the practice and are not treated simply as 'the hired help'. That said, many hanker after the permanence, opportunities and challenges that partnership has to offer, including the financial reward, the business exposure, the opportunity to create the type of practice you have always wanted to be part of and the sense of being master of your own destiny.

In truth, most people's first jobs will probably be locum work, salaried positions or, increasingly, a mixture of both. Here are some thoughts on how best to secure an income post-MRCGP.

You're going to need a good curriculum vitae (CV). There are two components to this: writing a good CV and having something to write about. Both are essential if you are hoping for the phone to ring. A good start will be asking your practice manager (PM) to let you see any CVs he or she has on record. PMs get sent a lot of CVs and generally hang on to the good ones. Ask to look at a few and get them to go through what was good and bad about each. This will give you a feel for how to approach creating the structure of your own life story. You will see that CVs are short. How short is a matter of debate, but avoid going over 2–3 sides of A4.

Having something to write about is easier if you have anticipated having to do it. Creating good CV points takes time; courses, publications, business skills and teaching experience cannot be conjured up overnight. Ideally you should be thinking about this from day 1 of training.

Having crafted a beautiful résumé, get honest feedback on it. Ask your trainer, your practice manager, your programme directors, other GPs ... the more feedback the better. Creating the perfect CV is generally an iterative process rather than something you can do at one sitting, so ALLOW TIME FOR IT. Don't leave it till the night before the deadline.

BOX 64.1: CV SUGGESTIONS

The job you are applying for may have many applicants so your CV needs to look professional, catch the eye of employers and efficiently convey why you are the person for the job. Below are some suggestions in keeping with these aims.

- Try to limit the length of your CV to two or three pages.

- Consider starting your CV with a 'Profile' of yourself. Constituting perhaps half a side of A4, the aim of this is to concisely explain your current situation and responsibilities, highlight your main skills, attributes and experience, as well as outlining your future plans and areas of interest. This allows recruiting practices to get a feel for who you are and what you have to offer before they've even read beyond the first page of your CV.

- When listing your attributes relate them to some sort of evidence rather than just relaying them as your own (possibly inflated!) view of yourself. For example, rather than stating 'I'm a great team player and patients love me', you could write 'The good relationships I enjoy with both colleagues and patients are reflected in excellent "360 degree" and patient questionnaire feedback'.

- Get your trainer/trusted GP partner to look at your CV with a critical eye. Ask this person if he or she was recruiting and had 50 CVs to look through, would yours stand out? If not, what could you change or highlight?

- Get friends and colleagues to check your CV's grammar, spelling, sentence structure, flow and layout. Then check it again. And again.

- The 'hobbies and interests' section is to let employers know you are a rounded person with stuff other than work in your life to act as a buffer against burnout, so don't worry if you're not an Olympic sailor. If you are a workaholic recluse, however, you may want quickly to adopt some more exciting pastimes.

If you are staying in the locality of your training then hopefully you will have realised that your whole training programme was a very long interview and opportunity to establish a reputation locally that stands you in good stead to get a job afterwards (or not as the case may be!). The hospital/GP world is a small and interconnected one. When your name comes up over coffee, let the first comments from your last hospital supervisor be a glowing recommendation rather than a curse. This hopefully illustrates the importance of giving your all in every job regardless of how much you are enthused in the attachment.

For this reason it's also best to try to get on a training scheme where you want to work and conversely considering changing plans to look for a job where you end up doing your vocational training scheme. That said, getting a job where you trained is not for everyone. Your circumstances may have changed and it may be time to move on. Don't panic. The core principles for finding work are the same and are outlined below.

When looking for work, as well as the usual sources like the GP magazines, you should also recognise that lots of jobs come up informally – ask your trainer/practice manager to 'keep their ear to the ground'. When replying to adverts one author of this chapter found arranging an informal visit was a useful way of getting a feel for a practice. Some practices were friendly and interested, while at others he was shown the building but none of the partners actually made the effort to speak to him.

In terms of finding the right job (as opposed to any job) GPs are generally friendly people. You should look for a practice with people you feel you can get on with – this will be a more important consideration for most recruiting practices than a candidate with multiple diplomas. Ask during informal visits how people (particularly the partners) at the practice get on. A hesitant or vague answer can be very telling! Don't be afraid not to apply for a job if it doesn't feel right after visiting, but be diplomatic – you may still be seeing these people on a regular basis throughout your working life if you get a job nearby!

If all goes well you may be called for an interview. In days gone by this was often an informal chat, but these days this has been largely replaced by a structured panel interview with all partners and practice manager, possibly any salaried doctors and possibly a representative member from the patient participation panel, so make sure you prepare for this.

Practising interview questions with colleagues is very useful, so ask your trainer to do a mock interview with feedback. Make sure you are up to date with the 'hot topics' of the day. Ensure you know why you want to work for them, have an opinion on the Quality and Outcomes Framework (QOF) and commissioning, and have a vision of how general practice will survive in the future.

Try to develop a skill during your training years that could be a potential source of income for a practice – minor operations, contraceptive coils/implants (Diploma of the Faculty of Sexual and Reproductive Healthcare) and joint injections. Have a think about what your interests are and try to demonstrate them during you training. You will be asked about them at interview.

BOX 64.2: THE INTERVIEW

Having crossed the first hurdle of making your CV stand out, the gauntlet of an interview lies before you. As with your CV, preparation is everything here as there are only so many areas a practice can ask questions about, so if you have invested time in practising answers you are likely to feel more confident and relaxed. Do not see the interview as merely a passive process putting you at the mercy of the panel; it is also a forum where you can communicate and emphasise why you are the candidate for the job. Virtually any question can be used as an opportunity to highlight your attributes, skills and experience if harnessed in the correct way. Make sure you have a couple of questions up your sleeve to ask at the end of the interview when you will almost certainly be offered the chance to ask the panel something. Get colleagues/trainers/friends to run mock interviews for you. Ask them to be honest about how you come across.

Thinking about how you would address the following questions (all lifted from genuine GP interviews) could form the start of your interview preparation:

1. What are your main strengths?

2. What are your main weaknesses?

3. How would your friends describe you if asked in a pub/restaurant?

4. What do you see as the main challenges facing general practice at the moment?

5. What is your view on commissioning/Care Quality Commission/revalidation?

6. In what ways will you bring money into the practice?

7. Outline your management experience so far.

8. Tell us about your special interests. How will they benefit the practice?

9. What do you see yourself doing five years from now?

10. Why aren't you emigrating to Australia to work as a GP?

After the interview you will either have a job or not. If not, ask for honest feedback as to why. Was it a problem with the CV or at interview or just a stronger candidate? (If so, why were they stronger?) Do this in a constructive way – this is one professional getting feedback from another so they can improve their future performance.

Reflect on the feedback and make the required changes, then pick yourself up, dust yourself off and get back on the hunt. *Remember*: even if you are doing all the right things and are a good candidate, ultimately getting the right job is often about being in the right place at the right time.

65

APPRAISAL AND REVALIDATION

Niall Cameron and Michael Norbury

Revalidation is the process by which doctors demonstrate to the General Medical Council (GMC) that they continue to be fit to practise. Effective participation in enhanced appraisal is an essential element of this process.

Appraisal is an opportunity to demonstrate your professionalism and commitment to maintaining your skills and knowledge as a GP. It allows you to demonstrate your participation in effective and high-quality patient care.

Appraisal requires that all doctors spend some time every year thinking about their clinical practice and how it could be developed. Clearly, this is more important now than ever, given the rapid pace of change within both clinical practice and the health service generally.

Most doctors are naturally reflective. They are inquisitive about how their practice impacts on health outcomes and strive to enhance the quality of care they deliver to patients. Appraisal allows you to discuss with a trained colleague in a supportive and developmental manner all aspects of your clinical practice and the factors that impact upon it.

Appraisal is designed to be dynamic and flexible. The ePortfolio, with which you will be familiar, is a record of prescribed learning activities necessary to satisfy the requirements of Workplace-Based Assessment for MRCGP. Appraisal is the process that takes over where the ePortfolio stops on attainment of your MRCGP.

Newly qualified doctors face a number of challenges. Some will have moved away from the area in which they trained, which may result in losing regular contacts and peer support developed during training, as well as having to come to terms with new ways of working.

Recent data from the RCGP First5 team confirm that most newly qualified GPs are likely to be pursuing a portfolio career. This may involve a combination of sessional work, salaried posts, out-of-hours work and peripatetic locum work, while there are those who may actively pursue partnership working.

While portfolio work has many attractions and provides opportunities for valuable experience and consolidation of clinical skills, it comes with the potential risk of ill-defined career progression with no obvious support structures. There are risks too of finding it difficult to access continuing professional development (CPD) activities, to get resourcing (funding) and to ensure protected time for learning. Appraisal can be viewed as your once-yearly opportunity to pause, reflect, consider and discuss such issues with your trained appraiser.

1. Be organised – create an appraisal folder either electronically or in paper format and add to it anything throughout the year that you think might be useful for your appraisal, such as certificates for courses attended, relevant letters (compliments, complaints, letters relating to significant health outcomes in patients you directly referred/admitted) and thoughts or experiences you have had that are significant. Make sure that you anonymise any patient-identifiable information.

2. If you have access to an online portfolio then update this as you go along, recording BMJ and RCGP learning modules and meetings/courses attended. Do not leave it until your appraisal is due.

3. Become familiar with your local appraisal system and arrange a username and password sooner rather than later:

    ›   England: http://appraisals.clarity.co.uk/ (or local deanery portal)

    ›   Scotland: www.scottishappraisal.scot.nhs.uk

    ›   Wales: https://gp.marswales.org

    ›   Northern Ireland: www.nimdta.gov.uk/general-practice/gp-appraisal.

4. The RCGP appraisal revalidation portfolio is designed to lead directly on from the trainee ePortfolio: https://gpeportfolio.rcgp.org.uk. It is *free* to RGCP members.

5. Contact your local appraisal administrator as he or she will be your first port of call for all queries you have. Make sure you keep him or her up to date with contact details.

6. Consider using one of the many online tools to keep track of your online learning while seeing patients. Websites such as GPnotebook can track your educational needs based on your day-to-day searches.

7. Be aware that simply downloading your online searches or collecting certificates for the year are not enough to satisfy the requirements of appraisal. Ensure that you reflect on the courses you've attended rather than just proving that you attended a course. Say how your reflection has either affirmed good practice or how it will change your practice as a result.

8. Wherever possible ask that course certificates, prescribing data, attendance certificates, etc. be sent to you electronically, as uploading them to your online appraisal portal will be a lot simpler. Consider investing in a desktop scanner so you can scan and upload relevant pieces of evidence that are not in an electronic format. Your appraiser can usually then log in to view your evidence once you have 'released it' for his or her viewing in advance of your appraisal.

9. Find out what support is available locally. Try contacting the deanery, RCGP faculty board and local locum groups. All are likely to offer support and ongoing CPD opportunities.

10. Look at national resources, such as the RCGP First5 web pages (www.rcgp.org.uk/membership/join-rcgp-newly-qualified-gps.aspx) and the National Association of Sessional GPs (NASGP) website, which also includes lists of local sessional GP groups and chambers (www.nasgp.org.uk).

11. Consider using online providers of CPD activities such as the essential updates run by the RCGP (www.elearning.rcgp.org.uk) or BMJ learning modules (which also have a built-in personal development section and a reflective CPD log).

12. Appraisal 'toolkits' are available for sessional GPs and out-of-hours GPs. The toolkit will help you produce evidence wherever you are based. One example is: www.scottishappraisal.scot.nhs.uk.

13. Most doctors will use information from their regular practice to inform appraisal. Where this is not possible keep a reflective log-book of where you have been working, and develop a system for recording interesting or complex clinical or organisational issues. Trying to do this retrospectively is impossible.

14. A log-book that describes issues you have encountered and your reflection on these, and any changes to your practice, can provide rich material for your appraisal. Make sure any patient-specific information is anonymised.

15. If you are not practice based, consider different ways of collecting information for your appraisal. For instance, if you work for an out-of-hours organisation ask what resources (including protected time to prepare for and undertake your appraisal) and data are available to help with your appraisal.

16. CPD should be a balanced mix of both organisational and clinical issues.

17. You should be appraised where you do most of your work, with a focus on your main clinical role. However, as part of your appraisal be prepared to discuss all areas in which you work as a GP including any extended roles together with appropriate evidence.

18. Check the date on which your appraisal is due, mark it in your diary and remember to submit your appraisal documentation 6–8 weeks before so your appraiser can review it. Remember to agree on a venue and set aside sufficient time for preparation. The interview will usually last for at least two hours.

19. Find out who your appraiser will be and, if you have concerns about your allocated appraiser, contact your local appraisal administrator.

20. Look at the GMC website, particularly the section relating to the latest detailed information on *Good Medical Practice* and how this informs appraisal and revalidation.

21. Be selective about what you include in your appraisal. Your appraiser is unlikely to thank you for several large ring-binders of evidence and will much prefer high-quality reflection on several core pieces of evidence.

22. Consider joining or forming a Practice Based Small Group Learning (PBSGL) group (www.gpcpd.nes.scot.nhs.uk/pbsgl.aspx), a local or online journal club (such as the Cochrane Journal Club, www.cochranejournalclub.com) or a 'young practitioners' group. If you were in a study group during your training then consider converting it into an ongoing CPD group. Contact with such a group provides the opportunity for peer discussion of significant event analyses (SEAs) and audit. Check whether external peer review opportunities exist in your area (such as at www.gpcpd.nes. scot.nhs.uk/west-overview/peer-review-resources.aspx) or consider using the RCGP audit peer review system at www.rcgp.org.uk/clinical-and-research/clinical-resources/clinical-audit/peer-review-programme.aspx

23. Think about your ongoing learning needs and personal development plan (PDP). Having the freedom to direct your future practice and development post-MRCGP can be immensely satisfying. There are formal and informal approaches to identifying knowledge, skills or attitude gaps in your practice that can inform your learning needs. Your appraisal should cover areas of strengths and weaknesses, and challenge you to develop a plan to address and develop these.

24. Ensure your CPR certificate is up to date and find out what other compulsory local requirements there are, e.g. training in child protection/vulnerable adults.

25. If you work as a sessional GP but have a practice or organisation for which you frequently work, approach them to ask if you would be able to join them for their regular CPD events or protected learning sessions.

26. The key outputs are the summary of your appraisal meeting and the PDP for the year ahead. These should both be agreed and signed off by you and your appraiser.

27. Your appraisal discussion and documentation are confidential to you and your appraiser, although the documents summarising your discussion can be reviewed by the relevant clinical director, appraisal leads and responsible officers.

28. In situations where significant concern is raised about a doctor's practice your appraiser is obliged to share these concerns and in some situations all appraisal documents may be reviewed by the responsible officer.

29. Remember that, just as for your trainee ePortfolio, you will need to demonstrate or show your appraiser evidence of where you have met, or are progressing towards meeting, your PDP. Remember to keep your PDP objectives specific, measurable, achievable, realistic and time bound – SMART.

30. Engage enthusiastically with the process. People generally find that the more they put in the more they get out.

31. You will be expected to complete patient feedback questionnaires and Multi-Source Feedback questionnaires. Having the support of your practice-based colleagues and patients will make this exercise much easier and more useful.

32. You should complete SEAs where relevant and include these in your annual appraisal discussions.

33. You will need to be involved in audit. There are usually resources to support this process, particularly in relation to improving prescribing. You do not necessarily have to have led the audit to include it in your appraisal documentation, but you do need to have been involved in the change resulting from completion of the audit cycle.

34. The appraisal process will require you to discuss health and probity with your appraiser. Read the GMC guidance and think about what this means to you.

35. Complete the feedback form you will receive after your appraisal. This allows you to feed back to your appraiser and comment on the process.

COINTREAU FOR BREAKFAST

Twenty years ago, when GPs were Real Men and did their own on-call, I was driving to work one morning when diverted to a council house in a rough part of town. A lady was causing a disturbance. I pushed open the semi-staved in front door. Piles of rubbish and excrement in the hallway. Basins of urine. I hitched up my smart leather trench-coat, dabbed a bead of sweat as it rolled down my glistening pate, and entered the front room. My patient was a semi-naked woman with one eye, quaffing from a bottle of Cointreau. *Or Anges Warmed By Zee Tropical Sun!* Even where I work this is not a good prognostic indicator. She swivelled around and The Eye widened in terror. 'Aaaaaargh!!!' she screamed, 'THE MEKON HAS LANDED!!!' In those grim paternalistic days that was certainly enough to get you Sectioned. So off she went.

Red Roses *collection curated by Alec Logan and illustrated by Helen Wilson.*

66

GENERAL PRACTICE AND MONEY

Gordon Cruickshank

FINANCE

The bulk of a practice's income will come in the form of a monthly remittance from the NHS. These payments vary in size throughout the year, with the calendar quarter payments being higher, particularly June when the balance of the Quality and Outcomes Framework (QOF) funds is paid.

Some practices keep an absolute minimum in reserve and distribute the maximum possible to the partners each month. This is done on the basis that the funds are better in the partners' hands rather than staying in the practice, leaving the individual partners to deal with saving for their own tax bills.

Others operate in a more reserved fashion, holding reserves to cover such things as tax. These practices often work on the basis that the partners take a regular fixed monthly income, leaving some profits in the practice. Any excess profits are distributed after the year end once the annual accounts are completed.

Both methods work, but if your new practice is run on the first basis then it is important that you recognise that you will have an irregular income and that you have to make provision for your own tax and National Insurance. You need to put aside at least 33% of your income to cover tax and National Insurance. This percentage needs to rise to around 41% if you have student loans outstanding. Because of the uneven income you may need to set aside a higher percentage of your income in the better months.

In both cases you will have to build up capital in the practice to the same level as the other partners, probably over the first couple of years. This can be paid in as a lump sum or by restricting your drawings from the practice until you have reached parity with the others.

PROFITS

Generally profits are allocated to the partners on the basis of the number of sessions done, although there are other methods of sharing these. Some practices include seniority in total profits to be shared, while others allocate seniority payments to the individual partners to whom they relate. You need to know how it is dealt with in the practice that you are looking at.

If the practice owns its premises, there will be payments received for rent. These normally get shared among those partners who own the property depending on their shares. You may be asked or required to purchase a share of the partnership property – usually from an outgoing partner (and usually via a bank loan). If you do, you would be entitled to your share of this income, which you can use to fund the loan repayments. Any interest paid is offset against your profits for tax purposes (but not the capital elements of the repayments).

If Extended Hours are carried out, these may be shared in proportion to who carries out the duty as some partners opt out of this.

TAX

The tax year runs from 6 April to 5 April and, after the first few years, your share of the practice profits for the accounts year that ends in the tax year is included in your self-assessment tax return. (If the practice accounts run to 30 June 2013, your share of the profit for that year is taxed in the tax year that runs from 6 April 2013 to 5 April 2014.)

Tax for a tax year is paid in three parts. On 31 January during the tax year you make a payment on account of your liability – normally based on your liability for the previous year – and on 31 July following the tax year you make a second payment on account of the same amount. Your tax return has to be submitted by 31 January following the end of the tax year (2014 has to be submitted by 31 January 2015). At that time – 31 January after the tax year – you pay any balance of tax for the year. Your liability is calculated from the return, the two payments on account are deducted and if there is more to pay it is due by 31 January. If there is a refund due it is repaid shortly after your return goes in.

Special Rules apply for the first few years:

› year 1 – you are taxed on your income from when you start to the next 5 April

› year 2 – you are normally taxed on your income for the first 12 months of business

› year 3 – you are taxed on your income for the practice accounts year.

You can see there is a bit of double counting in the above to get you into the tax system. This creates what is known as overlap relief, which gets saved up and deducted from your final profit from this self-employment. Unfortunately, you usually find that the daily rate of profit in the earlier years is much lower than the rate when you retire so there is usually a slightly higher tax bill at the end.

You can claim certain non-practice expenses like professional subscriptions, medical equipment, course fees and motor costs. These costs will be needed by the practice accountants to finish off the practice accounts. You should keep hold of your receipts for these for a period of five years in case of investigation.

You have to be careful with motor expenses as you are only entitled to tax relief on business journeys. Travel to and from the surgery is private and most GPs find that their business mileage is only for house calls and for any travelling to and from courses. It is important that you retain a mileage log to record your business journeys – HMRC is insisting on these to justify claims. You can either keep all of your car running costs for the year, tot them up and then apportion that total to the business element, or you may find it easier to take 45p per mile for your business miles. It usually doesn't make a great deal of difference unless you are doing house calls in a particularly heavily depreciating vehicle.

Unless you are in a rural practice or live very close to the practice premises, it is unlikely that your genuine business mileage will exceed 20% of your total mileage.

PENSIONS

When you start in partnership an estimate will be made of your pensionable earnings (which are around 88% of your taxable earnings) as your exact income will not be known until the practice accounts are completed. An estimated contribution should be deducted each month for you – please make sure that this has happened, particularly if your new practice fully distributes income on a monthly basis. If it is not deducted and you have been paid the contributions, these will be deducted from you by the practice when the pension scheme catches up with you.

Contributions are tiered depending on income levels, ranging from 18.5% at low income levels, to a maximum of 26.8% of pensionable earnings if that income exceeds around £110,274 (2014 level). You should be aware that pensions are a chunky deduction and if you are full time you should expect to pay between £19,000 and £22,000 p.a. Tax relief is available on these contributions at a higher rate, which slightly softens the blow.

The pension year is the year to 31 March and every GP has to submit a statement of pensionable earnings by 28 February following. This is usually prepared by the practice accountants. That form calculates what contributions you were due for the year to the previous 31 March. Your actual contributions are compared with what you are due and any shortfall is collected from the medical services payment in March.

They will also review what has been collected to date for the current year and adjust it in March in line with the previous year.

This can lead to quite large underpayments. If you have a five-partner firm who have each underpaid £3000 for the previous year and the current year's contributions have not been reviewed, that firm could have an *increase* in its pension deductions of £30,000 in a single month (which is not a happy situation if the practice has no reserves and fully distributes profits each month). In the past, some partners who have been caught out by this received no pay for a couple of months. Not a pleasant situation!

GOLDEN HELLOS

If you are eligible for one of these it is best not to receive this in your first period of self-employment as it will be taxed and pensioned more than once. GPs who receive a £10,000 golden hello in their first year in practice could find themselves in this position.

For example:
The practice year end is 30 June and new partner joins on 1 July. Golden hello is received in first year.

This is taxed as follows:

First tax year is based on period to 5 April so £7500 of the golden hello is taxed in year one (nine months up to 31 March). In tax year 2 the full amount is taxed again.

Also pension contributions are due at say 25.8% on 88% of it – year 1 £1703, year 2 £2270 – total £3973.

Tax relief is due on the pension contributions. The net position is shown on Table 66.1.

TABLE 66.1: NET POSITION

Golden hello received		£10,000
Tax year 1 (40% of £7500 - £1703)	£2319	
National Insurance 2% on £7500	£150	
Year 1 pension contribution	£1703	
Tax year 2 (40% of £10,000 - £2270)	£3092	
National Insurance year 2	£200	
Year 2 pension contributions	£2270	
Total deductions		£9734
Net income		£266

If a golden hello is available, try if you can to be a salaried GP until it is paid. Tax, National Insurance and pension are deducted at source but only once. If not, then if you join the practice at a time other than its year end and don't apply for the payment until after the first practice year end, you can save some of the extra tax and pension in year 1. It is worth getting advice before you apply for the golden hello on its timing.

SUMMARY AND TIPS

> Make sure that you are saving enough for tax and don't dip into your tax fund unless it is very short term.

> If the practice fully distributes its income try to build up an emergency fund.

> Find out how seniority is shared.

> Keep receipts for expenses and a mileage log to record business miles.

> Get that information to the practice accountants shortly after the practice year end.

> Make sure that you are happy with the pension deduction each month – if you are full time and you are not paying £1500 to £2000 per month you are not paying enough.

> Make sure that the practice accountants are happy with the current level of superannuation payments.

> Don't take a golden hello in the first set of accounts – get it as an employee if possible.

> If you are due a tax refund get your tax return back to your accountant a.s.a.p. – you do not see the cash until the return gets submitted.

> Tax repayments go to the individuals, even if the partnership hold on to funds to cover tax and National Insurance.

> If you do part-time hours, your pensionable earnings ignoring seniority must be at least two-thirds of average GP earnings to qualify for full seniority.

67

HEALTH IS GLOBAL

Luisa Pettigrew, Ha-Neul Seo and Trish Greenhalgh

Over the last century, improvements in technology have resulted in an exponential rise in the volume and speed with which information, goods and people can travel. For many countries this has contributed to economic growth, increased migration and urbanisation. While we have witnessed overall improvements in life expectancy, new health epidemics have emerged and health inequalities have been exacerbated both between and within countries, faster than ever before. What the term 'global health' entails has been debated at length, but in essence can be defined as 'an area for study, research, and practice that places a priority on improving health and achieving equity in health for all people worldwide'[1] in which 'health issues are affected by a complex array of direct and indirect global forces, and solving problems often requires multilateral co-operation across a range of sectors'.[2]

WHAT DOES THIS HAVE TO DO WITH PRIMARY CARE?

Universal access to health care is one of the core aims of any health system. However, on a global scale, this is far from being realised today. There is an estimated global shortage of 4 million health workers. Malaria, TB and HIV still kill millions of people each year. As a woman your chances of dying due to pregnancy are 83 times greater in Somalia than in the UK.[3] The rapidly growing global burden of non-communicable chronic diseases affecting low-, middle- and high-income countries alike and the increasingly recognised burden of mental health worldwide is significant. In many countries rising healthcare costs, driven by new health interventions and ageing populations, and compounded by economic crisis, are totally unsustainable.

Primary care teams are ideally placed to address many of these issues as they can provide community-based, person-centred, continuous, comprehensive care. Whether in Glasgow or Gaborone the social determinants of health are often major drivers of inequalities in health, and primary care teams with exclusive understanding of the communities they serve are often in a key position to advocate on behalf of patients. Evidence indicates that health systems based on primary care offer a more equitable distribution of health in populations and are more cost-effective than systems that are fragmented and oriented around specialty care.[4] It can therefore be said that primary health care is needed *now more than ever!*[5]

WHAT DOES ALL THIS HAVE TO DO WITH YOU?

Medical training is a treadmill. It is easy to become UK-centric, thinking that health issues outside the UK have little to do with you. But as individuals and health professionals the authors of this chapter would argue that we have a duty to advocate for better health for *all*. We simply cannot enjoy the benefits of a privileged education, global commodities, communication and travel while ignoring the reality others are living, thinking that there is nothing we can do, or that it is not even 1% our responsibility.

Moreover, the UK is no exception to the trend towards increasing ethnic diversity, nor is it immune to the (re)emergence of communicable and non-communicable diseases linked to global forces. Therefore learning about global health will better prepare you to care for your UK patients. Overseas experience also will broaden your horizons and enable you to develop new clinical and non-clinical skills; not through ethically dubious or imperialistic medical practice, but through carefully considered and locally led work. In addition, with UK health reforms in motion it will be increasingly important that GPs understand how different health systems function in order to make informed decisions regarding limited NHS resources. Finally, international work can renew enthusiasm and appreciation for the NHS and general practice. For these reasons there is a growing realisation of the need to support health professionals to engage with the global health agenda.[6-10]

WHAT CAN YOU ACTUALLY DO?

1. Learn about the global burden of disease alongside the roles of globalisation and social determinants of health. Reading may include the World Health Organization's (WHO) commission on the social determinants of health,[11] Millennium Development Goals[12] and summary of the 2011 UN summit on non-communicable diseases.[13] Watch Hans Rosling's '200 countries, 200 years, 4 minutes – the joy of stats' on YouTube.[14] It is excellent!

2. Learn about the key components of a well-functioning health system. Again, the WHO is a good starting point.[15] Learn about the role of primary care worldwide.[4,16] Barbara Starfield's 2005 paper 'Contribution of primary care to health systems and health' is probably the most widely cited primary care research paper of all time.[4] Read it! Other important primary care-related publications include the 1978 'Declaration of Alma-Ata',[17] the WHO European Observatory's *Primary Care in the Driver's Seat?*[18] and the 2008 *World Health Report*.[5]

3. To help you do all of this learning, consider undertaking a global health-oriented qualification, e.g. Master of Public Health, Global Health, Health Policy or International Primary Care.[19] Think about a PhD!

4. Meet people. Get involved in professional organisations that have an international dimension to their work. The World Organization of Family Doctors (WONCA) runs conferences across the world and offers an international professional network.

5. Take part in an exchange. WONCA Europe's network for trainees and newly qualified GPs, the Vasco da Gama Movement, offers the two-week international 'Hippokrates' exchange programme. You can even take part as a host without needing to leave the UK.

6. Think globally, act locally:

    ›   work with refugees and asylum seekers in the UK. Consider a special interest in migrant health[20]

    ›   consider a special interest in travel medicine

    ›   support health advocacy organisations that campaign in areas such as fair trade, access to essential medicines or improved sanitation[21]

    ›   donate to worthwhile organisations.

7. Work overseas. However …

    ›   Consider carefully what you want to do and why. Developing or developed country? Development or relief work? Service delivery, education, research, management or all of these? For how long? Organised off your own back or through a recognised organisation?

    ›   Be aware of the ethical implications of what you plan. What are the local needs? What can you offer? What will the impact be? Is it sustainable?

    ›   If considering research, ask yourself how the local population will benefit and how your findings will be useful. The argument 'There wasn't an ethics committee that far up the Amazon' will not wash with a journal editor.

    ›   Organising time out of programme (OOP) during training can be complicated. Approach your training body at least 12 months in advance.

Be aware that time OOP that 'enhances clinical experience for the individual … and/or supports the recommendations in global health partnerships'[22] *should be supported* by training bodies.[6]

› If planning to go after Certificate of Completion of Training (CCT) know UK appraisal and revalidation requirements before going. Check the Royal College of General Practitioners (RCGP) and General Medical Council (GMC) websites for updates.

› Will you earn a salary while away? Possible funding sources such as the RCGP International Travel Scholarships, non-governmental organisations (NGOs) and other charities may help.

› Seek guidance from the British Medical Association (BMA) and NHS Pension Scheme regarding your contributions.

› Prepare. Learn the language. Do a Diploma in Tropical Medicine and Hygiene, Medical Care for Catastrophes or Medical Education.

› If going to a conflict zone, go with a recognised agency that offers training in security and humanitarian laws.

› Organise appropriate travel insurance, vaccinations, medical indemnity and licence to practise.

› You may be asked to undertake work beyond your level of competency. Carefully weigh up the potential consequences of your actions.

› Be prepared for the unexpected, and know how to access support. Even scrupulous preparation cannot prevent culture shock.

› Keep a record of your work for your professional portfolio.

› Plan a return trip to establish the sustainability of what you did. Reflect on your time away. Has your experience changed your practice, shaped your future or possibly the future of others?

8. Finally, share your experiences and advocate for change: blog, tweet, publish in a medical journal, present locally and/or internationally. Make change happen. By doing so you too can positively contribute to the global health agenda.

LINKS OF INTEREST

- BMA > International: www.bma.org.uk.
- BMJ Careers > International Jobs: www.careers.bmj.com.
- Medact, global health research and advocacy charity: www.medact.org.
- Médecins du Monde/Doctors of the World: www.doctorsoftheworld.org.uk.

- Médecins Sans Frontières (MSF): www.msf.org.uk.
- Merlin: www.merlin.org.uk.
- RCGP International: www.rcgp.org.uk/rcgp-near-you/rcgp-international.aspx
- Tropical Health and Education Trust (THET): www.thet.org.
- Vasco da Gama Movement: www.vdgm.eu.
- Voluntary Service Overseas (VSO): www.vso.org.uk.
- World Organization of Family Doctors: www.globalfamilydoctor.com, www.woncaeurope.org.

FURTHER READING

- Farmer P, Basilico M, Kleinman A, *et al*. *Reimagining Global Health: an introduction*. Berkeley, CA: University of California Press, 2013.
- Gedde M, Edjang S, Mandeville K. *Working in International Health*. Oxford: Oxford University Press, 2011.
- Pettigrew L, Heath I. International primary care. In: P Hutt, S Park. *A Career Companion to General Practice: developing and shaping your career*. Oxford: Radcliffe Publishing, 2011, pp. 143–72.
- Special Edition: Global Health. *InnovAiT* 2012; **5(8)**.

REFERENCES

1. Koplan JP, Bond TC, Merson MH, *et al*. Towards a common definition of global health. *Lancet* 2009; **373(9679)**: 1993–5.

2. Department of Health. *International Health: Department of Health objectives and ways of working*. London: DH, 2009, http://webarchive.nationalarchives.gov.uk/20130107105354/http://www.dh.gov.uk/en/Publicationsandstatistics/Publications/PublicationsPolicyAndGuidance/DH_106249 [accessed March 2014].

3. World Bank. Maternal mortality ratio, 2008, http://data.worldbank.org/indicator/SH.STA.MMRT?order=wbapi_data_value_2008+wbapi_data_value+wbapi_data_value-first&sort=asc [accessed March 2014].

4. Starfield B, Shi L, Macinko J. Contribution of primary care to health systems and health. *Milbank Quarterly* 2005; **83(3)**: 457–502.

5. World Health Organization. *The World Health Report 2008: primary health care (now more than ever)*. Geneva: WHO, 2008, www.who.int/whr/2008/en/index.html [accessed March 2014].

6. Tooke J. *Aspiring to Excellence: findings and final recommendations of the independent inquiry into Modernising Medical Careers*. London: MMC Inquiry, 2008.

7. Crawford L. MMC and overseas work. 2009. http://careers.bmj.com/careers/advice/view-article.html?id=20000007 [accessed March 2014].

8. Banatvala N, Macklow-Smith A. Bringing it back to blighty. *British Medical Journal* 1997; **314(7094)**: S2–7094.

9.   Crisp N. *Global Health Partnerships: the UK contribution to health in developing countries.* London: DH, 2007, http://webarchive.nationalarchives.gov.uk/20130107105354/http://www.dh.gov.uk/en/Publicationsandstatistics/Publications/PublicationsPolicyAndGuidance/DH_065374   [accessed March 2014].

10. Department of Health. *Health is Global: a UK government strategy 2008–13.* London: DH, 2008, http://webarchive.nationalarchives.gov.uk/20130107105354/http://www.dh.gov.uk/en/Publication-sandstatistics/Publications/PublicationsPolicyAndGuidance/DH_088702 [accessed March 2014].

11. World Health Organization. *Closing the Gap in a Generation: health equity through action on the social determinants of health.* Geneva: WHO, 2008, www.who.int/social_determinants/final_report/csdh_finalreport_2008_execsumm.pdf [accessed March 2014].

12. United Nations. Millennium Development Goals. 2000, www.un.org/millenniumgoals/bkgd.shtml [accessed March 2014].

13. United Nations. 2011 high-level meeting on prevention and control of non-communicable diseases. 2011. www.un.org/en/ga/ncdmeeting2011/ [accessed March 2014].

14. Rosling H. 200 countries, 200 years, 4 minutes – the joy of stats. www.youtube.com/watch?v=jbkSRLYSojo [accessed March 2014].

15. World Health Organization. Health systems. 2013. www.who.int/topics/health_systems/en/ [accessed March 2014].

16. Kringos DS, Boerma W, van der Zee J, *et al.* Europe's strong primary care systems are linked to better population health but also to higher health spending. *Health Affairs* (Millwood); 2013; 32(4): **686–94**. doi: 10.1377/hlthaff.2012.1242.

17. International Conference on Primary Health Care. Declaration of Alma-Ata. 1978. www.who.int/publications/almaata_declaration_en.pdf [accessed March 2014].

18. Saltman RB, Rico A, Boerma WGW (eds). *Primary Care in the Driver's Seat? Organizational reform in European primary care.* Maidenhead: Open University Press, 2006.

19. Prospects, www.prospects.ac.uk/.

20. Public Health England. Migrant health guide. www.hpa.org.uk/MigrantHealthGuide/ [accessed March 2014].

21. British Medical Association International Department. *Improving Health for the World's Poor: what can health professionals do?* London: BMA, 2007, www.idcsig.org/BMA%20Report%20-%20Improving%20Health.pdf [accessed March 2014].

22. NHS. *The Gold Guide: a reference guide for postgraduate specialty training in the UK.* 2010. http://specialtytraining.hee.nhs.uk/the-gold-guide/ [accessed March 2014].

68

HOW TO BECOME A GP TRAINER

MeiLing Denney

WHAT IS A GP TRAINER?

A GP trainer is someone who has the training and accreditation to undertake training of a GP specialty training registrar (trainee/Associate-in-Training) in the practice setting. This may seem obvious, but nowadays the term 'educational supervisor' is often seen to be synonymous. In fact a practice may contain several GP trainers, but not all of them may be educational supervisors. (A clinical supervisor is someone responsible for training in a hospital post, and may train for general practice as well as other specialties.) An educational supervisor is allocated to each GP registrar, and some training practices may rotate this role between its trainers. The practice may also be involved in the education of medical students – these GPs are usually referred to as undergraduate tutors. It is more difficult, but not impossible, to be a GP trainer as a sessional GP as you are expected to have a long-term commitment to a particular practice.

POSSIBLE MISCONCEPTIONS ABOUT GP TRAINING AND AVOIDING UNREALISTIC EXPECTATIONS

Many GP registrars have been inspired by their trainers and their training experiences, and wish to become part of the GP educational community as soon as possible. It's important to have a realistic idea of what this involves, and the pros and cons of taking it on. As a GP registrar, you may have had an ideal relationship with your educational supervisor and your training practice, contributed significantly to the everyday running of the surgery, and had a trainer with wisdom, enthusiasm and protected time to devote to you. That's great, but training is not always a bed of roses. It is important not to go into GP training primarily to get a free extra pair of hands in the surgery, sign up to an interest without having the resources to devote to it, and see it as simply an escape from patients or practice meetings. This is because training is a substantial commitment, and all GP registrars require supervision, some of which may need to be considerable at times. The degree of supervision required depends on the stage of training, and varies from trainee to trainee. Taking on a remedial GP registrar can be very rewarding, but the service input is likely to be less and the supervision requirements higher. Far from escaping, you are more likely to become immersed in the practice as you develop the practice as a learning environment and bring in various members of the practice team to contribute to teaching. In short, attitudes and realism are important.

THE ROLES AND RESPONSIBILITIES OF A GP TRAINER

A GP trainer has a complex and varied job and, in a similar way to general practice, this is one of the reasons why it is so interesting. As a trainer, the teaching aspects potentially involve everything related to the work of a GP, including clinical management, communication skills, patient issues, the community, the interface between primary and secondary care, out of hours, the primary healthcare team and the extended team, computer and IT skills, and the business of general practice – remember the curriculum! Then there are the assessments – the Applied Knowledge Test (AKT), the Clinical Skills Assessment (CSA) and the Workplace-Based Assessment (WPBA). It is this latter where you have particular responsibility, balancing your role as teacher with that of assessor. You also need to inspire your trainee, and instil an appropriate set of values and aspirations. You are training part of the GP workforce of the future, and you have a responsibility to the profession and the patients. General practice is always changing and developing, and you need to have an eye to the future with respect to training, so teaching leadership, team management and wider societal issues are also important. Pastoral care is included, and you may find yourself having to advise on health problems, personal issues and career choices. You will need to liaise with others within and outside the practice, including the deanery and the hospital clinical supervisors. Lastly, there is your own continuing professional development (CPD) to consider – attending trainer group meetings, specific workshops and deanery educational conferences.

HOW TO BECOME A GP TRAINER

The first step is information gathering. There is usually a lot of information on deanery websites, and you should also speak to your local training programme director. Other trainers can give you their own perspectives of the role. Specific requirements vary from region to region, but you would usually be expected to attend a prospective trainers' course, which can quite often take up to a year to complete. Sometimes completion of these gives you credits that can count towards a Postgraduate Certificate of Medical Education or diploma course. The courses may be quite theoretical, giving you a good grounding in educational theory and practice, but you may find that on completion of the course you still need to get to know the 'nuts and bolts' of GP training. There are courses and books that deal with these; you may also just have to learn this on the job. You often need to submit a video of your teaching or consulting along with your reflections, and some deaneries require that you show that you have completed other relevant tasks such as an audit. You may also be expected to be able to put MRCGP after your name, i.e. be in good standing with the College. It is a good idea to get in touch with your local trainers' group – these are usually invaluable sources of help. Joining the trainers' group puts you in contact with your scheme programme director as well, and it is often a stated prerequisite that you attend the group for a certain number of sessions or months prior to applying to become a trainer. For the latter, you need to fill in an application form, and expect a face-to-face meeting with the deanery team, which may be held in the practice. First-time approval periods for new trainers and new practices are usually one to two years, and after the initial accreditation visit you can usually expect to be visited again after a year when hopefully you will be re-accredited.

WHAT TO LOOK FOR IN A PRACTICE IF YOU ARE INTERESTED IN TRAINING

It is easier to become a new trainer in an existing training practice than bringing a non-training practice up to training standard, although doing the latter can be extremely rewarding. In an existing training practice it is a good idea to discuss your ambitions to become a trainer with the other GPs – it is not a given that they will support your aspirations. In all practices it is essential to ensure that the doctors, the practice manager and all the staff are signed up to the idea. They will all need to make adjustments to accommodate a GP registrar, and many of them will also be involved in the teaching. Assess the practice ethos and attitudes to training, and the quality of the training environment. Practices differ in the involvement of the other doctors in teaching. In some the educational supervisor does everything, so you may not get much experience in hands-on teaching for some time even if you become a trainer. In others, you will be able to participate in teaching whether you are a trainer or not.

Now for some caveats. When you start off in general practice there is a lot to learn, and you will need to learn about practice management, staffing, coping with pressure and paperwork, and achieving a reasonable work–life balance. A host of people will be hoping and expecting you to take on tasks and roles within the surgery. It can be easy to say yes to too much too soon. Many deaneries have a minimum requirement of two years' experience in general practice, but you may have spent these years as a locum or working in out-of-hours centres, and so may still need to acquire GP-relevant knowledge and skills through a longer-term position in a surgery. It might be worth taking your time settling in before taking on the mantle of GP training, rather than taking it on too soon and risk feeling overwhelmed.

Besides, there are often other teaching opportunities to be had before taking the step to become a GP trainer. These include: medical student training within the practice; teaching and mentoring other healthcare professionals undertaking certificates and diplomas in a GP setting; informal teaching of GP registrars if you are in a training practice; and teaching and examining as part of a university role.

SUMMARY

General practice training is both challenging and fulfilling. It can inject new life into practice, and bring new insights into your own work as a GP. Every GP registrar is different and you will have the opportunity to tailor your teaching to suit different learning styles. You will also gain from learning about GP registrars from different cultural or educational backgrounds – some may have migrated from other specialties, while others may have trained abroad and have a wealth of interesting experiences. To get the most out of training, and be able to deliver the best experience for your GP registrar, you need to ensure that you have a realistic idea of the role, and you are adequately prepared. It is essential to have the GPs and other members of the primary healthcare team onside, and just as important to involve your spouse or partner if you have one. You need to enlist the support of your deanery/educational organisation before applying to become a trainer, and make sure that you have enough time and energy for the task. Most GP trainers would say that they do not do the job for the money, but for the other rewards. You get the satisfaction of seeing a GP registrar develop, enhance your career portfolio by developing yourself as an educator, and it brings refreshment to your own work as a GP. The rest of the practice benefits by being involved with teaching and being a member of the training community, and many former GP registrars subsequently apply for long-term positions at the practice.

FURTHER READING

- Gill J. *Secrets of Success: getting into GP training*. Oxford: Oxford University Press, 2011.
- The GP curriculum, www.rcgp.org.uk/GP-training-and-exams/GP-curriculum-overview.aspx.
- Mehay R. *The Essential Handbook for GP Training and Education*. Oxford: Radcliffe, 2012.
- Middleton P, Price M, Field S. *The GP Trainer's Handbook: an educational guide for trainers by trainers*. Oxford: Radcliffe, 2011.

INTERESTING QUESTIONS, INTERESTING ANSWERS

Question 1 – *What do you do for a living?*

Telephone consultation, a Monday morning, quiet (hah hah!!!):

'Back to work tomorrow. Diarrhoea stopped yesterday, need a line.'

Salmonella surrendering. 'So what do you do for a living?'

'I'm a catering manager, offshore.'

'Where?'

'The Forties.'

Yup. That's a whole quarter of UK oil and gas output.

Sometimes an extra day off work is no bad thing.

Question 2 – *For how long do you think you should take these tablets?*

I started three very different patients on antidepressants this afternoon. For some reason I asked all three the same question. The three supplied exactly the same answer.

'For as short a time as possible.'

Question 3 – *What is the percentage chance that you'll have a heart attack or stroke in the next ten years?*

In Scotland we score cardiovascular risk with a nifty tool called ASSIGN. Smoking and diabetic status, blood pressure and lipid results are sensed by my computer and an ASSIGN score, my patient's chance of having an MI or stroke in the next ten years, appears in the bottom left corner of my monitor. It's bold and red and expressed as a simple percentage. Even I can understand that. So can my patients. Ghoulish, like most computery things, but comprehensible.

Red Roses *collection curated by Alec Logan and illustrated by Helen Wilson.*

Twice last week I discussed ASSIGN scores, one face to face, second by telephone. I explained the rules of the game. Didn't let on that the answer was blinking at me. Then asked the question.

Patient 1 was 60 and a harassed electrician. '50%?' Nope, 15%. Phew!

Patient 2 was same age as me, 50, but a little overweight. Cholesterol 6.2, average in our regional gene pool. MI risk? '60%?' Well, actually, 3%. And of course, to put it another way, that's a 97% chance of not having an MI in the next 10 years. 'Have a good weekend.' I hear the sound of skipping over the phone. Great start to a Bank Holiday weekend. For both of us.

Red Roses *collection curated by Alec Logan and illustrated by Helen Wilson.*

69

HOW TO STAY OUT OF TROUBLE

Rob Hendry

Very few doctors set out in the morning with the intention of doing anyone any harm and it is therefore very distressing when allegations are made that you have done so. There can be few more unpleasant experiences than receiving a recorded-delivery letter from the General Medical Council (GMC) or being summoned to see the Medical Director because concerns have been raised about your fitness to practise. When one considers the number of interactions GPs have with patients and their families as well as with colleagues, the risk of complaints is relatively low. However, by giving a little thought as to how to manage your risks you can not only decrease the likelihood of a complaint or a claim but also improve the service you offer to your patients and enhance staff and professional relationships. I recall many years ago being told that I would be unlikely to get into trouble as a doctor if I was able, affable and available. Having been a full-time GP for 12 years and having worked in medical defence organisations for the past 16 years, I believe this advice remains true today and points to the fact that the way we behave as professionals has an effect on how others behave towards us. What follows is an entirely personal view, based on my experience of working with doctors who find themselves in various types of medico-legal difficulties.

Before turning to consider the practical steps all doctors can take to reduce their risk of getting into trouble, it is helpful to give some thought as to what motivates patients to take action against their doctors. Interestingly the literature reports that only 2–3% of patients who suffer medical negligence ever raise a claim, while more than 60% of complaints are found not to involve a clinical error. As one editorial put it neatly, 'If you make a mistake you are unlikely to be sued. If you are sued it is unlikely you will have made a mistake.' Even more interestingly we know that more than 50% of patients who sued were so dissatisfied with their care that they wanted to sue before the alleged event occurred. It is clear that there are often predisposing factors in the relationship between doctor and patient that will dictate the likelihood of trouble developing.

It is in the nature of medicine that things will go wrong from time to time. Patients will have outcomes neither we nor they would have wished for and we will all make errors. The way these adverse events are managed as well as the pre-existing relationships significantly impacts how the patient reacts. I still vividly recall visiting a family shortly after one of my patients died. I blamed myself for not admitting him to hospital and told the family so. During an emotional discussion the family spent most of the time comforting me and they remained my patients for many years.

Of course it is not only patients who can take action against you. When concerns about your fitness to practise are raised by colleagues the implications can be infinitely worse. It is well worth paying attention to how you interact with your colleagues, especially ones you don't particularly like if you want to avoid the misery of a GMC referral or a disciplinary inquiry.

There is a wealth of literature on risk management and dispute management. What follows is a very personal set of tips derived from my experience as a GP and working for a defence organisation. It is impossible to eliminate all possibility of a complaint being made about you, but the risks can be managed. Adopting a practical approach to risk management will hopefully allow you to stop worrying about litigation and get on and enjoy the practice of medicine.

COMPETENCY

› Know the limits of your competency. Patients expect their doctors to be competent in what they say they can do, but not be supermen/women. If you feel you are out of your depth don't be afraid to ask a colleague or refer the patient.

› Keep up to date. This is not an easy thing to do with the current cascade of information, but the advice given elsewhere in this guide should be followed.

› Keep an open mind. In medicine in general and general practice in particular, illnesses often evolve over time. Be careful not to discount new signs or symptoms that do not fit with your provisional diagnosis – you may have to change it.

› Remember rare things do occur. We were always taught that 'common things occur commonly'. While this is true, there is an awful lot of rare conditions out there that will present to a GP somewhere. Again, if the picture doesn't quite fit, be suspicious rather than frustrated by your patient.

› Have a high index of suspicion of rare conditions where an early diagnosis can make a big difference, for example meningococcal septicaemia, diabetic ketoacidosis in previously undiagnosed children and adolescents, testicular torsion and ectopic pregnancy.

> Remember 'all women of reproductive age are pregnant until proven otherwise'. These wise words from a professor of O&G have saved me, and the patient, on at least two occasions.

> If a test is worth doing then the result is worth seeing. It is always very embarrassing when an abnormal result is ignored that would have clinched a diagnosis. It is easy nowadays to order lots of tests, but you need a fail-safe system for dealing with the results as they return.

> Keep clear, contemporaneous records. It may be many months before a problem comes to light and you are asked to account for your actions. Courts accept that GPs will not get everything right. You will be expected to give a logical explanation of why you followed the course you did. Clear, structured notes are invaluable.

> If you want to add to a record later it is reasonable to do so but make it clear when and why you have made the addition.

> If protocols exist, know about them. Again it is highly embarrassing if you are asked why you didn't follow an agreed protocol and the only answer you can give is that you didn't know it existed. You may choose not to follow a protocol, but you must be able to give a logical explanation for your decision.

PROFESSIONALISM

> Speak to your patients and colleagues as you would wish to be spoken to. We know that patients often cite feelings of not being listened to, or being devalued or misunderstood when they complain. You may be feeling tired, fed up and irritated by the time you reach the end of a surgery, but ask yourself if this is how you would want a professional to speak to one of your loved ones.

> Keep patients' confidences. Subject to the usual caveats about public interest disclosures, take care to maintain confidentiality. Breaches are seen as betrayals of trust.

> Look like a doctor. Patients expect their doctors to be clean so wash your hands.

> Involve patients and where appropriate their family or carers in making decisions about their care. Make sure they understand the risks and benefits of proposed treatment and have a chance to ask about alternatives.

> Set reasonable expectations with your patients. It is often tempting to over-promise what you can do for patients. This is particularly so for doctors who get involved in cosmetic work. Where patients feel let down they are more likely to complain.

› Manage conflict effectively. Conflict with patients and colleagues is inevitable from time to time, so it is wise to think about how you manage difficult conversations. If there is an issue you want to speak to a colleague about choose your timing carefully and prepare how and what you want to communicate. If you find this difficult why not go on a training course?

› Be prepared to give and receive feedback. During your training the importance of reflective learning will be stressed. It is helpful to create an environment where issues are dealt with early. Praise and positive feedback to colleagues and staff are also important and often ignored.

› Develop situational awareness. One of the cornerstones of risk management is to be on the alert for potentially hazardous situations. Ask yourself, 'Is there anything about this situation that increases my risks?' Consider the case of a male GP who made a late home visit to a young female patient he hadn't previously met who complained of abdominal pain. The front door was unlocked and he found her alone in her bedroom. She asked him not to put on the light because she had a migraine. Notwithstanding all this he carried out a 'thorough examination' in the dark. The patient's husband later complained to the GMC about the doctor's inappropriate behaviour. This lack of situational awareness created a great deal of anxiety for the doctor and a considerable challenge for his barrister.

› Consider the use of chaperones. As an extension of the principle of situational awareness be mindful that the use of chaperones is appropriate when carrying out 'intimate examinations'.

› Beware of the 'red mist'. Another hazardous time is when we get angry. This is more likely if you are tired, hungry, unwell, in a rush to get away or worrying about problems outside of work. If you receive a request for a late visit just before you go off duty and the concert you are looking forward to starts in an hour, be careful about the decision you make.

› Be aware of times of increased risk in 'the patient journey'. We know that certain points in a patient's care have increased chances of error occurring. For example, when patients are discharged from secondary care there is an increased risk of medication errors. It is wise for practices to identify these possible error points and set in place fail-safe systems to reduce the chance of errors.

BEHAVIOURAL

› Be honest. The quickest way to end a glittering career in medicine is to act dishonestly. This applies not only to your professional activities, but also in your private life. I am often struck by the tragedy of doctors who destroy their careers for pitifully little gain. Sadly every year we see examples of prescriptions in false names for drugs of addiction, fraudulent research, falsified CVs, false claims for items of service and doctored records. The gains made are minimal and the consequences dire. In addition the GMC will look dimly on crimes of dishonesty in a doctor's private life, such as insurance fraud and theft.

› Demonstrate insight. Nothing is more unsettling to those around you than if they believe you lack insight into your shortcomings. If a Medical Practitioners Tribunal Service (MPTS) Fitness to Practise panel concludes you lack insight it is time to think of careers outside medicine.

› Maintain good working relationships with your colleagues. Spending your time proving to your colleagues that you are right and they are wrong rarely leads to a happy working environment.

› Look after your health. It is not just the patients who get ill. GPs often present late with mental health problems and addictive disorders. Never be tempted to treat yourself – go and see your GP. It's what they are good at!

› Look after and learn from your colleagues. One of the pleasures of general practice is sharing your experiences with those you work with. Remember learning between junior and senior colleagues is a two-way process, with each having skills and knowledge to benefit the other.

› Be aware of the current guidance from the GMC. These are the standards by which you will be judged.

WHEN THINGS GO WRONG

Despite your best efforts things will occasionally go wrong and errors will be made.

› Recognise the problem early and rectify the situation if possible. Take whatever steps are necessary to prevent further harm. Do not ignore the situation in the hope that no one will notice.

› Speak to the patient and his or her family as soon as you can and acknowledge what has happened. Let them know what you are going to do and what the implications for them are. Give them time to tell their story and what it means to them.

› Say sorry. It is a myth that medical defence organisations tell their members not to apologise. An early and sincere apology (if appropriate) is often very powerful in maintaining trust and mutual respect.

› Do not abandon the patient. It can be awkward seeing patients you have harmed, but it is important that they don't feel you have given up on or run away from them. Ensure they are properly followed up and supported, and have a chance to discuss ongoing concerns and anxieties.

> Report the matter to your colleagues. Practices should have a system for dealing with adverse incidents. Doctors are often surprised by how stressful receiving even a fairly trivial complaint can be and early discussion with your colleagues is often very therapeutic. Remember your collegiate duty to support them in similar circumstances.

> Investigate what happened. Are there steps that can be taken to reduce the chances of similar errors in the future?

> Produce a detailed account of what happened as soon as possible. This can be very helpful if you are asked for an account of what happened later. Your memory of events will become clouded with the passage of time and with speaking to others about what happened.

> Learn from your mistakes and ensure the rest of your team do too. It can be helpful reflecting on adverse incidents with colleagues and with your appraiser.

> Speak to your medical defence organisation. It is helpful to take early advice from your medical defence organisation. This is particularly important if you have to produce reports for outside agencies such as the coroner or procurator fiscal.

> Don't forget the 'near misses'. They are the 'free lunches' of risk management.

RECOMMENDED READING

- General Medical Council. *Good Medical Practice*. London: GMC, 2013, www.gmc-uk.org/guidance/index.asp – you need to know what your regulating body expects of you.
- British Medical Association Ethics Department. *Medical Ethics Today: the BMA's handbook of ethics and law* (third edn). Chichester: Wiley-Blackwell, 2012 – expensive but a good reference book for the practice.
- Ury WL. *The Third Side: why we fight and how we can stop*. New York: Penguin, 2000 – excellent book for all the family to read.

APRÈS SKIING

'So how much do I owe you?' says handsome European.

New patient.

'Nil', says me. 'NHS and a' that.'

'And how are you?'

'Fine', says I.

'And what are you doing after work today?'

'Picking the children up from nursery.'

I smile. I smile all the way home.

Red Roses *collection curated by Alec Logan and illustrated by Helen Wilson.*

70

SESSIONAL LOCUM WORK

Neil Iosson

Working as a locum is increasingly popular for many GPs at different stages of their careers including starting out, career breaks or after retiring from full-time practice. It offers great flexibility to work only when you want to, avoids many of the background administration and management tasks that plague salaried and full-time GPs, and is a good way to try out different practices in your area and different ways of working before settling for longer-term work.

GETTING STARTED

1. You will be self-employed, so will need to register as self-employed with HMRC (www.hmrc.gov.uk/selfemployed/register-selfemp.htm) and pay tax and National Insurance when they ask for it. The NHS pension rules mean it is rarely worth setting yourself up as a limited company.

2. You are also responsible for your own indemnity insurance so let your organisation know what you plan to do and how much you plan to work.

3. If you haven't already registered as a 'performer' of primary healthcare services, you need to contact your local Primary Care Organisation (PCO) or Health Board – or its successor – to do this.

4. Make sure you have a bag with equipment for home visits (BP, pulse, oximeter, ophthalmoscope, etc., etc.). The practice will supply emergency drugs when necessary. You need a reliable car unless you can use public transport and know you will not need to do visits.

5. Design a simple one-page CV that highlights your current training and added skills (joint injections, family planning, other qualifications, etc.) so that potential employers can see that you are professional and safe. They won't be interested in your Blue in rowing or GCSE in religious studies!

6. Scan important certificates so you can quickly email them when needed (GMC, CRB, performer's letter, indemnity, etc.).

7. How much will you charge? There is no set scale of fees – that is anti-competitive and illegal – so every locum has to set his or her own. Charge too little and you will gets lots of work but be cheating yourself of income. Charge too much and you won't get many bookings. A search of the web will probably find some fees by other locums and *Pulse* magazine does a survey each year by region. Write a ratecard and add terms and conditions so you can send this to employers to form your contract.

8. Market yourself. Contact practices and let them know you are around. Print some business cards. You could set up your own website. There are many options for getting work. You could:

   a) Work independently with practices

   b) Join an online service such as http://gpnetworks.co.uk/ or https://locumorganiser.com/ who have an electronic diary and offer a 'dating service' to get locums and practices together

   c) Apply to join a chambers (who will find you work in return for a commission) (e.g. www.pallantchambers.co.uk)

   d) Sign up to an agency. They will offer work to you and usually pay a set rate (although it can be negotiated up if they are desperate). Agency work is different because you are a contractor and cannot use this pay for the NHS pension.

9. Monitor your email and phone regularly. Practices want to have the certainty of knowing the surgery is covered so if you are slow to respond they may give the work to someone else. Smartphones are a great way of keeping in touch on the move. Many chambers and online services will sync with your Google or iPhone diaries to keep it simple.

10. Confirm all bookings in writing (by email) and make sure the day, date and time (and fee) are agreed with the practice. A good filing system for your emails can be a fallback if your diary fails.

11. Have an infallible system for recording bookings. Practices HATE having locums not turn up. You must avoid double bookings or not recording bookings. Services like https://locumorganiser.com/ do make it much easier by recording it centrally and syncing to a diary. A pen and paper diary are fine – but what would happen if you lost it?

DOING THE JOB

12. Especially when you are learning the ropes – take it easy. You will find it stressful working in different computer systems, offices, PCO areas and working with varying forms, local services and practice procedures. Allow overrun time and if you often run late then ask the practice to schedule a catch-up break and tack the extra patients on at the end. They want happy patients and on-time surgeries so it usually isn't a problem.

13. Until you are used to the practice and how to access local services it's best to avoid doing on-call/duty sessions.

14. If the clinical system isn't one you are used to then ask for some training time beforehand and to allow extra time to see the patients.

15. Arrive early. When you get there make sure you bring all the basics you need. Ask the reception team about all the passwords you will need. Find toilets (patient and yours!), coffee room and where to get help if you need it.

16. Some practices have a locum pack that includes all the information you need and the forms. This makes life much easier – but sometimes isn't up to date.

17. Most patients realise that a locum doesn't know them inside out and will be happy just to ask for simple things but others take advantage to get a 'second opinion'. You will have enough things on your plate keeping on time so don't let patients discuss more than one problem during the appointment – no matter what Dr Evans does normally!

18. Ask if you aren't sure how to do something. Partners and staff would prefer you to ask than make mistakes that cause extra work for them or cause patients harm.

19. If the practice is dispensing then ask about their formulary and any local rules they have.

20. Your notes need to be clear and explicit – it is almost certain that the next clinician to see the patient will not be you. Hand over anything vital to a permanent clinician if necessary before you leave.

21. Often you will be asked to sign repeat scripts – the Medical Protection Society (MPS) says you shouldn't do this without reading each patient's notes. Personally, if I think the practice seems to be organised about monitoring its patients I will sign most scripts after reading them. I usually don't sign benzodiazepines or strong opioids without reading the notes. Don't be afraid to hand any back you don't want to sign. If something goes wrong, your signature will make you liable!

22. At the end of the surgery always ask if there is anything else that needs to be done. Be bright, cheerful and helpful to everyone. If you annoy the receptionists then they can easily choose another locum next time. …

23. Most surgeries will have given you a reasonable amount of work – occasionally they will ask you to do too much for the time allocated or ask you to do things you are not comfortable with. Mostly this is because the people booking you are administrators and not clinicians. Politely explain the problem. You shouldn't expect to get paid more, but it is helpful to the practice to let them know. Hand over to a clinician anything you can't/won't do. When you next arrange a booking you can agree exactly what you will and won't do. If a practice was really terrible or made you feel unsafe – don't go back.

24. Make a note of how far you drove, including to and from the practice as well as for visits and any other expenses. Keep receipts for everything. You will be able to charge this against tax (or to the practice) depending on what you have agreed.

GETTING PAID

25. Write a professional invoice and store a copy on your computer. You can send out invoices when you do the work or in batches (I do it monthly).

26. All NHS work is pensionable (unless through an agency or most out-of-hours work) so the PCO will pay the employer's contribution for you (about 14%) and you pay your bit. Every practice you work for needs to complete a Pension Form A and send it back to you. Every month you need to collate these on Pension Form B and send it to your PCO GP pensions department. The forms and a detailed explanation are at www.nhsbsa.nhs.uk/Pensions/2665.aspx.

27. Keep a track of which invoices have been paid and chase any late payers. Surgeries are generally not bad debtors but some can be a bit disorganised!

28. Services like https://locumorganiser.com/ allow you to use your online diary to generate and send the invoices electronically and track the payments. They will also do all your pension forms and present your figures ready for an accountant. I would highly recommend using them because it simplifies all the admin and makes it much quicker.

OTHER THINGS

29. It can be quite isolating working as a locum. You are in different places all the time with different staff. Try to say hello and get to know the partners when

you can. It is worth finding out if there are any education sessions run in your local area (private hospitals run a lot and there may be non-principal groups and sessions from your NHS hospital as well) both for training and to meet other GPs.

30. Sometimes you will see a practice or GP that is underperforming or acting dangerously. The GMC makes it your responsibility to act to protect patients and that may involve notifying the practice manager or sometimes the clinical director of his or her PCO.

31. Appraisal is trickier as a locum – try to record as much evidence as you can of training, reflective learning and complaints/compliments. Each year the PCO will contact you to arrange an appraisal (which you get paid to do).

32. You will need to pay tax twice per year. At the end of your first year the bill will be BIG and the taxman won't wait to be paid. Make sure you save a good proportion (a third to a half) of your gross earnings so you can pay the tax bill when it arrives.

33. Unless you are very good with money, an accountant will help you claim all the expenses you are entitled to and pay the minimum tax necessary. Choose someone who knows about GP work.

34. Enjoy it. It's a fantastic opportunity to sample different surgeries and working practices and learn from what works well and what doesn't.

71

KINDNESS AS A BASIC CLINICAL SKILL

Helen Salisbury and Richard Lehman

Kindness is a key ingredient in good medical practice.[1] Ask any patient what he or she looks for in a good doctor, and the word 'kind' is almost certain to appear near the top of the list. Yet it is something we usually avoid talking about as professionals, perhaps for fear of sounding sentimental. It is not specified anywhere by the General Medical Council (GMC) regulations, nor defined in any guidance, but nevertheless it is something that people instinctively look for when they are ill, anxious or vulnerable. Here we shall argue that it is not an optional extra, or just a welcome personality trait, but an essential and learnable skill that all health professionals need to acquire.

Kindness is difficult to define but easy to recognise. Since we are all programmed to sense kindness from before the time we can speak, there is in fact no need to waste time over a definition. Most people readily understand the question 'Does this pass the grandmother test?' meaning: would we want someone we care about to be treated in this way? Yet despite our aspirations, we spend very little time focusing on what constitutes kindness in medical practice and what stops us achieving it.

One element of kindness is empathy. In selecting medical students we try to focus on candidates' capacity for empathy, and research has shown that students become worse listeners as they progress through medical school.[2] The challenge of practice is to remember the instinctive reactions we had on first meeting patients, the interest and the empathy, and to recreate them in every consultation – but now of course coupled with useful expertise. The natural reaction when someone tells you he or she is in pain is to express sympathy, but our training rapidly teaches us to ask instead 'When did it start? Where exactly is it?'

In clinical teaching patients are often labelled by diagnosis and other characteristics, but all labelling tends to objectify and dehumanise the people we deal with. Yet if we bear in mind that it is real, complete people who are of central importance in our professional life, empathy follows naturally. Clinical teaching needs to redress the balance by affirming the professional necessity of putting people together as well as taking them apart. Clinical learners, from students to professors, need encouragement and permission to regain their instincts of connectedness and kindness.

Kindness takes energy and motivation. It may be easy to feel full of patience, genuine concern and interest when we come to work after a refreshing break, but this may have worn thin by 6 p.m. on Friday with a very demanding patient on the fifth item of his or her list. In order to be consistent, to make kindness a professional attribute that our patients may expect from us, we must anatomise the behaviours that it comprises, and learn to reproduce them consciously.

Here are some basic rules for applying kindness to your daily practice:

INTEREST IN THE PATIENT AS A PERSON

This may be shown by asking questions about a patient's work or family life, often usefully in the context of how his or her complaint is affecting these areas.

EXPRESSION OF EMPATHY

When patients are describing the pain or disability they are suffering, the loss or anxiety, sometimes a change in facial expression will suffice, and sometimes a verbal expression of empathy is needed. Be careful that whatever expression you choose continues to sound genuine. (One author of this chapter has a particular problem with 'I'm sorry for your loss' – it always sounds as if it has been borrowed from an American police drama.)

WARMTH

This is conveyed in body language, tone of voice, in smiles and in reassurance that the patient is not wasting your time.

PATIENCE

A consistent theme in appraisal of doctors by patients (and by observant students) is that the good doctors give the impression of having time to listen to their patients, although everyone knows they are really very busy. Although we are all constantly pressed for time, this impression can be helped immeasurably by just keeping quiet after the opening question and letting the patient talk without interruption. Suppressing any overt expression of impatience as your patient takes five minutes to disrobe or the translating relative is excessively longwinded is also helpful.

GENTLENESS

This should be too obvious to mention but I will anyway. Always ask about pain before examining, touch gently, watch for wincing and apologise for any pain you cause.

NON-JUDGEMENTAL ACCEPTANCE

Patients often feel bad about themselves, about their weight, their alcohol or drug use, their gambling or their relationships. Whatever your own personal opinions, part of the job is to hold your patient in unconditional positive regard. In practice, this means guarding against facial or verbal expressions that undermine this and finding out from the patient what he or she wants or intends to do rather than jumping in with your advice. It also means avoiding the use of dismissive labels about patients to others in the practice team, because even in joking use these legitimise an 'us versus them' culture based on stereotypes and value judgements.

RESPONSIVENESS

This includes responding to direct requests but also to the hints and cues that there are further worries not yet satisfactorily addressed. 'So you're sure it's not something more serious?' invites not repetition of reassurance but exploration of underlying worries. Sometimes it will seem quicker not to ask but it will be kinder to do so. Our body language needs to reflect openness and active listening throughout the consultation.

Kindness, or its opposite, can be demonstrated in almost every aspect of the consultation. From the moment I walk out to the waiting room to call the patient in, my tone of voice and my body language betray my mood. If I am running late, am exasperated by the previous patient and have failed in my emotional housekeeping,[3] I may come across as rushed and impatient. If I am conscious of this risk, I will slow my walk as I reach the waiting room, smile as I apologise for the delay and chat to the patient as we walk back to my consulting room.

What can rob us of the kindness we aspire to? There are external and internal enemies. We may be concentrating so hard on getting the medicine right (What was the latest National Institute for Health and Care Excellence (NICE) guideline? What is the current favoured antihypertensive?) that we forget about the patient in front of us. Sometimes we are so stressed by lateness, or by fear that we may make an error, that our own emotional state prevents us from being kind.

Organisational culture can also influence the way we behave.[1] If the prevailing attitude in your A&E department to self-harmers is that they are inadequate people who waste valuable medical time, then it is difficult to avoid this affecting the way you interact with such patients. There is a strand of studied, self-protective cynicism within some medical literature and practice that paints patients as entirely other, even as the enemy (as in Samuel Shem's satirical novel about medical training in America, *The House of God*).[4] Fortunately, this is rare in general practice.

Kindness can be embodied not just in our professional behaviour but in everything that we provide for patients. The physical environment of our premises can emphasise comfort and reassurance rather than bare utility. Our practice teams can be praised for their kindness and flexibility towards patient needs, rather than by how well they protect us from disturbance as important health professionals. The fact is that general practice at its best already implicitly upholds all the basic principles of kindness. But as GPs increasingly get sucked into basing decisions about patients on cost and utility, we need to be more explicit about affirming the place of kindness as a core value in our daily contact with people who are ill and vulnerable.

REFERENCES

1. Ballatt J, Campling P. *Intelligent Kindness: reforming the culture of healthcare*. London: RCPsych Publications, 2011.

2. Chen DC, Kirshenbaum DS, Yan J, *et al*. Characterizing changes in student empathy throughout medical school. *Medical Teacher* 2012; **34(4)**: 305–11.

3. Neighbour R. *The Inner Consultation* (2nd edn). Abingdon: Radcliffe Publishing, 2005.

4. Shem S. *The House of God*. New York: Dell, 1978.

KINDNESS

I got a letter from a patient yesterday remarking that when I visited her last week, when she was in the grips of infective exacerbation of COPD, I'd held her hand and said, 'Poor you, it must feel awful.'

Her comment: 'No doctor I've ever seen has ever said anything like that before. They aren't normally kind.'

Flashback to medical school. …

Third year. A&E placement at a notorious South London war zone. I was paired with a colleague, Helen, even softer than me but twice as formidable.

Old lady brought in, palliative, broken, wanted to go home to die. Helen did battle with bed managers who would rather she died quickly in a side room than having to organise someone to go into her home and sit with her (this before the intermediate care hotlines etc. that now exist).

Waiting in the side room, I chatted and listened to this poor lady. As Helen returned, the patient looked deep into me and said, simply, 'Hold me.'

I knew what she meant but pretended not to. I held her hand.

'No! HOLD ME!' she said, not unkindly, but firmly.

I looked at Helen; she looked straight back. Wordlessly she got up and closed the door to the side room.

I got up and held the lady with all my might while she sobbed.

Helen watched the door. Both of us instinctively knew that this act of kindness to a dignified lady with only hours to live would have been viewed negatively by our 'superiors'.

Unprofessional.

We got her home, in the end, to die.

I was a mature entrant to medicine, as was Helen.

We had to unlearn a lot to fit in.

Red Roses *collection curated by Alec Logan and illustrated by Helen Wilson.*

72

SOCIAL MEDIA
A STARTUP GUIDE

Michael Banna (@DrMikeThe2nd)

The late legendary powerhouse diva Whitney Houston once said something about not being afraid, despite knowing that there is much to fear. This is kind of how I feel about social media. Many of us have very fixed ideas of what it is about, and it certainly has its negatives, but amongst the duck-faced selfies and heavily filtered breakfast pictures (and that's just my Facebook page), there is a wealth of information, interaction and debate, literally at our fingertips. Social media is whatever you want it to be – you can watch, participate, socialise, debate, promote or ignore, but there is no doubt that it is a big part of our future.

One of the great things about social media is its levelling of the playing field, with whatever hierarchies that still exist in the real world effectively being broken down. On Twitter, medical students can banter with professors and formerly 'staffroom only' discussions are opened up to people from all walks of life. This removal of the 'us and them' culture of yore has both its advantages and its pitfalls. We will be able to understand more about what bothers our patients, what their views are on health care, and more importantly why. It is an immense resource to be tapped into. On the other hand, it can leave us vulnerable if we are not careful, and as a result of this the General Medical Council (GMC) has recently published some (currently much discussed) guidance on how we should behave (www.gmc-uk.org/Doctors__use_of_social_media.pdf_51448306.pdf). The Royal College of General Practitioners (RCGP) has also developed its own Social Media Highway Code, which was published in February 2013 (www.rcgp.org.uk/social-media). *Don't forget that you can simply read comments; you don't actively have to participate.*

At the moment, Twitter is the juggernaut of social media medicine, and it is growing by the day. Little tiny micro-blogs, information nuggets and 'stream of consciousness' rants can be greatly entertaining and informative, but can also give a false impression of disposability. The RCGP (and specifically its Chair) tweets, as does the GMC and many others who provide daily commentary on our profession. But Twitter is not the only social network, and with time there are bound to be more cropping up. Some use LinkedIn, and the old stalwart Facebook also still exists. Tiko's GP Group has over 2000 members who post pictures of rashes, discuss cases, salaries, workload, politics, etc. Confidentiality is an issue here, and case discussions must be anonymised and consensual, but personally I am still a bit frightened of discussing specific cases on the internet. The main criticism levelled at Facebook is the sometimes ambiguous privacy options, and these can certainly be an issue if you are not careful. However, while Twitter is a totally open forum (unless you lock your account), as long as you behave as well on Facebook as on Twitter you should be safe. The GMC also advises using your actual name and identity rather than aliases, as you are more likely to watch what you say if you are easily identifiable (and you are still identifiable if you use aliases anyway).

One of the biggest selling points of Twitter for me is the juxtaposition (and not just because I really like that word) of the professional and the personal. One minute you can be having an intense political discussion, and the next you could be getting help on how to make a banana cake more banana-y, or debating the merits of houmous vs. taramasalata. I tend to get involved a lot more in the latter (1. Add more bananas, 2. I'm a houmous man). The GMC has made it clear that it doesn't wish to dictate how we behave on 'personal' accounts, but the lines here are usually blurred, and professionalism must be considered. I often imagine how the mother of an unwell child I see might feel if she stumbled across tweets from me about how late I got home the night before. My general feeling is that if I'm happy for my boss and my granny to see something, it's okay. But we all have our safety thresholds set at different levels, and it's important to find your own – just because a media doctor can get away with saying something, it doesn't mean you can too. Equally don't be afraid to point out to someone if you think they overstepped the mark. This is a new arena and we are all finding our comfort zones. Help others and they may well one day save your bacon.

I have found that one of the major perils of social media is the request for medical advice, which should of course be avoided. Responding in a way that doesn't put you at medico-legal risk but is still polite and supportive to the person who is asking for help is a big grey area that is hard to get right. Of course it's easy to say 'go and see your doctor', and in most cases that will be safe and appropriate, but having been faced with questions about street drugs, suicidal thoughts and cosmetic surgery amongst other things, I certainly don't have all the answers. I've debated this at length; 'Just don't give ANY medical advice, EVER', say my friends. So, what if someone asks you what they should do about their central crushing chest pain? I think all we can do is make sure that anything we say is kept safe, general and at arm's length. But like Whitney meant (I assume), do not be afraid of social media – get stuck in, be careful, but enjoy it!

To round this off, I asked for tips for medics on social media from my Twitter followers (terribly #modern, I know). I received advice from lay people and doctors across a wide range of specialties: some great and included above, some unprintable. Many thanks to @ctmaddison, @drewseybaby, @welshgasdoc, @Trisha_the_doc, @DoctorChristian, @thefourthcraw, @Danielf90, @stublue, @AlysColeKing, @HenryGoldstein, @gourmetpenguin, @fluffmed, @evasdaddy, and everyone who replied and retweeted!

73

SHARED DECISION MAKING MADE EASIER

USING A THREE-STEP FRAMEWORK

Glyn Elwyn and Richard Lehman

In his 2008 John Hunt Lecture on accepting honorary fellowship of the RCGP, Donald Berwick, founder of the Institute for Healthcare Improvement in Boston and an international expert in patient safety, recollected his father's small-town Connecticut general practice in the 1950s:

> At dinnertime, the telephone rang. A patient was calling. I watched my father listen, and then scowl. 'I'm the doctor', he seethed. 'You're not. You'll get penicillin when I say, and not a moment sooner.'

He slammed the phone handset down so violently that its plastic cradle shattered, sending shards into my beef stew.

Towards the end of this wonderful speech,[1] Berwick describes a contrasting medical professionalism that has replaced the dutiful authoritarianism of his father's generation. Today's doctors need to 'embrace of the authority and autonomy of patients and families in a wholly new distribution of power and knowledge'.

ATTITUDES

You will have had it drummed into you by now that everything you do can be boiled down to attitudes, knowledge and skills, and that is as true of shared decision making as the rest of clinical medicine. You will already be familiar with the need to identify patients' ideas, concerns and expectations. These steps are of course an integral part of sharing decisions, because a patient's understanding of his or her problem will be critical to the way he or she perceives the existence and relevance of treatment options.

Berwick describes two extreme attitudes towards shared decision making, which we can still see in many of the doctors we work with. 'No decision about me without me' might have made a fine political slogan for Andrew Lansley when he was Secretary of State for Health, you may say, but how on earth can you make that work in a ten-minute consultation? Fortunately, there are ways to do it. We can give you some tips here on how to do real decision making in real time, using three steps, although sometimes these three steps might not all fit into the same encounter. Good decisions need some time, and patients, like all of us, need time to talk to others when facing dilemmas.

But first we will assume that you accept the principle that, wherever possible, the patient needs to have the opportunity to choose and become empowered, to take responsibility for his or her health, and to decide which course of action to follow. If you don't accept that principle, then think carefully about whether general practice is the right career choice for you. The move to ensure that the perspectives and priorities of patients are given centre stage is likely to become even more important than it already is in medical practice.

The moral basis of this argument has been discussed extensively,[2] and we won't go there now, but in addition there are arguments based on safety and social acceptability, and we won't go into those either. In this short piece, we will simply assert that shared decision making is a basic principle of good medical practice, and assume that you agree.

This is not at all the same as asserting that patients must always be expected to take on a decision-making role in all clinical situations. Many patients don't want to share decisions for very good reasons and there are some situations – usually either very trivial or very life-threatening – where shared decision making is either inappropriate or impossible. It is also true of course that some cultures do not embrace the idea of individual autonomy as much as others. The goal is to be sensitive to this and to involve individuals in decisions to the extent that they desire, and not to shoulder them with responsibility that is too much of a burden.

KNOWLEDGE

Shared decision making is based on the sharing of knowledge. Traditionally, there was an enormous gulf between the knowledge of the doctor and the knowledge of the patient, but this gulf is closing all the time, and is now quite often reversed. Nearly everyone now goes straight online if they want to know about their medical condition. While there may be a generation that might be less able to navigate their way to high-quality information, there is increasing evidence that even the elderly use search engines to find material to read before they attend for care, or ask their younger relatives to do so. The next generation of GPs will need to be as adept at doing advanced searches in Google as their patients will become. In passing, we would say that this is a strong argument for working to improve web resources such as the National Institute for Health and Care Excellence (NICE) and other NHS resources to create reliable sources of information for shared decision making between patients and health professionals. Some will also argue that it might be possible for Wikipedia to become a great source of patient information, but it would need much more input from clinicians prepared to add evidence-based content before it could be widely recommended.

The doctor usually has the benefit of greater experience and breadth of knowledge, but this may not apply to you if you are at the start of your career. You may have vastly less experience than your patient of his or her particular condition. You have no way of knowing the patient's goals, expectations, priorities and fears unless you ask him or her – and pay close attention to what he or she tells you. The patient's preferences matter most, but it is also your job to find out how well-informed these preferences are. You need to make sure that preferences are based on a reasonable understanding of what is likely to happen, for bad and good, if you decide on particular treatments. That is what forms the agenda for your next steps – not your often mistaken preconceptions, or some prescriptive guideline drawn up by a distant committee of authority figures.

Another way in which you may assume your knowledge is greater than your patient's is in the matter of local providers of care. If you follow the static career path still typical of much UK general practice, you may stay in one place long enough to form strong opinions on the strengths and weaknesses of local colleagues and hospital departments. But increasingly patients can access outcome information about local providers and want to make their own choices.

It goes without saying that you cannot contain in your head all the knowledge that you need for properly informed shared decision making. Take pride in looking things up in the right places, together with your patient. In an age when no one can ever hope to remain up to date, the best skill to have is to know how to navigate information sources, how to find accurate, reliable information, and how to appraise it for its quality and relevance to the patient in front of you. Being able to explain this process openly to patients, perhaps to use Google in the encounter itself, is something you might want to explore. It has a transforming effect on the conversations you might have with patients and deepens the level of honesty and trust if you approach it in the correct way.

SKILLS FOR SHARED DECISION MAKING

Effective shared decision making is a skill that needs to be learnt, and honed by self-awareness and the help of others. It cannot be practised without a good grounding in effective communication. We hope that you will have gone through this grounding from medical school onwards, though when it comes to the specific skills of shared decision-making skills, we cannot pretend that they are yet taught as widely or effectively as they should be. There are many consultation models, of course, including the work by Nigel Stott,[3] David Pendleton,[4] Roger Neighbour[5] and others. The skills and stages of shared decision making are not in conflict with any of these models, but add to them by drawing more attention to what has been called the 'neglected second half of the consultation'.[6]

Here we describe a three-step model developed by the authors of an open-access paper in the *Journal of General Internal Medicine*,[7] and in a more recent BMJ article by Mulley *et al.*[8] There are other shared decision-making frameworks,[9-11] but most practitioners do not find them easy to put into practice. You will see that the three-step model recommends the use of brief decision support tools, such as Option Grids.[12] Option Grids are one-page tools designed for patients to use with their practitioners. They use the idea of 'frequently asked questions' to help patients compare treatment options, using simple, concise language.[13] There are over 20 of these Grids now published and more to come. We suggest that doctors should familiarise themselves with these in the course of their daily practice. An example of an Option Grid is provided (see Figure 73.1, opposite).

The Health Foundation commissioned work to examine how best to introduce shared decision making into routine practice. One of the most helpful developments was the idea of a three-step process that practitioners could remember and follow.[7] It was called the three-talk model, because it described three stages to be followed: Team Talk, Option Talk and Decision Talk. We go into more detail for these stages here. Figure 73.2 (see p. 368) shows a simplified sequence of these stages, illustrating that the goal is to get patients to move from initial preferences to informed preferences.

FIGURE 73.1: AN EXAMPLE OF AN OPTION GRID

option grid

Breast cancer surgery

Use this grid to help you and your healthcare professional decide whether you should have a mastectomy, or a lumpectomy with radiotherapy.

Frequently asked questions	Lumpectomy with radiotherapy	Mastectomy
Which surgery is best for long-term survival?	Survival rates are the same for both options.	Survival rates are the same for both options.
What are the chances of cancer coming back in the breast?	Breast cancer will come back in the breast in about 10 in 100 women in the 10 years after a lumpectomy. Recent improvements in treatment may have reduced this risk.	Breast cancer will come back in the area of the scar in about 5 in 100 women in the 10 years after a mastectomy. Recent improvements in treatment may have reduced this risk.
What is removed?	The cancer lump is removed, with some surrounding tissue.	The whole breast is removed.
Will I need more than one operation?	Possibly, if there are still cancer cells in the breast after the lumpectomy. This can occur in up to 20 in 100 women.	No, unless you choose breast reconstruction.
How long will it take to recover?	Most women are home within 24 hours of surgery.	Most women are home within 48 hours of surgery.
Will I need radiotherapy?	Yes, for up to six weeks after surgery.	Radiotherapy is not usually given after a mastectomy.
Will I need to have my lymph glands removed?	Some or all of the lymph glands in the armpit are usually removed.	Some or all of the lymph glands in the armpit are usually removed.
Will I need chemotherapy?	You may be offered chemotherapy, but this does not depend on the operation you choose.	You may be offered chemotherapy, but this does not depend on the operation you choose.
Will I lose my hair?	Hair loss is common after chemotherapy.	Hair loss is common after chemotherapy.

You can find more information at www.bresdex.com.

 Editors: Glyn Elwyn, Lisa Caldon, Kari Rosenkranz, Dale Collins Vidal, Marie-Anne Durand, Stephanie Sivell, Malcolm Reed
Evidence document: http://www.optiongrid.org/resources/breastcancer_evidence.pdf
More information: http://www.optiongrid.org/about.php
Last update: 13-Jan-2013 **Next update:** 13-Jan-2014 **ISBN:** 978-0-9550975-6-0
Creative Commons Licence: Attribution-NonCommercial-NoDerivs 3.0 Unported.

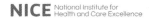

NICE National Institute for Health and Care Excellence

FIGURE 73.2: TEAM, OPTION AND DECISION TALK: SHARED DECISION MAKING MADE EASIER

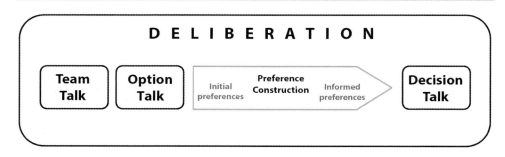

TEAM TALK

Team Talk is about making patients aware that reasonable options exist and that you as a practitioner will help the patient understand how to consider these options in more detail.

Components of the team talk include the following.

1. *Step back*. Summarise and say: 'Now that we have identified the problem, it's time for us as a team to think what to do next.'

2. *Offer choice*. Beware of patients misconstruing the presentation of choice and thinking that the clinician is either incompetent or uninformed, or both. Reduce this risk by saying: 'There is good information about how these treatments differ that I'd like to discuss with you so that we can work together to consider them.'

3. *Justify choice*. Emphasise: a) the importance of respecting individual preferences and b) the role of uncertainty.

4. *Personalise preferences*. Explaining that different issues matter more to some people than to others should be easily grasped. Say: 'Treatments have different consequences. Some will matter more to you than to other people.'

5. *Explain uncertainty*. Patients are often unaware of the extent of uncertainty in medicine: that evidence may be lacking and that individual outcomes are unpredictable at the individual level. Say: 'Treatments are not always effective and the chances of experiencing side effects vary.'

6. *Check reaction*. The choice of options may be disconcerting and some patients may express concern. Suggested phrases: 'Shall we go on?' or 'Shall I tell you about the options?'

7. *Postpone closure*. Some patients react by asking clinicians to 'Tell me what to do.' We suggest *postponing* or *deferring closure* if this occurs, providing reassurance

that you are willing to support the process. Say: 'I'm happy to share my views and help you get to a good decision. But before I do so, may I describe the options in more detail so that you understand what is at stake?'

OPTION TALK

8. *Check knowledge.* Even well-informed patients may only be partially aware of options and the associated harms and benefits, or be misinformed. Check by asking: 'What have you heard or read about the treatment of prostate cancer?'

9. *List options.* Make a clear *list* of the options as it provides good structure. Jot them down and say: 'Let me list the options before we get into more detail.' If appropriate, include the option of 'watchful waiting', or use positive terms such as 'active surveillance'.

10. *Describe options.* Generate dialogue and explore preferences. Describe the options in practical terms. If there are two medical treatments, say: 'Both options are similar and involve taking medication on a regular basis.' Point out where there are clear differences (surgery or medication), where postponement is possible or where decisions are reversible. Say: 'These options will have different implications for you compared with other people, so I want to describe. ...'

11. *Explain the harms and benefits.* Being clear about the pros and cons of different options is at the heart of shared decision making. Learn about effective risk communication, framing effects and the importance of providing risk data in absolute as well as relative terms. Try giving information in 'chunks' (chunking and checking).

12. *Provide patient decision support.* These tools make options visible and may save time. Some are sufficiently concise to use in clinical encounters. Examples of these short tools are Issues Cards, Decision Boards and Option Grids. More extensive patient decision support tools may play a crucial role. Say: 'These tools have been designed to help you understand options in more detail. Use them and come back so that I can answer your questions.'

13. *Summarise.* List the options again and assess understanding by asking for reformulations. This is called a 'teach-back' method and is a good check for misconceptions.

DECISION TALK

14. *Focus on preferences.* Guide the patient to form preferences. Suggested phrases: 'What, from your point of view, matters most to you?' Help the patients consider which aspects of the options help them decide for one or the other, according to their own priorities.

15. *Elicit a preference.* Be ready with a back-up plan by offering more time or being willing to guide the patient, if the patient indicates that this is his or her wish.

16. *Move to a decision.* Try checking for the need to either *defer* a decision or *make* a decision. Suggested phrases: 'Are you ready to decide?' 'Do you want more time?' 'Do you have more questions?' 'Are there more things we should discuss?'

17. *Offer review.* Reminding the patient, where feasible, that decisions may be reviewed is a good way to arrive at closure.

Acknowledgement: the Team, Option and Decision Talk model was developed and used in a programme designed to implement shared decision making in the NHS, commissioned by the Health Foundation, namely Making Good Decisions in Collaboration (MAGIC).

REFERENCES

1. Berwick D. The epitaph of profession. *British Journal of General Practice* 2009; **59(559)**: 128–31.

2. Wear S. *Informed Consent: patient autonomy and clinician beneficence within health care.* Washington, DC: Georgetown University Press, 1998.

3. Stott NCH, Davis RH. The exceptional potential of the consultation in primary care. *Journal of the Royal College of General Practitioners* 1979; **29(201)**: 201–5.

4. Pendleton D, Schofield T, Tate P, *et al. The Consultation: an approach to learning and teaching.* Oxford: Oxford University Press, 1984.

5. Neighbour R. *The Inner Consultation.* London: MTP Press, 1987.

6. Elwyn G, Edwards A, Kinnersley P. Shared decision-making in primary care: the neglected second half of the consultation. *British Journal of General Practice* 1999; **49(443)**: 477–82.

7. Elwyn G, Frosch D, Thomson R, *et al.* Shared decision making: a model for clinical practice. *Journal of General Internal Medicine* 2012; **27(10)**: 1361–7.

8. Mulley AG, Trimble C, Elwyn G. Stop the silent misdiagnosis: patients' preferences matter. *British Medical Journal* 2012; **345**: e6572.

9. Charles C, Gafni A, Whelan T. Shared decision-making in the medical encounter: what does it mean? (or it takes at least two to tango). *Social Science and Medicine* 1997; **44(5)**: 681–92.

10. Towle A, Godolphin W. Framework for teaching and learning informed shared decision making. *British Medical Journal* 1999; **319(7212)**: 766–71.

11. Makoul G, Clayman ML. An integrative model of shared decision making in medical encounters. *Patient Education and Counseling* 2006; **60(3)**: 301–12.

12. Elwyn G, Lloyd A, Joseph-Williams N, *et al.* Option Grids: shared decision making made easier. *Patient Education and Counseling* 2013; **90(2)**: 207–12 (epub 2012).

13. Greenhalgh T. Option grids: an idea whose time has come? *British Journal of General Practice* 2013; **63(608)**: 147. doi: 10.3399/bjgp13X664315.

LIST

Friday morning. The next patient who came in also brought me a rather unique list, quite unlike any I had seen before. It was written on the back of a tiny till receipt and was barely an inch long, with an untidy torn edge. The patient handed it to me as she sat down. In neat, handwritten capital letters, it read simply:

SHOULDER
TUMMY
NITS
TITS.

I read it out loud and could not contain a smile. It may even have grown into a tiny giggle. ... I think the patient saw the funny side.

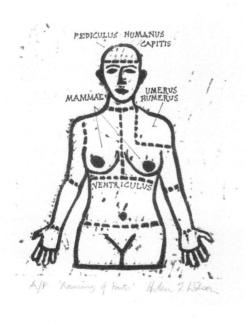

Red Roses collection curated by Alec Logan and illustrated by Helen Wilson.

74

STAYING UP TO DATE
A PERSONAL VIEW

Neal Tucker

A decade ago, as a final-year medical student I had an attachment with a retiring consultant. He told me about his own training as a junior doctor. Patients with severe heart failure would be admitted to hospital, copper pipes would be inserted in to their oedematous legs and their feet placed in buckets to catch the ensuing downpour. That year a new medicine was released. Its name? Furosemide. This magical drug revolutionised the treatment of heart failure. Word got around. Doctors stopped sticking metal tubes in people's legs.

Medicine has come a long way in the past 50 years. Knowledge is key. As doctors we strive to provide the best care we can for our patients, and this includes having the most up-to-date knowledge of the best treatments available. If interest in medicine, obligation to our patients and self-worth were not incentive enough, more than ever our patients demand this best care from us (as do their lawyers on occasion). In addition revalidation will oblige us to demonstrate 50 learning credits (each an hour of education) annually.

The amount of information and number of sources from which it is coming has never been higher. Can we possibly consume all this information while doing the day job, getting the kids to bed and still watching *The X Factor*? Not a hope. PubMed has >21 million citations. The challenge has become sifting through it all to get to the good stuff.

However, there are ways and means. It doesn't have to be complicated, it doesn't have to take long and, you never know, learning can actually be fun.

THE JOURNALS

> The Royal College of General Practitioners' (RCGP) own *British Journal of General Practice* (BJGP), *British Medical Journal* (BMJ), *New England Journal of Medicine* (NEJM) and the *Lancet* are all notable examples.

> They contain news, views, the latest research, broader reviews and summaries of the most important new guidelines.

> You can't read them all and nor would you want to. Much of the published material will have little relevance to the jobbing GP and his or her patients. Be sensible with your time; be selective.

> As an Associate-in-Training (AiT) you will receive *InnovAiT* each month – this is a good place to start.

> As an AiT/RCGP member you will automatically receive the BJGP each month –read it!

> Most journals charge to view them but as an NHS worker you are entitled to access to many of them via NHS Evidence with an ATHENS log-in. If you're still hospital based then contact your medical library or register online at https://register.athensams.net/nhs/nhseng/.

> Critically appraise everything you read in the journals.

THE GUIDELINES

> The National Institute for Health and Care Excellence (NICE) and Scottish Intercollegiate Guidelines Network (SIGN) are phenomenal resources producing guidelines that are used throughout the world. The quick reference guidelines are a must for all trainees (aspects of them will come up in the Applied Knowledge Test [AKT] and Clinical Skills Assessment [CSA]).

> Both can be accessed online: www.nice.org.uk and www.sign.ac.uk. SIGN also makes an iPhone app for its quick reference material.

> The Cochrane Collaboration is also world renowned for its evidence-based medicine reviews on a massive range of practical topics. It's open access at www.cochranelibrary.com.

> Don't forget the *British National Formulary* (BNF) – you will use it every day in practice.

THE COURSES

> You're a busy person so let someone else do the hard work for you.

> Take study leave and spend the day on a course – you'll have a break from wall-to-wall empathising and improve yourself as a doctor. In the end, your patients win.

> Want to avoid picking up a guideline or journal for the whole year? Come on an update course and get it all in one day. There are a number available, such as NB Medical's Hot Topics course, www.nbmedical.com. (I should point out that I present on this course and so am inherently biased). A year's worth of the most relevant research and guidelines is collated by GPs for GPs in to a single resource for everyday practice.

> Be wary of free courses. They may be very good but it's not cheap to put on a course – ask yourself where the funding comes from and how might that influence the content?

THE NEWSPAPERS

> If you have the *Daily Mail* there will be a medically related piece each day connecting cancer to an inanimate object. Read it, then look in a mirror and ask yourself why you have a copy of the *Daily Mail*.

> To beat the general journalistic rot, sign up to 'Behind the Headlines', produced by NHS Choices (www.nhs.uk/News/Pages/NewsIndex.aspx).

> There are a number of GP newspapers (*GP*, www.gponline.com, and *Pulse*, www.pulsetoday.co.uk, being the major players) who impart news each week and have broad-based educational sections.

THE INTERNET

> Apart from easy access to millions of articles of literature, online learning has flourished.

> www.patient.co.uk and www.gpnotebook.co.uk are good, reliable resources for immediate answers to your PUNs and DENs. Clinical Knowledge Summaries is a good resource from the NHS, but funding has ceased so from March 2011 there have been no more updates.

> Online educational modules are a great way to improve your knowledge in specific areas and offer a more interactive experience.

› The RCGP has extensive online learning at http://elearning.rcgp.org.uk/.

› Many websites offer free online education modules, including www.nb-learning. com (free to UK GP trainees; see website for details) and www.doctors.net.uk. Check if there are sponsors involved and consider how this might affect the content.

› Several other websites also have extensive online learning resources, often behind a payment barrier, for example BMJ Learning and *Pulse* Learning.

THE SOCIAL MEDIA

› So you thought staying up to date was just about the medicine? Think again. What happens in the world of politics has massive implications for all doctors.

› The new Health and Social Care Bill may have a much more profound effect on your patients' health than the next super-duper heart pill released.

› Twitter is becoming a *tour de force* worldwide. Want to stay up to date with both research and politics in general practice? Join in: start following and get tweeting. @BJGP and @GPHotTopics are good places to start.

THE GROUPS

› As an AiT arrange learning sets and set research topics and then educate each other.

› After training, First5 is an RCGP initiative supporting trainees who are, as the name suggests, in their first five years post-vocational training scheme (VTS). Local meetings (usually monthly) will often have an educational component, plus it's a great place to have a moan when your partner gets fed up of it.

› Most regions have a GP educational programme that helps provide continuing professional development (CPD) to local GPs, though whether this continues after the current government's NHS reforms remains to be seen.

THE FUN

› You've spent three years making friends. Don't lose them – keep your VTS group going!

› Set a date once a month and get together. It can be hard to find the time with new jobs, children, hobbies, etc. but it's worth it.

›   Remember that learning should be fun – relax in a coffee shop, public house or in your own home. Sit back, crack open a bottle of wine and start sharing.

›   It doesn't have to be over-planned. Case histories, NICE guideline, *ad hoc* Balint sessions – whatever works for you.

›   In the long run you'll only have to do half the amount of work to stay up to date. Plus it's a great time to find out how each other's practices function, locum tactics, contracts, gossip about *The X Factor* and everything and anything else on your mind. Enjoy!

So, now you are armed with everything you need to stay up to date. No one can predict what medicine will be like by the time we retire but that's what keeps it interesting. Here's to lifelong learning.

75

WORKING OUTSIDE THE UK
A POSTCARD FROM AUSTRALIA

Matthew Oliver

After finishing the GP registrar year and looking around for my next career stage I realised I was not ready for the responsibilities of partnership. Locuming (while fun for a few months) just wasn't providing me with the intellectual or emotional challenges that had driven me in the preceding year. Also driving to work in my little beat-up car for an hour every day, listening to John Humphrys on Radio 4 explaining how the UK economy was on a collision course with Armageddon, while the weather outside was anything but tropical, also made my feet itch for something a bit different. So after some extensive *Move Down Under* research, a quick Google search ('what is the best climate in Australia'), a chat to a few employment agencies, six months of paperwork/medicals/visa checks, a few tearful goodbyes, and we were on the plane to Oz for some surf, sun and skin checks ... and I haven't looked back since!

I was a bit nervous before going, having read about some of the experiences of rural GPs managing entire hospitals by themselves, drilling skulls, delivering babies while topping up the epidural and, yes, there are options to go to the outback and do these things (house and car provided). But there are also options to spend time in a semi-rural area and continue practising in a very similar environment to what any GP would be used to in the UK, but with the bonus that you can surf before, during and after work!

The process by which foreigners are allowed to choose their location of work in Australia is worth knowing. Effectively the government sets areas called DWSs (districts of workforce shortage), which are chosen based on the number of doctors per capita of population. Generally this means you can only work about one hour from capital cities, and not in the most famous areas like Byron Bay. The outback is really a fascinating place though and this is where most doctors are desperately needed. Some of the health needs among Aboriginal and Indigenous peoples are akin to Third World medicine, and it's an area where a good doctor can make a real difference, so if that appeals I would really encourage you to check the rural doctors' website at www.nswrdn.com.au/. Another website to explore is www.gpaustralia.org. au/content/information-international-medical-graduates-imgs, which explains in more detail the pathway foreign GPs can take (although a good agent will explain this to you hopefully).

I'm currently contracted to a corporate business, which has both positives and negatives, and if I had the option again I would prefer to join a more partnership-style practice. These still exist in Australia but are becoming few and far between. I get paid per patient contact (suddenly those extra patients added at the end of a list are not so onerous) so any extra work I do is remunerated, but paperwork is still a never-ending chore. Best of all there's no Quality and Outcomes Framework (QOF) boxes telling you what to do in the consultation. It means that I'm always happy to see patients!

Australia operates a kind of mix between private and public health care. Some doctors only charge a private fee, which they can set as high as the market allows. Patients can claim a part of that consultation fee back from Medicare, which is the Australian version of the NHS, and the fee currently stands at $35 (equivalent to approximately £19.50 at time of writing) for a 5–20 minute consultation. Other doctors only 'bulk-bill', that is, get paid a fee from the government for the patient consult (effectively the patient signs his or her right of the $35 back to the doctor). Most doctors fall somewhere in between, charging a private fee but also offering bulk-billing for those in need. Sounds complicated? This gets even more complicated in that there are huge amounts of 'Medicare numbers', which Medicare sets from A (artificial erection device, insertion of [37426,37429]) to Z (Z-plasty in association with Dupuytren's contracture [46384]). You then have to go looking for these numbers if you do anything more complicated than a basic consultation, to ensure you get paid your due.

Overall I'm paid more here than my training practice partners were in the UK, but do not get a pension – so don't let finances be the only reason for your move. One thing I found frustrating upon arrival was the disdain with which many GPs are treated by their specialist colleagues – it seems we are thought of as somewhere between wet, slimy things living under rocks and cavemen still clothed in furs who have not invented fire yet. Part of the reason for this is that specialists earn astronomical amounts, and many GPs do not choose their career path but have it forced upon them (emigrating to take up the role, failing exams).

Since I arrived I've learned a lot about skin cancer and I am enjoying basic minor operations. (This is a skill nearly all Aussie GPs seem expected to have a basic grasp on, and many of my colleagues are doing facial flaps and big excisions all in the surgery.) A difficulty is that most patients still register with their own doctor so you need to find a very under-doctored area, or join a big practice to build your patient list. Otherwise you may need to start another hobby to pass the time, at least in the first few months – this is how Sherlock Holmes was born, so free time is not always a bad thing. It is challenging coming from the NHS where demand generally exceeds supply, and healthcare delivery is free at the point of access, to suddenly find oneself in a partly private healthcare system and to start charging patients, and being able to choose what that charge is. But it gets easier!

Some boring bits: have a good think before you go because you may well want to stay. Even if you don't, I don't think a year in another culture will do any harm to one's career prospects. There are loads of possibilities out there – my choice was one of the more ordinary. If you look carefully you can find blogs from GPs in rural South Africa, doing Médecins Sans Frontières, working for Big Pharma – the choice is effectively as wide as your imagination. Just be careful to check (and get in writing) an agreement from your Primary Care Organisation (PCO) allowing your leave of absence and to keep your name on the Local Performers List or you could find returning to the UK extremely irritating – guidance can be found at www.gmc-uk. org/doctors. Also, while abroad, you should continue your revalidation, or at the very least write down some examples of lives you've saved and seminars you've been to. Where I'm practising lots of continuing professional development (CPD) is provided by drug companies and there are certificates available as proof of attendance (although sometimes you feel your soul is being corrupted by attending these talks).

I would advise finding a good employment agency (there are plenty around at career fairs and on the web) who will do all the hard work of filling in forms and liaising with the relevant medical colleges and immigration. Just make sure that any illness you have, e.g. cough and night sweats, you've had for the last few months is checked before going for your medical. Talk to those who have done it before, and try to get some help from local doctors to make the first fortnight transition as pain free as possible. Then the fun starts.

And fun it *has* been for me. I moved out with my wife (also a doctor, currently on a GP training scheme in the UK) and two girls aged four and two. She easily got a job at the local Emergency Department, and is enjoying that but is keen to get on to an Australian training programme. We need to be 'permanent residents' to be able to apply for such a thing, with priority obviously given to those who intend to stay in Oz. It would have been better if we'd both finished our training in the UK before flying out (in purely financial terms), but would have made the schooling and leaving friends and family more difficult for the girls. Saying that, most doctors are paid very well in comparison with the UK – we know two doctors just out of F2 who are earning over $100,000 each as effectively Emergency Department SHOs! Our two children are loving the outdoor lifestyle, lack of traffic and dirt, and are already learning to surf, swim and wear thongs (the footwear variety). Will we stay? Time will tell if we emigrate for good, but currently we are very content in our current position and hope to remain here for the foreseeable future.

I wish you all the best in your adventures – and hope John Humphrys is wrong!

76

SOCIAL VIOLENCE

Jane H. Roberts

Violence in society is endemic and no respecter of geography, with affluent suburbs, market towns and inner cities all affected. However, there are two issues that make the relationship between violence and health more important than it has been. The first is the pervasiveness of everyday violence. The second is the increasing knowledge of the neurobiology of trauma. We now know much more about its damaging impact on the development of the brain and on the formation of our earliest and later our most intimate relationships.

Aggression is a fundamental human emotion and is at times essential for our survival but if it is displaced, or becomes the currency of communication, then its consequences are far reaching. Although we tend to think of violence occurring between individuals or social groups, as doctors it is important to take a broader perspective and look at the bigger picture. Violence between individuals is usually embedded in societal violence. Consider some of the global 'hot spots' such as the townships of South Africa or the former plantation settlements of Jamaica and we can trace a history of violence that happened at the highest level. It is not surprising that the legacy of apartheid or slavery, brutal regimes that denied the most basic of human rights to the majority of their citizens, is to leave a society riven by conflict.

Anthropologists describe this phenomenon as 'structural violence':[1] the institutionalised inequalities that permit, even encourage, social structures to develop and maintain distinctions around race, class and sex resulting in social injustice. In the UK, this translates into a 100-fold differential between the highest and the lowest earners.[2]

What is the impact of this on our society and upon the lives of patients?

GROWING UP IN VIOLENCE

One in three children grow up in poverty living in communities where the effects of 'structural violence' are most evident.[3] The health impacts are striking. Key adverse health outcomes would be reduced by 18–59% if all children were as healthy as the most socially advantaged.[4] Children who grow up in households and communities where violence is pervasive have to make neuro-cognitive adaptations to cope with their stressful environments. Chronic stress, through the violence of neglect or abuse, can lead to changes in brain structure and intense or prolonged physiological stress responses.

Some children cope better because of protective, loving early attachments and a different genetic inheritance. The plasticity of the brain means negative adaptations can be modified so all is not lost but children exposed to violence need us to be attentive listeners and to act promptly when we suspect maltreatment.

A comprehensive checklist of physical and psychological signs of bodily, sexual, emotional abuse and neglect can be accessed in the new British Medical Association (BMA) Child Protection Toolkit, available as an app.[5] This indispensible tool has a logarithm for doctors who have concerns about a child but who are unsure of how to proceed. The National Institute for Health and Care Excellence (NICE) guidelines *When to Suspect Child Maltreatment* are also a useful resource.[6]

Make sure you know who are your local lead practitioners for safeguarding children (usually a nurse specialist and a GP). Each practice should have a nominated lead. Store their contact details and discuss early any concerns you have about a child in order to access help promptly.

BOX 77.1: CHILD SAFEGUARDING BODIES

If you suspect a child is in immediate danger you must act immediately to protect the child and contact one of the three statutory bodies with responsibilities in this area:

- National Society for the Prevention of Cruelty to Children, tel. 0808 800 5000
- social services, tel. available from the Local Authority's council switchboard
- police, tel. 999.

For young people, violent social environments pose additional threats. At a time of rapid developmental change, both physical and psychosocial, they might also be faced with threats to their immediate survival. Territorial 'turf' wars underpin the rise in knife crime that is made worse by decreasing opportunities for young people to study, pursue vocational training or secure employment. Institutional racism[7] against young black men compounds the situation.[8] Remember that the tough exterior you see in surgery may well belie a teenager who is fearful and unsupported, and who would benefit from your receptive listening and compassionate interest in his or her situation.

DOMESTIC VIOLENCE

Women consulting their GP have a higher prevalence of domestic violence, which has long-term and enduring affects on their health, especially mental health. For children the damage can be intergenerational. Have a low index of suspicion and know how to access domestic violence advocacy promptly.[9] It can save lives.

Keep a record of the contact details for your local refuge for women and children, and display posters in your surgery. Offer other resources such as the Women's Aid 24 hour national helpline (0808 2000247). Local police forces have individual arrangements for policing in domestic violence, e.g. the Metropolitan Police Service has a Community Safety Unit. Make sure you know how you can quickly contact your local liaison police officer.

FLEEING VIOLENCE

People escaping violence from zones of conflict who seek asylum in the UK face multiple risks. They are vulnerable to abuse during escape and their reception in 'host' countries is often hostile. As doctors our priority is the preservation of health and not to police. The BMA confirms that there is no requirement to confirm someone's immigration status to access primary care services.[10] Children detained in UK immigration centres have experienced state violence and the Royal College of General Practitioners (RCGP) opposes this abhorrent practice.[11]

In conclusion, we cannot change the social injustice of the world as individual doctors but we can make a difference in the consultation. Remaining compassionate and avoiding cynicism is a first step. By understanding more about the harsh reality of many people's lives we will judge less and strengthen resilience, which in turn improves health. If, however, you do want to change the world there are a number of excellent resources to get you started. ...

RESOURCES

- UCL Institute of Health Equity, www.instituteofhealthequity.org/. Building on the work of Professor Sir Michael Marmot this newly created institute at University College London will seek to increase health equity through action on the social determinants of health.
- Heath I. *Divided We Fail: the Harveian oration 2011*. London: RCP, 2011, www.rcplondon.ac.uk/sites/default/files/harveian-oration-2011-web-navigable.pdf [accessed March 2014].

- Kirkengen AL. *The Lived Experience of Violation: how abused children become unhealthy adults.* Bucharest: Zeta Books, 2010.

- Kids Company, http://kidsco.org.uk. A London-based charitable organisation run by Camila Batmanghelidjh since 1996, it is involved in collaborative research with University College London and the Tavistock Clinic to study the structural and functional aspects of trauma on the young brain.

- Partners in Health, www.pih.org. A USA-based international organisation that supports social justice in the development of good healthcare facilities.

- Farmer P. Partners in health [YouTube video of Dr Farmer talking about his work in Haiti and Rwanda], www.youtube.com/watch?v=deF6q9VDv-Y [accessed March 2014].

- Medical Justice, www.medicaljustice.org.uk/. Medical Justice exposes and challenges inadequate healthcare provision to immigration detainees. It is a charity comprising volunteer doctors, lawyers and ex-detainees that provides training for doctors to visit detainees in the UK.

- Medics against Violence, www.medicsagainstviolence.co.uk. A charity of health workers in Scotland, set up by maxillofacial surgeons with Scottish government support. They run educational awareness programmes in schools to influence attitudes to violence among Scottish youth, particularly in relation to knife carrying, knife crime and gang membership. Addressing domestic abuse is part of the remit with free training offered to dentists.

REFERENCES

1. Farmer P. *Infections and Inequalities.* Berkeley, CA: University of California Press, 1999.

2. Hills J. *An Anatomy of Inequality in the UK.* London: London School of Economics, 2011.

3. Child Poverty Action Group. Child poverty facts and figures. www.cpag.org.uk/povertyfacts [accessed March 2014].

4. Spencer N. Reducing child health inequalities: what's the problem? *Archives of Disease in Childhood* 2013; **98(11)**: 836–7. doi: 10.1136/archdischild-304347.

5. BMA Child Protection Toolkit for Doctors, available from Apple iTunes apps store @ £0.69.

6. National Institute for Health and Clinical Excellence. *When to Suspect Child Maltreatment* (quick reference guide). London: NICE, 2009.

7. MacPherson W. *The Stephen Lawrence Inquiry* [the MacPherson Report]. London: TSO, 1999.

8. Equality and Human Rights Commission. *Stop and Think: a critical review of the use of stop and search powers in England and Wales.* Manchester: EHRC, 2010, www.equalityhumanrights.com/uploaded_files/raceinbritain/ehrc_stop_and_search_report.pdf [accessed March 2014].

9. Feder G, Davies AR, Baird K, *et al.* Identification and Referral to Improve Safety (IRIS) of women experiencing domestic violence with a primary care training and support programme: a cluster randomised controlled trial. *Lancet* 2011; **378**: 1788–95. doi: 10.1016/S0140-6736(11)61179-3.

10. de Zulueta P. Asylum seekers and undocumented migrants must retain access to primary care. *British Medical Journal* 2011; **343**: d6637.

11. Royal College of Paediatrics and Child Health, Royal College of General Practitioners, Royal College of Psychiatrists. *Intercollegiate Briefing Paper: Significant harm. The effects of administrative detention on the health of children, young people and their families.* London: RCPsych, 2009.

WORKLOAD

Soon after completing my GP training I set up a practice in a needy housing estate, working from a Portakabin. Numbers rose steadily, workload also, and my stress levels. After three or four years I was finding it hard but I felt on top of things until one afternoon a young mother, divorced, with two children and a healthy degree of self-confidence asked me, 'What's wrong with you these days? You don't seem to have time to listen to people like you used to. People are talking about leaving the practice.' I was mortified, ashamed, upset – and eventually more grateful to her than to any other patient I can think of before or since. I got a part-time partner, the practice thrived, and Annie and I enjoyed a special bond – based I think on mutual respect and an unspoken fondness – that endured over the next ten years till I moved on while she, I hope, continued to speak her mind.

Red Roses *collection curated by Alec Logan and illustrated by Helen Wilson.*

PART IV

PERSONAL DOCTORING

77

PERSONAL MEDICINE

James Willis

General practice is much more than the general practice of medicine, although the compartmentalisation and baffling complexity of contemporary medicine has made the broad, inclusive perspective of the skilful generalist more important to patients than it has ever been. The thing that makes general practice special, however, that makes it uniquely valuable, that makes it at least as high an aspiration as any other in the whole of medicine, is the fact that it consists, at its very heart, of a personal relationship between the individual patient and his or her doctor.

And the problem, voiced over more than half a century by people like Theodore Fox, James McCormick and now Iona Heath, is that everything in the modern world is moving away from this kind of approach, because the modern world, at least at its official level, has lost the means to value that sort of thing. One way of expressing the problem is that the modern world has lost its heart, because technology has *improved* on fuzzy, fallible, messy things like hearts and made them obsolete.

But medicine is concerned with hearts.

'Oh no, I want to see my *own* doctor', says my friend, who is lucky enough still to have the choice.

'And what do you mean by your "own" doctor?'

'Well, you can't be just a name. He's got to know something about your character. He's got to know you. The inside you.'

She's using 'inside', you see, in the same sense I'm using 'heart' – she doesn't mean she wants a laparotomy. But you might have difficulty explaining that to a machine. And that's important because some people today are behaving like machines, and making a virtue of doing so. And if things go on as they are it won't be long before some doctors are doing the same. And if that happens they may find it hard to understand why patients no longer recognise them as doctors. Or at least not proper ones.

My first medical chief, Sir John Nabarro at the Middlesex, habitually referred to GPs as 'proper doctors'. And it was a mark of the wise doctor he himself was that he said this in the sense I am using it here, when the whole edifice of medicine conspired, even more than it does today, to glorify hospital practice. Everyone knew that 'Nab's housemen', as we were called, always went on to hospital careers. But I had seen something different in general practice, and he respected my different ambition. Unlike anyone else in my year at the Middlesex I had spent my student elective in general practice. During an electrifying month spent visiting doctors around the country, I had found a warmth, humanity and a transparent love of the job unlike anything I had seen in hospital. Theodore Fox defined the essential characteristic of the GP role as 'looking after people as people and not as problems'[1], and I knew exactly what he meant. And I also saw then that the difference was absolute – not a matter of degree, but of kind.

Another thing I had recognised as special about general practice was the way it embraces two entirely different worlds. The GP has a relationship with his or her patients that is intimate in every sense, with privileged access to their minds, bodies, homes, to their families and communities, and which extends, crucially, over years and over generations. But at the same time there is a deep immersion in a rigorous scientific discipline and in cutting-edge technology.

At the risk of making this essay too personal (although isn't that rather the point – to reassert the validity of the personal approach?) I will illustrate this by saying that along with my commitment to personal practice I was, and remain, nothing less than a technology freak. From the moment I got my first computer, a Sinclair ZX80, in 1980 – hence the name – I have been fascinated by the potential of these revolutionary tools. After evening classes in basic programming at Southampton Tech I quickly started writing programs for my practice. One of these programs actually won the 1989 John Perry Prize of the British Computer Society, which is still billed as the most important prize in general practice computing. It was for my self-administered health screening questionnaire, which I called *Health Screen*, which came to be adopted by practices around the country and one in Pakistan.

But right from those early days my real interest was in trying to see where the immense power of these unprecedented machines was leading us, and in trying to ensure that people who understood the human side of general practice continued to have some input into how they were to be used. I warned, repeatedly, and sadly to little avail, against the danger that computers would be used to fix an inhuman, mechanistic misunderstanding of general practice 'in tablets of silicon'. In other words, that they would be used to model general practice in digital rather than analogue terms. And I pointed out that this was another absolute distinction, even when the models so created appear on the surface to be identical. Underneath the machine and the human would always be entirely different kinds of things, with entirely different strengths and weaknesses.

This interest in balancing the two worlds – the 'Two Cultures' indeed – has stayed with me throughout my career and into retirement, when I obtained, amongst other activities, a BA in Humanities with Literature (First Class!) from the Open University. As a result of all this experience I have come to see the world as being on a cusp: a tsunami of technical innovation has swept through it in one generation, and continues to sweep with no stability anywhere in sight. In this situation I believe GPs have a unique contribution to make; their position, with a foot so deeply in each of these camps, gives them a special viewpoint and a special authority, if only they have confidence in their role.

And that means sticking to the knitting, and not abandoning, in some vain quest for modernity and legitimacy, the one ingredient of their role that makes it special. The technical bits of the role are essential of course, but they are merely the tools – what is essential is the holistic embrace of the humanity of the work. Where the modernist emphasis is on exclusivity and focus, the GP approach is inclusive. Where the specialist deals in parts, the GP deals in wholes. The difference is another absolute and if GPs abdicate this position, or are required to do so by politicians, administrators or even by colleagues stuck in the technical mindset currently so dominant and so convinced of its own superiority, then they do so at their peril. And to the immeasurable, inherently unprovable, but nonetheless tragic, disadvantage of their patients.

Which brings me back to my friend who wants to see her 'own' doctor. I am not saying we all want a personal relationship with every doctor we see in every situation and at every stage of our lives. Of course we don't. I am not saying that medical practice can only be conducted effectively in systems that provide personal medical care of the kind the British public have traditionally enjoyed. Plenty of countries provide nothing of the sort for their citizens, but compared with us this means they are greatly impoverished.

What I am saying is that the personal relationship, extending over a period of time, adds a dimension to the interaction between patients and their doctors that is simply too precious to lose, and the worst reason for losing it would be because it has an element of magic about it. Which of course it has. Words like *trust* and *confidence* are the ones people use when referring to their relationship with their *own* doctor. That is what makes it such a privilege to have your patient say, 'You're my doctor – tell me what you think.'

What your patient is asking here is for you to weigh up their situation – their *whole* situation, that is, not just the diagnostic label that happens to be uppermost at a particular time – in a way that is indeed rather magical. They assume you will have your professional expertise, laboriously acquired – through training, through textbook learning, and also through personal experience, something that is often denigrated today but is no less important for that. And yes, I hadn't forgotten evidence; of course they want you to use that as well. And notice how your patient's trust is not diminished in the slightest when they see you checking facts along the way. If anything it is the reverse, confirming, if confirmation is needed, that they have come for something that goes far beyond mere information.

What they have come for has to do with understanding, judgement, integrity, wisdom. But the trouble is that these concepts are members of a class of phenomena that it is difficult for the technical world to appreciate because they are all things that are inherently impossible to define or measure. And that quite literally rules them out of official consideration in a culture which has decided that progress requires it to blind itself to nebulous things of that kind.

But, unfashionable as it may currently be, understanding-based medicine, applied with wisdom, in the context of an ongoing personal relationship, is the hallmark of the true GP. And the challenge in the coming years will be, I suggest, not endlessly to seek ways of measuring and proving the validity of these things, as though trapped in some doomed medieval quest for something that can never be found, but to win the argument that we are dealing here with something different in kind, something that will always elude definition but which remains utterly essential to what we call humanity. And that the fact that this human, personal relationship can be combined, in a deeply mysterious way, with a rigorous scientific discipline is demonstrated, minute by minute, hour by hour, and day by day, by the best kind of general medical practice.

There is no higher aspiration in medicine, and, done properly like that, general practice will remain the best and most rewarding job in the world.

Is it not obvious that the day of the personal, generalist doctor is passing? Isn't the job being done, and done better, by nurses, specialists, walk-in centres? Weren't we rather unusual in this country in even aspiring to continuing care from a generalist, personal doctor? Has not that aspiration already been virtually abandoned in many, if not most, larger practices in Britain, as part of the dramatic change towards part-time work and specialist interests? And has not the equally dramatic change from professional autonomy to subservience to government directives changed the fundamental nature of the job so that it can indeed be done by technicians following systems of rules?

Is not the truth of the matter that, except for a few pockets of resistance in the Celtic fringes of the British Isles, the day of the personal, generalist doctor – as we have understood it since the beginning of the modern era – has already passed?

Well, people have been saying that sort of thing for a long time. When I entered practice, in 1969, in the area that had been set aside for the new city of Milton Keynes, I found that the Development Corporation, advised by the County Medical Officer for Buckinghamshire, was planning to group all the city's GPs into 12-doctor partnerships, each in its standard health centre, and each doctor having a specialty. This was a model that had been pioneered in Livingston New Town, during an era when a certain kind of forward-looking GP (in other words GPs who were looking forward in one particular direction) had taken to wearing white coats. I used to call it the 'aspiration to hospital medicine syndrome', and saw it as a complete failure to understand what was special about general practice.

So – idealistic young GP, me, put up my hand at a meeting: This plan, I said, seemed to be based entirely on a sentence in the Todd Report on Medical Education, which stated, without support, that GPs of the future would work in large group practices. I challenged this with great passion because I had come to the new city believing continuing care from personal doctors would be one of the most important forces creating community and welding it together.

And fresh as I was from my traineeship in Lyndhurst in the New Forest I knew exactly what I was talking about. I had spent a year watching my trainer, Tony Danby, perfectly illustrate Dr Ian Tait of Aldeburgh's famous statement that to have a professionally well-educated personal doctor is one of the most valuable gifts a modern society can provide for its members. And it was obvious to me that the modern society of Milton Keynes was going to need this *more* than Lyndhurst, not less.

And here I am, 40 years later, still waving my hand in the air, more convinced than ever that we all need this sort of thing now more than we ever did before.

So what is it about the GP role that *cannot* safely be handed over to nurses – to technicians – to systems – to specialists? Easy – continuing, personal relationship to the patient, and generalism.

Interestingly, generalism was a term virtually unknown in those early days. I know because I was one of the first to start using it, and I used it provocatively, because we heard so much about 'specialism' as a self-evident good, and I thought that we should also be *named* and celebrated. We didn't quite go as far as 'generalist pride' marches, but that was the general idea.

But now, when the word 'generalism' has passed into the language and has almost lost its power to challenge by becoming a platitude, the essential heart that it forms to the GP role is still there, deep inside, never showing on the surface, and never in the short term. Which is tough because the modern world does rather tend to live on the surface and in the short term.

One of the unwanted effects of the modernisation of general practice that has taken place in the last few decades is that we have constructed a kind of artificial model of the GP role that is so ingenious that from the outside and from a distance it is next to impossible to tell the difference from the real thing. It looks like a doctor and it acts like a doctor. But if you get up close and peel back the surface and look inside you find an alien anatomy of wires and circuit boards and whirring disk-drives.

Now, if *we* can't tell the difference, and managers and governments certainly can't tell the difference – *patients* – and I count myself amongst them now even though I avoid doctors like the plague – patients certainly can.

Patients recognise instinctively what they need in a doctor. And when I say doctor I do mean a 'proper doctor' – a GP – in other words a personal, generalist doctor.

And this is something for which there is a natural ecological niche. A niche that has existed in all societies and probably at all times in history. And although we have immeasurably enhanced the effectiveness of the role through the fabulous tools of modern technology, the key features of the role remain, at least as essential as they ever were. They are not ours to change. Nor can they be changed at the whim of managers and politicians, however well-intended some of them may be.

If we abdicate that role, or if we are *required* to abdicate it, one thing is certain – others will fill it. Indeed we can see this already happening in the anomalous popularity of unscientific medicine in our supposedly super-rational, evidence-based world. But if we do abdicate our role, or are required to abdicate it, we are also going to deny our patients and our society the unprecedented opportunity to benefit from the technical enhancement of that role which is even now within our grasp.

But the true role must incorporate certain key elements. First, in order to be effective, the doctor must have authority; he or she must have freedom of action; and the action must be based on understanding, never on rote. In other words he or she must make full use of the mysterious powers of the human mind, such as intuition and empathy, which are the antithesis of cold mechanism.

For doctors to wield the authority so necessary for their healing role they must be perceived by the patient to be independent. Of course this independence exists within limits. A loose-fitting framework of strictly enforced boundaries is the essence of professionalism, in the medical sense of that confusing word.

The patient needs a doctor who is learned, wise and free. That is what they mean when they come to you and say, 'You're the doctor': they want you to weigh up their whole situation in your mind and come up with an answer that is right for them. They take it for granted that you will use mysterious human powers, which *they* know exist, even if they couldn't put it into words, to put yourself in their position, 'get into their shoes', and produce an answer – or a series of possible answers – which are appropriate in their particular circumstances at that particular time.

One of the epiphany moments of my life – when I suddenly knew something fundamental was wrong with my understanding of medicine – may seem to you to have been quite trivial. It was when a young doctor working in a casualty department told me that they knew the treatment that a patient required but that they were not allowed to do it because it wasn't in the hospital protocols.

To me at the time this was something utterly new. Of course in the old days we took advice. I used to be particularly free in asking for it: I would call GP colleagues into my room; I would walk down the corridor in our health centre to where the consultants were doing their clinics and wait for them to be free between patients; I would often take down reference books from the shelf behind me (not in the library, which was far too far away); latterly I would look things up on the internet, the screen always turned so that the patient could see it – and all this I knew was seen by the patient as a sign of strength. But I NEVER took instructions. Not once in my whole career. It was always me who wrote the 'bottom line'.

That is what I understood to be required of the role of doctor, and this is what the patients undoubtedly expected of me. I submit to you that they still do, and that they would be shocked and you would lose a lot of your power to help them if they ever found out that this was no longer the case. This is not an optional extra of the doctor role – it IS the doctor role. If you don't do it you are something else – perhaps something rather like a protocol-following nurse. And *they* don't get patients saying, 'Come on, what do you think? You're the protocol-following-nurse' in anything like the way they say, 'Come on, you're the doctor.'

It is a question of who you are seen to be answerable to. As a patient I want my doctor to be answerable first to me, then to my family and to my community. Next I want him or her to be answerable to something higher, something that includes principles, and truth, and this of course includes scientific truth. I do not want to be doctored, for example, by the Minister of Health, whose qualifications for this role do not inspire me in the least. I want the government and the Department of Health to do their job, which is to provide the infrastructure, employ the doctor as my agent, and ensure that the boundaries of professional freedom are effectively policed.

When the patient says, 'You're the doctor' they are saying something of the utmost significance. They are saying that they are expecting you to base your answer on understanding. Understanding of the *whole* situation. Not just treating the patient as a whole person, but *being a whole person themselves* as they do so.

The patients would be shocked and let down (and we hear stories of this happening) if they felt they were receiving anything which smacked of an unthinking, formulaic response.

For medical practice shall not live by evidence alone. Understanding is a much more fundamental base than evidence ever was, or ever will be. Evidence is an absolutely essential basis for understanding, but it is only one of several that are no less essential. Practice also needs, for example, protocols – another of its elements, tools, aids. It also needs background knowledge of the patients, their families, their society, their local geography. It also needs a knowledge of their anatomy, their physiology, of possible pathologies, of pharmacology, all built up progressively from earliest biology lessons at school onwards, and thereafter laboriously maintained and updated – constituting nothing less than an evolving internal model of the whole of medical knowledge.

The way this vast body of understanding is held and integrated in our minds is deeply mysterious, but we know from our experience that while much of the material is held subconsciously the whole of it is brought to bear on whatever situation we happen to be dealing with at the moment, as we absorb the elements of that situation with our equally mysterious and equally subtle array of senses.

The whole thing works in a way that is profoundly different from any machine we have ever made, or, in my opinion, are ever likely to make. We certainly haven't made anything remotely like it at the moment.

So while it may be very tempting to think that the days when this sort of thing is necessary are nearly over and that we are close to the dawn of join-up-the-dots-and-there-will-be-a-right-answer-to-everything medicine, patients are not tempted by this prospect, however much of a relief it would be to the doctors, especially if the latter get better paid for going along with it. People go to their own personal doctor for something more and that something is understanding. They have all-too-much experience of dealing with automatic systems in other parts of their lives.

For example, many people today have experience of trying to get help with their computers – which are, after all, much simpler things than human bodies – and know from this the infuriating limitations of protocol-bound help. It leads them round and round in maddening circles and seems to have a supernatural ability to discuss every situation and problem except the one they are actually in. They know the incredible difference, and the sheer speed and efficiency, when they find themselves talking to a real person who understands their problem. By which I mean a real person who doesn't work through a series of codified steps – who has the whole thing there as a working model in their mind.

And the other thing patients know about automatic systems is that they crash – they go wrong. And when they go wrong they *stay* wrong until a human being who understands them comes along and sorts them out. And that is exactly what happens with automatic doctors – i.e. nurses following protocols that they either don't understand or aren't allowed to depart from. When something crops up that wasn't allowed for in the protocol, that system crashes – and the nurse tells the patient to see the real doctor. Or go to casualty. Or call an ambulance. And how much longer will it be before we no longer have ambulances either?

So there is a much more fundamental difference between a doctor and a protocol-following nurse than the ones that attract the government so much – that the latter are paid less and do what they are told. The difference is that the doctor has an authority based on independence, and bases his or her actions on an internal understanding. To have one of these remarkable beings available in your time of need is indeed one of the greatest gifts that a civilised society can provide for its members. And we are not about to see that need change. But whether it is provided for in the future remains to be seen; there are plenty of societies in the world that do not provide it to anything like the extent we have done. But I believe that in comparison to us they are immeasurably impoverished.

And the key, of course, is that word 'immeasurably', because our technical world has ceased to recognise, still less value, anything that cannot be measured. We are at a cusp in human history, no less, as the tools of information technology, utterly unprecedented in kind and power, pursue their unknowable course. General practice, with its unique stance, its unique breadth and depth, its foot in the most advanced technology, and its other foot deeply embedded in humanity at its most personal and intimate level, has the opportunity and the responsibility to affect that course and ensure that technology serves man and not the other way round.

Please, young doctors, go on putting your hands up at meetings – you couldn't be more nervous than I was all those years ago – and go on saying and go on saying how important these sorts of things are. But never forget that your words will carry immeasurably more authority if you are seen by everyone, including yourself, to be occupying the role of a proper doctor.

REFERENCE

1.   Fox TF. The personal doctor and his relation to the hospital. *Lancet* 1960; **1(7127)**: 743–60.

GLOSSARY

AA	Attendance Allowance
AAA	abdominal aortic aneurysm
ABC	airway, breathing and circulation
ABG	arterial blood gas
ABPI	ankle-brachial pressure index
ACF	Academic Clinical Fellowship
ACS	Acute Coronary Syndrome
ADRT	advance decision to refuse treatment
AiT	Associate-in-Training
AKT	Applied Knowledge Test
ALS	Advanced Life Support
ALSG	Advanced Life Support Group
ALSO	Advanced Life Support in Obstetrics
AMTS	Abbreviated Mental Test Score
ANA	anti-nuclear antibody
AP	antero-posterior
APER	abdominoperineal excision of the rectum
ARCP	Annual Review of Competency Progression
ASME	Association for the Study of Medical Education
ATLS	Advanced Trauma Life Support
AWI	Adults with Incapacity Act
AXR	abdominal X-ray

BASICS	British Association for Immediate Care
BCG	Bacillus Calmette-Guérin
βHCG	beta-human chorionic gonadotropin
BJGP	*British Journal of General Practice*
BMA	British Medical Association
BMJ	*British Medical Journal*
BNF	*British National Formulary*
BP	blood pressure
BPAP	bilevel positive airway pressure
BPPV	benign paroxysmal positional vertigo
CAF	Common Assessment Framework
CAMHS	Child and Adolescent Mental Health Services
CbD	case-based discussion
CBT	cognitive behavioural therapy
CCT	Certificate of Completion of Training
CCU	Coronary Care Unit
CMH	Community Mental Health Team
CMV	cytomegalovirus
CNS	central nervous system
COHb	carboxyhaemoglobin
COPD	chronic obstructive pulmonary disease
COT	consultation observation tool
CPAP	Continuous Positive Airway Pressure
CPD	continuing professional development
CPN	community psychiatric nurse
CPR	cardio-pulmonary resuscitation
CRB	Criminal Records Bureau
CSA	Clinical Skills Assessment
CSF	cerebrospinal fluid
CT	computed tomography
CTO	Community Treatment Order
CVA	cerebrovascular accident
CXR	chest X-ray
DENs	Doctor's Educational Needs
DFSRH	Diploma of the Faculty of Sexual and Reproductive Healthcare

DH	Department of Health
DKA	diabetic ketoacidosis
DLA	Disability Living Allowance
DMARDs	disease-modifying anti-rheumatic drugs
DNACPR	Do Not Attempt Cardiopulmonary Resuscitation
DNAR	Do Not Attempt Resuscitation
DOPS	Direct Observation of Procedural Skills
DRCOG	Diploma of the Royal College of Obstetricians and Gynaecologists
DVLA	Driver and Vehicle Licensing Agency
DVT	deep-vein thrombosis
DWP	Department for Work and Pensions
EBV	Epstein–Barr virus
ECG	electrocardiogram
ECT	electroconvulsive therapy
EDTA	ethylenediaminetetraacetic acid
EMQ	extended matching question
ENP	emergency nurse practitioner
ENT	ear, nose and throat
EPAC	Early Pregnancy Assessment Clinic
ERPC	evacuation of retained products of conception
ESA	Employment and Support Allowance
FAST	Face Arms Speech Test
FBC	full blood count
fMRI	functional magnetic resonance imaging
FY1	Foundation Year 1
FY2	Foundation Year 2
GDS	Geriatric Depression Scale
GI	gastrointestinal
GMC	General Medical Council
GP	general practitioner
GPwSI	GP with a Special Interest
GTN	glyceryl trinitrate
GUM	genitourinary medicine

HADS	Hospital Anxiety and Depression Scale
HCA	Healthcare Assistant
HMRC	HM Revenue and Customs
HONK	hyperosmolar nonketotic state
HPU	Health Protection Unit
IBD	inflammatory bowel disease
IM	intramuscular
INR	international normalised ratio
IPF	In-Practice Fellowship
ITU	Intensive Treatment Unit
IUD	intrauterine device
IUGR	intrauterine growth restriction
IUS	intrauterine system
IV	intravenous
IVU	intravenous urogram
JSA	Jobseeker's Allowance
LARC	long-acting reversible contraception
LFT	liver function test
LRTI	lower respiratory tract infection
LTFT	less than full time
LUTS	lower urinary tract symptoms
LVA	low-vision aid
MAU	Medical Admissions Unit
MDO	medical defence organisation
MDT	multidisciplinary team
MI	myocardial infarction
MIMMS	Major Incident Medical Management and Support
mini-CEX	mini-clinical evaluation exercise
MM	malignant melanoma
MMSE	mini-mental state examination
MNG	multinodular goitre
MODY	maturity onset diabetes of the young
MPS	Medical Protection Society

MRCGP	Member of the Royal College of General Practitioners
MRI	magnetic resonance imaging
MSF	Médecins Sans Frontières
MSF	Multi-Source Feedback
MUST	Malnutrition Universal Screening Tool
NAFLD	non-alcoholic fatty liver disease
NASGP	National Association of Sessional GPs
NGO	non-governmental organisation
NICE	National Institute for Health and Care Excellence
NIHR	National Institute for Health Research
NIHSS	National Institutes of Health Stroke Scale
NLS	Newborn Life Support
NOF	neck of femur
NSAIDs	non-steroidal anti-inflammatory drugs
O&G	obstetrics and gynaecology
OA	osteoarthritis
OCP	oral contraceptive pill
OCSE	objective structured clinical examination
OCSP	Oxford Community Stroke Project
OGD	oesophago-gastro-duodenoscopy
OOH	out of hours
OOP	out of programme
OPG	orthopantomogram
OT	occupational therapy
PAD	peripheral arterial disease
PBSGL	Practice-Based Small Group Learning
PCO	Primary Care Organisation
PCT	Primary Care Trust
PDP	personal development plan
PE	pulmonary embolism
PEC	Professional Executive Committee
PEPSE	Post-Exposure Prophylaxis following Sexual Exposure
PET	positron emission tomography
PFR	peak flow rate

PhEC	Pre-hospital Care Course
PICOTS	Population, Intervention, Comparison, Outcome measures, Time and Setting
PIP	Personal Independence Payment
PM	practice manager
PMB	postmenopausal bleeding
POP	progestogen-only pill
PR	per rectum
PSA	prostate-specific antigen
PSQ	Patient Satisfaction Questionnaire
PUL	pregnancy of unknown location
PUNs	Patient's Unmet Needs
QALY	Quality-Adjusted Life Year
QOF	Quality and Outcomes Framework
RCGP	Royal College of General Practitioners
RCOG	Royal College of Obstetricians and Gynaecologists
ROSIER	Recognition of Stroke in the Emergency Room
SAAG	serum-ascites albumin gradient
SAPC	Society for Academic Primary Care
SBA	single-best answer
SBP	spontaneous bacterial peritonitis
SCREDS	Scottish Clinical Research Excellence Development Scheme
SCT	stem cell transplantation
SDQ	Strengths and Difficulties Questionnaire
SEA	significant event analysis
SHO	senior house officer
SIGN	Scottish Intercollegiate Guidelines Network
SMART	specific, measurable, achievable, realistic and time bound
SpR	specialty registrar
SSRIs	serotonin-specific reuptake inhibitors
ST1	Specialist Trainee Year 1
ST2	Specialist Trainee Year 2
ST3	Specialist Trainee Year 3
STI	sexually transmitted infection
SVC	superior vena cava

TAC	Team Around the Child
TATT	tired all the time
TACS	Teaching and Assessing Clinical Skills
TB	tuberculosis
THET	Tropical Health and Education Trust
TIA	transient ischaemic attack
TIPS	Teaching Improvement Programme System
TLHP	Teaching and Learning for Health Professionals
TLS	tumour lysis syndrome
TPR	temperature, blood pressure, pulse
TSH	thyroid-stimulating hormone
TURP	transurethral resection of the prostate
TWOC	trial without catheter
U&Es	urea and electrolytes
UC	ulcerative colitis
UPSI	unprotected sexual intercourse
USS	ultrasound scan
UTI	urinary tract infection
VA	visual acuity
VARK	visual, aural, read/write and kinaesthetic
VC	videoconferencing
VTE	venous thromboembolism prevention
VTS	vocational training scheme
WCC	white cell count
WPBA	Workplace-Based Assessment

INDEX

A

abdominal aortic aneurysm (AAA) 39, 164, 165
abdominal pain assessment 69–71
abdominoperineal excision of the rectum (APER) 29
abscesses 71
    anorectal 31
    breast 18
    facial 113–14
academic general practice 279–81
    career ladder 282
    how to write a paper 297–300
    routes into research 282–3
    useful meetings and courses 283
acceptance 357
access to services, global scale 331
accountability 392
acopia 80
actinic keratoses 245
acute coronary syndromes (ACSs) 22–3, 64
acute kidney injury 64
acute medicine
    basics 11–12
    patients 12
    PDP pointers 14–15
    referrals and teamwork 12–13
    skills and development 13–14
adalimumab therapy 57
adjuvant therapy 102
adolescents, child and adolescent mental health
    (CAMHS) 253–9

advance decisions to refuse treatment (ADRTs) 125
agency work 351
alcohol dependence 57
alcohol withdrawal 64
alcoholic liver disease 58, 59
anaemia 63
anal fissures 31
analgesia, palliative care 124
aneurysms *see* abdominal aortic aneurysm (AAA)
anorectal abscesses 31
anorexia 257
anterior resection 29
antibiotics 235
    in chronic respiratory conditions 141
    drug interactions 63
    and oral contraception 51, 171–2
    in severe sepsis 65
anticoagulation 87
    in arrhythmias 23–4
antiphospholipid syndrome 87
antipsychotics 129
    use in older patients 99
anti-TNF therapy 57
Applied Knowledge Test (AKT) 195
    cost of exam 182
    questions 196–7
    timing 196–7
    what to take with you 197–8
appointment timings 176–7
appraisal 320–4

locum workers 354
Après Skiing vignette 349
arrest calls 14
arrhythmias 23–4
ascites 58, 59
ASSIGN scores 341–2
Associate-in-Training (AiT) programme 181
asthma 139
asylum seekers 382
atopic eczema 246
ATOS Origin, employment opportunities 296
atrial fibrillation/atrial flutter 23, 64
    oral anticoagulation 87
Attendance Allowance (AA) 295
audit 14, 206, 324
    choice of topic 207
    good practice 208–12
audit criteria 208–9
audit cycle 206–7
audit standards 209–10
Australia, employment opportunities 377–9
autonomy 237
    shared decision making 363–6

B

bacteriuria, elderly patients 234
bad news, discussion with patients and families
    123–4, 127
BCG, intravesical 160
benign paroxysmal positional vertigo (BPPV) 252
benzodiazepines 130
Berwick, Donald 363
bimanual examination 91–2
biochemistry 230
    Potassium Supplements vignette 232
    result reporting 231–2
    samples and requests 230–1
bladder cancer 160
bleeding
    epistaxis 34, 39
    gastrointestinal 59–60
    high INR 87
    postmenopausal 92
    during pregnancy 92
    rectal 30, 71
blood gases 40, 64, 141
blood products prescribing 86
blood samples 230–1
bowel dysfunction 122
bowel obstruction 70

breast surgery
    basics 16–17
    cancer 18
    mastalgia 18–19
    patients 17
    PDP pointers 19
    sepsis 18
burnout 237

C

cancer
    breast 18
    colorectal 27, 29–30
    head and neck 35
    lung 138–9
    malignant melanoma 39
    urological 160–1
capacity 81, 240
    legislation 99
car maintenance and mileage allowances 183
cardiology
    arrhythmias 23–4
    basics 20–1
    chest pain 22–3
    clinical skills 22
    heart failure 24
    investigations 21–2
    patients 21
    PDP pointers 24–5
cardioversion 23
    oral anticoagulation 87
care costs 286
career paths 307
case-based discussion (CbD) 191
catheterisation 158–9
cauda equina syndrome 155
Cerazette 51
Certificate of Completion of Training, cost 184
cervical cytology, DOPS 194
changing specialty 270–2
chaperones 17, 28, 346
    breast examination 73
    DOPS 194
    genital examinations 73
    gynaecological examinations 91–2
    urological examinations 158
chemotherapy 104
chest drains 141
chest pain 22–3
child and adolescent mental health (CAMHS) 253

consultation skills 253–5
eating disorders 257
internet and social networks 257–8
local services 255–6
'naughty' children 257
questionnaires and scales 257
referrals 256
resources 258–9
child protection 254, 381
children
emergency medicine 40
impact of social violence 381–2
joint pain 152, 155
sexual activity 75
see also paediatrics
chronic daily headache 249–50
cirrhosis, spontaneous bacterial peritonitis 58
claudication 164
clinical diaries 44
Clinical Skills Assessment (CSA) 199
access to services 203–4
communication 204
confidence 204
cost of exam 182
dress code 203
helping yourself 203, 205
marking scheme 201
preparation 199–200, 202–3, 204
timing 202
what to expect 200–1
what to take to the exam 200
clinical supervisors 337
Clostridium difficile 57
coagulopathy, in obstructive jaundice 60
Cochrane Collaboration 373
cognitive enhancers 100
cognitive impairment screening 100, 148
Cointreau for Breakfast vignette 325
colonoscopy 29–30
colorectal surgery
anal and perianal complaints 31
basics 27–8
cancer 29–30
inflammatory bowel disease 30
patients 29
PDP pointers 31
rectal bleeding 30
resections 28–9
stomas 28
colostomies 28
combined contraceptive pill 50–1
commissioning 284

care costs 286
getting involved 287–8
need for 284–5
outcome domains 285
role of primary care 286–7
communication
Clinical Skills Assessment 204
discharge planning 66
geriatric medicine 79–80
GUM clinics 74
haematology 86
palliative care 123–4
with relatives 65
respiratory medicine 140
stroke patients 148
vignette 264
community awareness 66
compartment syndrome 153
abdominal 165
competency 344–5
competency framework 188–9
complaints 343–4
avoidance of 344–7
complementary therapy 123
computers, dangers of 387–8
condom use 75
conferences
on medical education 313–14
RCGP Annual Conference 306
confidentiality 345
and social media 361
conflict management 130, 346
confusion, elderly patients 80–1
consent 238, 276
mental capacity 99
from study participants 298
young people 243
constipation, elderly patients 80
consultation observation tool (COT) 191–2
continuing professional development (CPD) 307–8
appraisal 320–4
staying up to date 372–6
contraception see family planning
controlled drugs 225
Coronary Care Units (CCUs) see cardiology
corticosteroids, osteoporosis prevention 57
costs
Associate-in-Training (AiT) programme 181
care costs 286
Certificate of Completion of Training 184
doctor's bag 182
exams 182

General Medical Council registration 184
medical indemnity insurance 181–2
relocation 183
study leave budget 183
travel 183
courses 374
'crash teams' 14
Crohn's disease 30, 57
cryotherapy 246
curriculum vitae (CV) writing 316–17
for locum work 351
cutaneous horns 246
cycle to work scheme 183

D

data collection, audit 210, 211–12
deanery
communication with 179
reimbursement of insurance costs 181–2
website forms 184
Decision Talk 369–70
deliberate self-harm (DSH) 40
older people 99
delirium 79, 98
dementia 97, 98
medications 99, 100
dental problems 114, 115
Department for Work and Pensions (DWP) 295–6
Depo-Provera 51–2
depression screening 148
dermatitis herpetiformis 245
dermatology 172, 244–7
minor surgery 274, 275–6
Ringworm vignette 248
dermoscopy 276
diabetes 44, 45
insulin regime adjustment 64
peripheral arterial disease 165
vignette 121
diabetic ketoacidosis (DKA) 45, 66
diagnosis 290–3
Direct Observation of Procedural Skills (DOPS) 193–4
Disability Living Allowance (DLA) 295, 296
discharge planning 66
geriatric medicine 80
Immediate Discharge Letter vignette 219
stroke medicine 148, 149
dissection, aortic 166
districts of workforce shortage (DWSs), Australia 377

dizziness 33, 252
'Do Not Attempt Resuscitation' decisions 65, 79
palliative care 125
respiratory medicine 140
doctor–patient relationship
Nothing vignette 294
patient's perspective 1–2
patients' expectations 391–3
personal nature 386–7
challenges 389
threat from computers 387–8
doctor's bag 182
doctoring 3–5
documentation
emergency medicine 38–9
general medicine 65
geriatric medicine 79–80
respiratory medicine 140
Dog's Life vignette 289
domestic violence 382
dress code
Clinical Skills Assessment 203
out-of-hours care 224
driving, and epilepsy 250
drug abuse 225
dry socket 115
duodenal ulcers 60
duty of care 238

E

ear, nose and throat (ENT)
basics 32
ears 33
nose 34
patients 33
PDP pointers 36
throat and neck 35
early pregnancy assessment clinic (EPAC) 92
eating disorders 257
ECGs 21–2
ST elevation 65
ectopic pregnancy 92
educational supervisors 176, 337
elderly patients
bacteriuria 234
fractured neck of femur 153
out-of-hours care 225
vignette 121
see also geriatric medicine; old-age psychiatry

electroconvulsive therapy (ECT) 100
electrolyte imbalance 46
embarrassment, bowel problems 29
emergency contraception 53
emergency medicine
    basics 37–8
    communication and documentation 38–9
    patients 38
    PDP pointers 41
    skills and management 39–40
    trauma and injuries 40–1
empathy 355, 356
Employment and Support Allowance 295
empyema 64
endocrinology
    basics 43–4
    diabetes 45
    electrolyte imbalance 46
    hypercalcaemia 46
    outpatients 44
    patients 44
    PDP pointers 46–7
    thyroid disease 45–6
end-of-life care 103–4
endoscopy 59, 60
epididymitis 39
epiglottitis 35
epilepsy 250–1
epistaxis 34, 39
Epley manoeuvre 252
ePortfolio 185–7
equipment, doctor's bag 182
errors 292
    avoidance of 344–7
    examples of 214
    in laboratory tests 232
    litigation 343–4
    management of 347–8
    openness 240
    see also significant event analysis (SEA)
ethico-legal issues 237–43
    in old-age psychiatry 99
    research 298
    testing 268
euthanasia 238
events medicine 301–4
evidence-based practice 267, 392
exams
    Applied Knowledge Test (AKT) 195–8
    Clinical Skills Assessment (CSA) 199–205
    costs 182
exceptional-circumstances panel reports 134

exchange programmes 333
expenses, tax relief 328
expert patients 85
eye disease
    thyroid-related 46
    see also ophthalmology
eye drops 108, 109
    systemic effects 110

F

Facebook 361
facial infections 113–14
facial rashes 246
faints 250–1
fallibility 239
falls assessment, elderly patients 78, 79
family planning
    basics 48–9
    emergency contraception 53
    method-specific guidance 50–3
    patients 49
    PDP pointers 53–4
fear, patient's perspective 1–2
femoral fractures 153, 154
fetal heart rate traces, classification 93–4
finances
    golden hellos 329–30
    income 326–7
    locum work 353
    pensions 328–9
    profits 327
    tax 327–8
    tips 330
finasteride 160
First5 initiative 306–8, 375
fits 250–1
food bolus obstruction 35
foreign bodies, nasal 34
'four principles' of ethical practice 238–9
fractures 40–1, 153–4
    maxillofacial 114
freedom, professional 391–2

G

gastric ulcers 60
gastroenteritis 235
gastroenterology
    basics 56
    endoscopy and GI bleeding 59–60

inflammatory bowel disease 57
liver disease 58–9
nutrition 59
outpatients 60
patients 57
PDP pointers 60–1
General Medical Council (GMC)
advice on social media use 360, 361
registration cost 184
general medicine
basics 62–3
communication and documentation 65
discharge planning 66
medical emergencies 65–6
on-call 64
patients 63–4
PDP pointers 66–7
general surgery
basics 68–9
on-call 69–71
PDP pointers 71
ward and theatre 69
generalism 390
genital examinations 73–4
genitourinary medicine (GUM)
basics 72–3
clinical issues 74–5
communication issues 74
patients 73
PDP pointers 75–6
gentleness 357
geriatric giants 78–9
geriatric medicine
basics 77–8
communication and documentation 79–80
confused patients 80–1
diagnostic quandaries 80
patients 78
PDP pointers 81
vignette 83
see also elderly patients; old-age psychiatry
gifts 239
global health 331
links and further reading 334–5
significance for primary care 331–2
what you can do 332–4
golden hellos 329–30
GP rotation 169, 172–3
basics 170
home visits 170
obstetrics and gynaecology 171–2
paediatrics 171
the practice 170–1
referrals 172
training 172
GP trainers 176, 337
GP training 340
getting involved 338–9
possible misconceptions 337–8
roles and responsibilities 338
trainers' groups 339
training practices 339
when to start 339–40
guidelines, staying up to date 373
gynaecology see obstetrics and gynaecology

H

haematology 84
basics 85
emergencies 88
oral anticoagulation 87
patients 85–6
PDP pointers 88–9
prescribing 86
haematuria 161
haemorrhoids 31
hand injuries 152
Hartmann's procedure 29
headaches 249–50
health concerns 347
heart failure 24
treatment revolution 372
hemicolectomies 28
hepatic encephalopathy 59
Hickam's dictum 292
hip pain, children 152, 155
history taking 62–3
HIV (human immunodeficiency virus) 74
hoarseness 35
holistic practice 202–3, 388–9
home visits 170, 220–1
guidelines 221–2
Pork Chop? vignette 223
honesty 239, 346–7
hospices see palliative care
hospital posts, basic points 8–10
'How' questions 254
humanity 279–80
hypercalcaemia 46
hyperkalaemia 46
hypernatraemia 64
hyperosmolar nonketotic state (HONK) 45

hyperthyroidism 45–6
hypokalaemia 46
    diabetic ketoacidosis 66
    during steroid therapy 57
hyponatraemia 46

I

ileostomies 28
impetigo 246
implants, contraceptive 52
incapacity, statements of 295
income 326–7
infection control 236
inflammatory bowel disease (IBD) 30, 57
infliximab therapy 57
insight 347
insulin regime adjustment 64
insurance costs 181–2
international normalised ratio (INR) 87
internet, learning resources 374–5
interviews 318–19
intestinal perforation 70
intrauterine devices (IUDs) 52–3
iRefer 227

J

job applications 315–18
job interviews 318–19
joint aspiration 155
joint injections 276–7
journals, staying up to date 373
justice 239

K

keratoacanthoma 245
kindness 240, 355–8
    vignette 359

L

laboratory tests *see* biochemistry; microbiology
lactation, breast sepsis 18
laryngectomy 35
lasting power of attorney 240
learning, staying up to date 372–6
learning cycle 312

learning styles 311
leaving GP training 270–2
left hemicolectomy 28
leg ulcers 235
legislation *see* ethico-legal issues; medico-legal issues
less than full time (LTFT) training 178–80
lesson plans 310–11
lichen simplex 245
lifelong learning, staying up to date 372–6
lignocaine, maximum safe doses 112
limb ischaemia 70, 164–5
listening 4–5
List vignette 371
literature searches 298
litigation 343–4
    avoidance of 344–7
liver disease 58–9
liver screen 58
local authority public health placements 134
locum work 353–4
    doing the job 352–3
    getting paid 353
    getting started 350–1
loss of consciousness 41
lung cancer 138–9
lymphoedema 166

M

malignant melanoma (MM) 39
mastalgia 18–19
maxillofacial surgery *see* oral and maxillofacial
    surgery
media statements 134
Medical Admissions Unit (MAU) *see* acute medicine
medical emergencies 65–6
medical indemnity insurance 181–2
medical students, teaching of 279–80, 309–14
Medicare, Australia 378
medico-legal issues
    litigation 343–4
        avoidance of 344–7
    minor surgery 276
    old-age psychiatry 99
melanocytic lesions 274
meningitis 250
mental capacity 81, 99, 240
mental health, child and adolescent mental health
    (CAMHS) 253–9
Mental Health Act 130
mesenteric ischaemia 166

metoclopramide 70
microbiology 233
 reports 234
 samples and requests 233–4
 the service 235
 specimen-related issues 234–5
migraine 249, 250
minor surgery
 attractions of 273–4
 joint injections 276–7
 medico-legal issues 276
 resources 277
 training 274–5
Mirena intrauterine system 52–3
missed-pill advice, oral contraceptives 51
mitomycin, intravesical 160
Modernising Medical Careers (MMC) 270
morphine, palliative care 124
motorised vehicle allowance 183
multi-source feedback (MSF) 192
Murtagh's process 292

N

nails, dystrophic 246
nasal foreign bodies 34
nasal fractures 114
nasal packing 34
nasal polyps 34
nasal trauma 34
National Institute for Health and Care Excellence
 (NICE), guidelines 373
'naughty' children 257
neck of femur fractures 153
negligence 240
neo-adjuvant therapy 102
neonatal units 117–18
nephrostomies 160
networking
 First5 initiative 307
 international 333
 job applications 317
neurology 249
 dizziness 252
 fits and faints 250–1
 headache 249–50
 Parkinson's disease 251
neutropenic sepsis 65, 88, 104–5
new baby checks 118
newspapers 374
Nexplanon 52

night sedation, elderly patients 81
nipple 'eczema' 245
Nothing vignette 294
nursing staff, teamwork 13
nutrition
 elderly patients 78, 80
 gastroenterology patients 59
 post-operative 69

O

obstetrics and gynaecology 90
 basics 90–1
 early pregnancy assessment clinic 92
 examining the patient 91–2
 in general practice 171–2
 obstetrics 93–5
 on-call 92–3
 patients 91
 PDP pointers 95–6
obstructive jaundice, coagulopathy 60
Occam's razor 292
occupational therapy 145
old-age psychiatry 97
 basics 98
 legal issues 99
 medications 99–100
 patients 98–9
 PDP pointers 100–1
 training 100
oncology
 basics 102–3
 chemotherapy 104
 neutropenic sepsis 104–5
 patients 103–4
 PDP pointers 105
 radiotherapy 104
 spinal cord compression 105
online learning 374–5
open fractures 154
openness 240
ophthalmic examination 109–10
ophthalmology 40
 basics 107–8
 commonly used abbreviations 107–8
 on-call 110
 patients 108–9
 PDP pointers 111
 thyroid-related eye disease 46
opioids, palliative care 124
Option Grids 366, 367

Option Talk 369
oral and maxillofacial surgery 112
    basics 112–13
    dental problems 115
    facial infections 113–14
    patients 113
    PDP pointers 115
    trauma 114
oral anticoagulation 87
oral contraceptives
    and antibiotics 171–2
    missed pill advice 51
orthopaedics
    basics 151–3
    fractures 153–4
    glossary of terms 151–2
    on-call 154–5
    patients 153
    PDP pointers 156
otitis externa 33
out-of-hours care 224–6
    rural areas 261–2
out of programme (OOP) time 333–4
outbreak investigation 135
over-diagnosis 268
overdoses 40
overseas experience 332, 333–4
    postcard from Australia 377–9
oxygen therapy 139

P

paediatrics
    basics 116–17
    child protection 254, 381
    emergency medicine 40
    in general practice 171
    joint pain 152, 155
    neonatal unit and new baby checks 117–18
    on-call 118–19
    patients 117
    PDP pointers 119–20
    sexual activity in children 75
    skills 117
    social violence impact of 381–2
    vignette 121
    see also child and adolescent mental health
    (CAMHS)
pain
    chronic 144
    'total pain' 122

pain relief, palliative care 124
palliative care 102, 220
    basics 122–3
    communication 123–4
    controlled drugs 225
    end-of-life care 103–4
    ethical and legal issues 125–6
    Kindness vignette 359
    patients 123
    PDP pointers 126
    prescribing 124
    teamwork and organisation 124–5
pancreatitis 70
papers, how to write them 297–300
Parkinson's disease 251
partnerships 240–1, 315
part-time training 178–80
part-time work, seniority payments 330
patience 356
patient-centred approach 386–94
    to testing 268
patient satisfaction questionnaire (PSQ) 193
patient's perspective 1–2
peer review opportunities 323
pensions 328–9
    and locum work 353
per rectum (PR) examination 69
peri-orbital cellulitis 34
peripheral arterial disease 164–5
peritonism 70
personal development plans (PDPs) 187
    appraisal 323–4
Personal Independence Payment (PIP) 296
personality disorders 129
pilonidal sinus 31
pitted keratolysis 245
plaster casts 154
pneumonia, empyema 64
polypharmacy, elderly patients 78
portfolio careers 321
posterior vitreous detachment 110
Potassium Supplements vignette 232
practical procedures 13–14
    chest drains 141
    in paediatrics 117
practice finances 326–7
    profits 327
pregnancy 171
    early pregnancy assessment clinic 92
    prescribing 94–5
    see also obstetrics and gynaecology

problem-free talking 255
producer capture 285
professional relationships 8–9, 347
    with dermatology department 275
    events medicine 302, 303
    during the GP rotation 170–1
    locum work 353–4
    with radiology departments 229
    during the registrar year 174
    in rural areas 261–2
professionalism 345–6
progestogen-only injectable contraception 51–2
progestogen-only pill (POP) 51
prognosis, discussion with patients and families
    123–4, 127
project management 134
prostate cancer 160–1
prostate-specific antigen (PSA) 160
prostatic enlargement, catheterisation 158–9
prosthetic valves, oral anticoagulation 87
protocols 392, 393
psoriasis 245
psychiatry
    basics 128
    conflict and difficult situations 130
    general management and personal
    development 131–2
    on-call 130–1
    patients 129
    PDP pointers 132
    psychopharmacology 129–30
    see also child and adolescent mental health
    (CAMHS); old-age psychiatry
public health placements 133
    in local government authority 134
    PDP pointers 136
    in Public Health England (PHE) unit 135–6
pyelonephritis 71
pyrexia, post-operative 69

Q
Quality Adjusted Life Years (QALYs) 241
Quality and Outcomes Framework (QOF) 241

R
radiology
    contrast-using investigations 40
    do's and don'ts 228–9
    professional relationships 229

reports 228
requests 227–8
the service 229
radiotherapy 104, 105
rapid tranquillisation 129
rashes see dermatology
rationing of treatment 241–2
record-keeping, medico-legal issues 345
rectal bleeding 30, 71
reduced-hours scheme 178–9
refeeding 59
referrals
    accepting acute medical referrals 12–13
    accepting general medical referrals 65
    accepting O&G referrals 92
    accepting paediatric referrals 118–19
    radiology requests 227–8
    to secondary care 172, 225–6
    child and adolescent mental health services
    (CAMHS) 255–6
reflective learning 186–7, 297
    learning from errors 348
    on teaching sessions 313
refugees 382
registrar year
    planning for the future 177
    the practice 175–6
    timings 176–7
    trainers (educational supervisors) 176
    training commitments 177
    Workplace-Based Assessments (WPBAs) 189
        the assessments 190
        case-based discussion 191
        competency framework 188–9
        consultation observation tool (COT)
        191–2
        Direct Observation of Procedural Skills
        (DOP) 193–4
        marking scheme 190
        multi-source feedback 192
        patient satisfaction questionnaire 193
relatives, communication with 65, 79, 123, 149
relocation costs 183, 184
remote areas see rural areas
renal calculi 71, 161
renal colic 161
repeat scripts 352
research 280–1
    how to write a paper 297–300
    overseas 333
    routes into 282–3
    staying up to date 373

useful meetings and courses 283
resources 241–2
respiratory medicine 138
    basics 138
    communication and documentation 140
    patients 140
    PDP pointers 141–2
    skills and management 140–1
responsiveness 357
resuscitation, training in 304
resuscitation decisions 65, 79
    palliative care 125
retinal examination 109–10
revalidation 307, 320
reviews, ePortfolio entries 186
rheumatology 143
    basics 143–4
    inpatients and on-call 144–5
    multidisciplinary team 145
    outpatients 145
    patients 144
    PDP pointers 145–6
right hemicolectomy 28
right iliac fossa pain, differential diagnosis 71
ringworm 246
    vignette 248
role of doctor 391–4
Royal College of General Practitioners (RCGP)
    appraisal revalidation portfolio 321
    First5 initiative 306–8, 375
    online learning 375
    Social Media Highway Code 360
rural areas 260
    in Australia 377–8
    communities 260–1
    further reading and resources 263
    leisure time 262
    making a career in rural practice 262–3
    medical issues 261
    on-call 261–2
    training in 262

S

safety, home visits 222
salaried posts 315–16
salbutamol 140
scaphoid injuries 40
Scottish Intercollegiate Guidelines Network
    (SIGN) 373
sedation 65

elderly patients 80–1, 99
    rapid tranquillisation 129
seizures 250–1
self-harm 254
seniority payments 327
    part-time work 330
sepsis 65–6
    neutropenic 88, 104–5
serotonin-specific reuptake inhibitors (SSRIs) 130
serum-ascites albumin gradient (SAAG) 59
sexually transmitted infections see genitourinary
    medicine (GUM)
shared decision making 363
    attitudes 363–4
    knowledge 364–5
    Option Grids 366, 367
    skills 365–6
    three-talk model 366, 368–70
shared management plans 202
shingles, facial 246
shoulder injuries 152
sickle cell crisis 88
sigmoid colectomy 29
significant event analysis (SEA) 213–14, 218
    barriers to success 217
    errors and system failures 214
    good practice 215–16
    human factors 214
    outcomes 216–17
    report writing 217
sinus infection 34
sitting in 176
situational awareness 346
skin disease see dermatology
slit lamp examination 109, 110
slot share 178–9
SMART entries, PDPs 187
smoking, and breast sepsis 18
smoking cessation, incentivising graph 139
social media 360–2, 375
social understanding 4–5
social violence 380
    impact upon children 381–2
    resources 382–3
speculum examination 73–4, 91–2
spinal canal stenosis 164
spinal cord compression 105
spontaneous bacterial peritonitis (SBP) 58
sputum samples 235
standards, audit 209–10
statins, drug interactions 63

statistics 134, 197
staying up to date 372–6
stents, urological 160
steroids, topical 246
stomas 28
stridor 35
stroke medicine 147
    basics 147–8
    patients 148–9
    PDP pointers 150
    referrals and teamwork 149
    skills and development 149
structural violence 380
study leave budget 183
subarachnoid haemorrhage 250
subdural haematoma 250
suicide risk 129
    older people 99
supererogation 242
support, sources of 239
suprapubic catheters 159
system failures
    examples of 214
    see also significant event analysis (SEA)

T

tamsulosin 161
tax 327–8
    golden hellos 329–30
    locum workers 354
teaching 279–80
    delivery 311–12
    evaluation 313
    getting involved 313–14
    planning 309–11
    resources 314
    see also GP training
teaching courses 313
Team Talk 368–9
teamwork
    emergency medicine 41
    events medicine 302, 303
    with nursing staff 13
    oncology 105
    palliative care 124–5
    psychiatry 128, 132
    rheumatology 145
    stroke medicine 149
technological change 3–4
teenagers

child and adolescent mental health
    (CAMHS) 253–9
    see also paediatrics
teeth, avulsed 114
telephone consultations 174
temporal arteritis 250
Ten Commandments
    for the new therapeutics 265
    for testing 266–9
tension headache 249–50
testicular torsion 162
'thin-slicing' 291
threatening situations 173
three-talk model 366, 368–70
thyroid disease 45–6
tonsillitis 35
trainers see GP trainers
training commitments 177
transient ischaemic attacks (TIAs) 165
trauma 40–1
    basics 151–3
    fractures 153–4
    on-call 154–5
    patients 153
    PDP pointers 156
travel, choosing a car 221
travel costs 183, 184
    tax relief 328
tremor 251
Tribunal Service, employment opportunities 296
troponin tests 22
trust 242, 388–9
tumour lysis syndrome (TLS) 88
TURP, post-operative bleeding 161
Twitter 360–2, 375

U

UK Medical Eligibility for Contraceptive Use
    (UKMEC) 48–9
ulcerative colitis (UC) 30, 57
uncertainty 242, 269
upper GI bleeding 59–60
urethral strictures 159
urgent laboratory tests 231
urinary retention 160
urinary tract infection (UTI), duration of treatment
    234
urine samples 234
urology
    basics 157–8

cancers 160–1
catheters 158–9
haematuria 161
nephrostomies and stents 160
patients 158
PDP pointers 162
renal stones 71, 161
testicular torsion 162

V

valvular heart disease, oral anticoagulation 87
variceal haemorrhage 60
varicose veins 166
vascular surgery
    acute arterial disease 165
    aneurysms and dissections 165–6
    basics 163–4
    chronic peripheral arterial disease 164–5
    lymphoedema 166
    mesenteric ischaemia 166
    patients 164
    PDP pointers 166–7
    venous disease 166
venous thromboembolism (VTE)
    oral anticoagulation 87
    prophylaxis 69, 140
video consultations 191–2
vignettes
    Age – a State of Being or a State of
    Becoming? 83
    Après Skiing 349
    Cointreau for Breakfast 325
    Dog's Life 289
    The Gaelic? The Gaza 264
    Hug 137
    Immediate Discharge Letter 219
    Interesting Questions, Interesting Answers
    341–2
    Kindness 359
    List 371
    Nothing 294
    Pork Chop? 223
    Potassium Supplements 232
    Reaching Agreement on the Reason for the
    Patient's Visit 55
    Red Roses 6
    Remarkable Consultations 121
    Ringworm 248
    Sequelae MI 26

Short and Sweet 174
    Thank You for Telling Me 127
    Workload 384
violence, domestic 382
violence, social 380
    impact upon children 381–2
    resources 382–3
violent encounters 130
vision, loss of 110
visual acuity testing 109
vocational training scheme (VTS), teaching
    opportunities 313

W

warfarin 87
warmth 356
Wernicke's encephalopathy 59
whistleblowers 242
work, fitness for 295–6
working hours 224
Workload vignette 384
Workplace-Based Assessments (WPBAs)
    the assessments 190
    case-based discussion 191
    competency framework 188–9
    consultation observation tool (COT) 191–2
    Direct Observation of Procedural Skills
    (DOPS) 193–4
    general points 189
    LTFT trainees 180
    marking scheme 190
    multi-source feedback 192
    patient satisfaction questionnaire 193
World Organization of Family Doctors
    (WONCA) 333
wrist injuries 152

X

X-rays of injuries 152

Y

young people 242
    child and adolescent mental health
    (CAMHS) 253–9
    see also paediatrics